GOING FOR GOLD

GOING FOR GOLD

The History of Newmont Mining Corporation

JACK H. MORRIS

The University of Alabama Press • Tuscaloosa

The University of Alabama Press
Tuscaloosa, Alabama 35487-0380
uapress.ua.edu

Hardcover edition published 2010.
Paperback edition published 2017.
eBook edition published 2010.

Inquiries about reproducing material from this work should be addressed to the University of Alabama Press.

Typeface: AdobeCaslon Pro

Cover image: A doré bar at Newmont's refinery at Carlin, Nevada; used by permission from Newmont Mining Corporation
Cover design: Michele Myatt Quinn

Paperback ISBN: 978-0-8173-5901-0

A previous edition of this book has been catalogued by the Library of Congress as follows:
Library of Congress Cataloging-in-Publication Data
Morris, Jack H.
Going for gold : the history of Newmont Mining Corporation / Jack H. Morris.
p.   cm.
Includes bibliographical references and index.
ISBN 978-0-8173-1677-8 (cloth : alk. paper) — ISBN 978-0-8173-8443-2 (electronic) 1. Newmont Mining Corporation. 2. Colorado—Gold discoveries. 3. Gold mines and mining—Colorado—History. I. Title.
TN413.Z6N496 2010
338.7'6223422—dc22
2009038142

CONTENTS

ILLUSTRATIONS

PREFACE

A thimbleful of gold for $1,023! Now that's a precious metal! Gold reached that peak on March 17, 2008, having two months earlier surpassed the previous record of $850 an ounce set in January 1980.[1] The price had doubled in just four years as growing demand and declining output met amid uncertain economic and political times. It was then pushed to the summit by the steep decline in the value of the U.S. dollar and turmoil in the credit markets. Yet, in 1999, with the price barely above $250 an ounce, gold was at a twenty-five-year low and pundits were calling it a relic with little relevance to current-day economics. As the span of these few years shows, gold is a volatile commodity. But what the pundits forgot is that gold also is money.

The ultimate symbol of power and authority for gods and kings and the cornerstone of monetary value, gold is woven through the fabric of human history. Exquisitely beautiful with unparalleled qualities of durability and versatility, gold has been offered in homage, demanded in battle, mined since the dawn of civilization, and horded by democrats and tyrants alike. The quest for the yellow metal drove Spanish conquistadors to explore the New World and centuries later helped populate the American West. Today, gold mining brings education, employment, and a higher standard of living to thousands of people in the most remote corners of the earth.

The world's fascination with gold has been coupled with a millennia-long dream of a Midas touch, the ability to turn common earth or clay into the most precious of metals. To the casual observer, that is exactly what Newmont Mining Corporation accomplished on May 4, 1965, when the first gold bar was poured at its Carlin Gold Mining subsidiary near Elko, Nevada.

By creating value from "nothing at all," the event revolutionized the gold industry and vastly expanded the amount of the metal that could be economically extracted from the earth's crust. As the first new gold mine to open in the United States in fifty years, Carlin breathed new life into Nevada's economy and propelled a company, once noted for its diversity, into world leadership in production of the yellow metal.

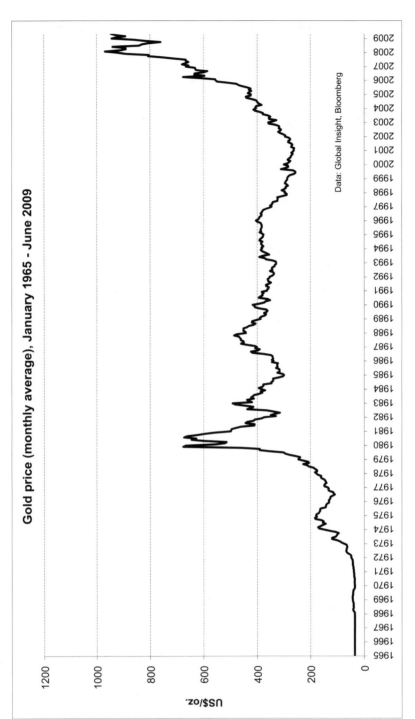

Gold price (monthly average), January 1965 - June 2009

Data: Global Insight, Bloomberg

US$/oz.

P.1. The gold price, once controlled by the government at $35 an ounce, peaked at $850 an ounce in 1980 and at $1,023 an ounce in early 2008. The monthly average, as shown here, has been slightly lower. The spot price passed $1,200 an ounce in December 2009. (Bloomberg)

The first gold bar, the size of a small loaf of bread, weighed 92 pounds and was valued at $47,000 at the then government-fixed price of $35 a troy ounce.[2] (It would have been worth nearly $1.4 million at $1,023 an ounce.) There was nothing to distinguish it from gold produced elsewhere in the world. Gold is a natural element, Au on the periodic table, and after refining out small amounts of naturally occurring by-product metals like silver and copper, the Carlin gold achieved the four nines (99.99 percent) purity that is the industry standard.

Likewise, the plant itself, while highly automated for its day, was not a breakthrough. Finely ground ore was mixed with cyanide-laced water in an extraction process developed in Scotland in 1887. Agitated in a series of large tanks, the chocolate-colored solution was filtered, mixed with zinc dust to precipitate the gold into a concentrate, and finally smelted into bars of gold bullion.

What was revolutionary was the ore itself. The gold was invisible, even with a microscope. The metal was so finely dispersed through the rock that it could only be detected by a fire or chemical assay. It took three tons of ore to produce just one ounce of gold—4,000 tons for that first bar of gold. Such tonnage required a large-scale operation and, as a result, Carlin became the first large open-pit gold mine in the world.

Today, Newmont is able to locate and economically mine ores containing less than 0.01 ounce per ton, or 100 tons for each ounce of the metal. Utilizing economies of scale, giant 240- to 320-ton trucks ascend ant-like from half-mile deep pits and processing plants crush rock to the consistency of talcum powder before chemically recovering the gold. The 50-mile by 5-mile geologic corridor across the high desert of northern Nevada now famous as the Carlin Trend has become one of the most prolific gold districts in history and low-grade disseminated gold deposits are mined the world over.

"The discovery of the Carlin deposit is one of the most significant events in worldwide mining and in the history of Nevada," wrote Nevada state geologist Jonathan Price in 1991. "Deposits on the Carlin Trend have set new standards for gold mining throughout the world. Large-scale mining, heap leaching (a low-cost recovery technique first utilized on a large scale by Newmont), and automation at various levels in mining, milling, and assaying processes have cut overall costs and allowed lower and lower grades of

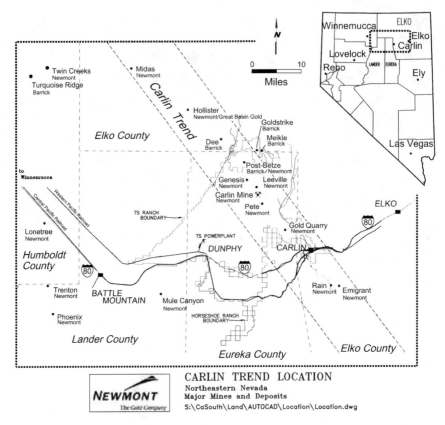

CARLIN TREND LOCATION
Northeastern Nevada
Major Mines and Deposits
S:\CaSouth\Land\AUTOCAD\Location\Location.dwg

P.2. The Carlin Trend, a 50-by-5 mile geologic corridor through northern Nevada that began with a Newmont discovery, is one of the most prolific gold districts in the world. Including the vast T/S Ranch, Newmont owns or controls 3,000 square miles of land in Nevada, making it the state's largest landowner after the federal government. (*Newmont*)

ore to be mined."[3] Since then, the Trend has seen the advent of autoclaves, roasters, and even naturally occurring bacteria to squeeze even more value from rocks previously thought worthless.

These innovations, however, have increased mining's impact on the environment. In the aggregate, mining uses only a fraction of the land required for other essential uses—farming, highways, and shopping centers, for instance. The city of Las Vegas, with 113 square miles, consumes more land than all the gold mines in northern Nevada. Still, open pits are huge; waste rock and tailings (the crushed ore left after metal processing) must be disposed of in mountainous piles or lake-size ponds. Poisonous metals such as mercury and arsenic are often found in conjunction with gold and are disturbed during the mining process. Water supplies both above- and underground can be threatened.

Newmont has been at the forefront in developing effective methods of environmental protection and works closely with Nevada, federal, and foreign regulators to ensure that its mines and methods are safe. It also strives to set standards of excellence in community affairs, especially when entering new countries, and is in the vanguard of mining concerns in embracing CSR, or corporate social responsibility, as a way of broadening its decision making to include a host of public interests. Nevertheless, environmentalists and human rights activists, who watch mining closely, are wary of even the best producers. The sheer size of operations creates an inevitable tension wherever gold is mined.

In April 2002, Nevada governor Kenny Guinn celebrated the 50 millionth ounce (1,555 tonnes) of gold produced on the Carlin Trend amid predictions that with known reserves, the Trend is expected to produce that much more gold, reaching 100 million ounces in the not too distant future. (Through 2007, the number had reached 68.5 million ounces, or 2,131 tonnes, of gold.)[4] Half of that gold has come from Newmont mines. The *Reno Gazette-Journal* reported at the time that "Economists estimate gold to date from the Carlin Trend—source of one-half of Nevada's entire gold production of 8.1 million ounces in 2001—equates to $34 billion in jobs, spending and other indicators."[5] There were 9,000 miners in Nevada in 2008, nearly 40 percent employed by Newmont, in jobs that averaged $81,500 a year before benefits, the highest industrial wages in the state.

In the history of gold mining, only three other districts—the Witwatersrand of South Africa, Muruntau in Uzbekistan, and Kalgoorlie in Australia—have produced 50 million ounces. Newmont has been involved in all three. From the mid-1980s until it was surpassed by China in 2006, Nevada was the third largest gold-producing region in the world, ranking just below South Africa and Australia but well ahead of Canada. In 1964, the year before the start-up of the Carlin mine, the United States produced 1.5 million ounces of gold, 3 percent of the world total, and was a net importer of the metal. Forty years later, U.S. gold production topped nine million ounces and accounted for 10 percent of the world's output, making the United States a major gold exporter.

Newmont's growth, spurred by additional discoveries and acquisitions, has been even more impressive—from a company with a market capitalization of $200 million at the time of the Carlin discovery to one worth $25 billion in early 2009. It is in the top tier of gold producers in the world and was ranked number one from 2002 until 2006 when it was overtaken by the merger of two Canadian companies, Barrick and Placer Dome. Its operations are enormous. In 2007, its mines moved 780 million tons of rock (more than two million tons per day) to produce 6.2 million ounces of gold (5.3 million ounces for its own account; the balance for its partners) and 454 million pounds of copper. Proven and probable reserves totaled 86.5 million ounces of gold in eight countries. It employed 35,000 people including contractors and controlled 43 million acres of land, giving it an exploration base greater than the size of Great Britain.

Carlin was not Newmont's first gold mine; it has had gold in its veins since its birth. Three of its first four chief executives grew up in gold camps. Yet, it was a recognized leader in mining long before gold became an important part of its portfolio.

Newmont was born in the early years of the twentieth century, the creation of William Boyce Thompson, a flamboyant Wall Street promoter who made millions by arranging financing for early mining ventures. He established Newmont as an investment house, much like a mutual fund with a portfolio of shares in a variety of mining firms. Until the end of World War II, it operated few mines on its own.

Plato Malozemoff, an astute Russian emigrant, became president in 1954 and set Newmont on a new course of expansion and diversification. Under Malozemoff, Newmont was primarily involved in copper but had interests in precious metals, lead, zinc, uranium, lithium, coal, oil, and even cement. Operations circled the globe.

By the mid-1980s, however, the company's exposure to multiple mines and metals was losing favor on Wall Street. Investors wanted greater returns and were growing impatient with underperforming assets. In 1987, corporate raider T. Boone Pickens launched a takeover attempt which Newmont repelled in a pyrrhic victory unmatched in the annals of corporate warfare.

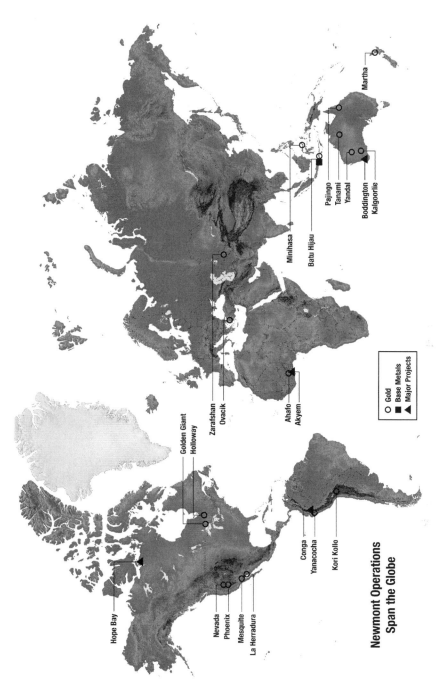

P.3. Newmont's operations span the globe with producing mines or mineral deposits on five continents. (*Newmont*)

The company paid out a special dividend of $33 a share, $2.2 billion in total, which drained its coffers and left it heavily in debt. To regain solvency, it sold most of the assets Malozemoff had spent a career acquiring and reestablished itself as a gold producer centered on Carlin. After Pickens, Newmont defended its independence against other raiders—the Oppenheimer Empire of South Africa, Britain's Hanson Trust, and Sir James Goldsmith. Today's Newmont is the golden Phoenix that rose from the ashes of those fights.

Underlying the company's rise—and attracting the barbarians to its gate—was a profound change in Wall Street sentiment toward gold and gold stocks following the return of the metal to free market pricing in 1971. With a spike in worldwide inflation and Russia's invasion of Afghanistan in 1979, gold soared. Within a few years, the high desert of Nevada was teeming with prospectors backed by easy money from Wall Street and the financial canyons of Toronto, Vancouver, and London.

Gold is a complex and uniquely valued commodity with demand tied not only to world fashion in jewelry and a multitude of electronic and industrial uses but to international currency exchange rates, inflationary trends, and global instability. Price moves, as well as the stock price of gold producers, are often countercyclical to the stock market. As a result, studies have shown that gold is an excellent tonic for portfolio balance. Taken in doses of 5 to 10 percent of a portfolio's net worth, gold and gold stocks diminish volatility and add to long-term investment returns.

For gold producers, higher metal prices translate into higher profits from current production and increased value of unmined ore reserves. But it also makes it economic to mine lower-grade ores, thereby increasing reserves. As a result, investors are willing to pay large premiums for stocks of pure-play gold companies—sixty times earnings at some points—that afford an opportunity to participate in upward movements in the price. By contrast, producers of industrial metals like copper traditionally sold at eight to twelve times earnings. The ability of Newmont management to exploit this phenomenon has been key to the company's recent success. It also puts the company under extreme pressure to perform to Wall Street's expectations.

Newmont's prominence is all the more remarkable because of the decline of mining in the United States and consolidation throughout the industry. ASARCO, Phelps Dodge, Kennecott, Amax, Anaconda, Cyprus, and Cerro, among others, were towering names in mining and financial circles for most of the twentieth century. Homestake was the largest gold mining company in the country and, until 2001, one of the oldest listed stocks on the New York Stock Exchange. Today, none of these companies survives as an independent entity, and Newmont is the only gold stock in the S&P 500 and the Fortune 500. In 2007, Newmont also became the first gold miner to be included in the prestigious Dow Jones Sustainability Index-World, which selects industry leaders based on the long-term economic, environmental, and social performance of 2,500 of the world's largest companies.

From the beginning, the company's reputation rested on its ability to attract and retain some of the brightest minds in exploration, mining, metallurgy, and finance. These men and women enabled the company to acquire and develop world-class assets and breakthrough technologies. While setting global standards for operating efficiency, the company has overcome a plethora of challenges, an occasional stumble, and a few missed opportunities. Leaders have had foresight and determination; they have been highly competitive, committed to excellence, and confident in their own judgment. The company's founder could be short tempered, Malozemoff was brusque, and at times the company has had a reputation for arrogance, yet over the years the corner office has been occupied by gentlemen who have acted with decency and honor.

Furthermore, from top to bottom, employees have been proud to be part of a company that is ethical and honest in a world where simple values are often sacrificed for short-term success. David Potter, an attorney with the company from 1972 to 1989, says Newmont was always principled: "The corporate culture that gave rise to scandals at companies such as Enron was totally foreign to Newmont."[6] Integrity remains a bedrock corporate value.

As Newmont's vice president of investor relations from 1994 to 2001, a period of international expansion but the lowest gold price in a quarter century, I shared in the struggles and triumphs of that time and grew to greatly admire the company and its people. I also developed a deep respect for Newmont's past and in retirement sought to gather its history. Many of the men who had fought the company's toughest battles and steered its transition to gold were approaching or already in their eighties and I felt an urgency to get their stories on paper before memories faded. The company provided financial support for the collection of oral histories from more than eighty retired and present officers, directors, and employees.

It was a wonderful assignment and provided a firsthand perspective on transforming events. Deep pride in the company and a recognition that personal achievements had occurred in the context of creating something special were common themes in these interviews. While some rambled as they reminisced, others had bell-clear recall. Richard Leather, who retired as vice chairman in 1992, spoke in perfectly parsed paragraphs. Unless otherwise noted, all quotes in this book come from those interviews.

Extending these firsthand observations into the company's early years were oral histories with Malozemoff and others conducted by Eleanor Swent at the Bancroft Library of the University of California, Berkeley. I also relied on *The Magnate,* Hermann Hagedorn's 1935 biography of Thompson; Robert Ramsey's 1973 history, *Men and Mines of Newmont;* and *Goldstrike!* by Bill Jamieson, the 1990 story of Oppenheimer's attack on Consolidated Gold Fields, Newmont's largest shareholder in the 1980s.

I am grateful to Newmont for its support and to all who took the time to share their stories. Yet, while this is Newmont's history, it is not a corporate document. Editorial judgment is entirely that of the author; management neither dictated nor constrained what is written here. I am no longer a spokesman for the company and have sought to tell the story as fairly as possible and let the decision makers speak for themselves.

Special thanks are due to former CEOs Gordon Parker, Ronald Cambre, and Wayne Murdy; to Richard Leather, and to Dr. James Taranik, director of the Mackay School of Earth Sciences and Engineering at the University of Nevada, Reno, a Newmont director since 1986, each of whom granted numerous interviews and endured repeated probes for information that added immensely to this document. Reviewing my manuscript and helping focus my interviews were Taranik; former vice president and corporate secretary Tim Schmitt and former executive vice president of exploration John Dow, both of whom brought the perspective of a twenty-six-year career; and Randy Eppler, former vice president of corporate development, who added a superb knowledge of Wall Street attitudes.

Despite this help, many stories will have been missed. Little time is spent on unsuccessful exploration, although discovery is largely a process of elimination. Additionally, with a top-down focus, much of the sweat and success of daily operations is omitted. I apologize to those whose contributions I have overlooked and readily acknowledge that the company's success has required an "all hands on deck" commitment. Relying heavily on personal accounts, this work touches on the differences of opinion and rivalries that make a company real and relevant. Yet no purpose would be served by trying to settle old scores.

Rather, my goal is to tell the story of a fascinating company with a look at how decisions, often critical to survival and cloaked by intrigue, were made by real people in real time. By doing so, I hope the reader can gain an appreciation for all who have made Newmont the company that it is, for its leadership in the birth and development of the modern gold industry, for the challenges that both Wall Street and environmentalists place on corporations, and for the metal that continues to fire universal passions.

1

EUREKA

The story of gold mining in North America is told in terms of mass hysteria—the California gold rush of 1848 and 1849 that brought an estimated 90,000 fortune seekers to San Francisco and Sacramento; the Klondike Stampede of 1898 and 1899 that saw thousands more trek by mule train or dogsled into the frozen mountains of the Yukon and Alaska; and the many gold rushes in the years between into the Black Hills of South Dakota, the Colorado Rockies, Idaho, Wyoming, and Montana. Each began with the lucky find of a nugget or abundant gold flakes in a stream bed or alluvial outcropping, followed by wild speculation and an influx of young men determined to beat the odds and strike it rich.

The Carlin discovery was different. It resulted from the intellectual curiosity and meeting of the minds of two people—Newmont geologist and prospector John Livermore and Ralph J. Roberts, a geologist with the U.S. Geological Survey, who had developed a theory of Nevada geology and mineral endowment through years of observation. And once found, the deposit was exploited not by grizzled forty-niners with picks and shovels but by geologists, metallurgists, and mining engineers using the best science, technology, and deep-pocket capital of a multinational mining company.

Both geologists prided themselves on their economic rather than purely academic approach. "I was always more interested in the practical side of geology, actually finding ore bodies," says Livermore, a 1940 graduate in geology from Stanford. "There are many fine geologists who are not very good at prospecting. You have to be good at reading the rocks and seeing the signs, being a good observer. I was also very interested in studying the literature."[1]

Roberts received his undergraduate degree in geology from Yale in 1939 and his doctorate ten years later with a dissertation on orogeny, the formation of mountains, in north-central Nevada. His work showed that mineral deposits in the area were not randomly located but found in structurally con-

1.1. A 1965 aerial view of the Carlin operations, the world's first large-scale, open-pit gold mine. (*Newmont Archives*)

trolled zones of deformation. In meetings with fellow geologists Roberts asserted, "You can concentrate prospecting along the mineral belts and save both time and money."[2]

Roberts theorized that gold, in hydrothermal solutions and magma, percolated up from the depths of the earth in the Tertiary period millions of years ago when the earth's crust was undergoing breakup. As mountains formed, oceanic shale and chert were moved into central Nevada by thrust faults and acted as impervious cap rocks, trapping the gold-bearing fluid, which spread into the surrounding rocks below the thrust plates. When erosion wore through this crust, the gold-bearing rocks were exposed.

In June 1961, armed with Roberts's theory, Livermore and fellow geologist J. Alan Coope began a search across the empty high desert of northern Nevada for unusual rocks and surface anomalies that might indicate the presence of gold. In less than six months they had zeroed in on the Carlin deposit. Quite fittingly, the discovery was made in Eureka[3] County. "I guess you could say we were fantastically lucky," Livermore says.

It was luck based on hours of preparation and dog-tired days of walking over the rugged terrain and hauling out backpacks of rock samples found lying on the surface or chipped from outcrops. It was lonely work. Covering 4,180 square miles, nearly the size of the state of Connecticut, Eureka County had a population of only 775 souls in 1960.

Carlin was not the first mine to exploit invisible gold, nor was it the first in which Newmont had an interest. But it was the first discovery specifically targeted at a sub-microscopic, or disseminated, gold deposit. Very fine gold was mined at the Mercur mine just south of Bingham Canyon, Utah, in the 1880s when a fire assay detected traces of gold in the mine's silver ore. In northern Nevada, Gold Acres in Lander County, the Gold Standard mine in Pershing County, and Getchell in Humboldt County (in which Newmont was an early investor) all produced small amounts of disseminated gold in the 1930s and 1940s.

Livermore worked briefly at the Standard in the late 1940s and did field studies at Getchell as part of a summer program at Stanford. He was intrigued by both and wondered how the forty-niners who had trekked past Getchell en route to the California gold rush had missed the signs.

"The original Getchell outcrop was a very large, bold mass of silicified iron-stained material, which usually would catch a prospector's eye," Livermore told the Bancroft Library's Eleanor Swent in an oral history interview. "It was right on a main trail that a lot of prospectors and other people had passed for years, and they would bang off chunks of rock and crush them up and pan them, which was the standard way of prospecting in those days, and they never would get any colors of gold."[4] The gold was so fine it would float out of the pan undetected. Eventually in the 1930s a prospector thought to assay the rock and the mineralization was discovered.

One of those passing the Getchell outcropping—and quite possibly Carlin as well—was Livermore's great-grandfather, fifty-five-year-old Horatio Gates Livermore, who left Boston for San Francisco in search of gold in 1849. But like many of those who participated in that piece of history, he was delayed in Salt Lake City, most likely by heavy snows in the Sierra Nevadas, and didn't arrive in California until the next year. By then the best claims were being worked and Horatio's panning along the American River above Georgetown came to naught. He turned to logging and eventually became a state senator.

John Livermore joined Newmont in 1952, and after several years at the corporate office in New York and assignments around the world, he returned to Nevada in 1960 to evaluate a lead-zinc-silver property at Ruby Hill in Eureka County that Newmont jointly owned with Cyprus and Hecla Mining. When that task ended, he decided to follow up his earlier curiosity about deposits of finely disseminated gold by researching U.S. government documents on local geology. One such paper was the *40th Parallel Survey* written in 1876 by Clarence King, who later became the first director of the U.S. Geological Survey. This pioneering effort, which took six years, documented the topography and geology along the transcontinental railway that paralleled the Humboldt River and Emigrant Trail. Reports were also written between 1936 and 1939 by W. O. Vanderburg, a mining engineer with the U.S. Bureau of Mines, who had studied lode and placer gold mines in northern Nevada. Although he stated that "sedimentary gold deposits do not possess easily recognizable indications," Vanderburg concluded that other deposits similar to Getchell, Gold Standard, and Gold Acres remained "to be discovered . . . where sedimentary formations, like shale and limestone lying in proximity to acid intrusives, are common."[5]

That was enough to ignite a prospector's interest. "The big question for me was how do you find these deposits? You can't look everywhere," Livermore recalled. It was at this point that Roberts provided the key. Roberts had participated in regional mapping studies of Nevada since 1939. In 1960, he published a two-and-a-half-page professional paper on the alignment of base and precious metal mineral districts in northeastern Nevada and their relationship to major thrust faults, particularly the Roberts Mountain Thrust. The name is a coincidence, the mountains having been named for Bolivar Roberts, superintendent for the Pony Express, which crossed the area in 1860–61.

"By very careful mapping, he had concluded that there was this enormous thrust structure where the rocks had been shoved horizontally about 50 miles to the east in the central part of Nevada," Livermore told Swent. Roberts then plotted known mineral deposits on the map and showed that many occurred near "windows" where older, overthrust rocks had faulted and eroded, exposing younger, mineral-bearing rock below. "That really got me interested, because now I had a model to follow to try to find some of these occurrences," Livermore said.

In the spring of 1961, Roberts gave a talk in Ely, Nevada, which Livermore attended. After several discussions between the two men to hone in on his theory, Livermore persuaded Fred Searls Jr., Newmont's chairman and a noted geologist in his own right, to undertake the search for invisible gold in the Carlin area. Coope, who was in Nevada to investigate possible gold properties near Valmy, was assigned as his assistant.

Newmont in 1961 was still a relatively small investment company with interests in a dozen mining operations, the largest being in southern Africa. An offer late that year to increase its holdings in Arizona's Magma Copper from 21 to 81 percent was accepted in early 1962. Revenue, almost entirely from dividends and security sales, totaled $18 million. Net income, after modest expenses for salaries, exploration, research, and taxes, was $15 million, of which almost half was paid out in dividends. The market value of its stock was $200 million.

Yet, the company's office at 300 Park Avenue in New York was an exhilarating place to work. Plato Malozemoff, who would shape the company's persona for three decades, was CEO and in his seventh year as president. Including Searls, there were only eight officers and a handful of staff. Offices were open and daily discussions ranged over a multitude of issues affecting the company's various holdings. Staffers were expected to be multitasked and reporting responsibilities were vague at best. Livermore, who had worked as a roving geologist on a number of projects that Newmont did not directly own, reported to Searls. Coope reported to Robert Fulton, a workaholic mining engineer, who headed exploration.

Exploration attention in the early 1960s was on base metals, particularly copper. With the cold war and rising demand for electricity, the U.S. Atomic Energy Commission had encouraged Newmont to open a uranium mine in the mid-1950s, but within a few years the outlook for yellowcake had dimmed. Now looking for new ventures, Newmont began to think of applying the techniques of modern copper mines—large-scale open pits mined with huge shovels and trucks—with relatively cheap and highly efficient cyanide gold extraction to western gold properties. Searls had brought Newmont into the Getchell mine and Fulton, like Livermore, had read Roberts's 1960 paper with interest.

Livermore and Coope began their search in deep secrecy, sometimes working at night.[6] But with only one small hotel, two cafés, and two gas stations in the railroad town of Carlin, the two geologists, Livermore a lanky six foot five and Coope very British in dress and speech who drove a blue MG, stood out and questions were asked. People in the larger town of Elko, twenty miles to the east, ridiculed the prospectors. The area had been "prospected for years," they were told. Newmont itself had mounted a short-lived search for lead and silver in Elko County in 1946. Years later Livermore admitted that the secrecy probably wasn't necessary. "We had the whole country to ourselves; no one else was much interested in gold in the early 1960s."

The reason was price and government policy. The gold price had been fixed at $35 an ounce in a Presidential Proclamation by Franklin Roosevelt in 1934. Then in October 1942, the War Production Board issued Order L-208, which halted most gold mining in the United States so that miners and material could be reassigned to more strategic metals. When the war ended and mines sought to reopen, costs had risen above the selling price. Livermore recalls that there were 1,100 gold mines in California alone in 1940. Most were tiny operations. Twenty years later only a handful remained in business.

The Empire-Star mine in Grass Valley, California, which had sustained Newmont during the Depression, closed in 1956. Still, in the early 1960s, Newmont was one of the top ten gold producers in the country with by-product output from Magma Copper and Idarado, a Colorado lead and zinc mine. Carlin lifted Newmont to second place after Homestake's underground mine in South Dakota.

The focus of Newmont's Carlin exploration was the Lynn district, an empty swath of blowing sagebrush and a few scattered cattle ranches some fifteen to twenty miles north of the town of Carlin. Mining in the area had been limited and not very lucrative. Fred Lynn had opened a placer mine along Lynn Creek, about 1.5 miles from the Carlin discovery, in 1907.[7] He and other placer miners extracted perhaps 10,000 ounces of gold from area creeks over the next fifty years. Livermore and Coope would have encountered the grizzled Hansen brothers, bachelors who lived in separate caves along Maggie Creek and always had a roll-your-own cigarette protruding from their lips and were still panning the creek each spring for a few dollars in gold. The Springers, from Pennsylvania, operated a small oxide copper mine while living in an old railroad boxcar. Bootstrap, an antimony mine, produced some 10,000 ounces of gold in the 1950s before operational difficulties forced its closure. Turquoise had been mined at Blue Star since the 1920s and traces of gold were found in some drill samples in 1960. But efforts by a Salt Lake City investor to mine this with used equipment failed after producing only four 200-ounce doré bars.

Studies of the Blue Star deposit correlated with Roberts's findings. According to Coope, "Upward-migrating hydrothermal fluids had been ponded beneath a low-dipping thrust structure."[8] Over time, gold migrated from the ponds into the surrounding quartz rock where it precipitated into concentrations of fine-grained gold. Unable to acquire the Blue Star property, a systematic prospecting effort was initiated along similar outcroppings a few miles to the south.

"Two things that are associated with gold are pyrite and silica, so we were looking for silicification," Livermore recalls. "The pyrite breaks down on the surface to iron oxide, so you are looking for a rusty color which indicates that there is pyrite at depth. Certain types of color are quite important. We found that the darker browns tend to be more encouraging than the lighter, yellowish browns." Furthermore, they had to be the right kind of rocks, sedimentary rocks, with calcareous siltstone being the most favorable host setting for gold.

Rock samples were sent fifty miles away to Gold Acres in Crescent Valley, where Harry Treweek and his wife, Clemmie, ran the only assay lab in the area in an old shack. The samples showed traces of gold, assaying 0.03 to 0.05 ounce per ton. Sitting one day on his "chair of geology," a large rock where he often ate lunch, Coope noted a friable, spongy brown rock among the silicified limestone and wondered if it had absorbed any gold. An assay, which showed a quarter-ounce gold, proved him right. That gold constitutes less than 0.4 millionths of 1 percent of the earth's crust explains why a geologist can get excited by a rock containing nearly 8 parts per million gold. Livermore quickly invited Searls and Fulton to come out for a look.

Searls, who established Newmont's first exploration staff and had been with the company since 1925, was a tough westerner who spent his days behind his desk in New York and then visited mines on the weekend. Few mines were acquired or deposits developed without the personal oversight of Newmont's aging chairman. As a young geologist, he had a reputation of arriving by train at a mine in the evening, spending several hours underground mapping the work that had been performed since his last visit, preparing a report, and leaving it on the manager's desk before catching the first train out the next morning. Fulton, equally hard-driving, boasted of working seven days a week and was not opposed to calling a staff member at 3 o'clock in the morning if he had an idea to discuss.

Together they arrived at Carlin in late September, looked over the barren land, and reviewed the gold samples. They were not impressed. Livermore wanted to stake the area to give Newmont legal protection if gold in economic amounts was found. Reluctantly, Searls gave in. "OK, John, if you want to stake this, go ahead," Livermore recalls being told. "Besides," Livermore laughs, "he didn't have another assignment for me."

Seventeen 20-acre lode claims were staked in October with the claims filed at the Eureka County courthouse one hundred miles away. The claims covered what would eventually be the main pit of the Carlin mine. A bulldozer was brought in and trenches dug to expose the underlying rocks. An assay in one trench showed 0.20 ounce of gold per ton over an eighty-foot sample. That was the Carlin discovery.

Heavy snows ended the 1961 prospecting season in late November. Livermore was promoted to manager of exploration for Newmont Canada, where he remained until leaving the company in 1970. Coope and Fulton returned to Carlin in April 1962 and soon acquired an adjoining eighty acres of land known as Popovich Hill. The property was brought to their attention by Bob Morris, who had been part of Carson City–based M M & S Mining that had been involved with the Blue Star mine. At the same time, Pete Loncar, who had supervised drilling programs for Newmont since 1946, began drilling on another prospect near Maggie Creek, about halfway between Popovich Hill and the town of Carlin. A percussion drill, which worked with compressed air like a jackhammer and was capable of drilling to a depth of about 130 feet, was acquired from a Reno road contractor. While not as precise as a diamond core drill, it cost only $2 a foot to operate versus $30 for a core drill. Carlin began on a frugal footing.

Ore samples were collected at five-foot intervals and split into three segments. One was delivered to the Treweeks for overnight assay, one went to a lab in Salt Lake City as a check and balance, and the third was stored as a backup. Results at Maggie Creek were not very encouraging given the gold price at the time. However, the deposit would later be mined in the 1970s and lead to the much larger find at Gold Quarry.

Once Popovich Hill was acquired, Loncar moved his rig north and began drilling a series of holes at 100-foot centers fifty feet from the property line of the T/Lazy S Ranch. "The day after we finished the third hole, I was surprised to see Harry Treweek personally bringing me the assay report," Loncar recalls. "Looking at it, I couldn't believe my eyes. We had struck one hundred feet of ore assaying 1.03 ounce per ton. Bob Fulton immediately flew off to Los Angeles to meet with the owners of the T/S Ranch about leasing their property and I leased another drill from a local man and put him to work a few hundred yards from the first drill."[9] The date was September 1962.

Drilling continued through 1963. Gerald Hartzel, who had just graduated from Carlin High School, was hired to carry four-by-four wooden stakes up the hills for the survey crew and haul out backpacks of rock samples for Coope and geologist Byron Hardie. "I still have my first pay stub for $2 an hour and remember when I got a raise of five cents an hour," says Hartzel, who retired as director of administrative services in 2001. "Things were done on a handshake," he recalls. "If you wanted a water truck for the drilling rigs you asked Lou Eklund [the local driller who by then had four rigs working on the property] what it would cost and he would say '$200 a month' and you would say 'fine' and he would deliver. Nothing was put on paper."[10]

By late 1963 an ore body of 11 million tons averaging 0.32 ounce per ton, or 3.5 million ounces of gold, had been proven up. "I knew we had to find something bigger than Gold Acres or Getchell, which had about a million tons of ore each, to be of interest to Newmont. But I never dreamed we'd find 11 million tons of high-grade ore," Livermore says.

Frank McQuiston, Newmont's chief metallurgist who had designed the first flotation circuit for gold recovery on the Mother Lode in California and built Newmont's first research lab in the 1930s, was brought in to supervise construction of a mill. Bechtel Corporation, which at the time was building the copper recovery plant for Newmont's 29 percent–owned Palabora copper mine in South Africa, was the general contractor.

Robert Shoemaker, Bechtel's metallurgist, later recalled McQuiston and fellow Newmont metallurgist David Christie walking into his office in San Francisco. "They said, 'We've got to have a gold plant and we've got to have it in a hurry.'"[11] Within days Bechtel had men on-site and ten months later, after working through the bitterly cold winter of 1964–65, the plant was finished and three million tons of overburden had been stripped from the mountain to expose the ore. Engineering drawings were cranked out only days before cement was poured or equipment installed. At one point 120 electricians brought from Reno 260 miles to the west were stringing wire through the facility. In all, 500 construction workers were on-site.

The mill, known as Mill No. 1, was designed to process 2,000 tons of ore a day, three times the amount of material Newmont had processed at two combined mills at Grass Valley in the 1950s. It was a combination of firsts and lasts. Carlin was the first to use a cyanide leaching and carbon recovery circuit outdoors in a freezing climate. It was also the first gold operation to use semi-autogenous mills, huge steel cylinders in which tumbling rocks grind against each other to pulverize the ore. But to save money, McQuiston acquired a couple of old ball mills from an Idaho copper mine that had not been used in thirty years. Loncar, who became general superintendent on completion of the mill, reported difficulty moving the first ore through the crushers as the ore was wet and full of clay, gumming up the works. But after a few modifications, the plant soon reached design capacity.

At the pit, ore was loaded by a 2½-yard shovel into two 35-ton Haulpak trucks for delivery to the mill. Although larger than anything in the gold industry at the time, the equipment was tiny by today's standards. To loosen the ore, blast holes were drilled sixty-five feet deep on 10-foot centers, packed with a mix of ammonium nitrate and fuel oil and then set off with a dynamite primer to fracture the rock. Each hole was assayed to determine if the rock was ore or waste and flagged with red and yellow ribbons. "That's when we discovered Pete was colorblind," recalls Hartzel.

Although operating on a 24-7 schedule, the boulder-to-bullion process required a total workforce of barely a hundred men. The automated mill, for instance, could be operated by a three-man crew on each shift. Shortly after start-up, the Operating Engineers Union organized much of the workforce. The biggest complaint was the condition of the unpaved road from Carlin and the long drive for the many employees who lived in Elko. Soon three buses were purchased to relieve the frustration. Willie West, wife of geologist Perry West and one of only three women who worked at the mine when it opened, shared a ride to work with the other women. The other miners called their car the "girlie wagon."

1.2. Mill No. 1 used the industry's first semi-autogenous, or SAG, mill (background) as well as traditional ball mills (foreground) where tumbling rocks or steel balls pulverized the ore into a fine powder prior to gold recovery. (*Newmont Archives*)

1.3. Pete Loncar (in hard hat), Carlin's first superintendent, directs stripping operations in 1964. (*Chester Higgins Jr.*)

On May 4, as a number of local dignitaries and Newmont officials gathered to watch, an electric furnace heated to 2,500 degrees Fahrenheit poured out the first bar of gold. "As the last drops fell from the ladle, some gold poured from the mold and fell onto the floor. Bob Fulton and I scrambled to our knees to pick up the beads," recalls Loncar. "We probably collected a teaspoonful of gold."

Three weeks later, President Malozemoff came to Carlin for the official dedication and declared the new operation "a miner's dream." Indeed it was. The entire project had cost Newmont just over $10 million, including $350,000 for exploration. In the first six months of operation, the Carlin mine produced 128,500 ounces of gold and earned a profit of $892,000 at the prevailing $35 an ounce price. The company recovered its entire investment in just three years.

In a pattern that was to be followed with increasing sophistication and sensitivity at later mines, the mining operation was designed to minimize its environmental impact and to safeguard the area's water sources. A large earth and rock dam was built in a canyon below the mill to contain discharge water, which was recycled for use in the mill. Automatic equipment

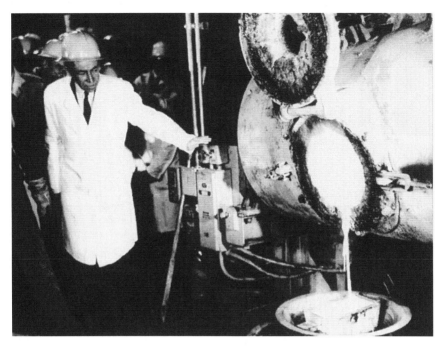

1.4. CEO Plato Malozemoff makes a ceremonial gold pour in May 1965, shortly after the opening of the Carlin mine. The event was photographed for *Life* magazine. (*Joe Monroe*)

was installed to destroy any cyanide that might spill over the dam by injecting chlorine into the solution. When Mill No. 1 closed in 1994 after processing nearly 26 million tons of ore and producing 4.7 million ounces of gold, there had never been an environmental spill.

As the nation's first large-scale, open-pit gold mine, Carlin set a new standard for low-cost, environmentally sound gold production. Equally important, it gave the company confidence in its ability to manage large mines and to grow successfully through exploration. In his 1973 history *Men and Mines of Newmont,* Robert Ramsey wrote that "Since 1900 when W. B. Thompson became interested in the Shannon mine in Arizona, Thompson himself, and later Newmont, have been involved in ninety-three major projects or investments in mining and petroleum fields. Very few of these have been the result of entirely new discoveries on the part of a Newmont geologist."[12]

For much of its history, Newmont acquired an interest in mines started by others or provided a conduit by which prospectors could obtain Wall

Street financing for their discoveries. Before starting his Carlin search, Livermore recalls a conversation with Malozemoff in which Newmont's legendary chief executive remarked, "We haven't come up with much ourselves in exploration the last ten years. I think we're better off just to buy mines."

Carlin changed that thought process. Over the past forty years, Newmont has led the industry in gold discoveries thanks to a series of talented exploration geologists backed by technological breakthroughs, a renewed open door policy toward foreign investment by many less developed countries, and a steady financial commitment from Newmont's board of directors. Their efforts continue to demonstrate that exploration is the most effective tool for creating lasting shareholder value.

Elko

Elko, Nevada, where 75 percent of all employment can be linked to gold mining, was named "the number one small town in America" during the height of the gold boom in the late 1980s. Employees of Newmont Mining agree with Norman Crampton, whose book *The 100 Best Small Towns in America* declared Elko a place "where the traditional values of family, community, faith, hard work and patriotism remain strong."[13]

The town was founded by the Central Pacific Railroad in December 1868 as crews pushed toward Promontory Point, Utah, where the golden spike joined the Central with the Union Pacific to create the transcontinental railroad. Since Newmont found gold thirty miles to the west in 1961, the population of Elko and its surrounding communities has tripled to 35,000.

Located at the edge of the Ruby Mountains halfway between Salt Lake City and Reno, the area was a hunting ground for Shoshone Indians and for French fur trappers who penetrated the area in the 1820s. With the completion of the railroad, Chinese workers moved in and planted vegetable gardens while Basque shepherds from the Pyrenees of Spain and France found it ideal for raising sheep at the end of the nineteenth century. Family-style Basque restaurants are still a highlight of the town.

The Commercial Hotel offered big-name entertainment as well as gambling in the early 1940s, years before Las Vegas or Reno casinos became entertainment meccas. The annual Cowboy Poetry Gathering draws hundreds of visitors to Elko each year.

Bing Crosby, who owned cattle ranches in the area, was honorary mayor of Elko at the time of the Carlin discovery—from 1947 until his death in 1977. He would occasionally show up at St. Joseph's Catholic Church for Sunday Mass, silencing the choir with his singing.

Some say the town's name was provided by Charles Crocker of the Central Pacific, who liked to name towns for animals and added the O to Elk. But in 1907, the *Elko Free Press* related the story of a dead Indian boy at whose funeral the Shoshone chanted "Elko, Elko" for "beautiful, beautiful." Either way, those who have spent part of their careers in the community would most likely agree with Peter Philip, who commented on his retirement as Newmont president in 1994, "Elko is the place where you cry when you get there and cry when you leave."[14]

2

COLONEL

When Newmont Mining Corporation issued its first annual report for 1925, the company looked more like a mutual fund than a mining house. It had no operations but held investments valued at $20 million in six mining and oil companies. That portfolio of assets generated $2.5 million in dividends and interest during the year, enabling the company to pay out $1.20 per share to its shareholders. There were 430,000 shares of stock outstanding, 300,000 owned by William Boyce Thompson, the company's chairman and founder, and a handful of officers and directors, and 130,000 sold in an initial public offering earlier that year that raised $5.2 million at $40 a share.

With the decision to list the company's stock on New York's Curb Exchange, the forerunner of the American Stock Exchange and the trading arena for the country's more speculative issues of the day, Thompson added the word "Mining" to a company he had incorporated under the laws of Delaware on May 2, 1921. Newmont Corporation had been a private investment vehicle for Thompson's collection of mining interests, but now that public shareholders were involved he wanted a more descriptive name for the company's activities, one that would forewarn of the risks involved.

Newmont's debut as a publicly traded company was major news in the New York and Boston financial press and mining journals. The company was described as "unique," in that it combined the attributes of a British mining house, investing in mining properties and exploration worldwide, with those of an investment trust, holding sizable shares and trading in profitable mining and oil companies. The *Wall Street Journal* reported that through the sale of stock "the public was permitted to share in the business judgment and investment sagacity of Colonel William Boyce Thompson" backed by "an engineering and geological corps that ranks with the best in the country."[1]

While Newmont dates itself from its 1921 incorporation, that was merely a reincorporation of Thompson's earlier investment vehicle, Newmont Company, which had been chartered under the laws of Maine in March 1916. Before that there had been the Gunn-Thompson Company established in New York in 1907 to finance the exploration and development of mining properties; the W. B. Thompson Company of Boston in 1902, which bought and sold mining stocks; and the Thompson Investment Company of Butte, Montana, created in 1897 to invest in real estate and mining.

With each new venture Thompson became more adroit at searching out attractive mining properties; building ties with the era's best geologists and mining engineers to investigate and develop each prospect's potential; forging alliances with New York's powerful money houses for financing; and finally promoting the mines through the public sale of stock. Thompson didn't explore; he listened. And when he heard something he liked he sent his experts to check it out. It was said he had "20/20 hearing."[2]

He was instrumental in and had a major part in organizing, financing, and developing some of the most important mines and mining companies of the twentieth century, including Anglo American Corporation, Kennecott, Magma Copper, Texas Gulf Sulphur, and Hudson Bay Mining and Smelting. Bringing eastern money to western mines made him exceedingly wealthy. The word Newmont is a contraction for New York, where Wall Street's canyons could be mined for money, and Montana, the home of his birth and mining heritage.

Thompson was born in May 1869—a time when Indian wars were raging across the Upper Plains—in Alder Gulch, Montana, a village of log cabins which with neighboring Virginia City had been the site of an 1863 gold rush. Thompson's father, one of ten thousand who converged on the area, left North Dakota with a covered wagon, four oxen, and a couple of cows. When he arrived over the Yellowstone Trail only the cows were left and the elder Thompson described them as "mostly horns and ribs." Finding the best claims occupied, he returned east to bring back a quartz-crushing mill. But by the time he made his second entry into Virginia City, the gold was gone, the miners were departing, and there was no need for labor-saving machinery. He was broke.

Thompson learned an important lesson from his father's experience. If he had sized up the situation before leaving, the elder Thompson would have realized that the gold's potential was limited. "I have spent thousands

of dollars on investigation before I invested a dollar in development," Newmont's founder told a reporter in 1920. "If an impulse came to move ahead
before I got to the bottom of things, I thought of my dear old dad, who
reached Virginia City with his quartz mill after the gold rush was over."[3]

The rough and tumble nature of Western mining camps was embedded in Thompson's early experience, both at Alder Gulch and later at Butte,
a copper-mining town where his father set up a sawmill and developed a
number of small mining claims. Thompson's biographer, Hermann Hagedorn, wrote, "Butte was whiskey and women and dice and profanity and the
quick 'draw.' And if you did not like it you could go to hell."[4] His parents
sent him east, to Phillips Exeter Academy in New Hampshire, and then
to Columbia University's School of Mines in New York City. He did not
distinguish himself at either institution, except by his proficiency at poker,
and did not graduate.

Back in Montana he sold lumber and coal, dabbled in real estate, and
formed Thompson Investment Company with his father and brothers. Then
in 1899, at age twenty-nine, he returned to New York with a briefcase full
of copper stocks. When his promotional efforts came to naught, he ventured into other things, "easy things" he hoped would "make a killing."[5] He
bought a formula for cough drops and imported ashtrays from Japan with
pictures of the Mormon Tabernacle for sale in Salt Lake City. With his wife
and young daughter he lived beyond his means at the Waldorf Astoria Hotel because he thought the address added prestige to his ventures.

Fortune turned that summer when he learned that the small Shannon
copper mine near Clifton, Arizona, was for sale. Thompson went to take a
look and became infatuated with both the mine and the American Southwest. Finding the Shannon's geology similar to an adjacent, profitable mine,
Thompson headed for Denver to negotiate with the owners. When he arrived, the asking price was $250,000. He left after paying $500 down and
promising future installments. The Shannon had expansion possibilities but
needed a smelter to convert its ore into marketable metal and a way to connect to the main railroad ten miles away. Thompson set out to raise the necessary funds, pounding the pavement in New York, Hartford, Boston, and
places in between.

In the spring of 1900, his father in Butte showed a telegram he had just
received to a friend and complained, "That damn fool boy of mine is do-

ing the most ridiculous thing I have ever heard of."[6] W. B. wanted $5,000 to charter a railroad car to bring potential investors to Arizona to visit the mine. It was one of the first investor relations tours in mining history and helped raise $750,000. After installing professional management and developing the property, Thompson sold his interest in 1904 for $75,000.

But that was chump change in an age of high-flying ventures, inflated stock promotions, and fast money. At the turn of the century, men of obscurity rose to power as oil barons, steel magnates, and financiers. John D. Rockefeller, J. Pierpont Morgan, Andrew Carnegie, Jay Gould, and E. H. Harriman stalked Wall Street and the centers of power. Consolidation seemed the focus of business, and companies of every sort were combining in giant trusts. In 1898, Morgan and executives from U.S. Steel formed International Nickel with plans, according to the *Canadian Mining Review*, "to consolidate and control the nickel production of the world."[7] In 1899 Henry Rogers, a Rockefeller protégé, formed a group that consolidated Anaconda and other copper mines in Butte into Amalgamated Copper Company and later that year organized the American Smelting & Refining Company (ASARCO), to control lead and silver smelting operations from New England to Colorado. These were known as the Copper Trust and the Smelter Trust.

Of more permanent influence, the new century also brought a flood of new technology and ideas to mechanize manufacturing, improve productivity, and apply scientific principles to fields as old as farming and mining. Two who profoundly impacted mining were Daniel Jackling, a graduate of the Missouri School of Mines, and Henry Krumb, who, like Thompson, had attended Columbia.

Jackling reasoned that if big ore bodies could be mined in a big way— using economies of scale—even low-grade deposits could be highly profitable. In 1906 he helped organize the Utah Copper Company to develop a huge porphyry copper deposit at Bingham Canyon. It was the nation's first large-scale, open-pit mine utilizing steam shovels and steam-driven drills, instead of relying on the physical labor of men with picks, wheelbarrows, and mule-drawn carts. A 6,000-ton-a-day mill, an unheard-of size for its day, incorporated ball mills where rotating steel cylinders filled with cascading steel balls pulverized the ore before processing.

Krumb was the first to apply scientific methods to develop an ore body.

He laid out a grid pattern for drilling and sampling that enabled Jackling to define the deposit and develop a mine plan before breaking ground. Krumb's methodology is still in use today. Thompson helped raise $1.5 million to finance Jackling's first smelter and became lifelong friends with both men. Krumb never worked for Newmont but was a consultant for many years and served as a director from the company's inception until his death in 1958.

Another important name in mining—Guggenheim—entered Thompson's circle early in his career—or better stated, he entered theirs. Meyer Guggenheim came to America in the 1840s and with seven sons established a mining dynasty. A lace merchant in Philadelphia, he loaned money to a couple of start-up silver mines in Leadville, Colorado, in the 1870s and when they failed, the family took possession. At the time Leadville and Virginia City, Nevada, were the biggest mining towns in the West.

The Guggenheims soon discovered that the real money in mining, at least at that time, came not in moving rock but in smelting ore, and they set out to dominate the smelter market. In 1900, just one year after its creation, they wrested control of ASARCO from Henry Rogers and in 1906, when Jackling's Utah Copper operation needed more funds, Daniel Guggenheim and his brothers stepped in to take control of Bingham Canyon.

America and the world were electrifying, which meant that copper for wiring, transformers, and transmission lines was in increasing demand. Plumbing was moving indoors and required copper pipes. In the forty-year span between the late 1880s and late 1920s, world copper consumption rose eightfold, and mining and smelting companies, including ASARCO and Utah Copper, became the largest corporations on the planet.

With rising copper prices, Butte was known as the "richest hill on earth," and the man from Alder Gulch dreamed of a "second Butte." He took an option on 40 percent of the Nevada Consolidated copper mine near Ely at $12 a share and quickly sold it to the Guggenheims at $12.50 for a $200,000 profit.

Next came Nipissing, a silver and cobalt mine 350 miles north of Toronto, where a vein 6 to 28 inches wide and 600 feet long waited to be exploited. Thomas Lamont, a New York banker and classmate of Thompson's at Exeter, suggested to the owners that Thompson was the man to promote their property. In 1906, Thompson took an option on 600,000 shares at an average of $4.33 a share and brought in a mining reporter, Starr Bullock from the *New York Sun,* to help spin the story. Soon Nipissing was heralded as the "silver sidewalk" and its stock price on the Curb soared to 12, 20, and then 33⅞.

With Thompson's encouragement the Guggenheims took an option for 400,000 shares at $25 each, paying $2.5 million as the first of four installments. Thompson and Bullock then led a party to Canada to tour the mine. While the Guggenheims' expert, John Hammond, was impressed, Thompson's own engineer, George Gunn, an old friend from Butte, detected that the glitter was mostly on the surface and that the vein narrowed at depth. Gunn felt obliged to share his views with Hammond; Thompson was determined to keep the two men apart and on the train trip back engaged Gunn in an all-night poker game. At North Bay, Gunn departed for the West on the Canadian Pacific after telling Thompson to sell his stock at the first opportunity. Later, as Thompson went to a phone at the station in Ottawa, he encountered Hammond, who asked that he place a buy order for him for 10,000 shares. Thompson executed both orders on the same call and then sent Gunn a fur coat as a thank you. In the end, Thompson pocketed $5 million and the Guggenheims, embarrassed when the stock price plunged, offered to reimburse investors who had bought in on their advice.

Apparently there were no hard feelings, since a year later the Guggenheims turned to Thompson to promote their Yukon Gold mine. In a repeat pattern, a reporter was engaged to provide hype, the stock rose, and then it tumbled amid charges and denials. Thompson left with more than a jingle and a smile. Even later, when the Guggenheims and J. P. Morgan put their copper interests together into Kennecott Copper Corporation, Thompson was asked to handle the marketing. A close friend, Clarence Barron, a Boston financial writer who acquired the *Wall Street Journal* and its parent, Dow Jones & Company, in 1902 and for whom *Barron's* financial magazine is named, was often called upon to draft news releases for Thompson's ventures and to put the story on the ticker before morning trading began.

These were the days before the Securities and Exchange Commission, when insider trading was common practice. Thompson was a wheeler-dealer, sitting at his desk hour after hour buying, selling, promoting, trading, cajoling. But he was also a market maker, particularly in public offerings, who would acquire an initial block of stock, sell as the price went up, buy back on declines, and put his own capital at risk in order to maintain liquidity and a semblance of order in a raucous market.

Later in life he liked to be called "Colonel." But Thompson's nickname in New York and Boston was "Boulder." He worked exclusively on the free-wheeling Curb Exchange and resigned after a short period with the New York brokerage firm of Hayden, Stone & Co. because it was obliged to follow New York Stock Exchange rules. "I may want to do some things those fuddy-duddies on the Stock Exchange won't like," he remarked.[8] Nevertheless, his blue eyes could look another straight in the face and he was known as a "straight shooter" in his promotions. "Never sell a man anything for more than it's worth," he told an associate.

He was a big man, corpulent some said, which seemed fitting for a man of power in the early twentieth century. President Theodore Roosevelt, whose trust-busting Thompson believed was rooted in an "ignorance" of business, was succeeded in 1909 by William Howard Taft, the two being the most corpulent men to ever hold the presidency. Boulder Thompson weighed 220 pounds and ate, drank, and smoked to the point of excess, often consuming at one meal enough to feed three men. He was said to smoke forty cigars a day and carried a plug of tobacco for times in between. Balding from his late twenties, he looked ten years older than his age. Yet he was good-humored, unless an underling's miscue brought forth a tirade of profanity, and was almost always optimistic. There was money to be made.

He invested in utilities, was one of the largest shareholders in Chase National Bank and Bethlehem Steel, launched a Cuban sugar company, and held a controlling interest in companies that made Pierce Arrow automobiles and Indian motorcycles. He built a sixty-seven-room mansion at Yonkers, along the Hudson, and bought paintings by Reynolds, Gainsborough, and Titian. He would rise at dawn and often worked late into the night at his office on Wall Street or attending functions at the Metropolitan or Union League Club.

For all of this, mining and mining stocks remained his passion. In 1908 he organized the Inspiration copper mine at Globe, Arizona, and poured $17 million into its development before extracting a pound of metal. He then got it all back plus $3 million more in one year and received millions more in succeeding years. Twenty miles to the west, he picked up the Silver

2.1. Newmont founder Colonel William B. Thompson, at Alder, his house in Yonkers, New York. (*Newmont Archives*)

Queen mine for $130,000. Both moves were on the recommendation of Henry Krumb.

Located at the edge of the squalid town of Superior, the Silver Queen was an abandoned copper mine with a record of producing only 50 tons of ore in thirty years. Thompson renamed the mine Magma, raised an initial $1.2 million, and began sinking a shaft. At the 650-foot level the main ore vein was 8 feet wide, 150 feet long, and assayed between $800 and $1,000 per ton in copper and silver. By 1913 the shaft had reached 1,400 feet and the ore was continuous. A 150-ton per day concentration mill was installed and a power line was brought in from the just completed Roosevelt Dam on the Salt River twenty-five miles north of Superior. A 75-horsepower electric motor manned the pumps to keep the shaft dry, while a 225-horsepower motor drove the air compressors that operated the hoist. These were state-of-the art for their day.

Production at Magma began in 1914 under Alexander J. McNab, a Canadian metallurgist Thompson had originally hired to run the Inspiration mine. Initially, concentrate was hauled out daily by a three-wagon train carrying thirty tons and pulled by a team of thirty-two horses and mules to a rail head at Florence, thirty miles to the southwest, where it could be shipped to ASARCO's refinery at Hayden. A year later, after a rail connection cut shipping costs to a fraction of the wagon team's $10 a ton, Magma president Walter H. Aldridge could report a rosy outlook to shareholders: "With a production of 50,000 tons of ore annually of average grade, there will result a profit of approximately $500,000 per year, assuming a selling price of copper of 14 cents a pound."[9]

With wealth came responsibility and Thompson gave with as much enthusiasm as he earned. He established thirty-six fellowships at Mellon Institute to study copper recovery methods; he built science and administration buildings for Exeter; he headed a committee to erect a permanent memorial to Teddy Roosevelt, despite his earlier misgivings about the man; he raised $20 million for the first Liberty Loan program during World War I and personally subscribed for $1.5 million; and he raised millions for the Republican Party. When future president Herbert Hoover established a relief fund for Belgium during the war, Thompson engaged New York's Rocky Mountain Club in the cause and raised $5 million after priming the pump with $100,000 of his own.

In 1917, in a mission that earned him the honorary title "Colonel," Thompson was asked by the American Red Cross to head a delegation to Russia to assess the needs of the people in the wake of the overthrow of the czar. Shocked by what he saw, he gave a million dollars. An interim provisional government had been established by Prime Minister Alexander Kerensky, a democratic socialist, but it was not expected to hold against the rising Bolshevik tide. Thompson sought to prop up the Kerensky regime, in part to keep Russia in the war against Germany, and urged the prime minister to accept some of the Communists' demands, specifically the redistribution of land from the great land barons to the peasants. While many in the United States and Britain were appalled, Thompson barked, "Distribute the damned land and settle the compensation later."[10]

After the Communist takeover, he urged President Woodrow Wilson to extend American recognition to the Soviet regime and in newspaper interviews argued that the Russian revolution was as necessary for its people as the abolition of slavery was for the United States. While Thompson thought he was being a realist, the public thought he had been "dyed red." Hagedorn argues that in his "inexperience . . . he permitted himself to appear as an apologist for the Bolshevik order."[11] Yet, he later received public praise for his cool competence during that political storm.

Raymond Robins, another member of the American Red Cross legation, described walking into Thompson's room at the Hotel de l'Europe in Petrograd (St. Petersburg) on the evening of November 2, 1917. The Bolshevik revolution was in full swing, gunshots echoed in the streets and the hotel was expected to be sacked. Instead of showing alarm, one of America's foremost capitalists was calmly smoking a cigar while poring over an engineering drawing of the Magma mine. "Panther," which was his nickname for Robins, "it looks to me as though on the 1,800 foot level we'd find good ore," Thompson remarked. "If the Magma is what I think she is, I'm going to put up the finest smelter in the world there."[12] Whatever his sympathy for the underclass, world events were beyond his control; better to focus on his newest mine and the millions to be made on Wall Street.

The end of World War I brought a collapse in metal prices and production at Magma was suspended in 1921. Instead of brooding, Thompson used the time to add reserves, increase capacity, and improve facilities. This included building the smelter he had discussed with Robins, which saved two cents a pound Magma had been paying the Guggenheims at ASARCO. Production resumed in 1923 with a workforce of 750 men. Magma proved to be a fabulously rich mine, with veins running 14 percent copper, earning Thompson a reputation for "making millions out of other men's scrap heaps."[13] Magma would be one of Newmont's most important investments for nearly seventy-five years.

Thompson's Exeter classmate Lamont, who had become a partner in J. P. Morgan, was a close business associate and the two men often referred deals to each other. With extensive investments in Mexico's Sonora Province, he lobbied the U.S. Senate on behalf of another Morgan partner and close friend, Dwight Morrow, to be named ambassador to Mexico. In May 1929, Morrow's daughter Anne married Charles Lindbergh, whose solo flight from New York to Paris two years earlier had made him the celebrity of the era.

Other close ties were with Hoover, the most influential mining engineer of the period, and Bernard Baruch, a noted Wall Street financier and presidential advisor. Baruch and the Morgan interests involved Thompson in the 1918 organization of Texas Gulf Sulphur Corporation, which was developing the Frasch process to inject superheated steam into sulfur wells to extract the molten material. With Baruch and Jackling, Thompson formed New York Orient Mines to explore for minerals in China and the Far East. Also investing in that part of the world was the British-based Burma Company in which Hoover was a principal shareholder until he sold his interest to Thompson and others. A $100,000 investment in 1924 in Noranda Mines, a Canadian gold producer, turned a profit of $1.5 million within a year.

Another venture with longstanding benefit to Newmont was Thompson's 1925 investment of $235,000 in Baruch's Orange oilfield in Texas. Ownership rights were tangled and Thompson sent his personal lawyer, Charles Ayer, to take a look. Ayer, an astute Californian who wore a stiff wing collar around his short neck and looked, according to some, like a barrister out of Dickens, resolved the issues and consolidated the various interests. But before a barrel of oil was produced, Thompson negotiated a swap of that property for an interest in Continental Oil Company of Maine, which on the Justice Department's breakup of the Standard Oil Trust had taken up Standard's interests in the Rocky Mountains. As a result, Newmont became the largest shareholder in Continental.

Ayer and Krumb also were instrumental in Newmont's help in organizing the Hudson Bay Mining and Smelting Company. Sent by Thompson to check out the Flin Flon copper deposit in northern Manitoba shortly after its discovery in 1914, Krumb sank $350,000 in a drilling program that, while exciting, failed to discover an economic ore body. When the booming metals market of 1928 brought in a new group to develop the property, Ayer insisted not only that Newmont be awarded a one-third interest in what became Hudson Bay Mining but that Thompson's copper expert, McNab, help manage the operation. Over the years, Newmont and its shareholders received $12 million from that investment.

By the time Newmont went public in 1925, Thompson was feeling the effects of his lifestyle and job pressures and began to step back. He had assembled what the *Engineering and Mining Journal-Press* called "an imposing array of financial and technical talent"[14] to continue the search for prime prospects to develop. At Newmont, Ayer had become president after a short stint by Thompson's son-in-law, Theodore Schulze. Fred Searls Jr., considered one of the country's top geologists and a man Thompson had brought on to explore one of his properties in China, was a vice president. Henry Dodge was secretary and treasurer. Directors in addition to Thompson and the above named included another vice president, David Thomas; Krumb; McNab, vice president of Magma; Stephen Birch, president of Kennecott; Vernon Munroe of the Morgan firm; John Kemmerer, a western coal mine operator and president of Utah Copper; and Albert Wiggin, president of the Chase Bank.

Magma Copper, with assets of $8.5 million, had been publicly traded for a decade and listed on the New York Stock Exchange since 1922. Although Newmont did not yet own any shares in Magma, the two companies shared offices at 14 Wall Street. Ayer was also president of Magma and Dodge was the company's secretary-treasurer. Thompson did not have a seat on the Magma board but was a principal shareholder and from his office adorned with bearskin rugs and the mounted heads of a buffalo, elk, and bighorn sheep, he remained the moving force behind both companies.

Hagedorn, Thompson's biographer, says his reputation went far beyond that of a flamboyant promoter. He was a member of the Federal Reserve Bank of New York and was given credit for initiating "enterprises which employed more than 100,000 men."[15] In 1921, he was appointed by President Warren Harding as the U.S. representative to attend Peru's one hundredth anniversary celebration. A few years later, Newmont became a large investor and managing partner in New Verde Mines in a search for lead, zinc, and silver in Peru.

Thompson traveled widely—to Europe, South America, and China—and in style. He bought the second largest yacht in the world and christened it the *Alder,* the name he gave his private railroad car and his mansion in Yonkers. At 294 feet, the *Alder* was just ten feet shorter than J. P. Morgan's *Corsair.*

He also started taking time to stop and smell the roses. He loved flowers and had prize-winning gardens and greenhouses at his estate in Yonkers. In 1924 he established the Boyce Thompson Institute for Plant Research on nine acres across the street from his home and eventually endowed it with $10 million. His goal was to bring science to agriculture and thereby improve the production of food for a hungry world. Now located on the campus of Cornell University, the institute is one of the most prestigious such research centers in the world. He built a second home, the Picket Post House, on a bluff in Arizona not far from Magma's operations at Superior. There he founded the 320-acre Boyce Thompson Southwest Arboretum, which today exhibits the world's finest collection of desert plants.

Thompson wasn't the only philanthropist among Newmont's founders. Krumb, who had no children, bestowed $16 million on Columbia University in thanks for a $200 scholarship he had received in 1895. The gifts were the largest ever received by the university and provided the endowment for the Krumb School of Mines.

In early 1929, Colonel Thompson felt that the stock market was overpriced and began selling his holdings. He thus avoided the worst impact of the market crash. Since suffering a stroke in 1926 he had been confined to a wheelchair and brooded about his mortality. When he died on June 27, 1930, at the age of sixty-one, he left an estate valued at $85–$150 million[16] and a legacy of public service and philanthropy matched by few. More important, he also left a company that has survived and prospered into the twenty-first century as one of the world's most respected mining houses.

All in the Family

The board of directors of Newmont Mining included heirs of William Boyce Thompson until 1986, when a decline in the copper price brought a diversification in family holdings.

In 1929 his only child, Margaret Schulze, joined the board and was listed in reports as "Mrs. Boyce Thompson Schulze." Two years later she married U.S. diplomat and banking scion Anthony J. Drexel Biddle Jr., whose previous marriage had been to Mary Duke, heiress to a tobacco fortune, and became, for corporate purposes, "Mrs. Thompson Biddle." In 1934, as her husband's duties took him abroad as ambassador to Poland, Mrs. Biddle relinquished her board seat. Her mother, Thompson's widow, Gertrude, had joined the board a year earlier and served until her death in 1950.

Mrs. Thompson also assumed another of her husband's positions, that of chairman of the Magma Arizona Railroad. The thirty-mile standard gauge railroad carried passengers, mail, freight, and copper concentrate between Superior, Arizona, and a branch of the Southern Pacific southeast of Phoenix. She was the first woman to head a railroad in the United States.

Mrs. Biddle, who had inherited some of her father's business skills and as the company's largest shareholder was deeply interested in Newmont's success, returned to the board in 1947 and served until her death in 1956.[17] Both of her children, Theodore Schulze Jr. and Margaret Downey, were Newmont directors. Schulze, the son of Newmont's first president, succeeded his mother and served until his untimely death in 1962. Mrs. Downey, wife of radio and television singer Morton Downey, was a director from 1950 until her death at age forty-two in 1964. Newspaper reports at the time called her one of the richest women in America with substantial interests in both Newmont and Magma Copper.

On her death, her daughter (by her first marriage to Polish Prince Alexander Hohenlohe) Catherine Hohenlohe, Thompson's great-granddaughter, became Newmont's youngest director at age twenty-two. In 1970 Catherine, by then Mrs. William Cook, resigned and was replaced by her brother, Washington attorney and Montana rancher Christian Hohenlohe, who served until 1977. He, in turn, was succeeded by Mrs. Cook's subsequent husband, George Jacobus, a Little Rock real estate developer and Palm Beach investor, who remained a board member until 1986.

3

VEINS

The Roaring Twenties were halcyon years for Newmont Mining Corporation as W. B. Thompson sorted out his investments between his private holdings and those of his publicly held companies and as his newly assembled team picked up the reins of management. In just four years since becoming a publicly traded company, net profits rose nearly sixfold to $11.8 million, or $23.35 a share, dividends increased from $1.20 to $4 a share, and with a stock price that peaked at $236 a share in August 1929, market capitalization topped $100 million.

In 1928, Newmont took a 15 percent interest in Magma Copper. It also held large positions in Kennecott Copper, Hudson Bay Mining and Smelting, Texas Gulf Sulphur, Continental Oil, Standard Oil of California, Standard Oil of Indiana and eight other mining and petroleum concerns, three of which were in southern Africa. Investments were selected as much for their potential for trading profits as for long-term growth, as even positions in core holdings were sold and bought back on a regular basis.

With the Great Depression, Newmont, like the rest of America, suffered a staggering blow. Demand for metals and oil fell and prices retreated, causing companies Newmont relied on for dividends to slash their payouts. Magma illustrated the problem. In 1929, 38 million pounds of copper were produced at a cost of just over nine cents a pound. With a selling price of 18.2 cents a pound, Magma earned a profit of $3 million and paid out $2 million in dividends, of which Newmont's share was $300,000. By 1932, production had dropped 44 percent to 21 million pounds and the copper price had fallen to six cents. Although Magma paid a small dividend, despite a loss for the year, Newmont received just $30,000, 90 percent less than three years earlier. Dividends were eliminated in the next year.

Following Thompson's death in 1930, Newmont suffered losses in 1931 and 1932, eliminated dividends to its shareholders between mid-1931 and mid-1934, and saw its stock price tumble to an all-time low of $3.875 a share in 1932. Salaries were slashed by 20 percent for those earning over $10,000 a year and president Charles Ayer, who preferred to be called "Judge," gave up his own salary. For the remainder of his career—he served on the board until his death at age ninety-eight in 1961—he never took another dollar in salary, relying instead on stock and dividends.

Thomas Lamont and the J. P. Morgan firm, Thompson's allies for years, were alarmed about the company in the absence of the founder's leadership. Ayer and geologist Fred Searls Jr. had outstanding competence in their fields, but could they weather a financial crisis this severe? Lamont along with director Albert Wiggin, president of the Chase Bank, pressed on the young company the services of Franz Schneider, an engineering graduate from the Massachusetts Institute of Technology and financial editor of the New York *Sun,* a publication Lamont owned. Within a year, Schneider was made a director and chairman of the executive committee and had responsibility for all financial decisions. Ayer, Searls, and Schneider ran the company as committee, a "three-headed dog" according to insiders, from 1931 until 1947 when Ayer was made chairman of the board, Searls president and CEO, and Schneider executive vice president. (Schneider, who later played a key role in the establishment of the natural gas industry in the United States, died in 1993 at age 105.)

Despite the bankers' concern, the company had an ace in the hole—gold. President Roosevelt's 1934 decision to set the gold price at $35 an ounce represented a jump from the $20.67 price at which gold had been fixed for the previous one hundred years. While other metals were being squeezed, the government was giving gold miners a 69 percent price increase. The reason had to do with gold's traditional standing as the currency of last resort. During the financial panic of 1933, banks closed by the thousands and people turned to gold as a safe haven for their savings. Twenty million dollars in paper currency was being turned in to the U.S. Treasury each week in demand for gold.[1] To stop the drain, Roosevelt declared a bank holiday, deflated the dollar by raising the gold price, and confiscated all gold coins and bullion held by U.S. citizens. Under his order, only the federal government could hold the metal and was the sole buyer of gold from U.S. mines.

Newmont, in one of those fortuitous moments in its history, had acquired a couple of gold mines in 1929. Not just any mines, but the two largest and most important gold mines in California history—the Empire and North

3.1. During the Depression, Newmont was governed by a three-man executive commit-tee known as the "three-headed dog." Chaired by Franz Schneider (right), the committee included president Charles Ayer (top) and geologist Fred Searls Jr., both of whom later be-came CEO. (*Newmont Archives*)

Star in Grass Valley. Searls had grown up in neighboring Nevada City, in the foothills of the Sierra Nevadas, and had been afflicted with gold fever since his youth. His 1906 honors thesis in geology from the University of California, Berkeley, was on the Empire mine. When the owner, who had known Searls for years, lost interest in mining due to the death of his daughter and his own illness, he offered it to Searls for the bargain price of $250,000. On hearing this, the owners of the adjacent North Star, which had been feuding with the Empire over land claims for years, offered to put up their mine and $150,000 in working capital for a 49 percent interest in the combined properties. Newmont acquired both mines and formed a new company, Empire-Star Mines, of which it owned 51 percent, to operate the properties. Newmont's ownership was later reduced to 37 percent as shares were issued to acquire additional gold mines.

The Empire mine dated from 1850, the North Star from a year later. Both were tapping deep quartz veins, in which gold-bearing ore was sandwiched in fault zones between harder granodiorite rocks. As the California forty-niners worked their gold pans in the riverbeds north of Sacramento, they moved upstream in search of the source, or Mother Lode, of this placer gold. When prospectors encountered large occurrences of gold in quartz outcrop-pings along the nearby hills, they staked their claims and began digging with picks and shovels. Early claims included such names as Ophir,[2] Magenta, Gold Hill, Crown Point, and WYOD (Work Your Own Diggings). But the hard rock wasn't easily moved by muscle alone; it took heavy equipment, explosives, steam power to lift hoists and power rock drills, pumps to keep the shafts dry, and costly stamp mills to crush the ore. In short, it took money and organization, the consolidation of claims, and the pooling of resources by investors. The Empire and North Star became the first gold mines in America to be operated as businesses rather than as an individual prospector's property.

By 1900, the Empire was the showplace of all California mines, with elaborate water-powered equipment having replaced the steam-driven workings of the past. Stone cottages for administrators surrounded thirteen acres of lawn and gardens and an artificial lake. In 1918, as the mine reached an inclined depth of 7,500 feet and ore was being extracted at a dozen levels, a 500-horsepower electric motor was installed to operate the hoist. On the surface, the ore was crushed in a 60-stamp mill in which 60 metal hammers weighing 1,575 pounds each dropped seven inches at the rate of 102 times per minute. Gold was separated from the crushed ore on vibrating tables and then amalgamated with mercury for final recovery. The entire operation was said to work like a Swiss watch.

Once Newmont acquired the property, an exploration program was launched, which found new reserves. The older North Star mill was closed and a 6,000-foot-long overhead tram was constructed to transport ore to the Empire mill. Frank McQuiston, who was hired as a metallurgist in 1934, improved the sequencing of ore treatment to speed processing, installed a new ball mill and jaw crusher, and replaced the shaker tables with the industry's first flotation plant for the chemical separation of gold from ore. With 1,290 employees mining and processing 1,500 tons of ore a day, the Empire-Star was the largest gold mine in California, which at the time was the largest gold-producing state in the nation. Most important, during the crucial years of the Depression, from 1931 until its wartime closure in late 1942, the Empire-Star paid Newmont $3.2 million in dividends.

Success at Grass Valley brought an intensified search for other gold mines. In 1931, six mines on the Mother Lode, including the Original 16 to 1 mine, were acquired. A gold deposit in western Ontario, named the Northern Empire, was brought into production in 1934 at a cost of $750,000 and in seven years paid Newmont nearly twice that much in dividends. Berens River Mines of Manitoba and other properties in Ontario and British Columbia also were added. John Drybrough, who brought Berens River to Searls's attention, became president of Newmont Canada in 1942.

In Nevada, Newmont took an interest in the Getchell mine. Nobel Getchell, a Nevada state senator, had grubstaked a couple of prospectors for several years before the two, reportedly after consuming a considerable amount of whiskey, stumbled upon an outcropping north of Golconda in 1936 and sent a sample to Reno for assay. It showed gold at better than 0.20 ounce per ton, or $7 to $8 for each ton mined. Unable to finance development on his own, Getchell turned to longtime Newmont friend Bernard Baruch in New York who put up $1 million and immediately asked Searls to examine the property. Liking what he saw, Searls got Newmont to join Baruch in taking a joint 38 percent interest. Production began the next year after installation of a 1,000-ton-per-day cyanide recovery plant. With operating costs of $1 a ton, the mine paid handsome dividends for a few years.

NIGHT SHIFT.
EMPIRE MINE
GRASS VALLEY. CAL

G.H. Miller
PHOTO

3.2. Workers prepare to descend on a tram into California's Empire mine in 1910, when it was one of the largest gold mines in the world. Newmont acquired the Empire and adjoining North Star mines in 1929. (*Empire mine*)

But near-surface oxide ore soon gave way to metallurgically complex sulfides that even McQuiston was unable to solve.

By 1939, Newmont had an interest in twelve gold mines and counted on the yellow metal for much of its income.

Having weathered the Depression and increased its portfolio to holdings in thirty-three mining and oil concerns, Newmont took another significant step in 1939 by applying for listing on the New York Stock Exchange. Its application was approved on December 27 and one month later, on January 27, 1940, the *Wall Street Journal* reported that Newmont "made its bow" on the Big Board. Trading that day, a Saturday, involved 100 blocks of 100 shares each, or 10,000 shares, at a closing price of 73⅛, up from Friday's close of 72 on the Curb Exchange. At the time, Newmont listed 2,411 shareholders.

While the company sought to resume gold production after 1945, none of the early mines could withstand the inflationary environment and labor pressures that followed World War II. At the Empire-Star, it was costing $45 to produce $35 worth of gold. Newmont chafed at government policies that prohibited its return to profitability. As president Searls told shareholders in the company's 1950 annual report, "the Government of the United States must eventually recognize the deterioration of the dollar and either pay a fair price for the gold produced or allow it to be sold [on the international market] to those who will pay such a price."

Additionally, the Cornish leasing system that had operated at Grass Valley for a hundred years had come under attack. Under the system, marginal underground stopes were leased to individual miners who, working on their own, often earned more than they would have as an employee. (Hence the name Work Your Own Diggings.) But after the war, the federal government sought to classify such miners as employees, subject to wage and hour policies, collective bargaining, and withholding for income and Social Security taxes.

Without relief, the Empire-Star mine closed, after a strike, in 1956. Over its 105-year history, the combined Empire and North Star mines had produced nearly 10.5 million tons of ore and recovered 5.8 million ounces of gold worth $135 million. A little over one-quarter of that gold was attributable to Newmont's twenty-seven years of ownership, most of it in the prewar period. In 1974 Newmont sold the land, equipment, and buildings to the California Department of Parks and Recreation for $1.25 million.

Today the Empire Mine State Historic Park, with restored buildings and 784 acres of land, provides a fascinating glimpse of the nation's early gold mining and the history of the Mother Lode.

To this day, however, Newmont still owns the mineral rights since Plato Malozemoff, Newmont's CEO in 1974, had an aversion to selling reserves. Attorney David Potter, who handled the sale, provides an interesting anecdote. There were nearly five hundred miles of underground workings at Grass Valley, which filled with water once mining stopped. This water poured out of a tunnel into a river. "I was terrified by the thought of what might happen if that tunnel blocked up and then burst forth flooding the entire Grass Valley," Potter says. "I drove myself crazy trying to figure out how to deed it to the state so that if something went wrong, it was their problem and not ours." His solution: "a funny section in the deed where the state's interest goes down 200 feet for a couple hundred yards."[3] In 2007, with gold above $800 an ounce, Newmont was considering another look at those reserves.

The Empire-Star mine is credited with Newmont's survival during the Depression. But its importance to the company, like Potter's deed, went deeper. It was the first mine that Newmont directly operated, and it provided the base from which the company developed its expertise in most mining disciplines. While other mines closed during the Depression, Newmont was able to keep an experienced mining team intact, which provided a strong competitive advantage in later years. The Empire-Star provided the training ground for a number of talented Newmont professionals, including McQuiston, who established Newmont's first metallurgical laboratory at Grass Valley in the 1930s; Robert Fulton, who was to head the company's global exploration effort; Marcus Banghart, who was instrumental in the development of operations in southern Africa; and Wesley Goss, who became president of Magma Copper. Later, Newmont's African entities, Magma Copper, and the Carlin gold operation would serve similar roles as key people were rotated through these operations as part of its development program.

The growing diversity of Newmont's interests, its willingness to fund research and exploration, and the challenges of an industry undergoing profound technological change helped attract talented men to the company. For much of the twentieth century, mining offered prestigious careers and mining schools with renowned professors attracted the best and brightest on campus. A key reason was the opportunity to travel, often to exotic locations. Mining has always been a global industry and in the days before foreign travel became commonplace, mining was one of the few tickets abroad for talented young men other than the military.

Early on, Searls sent exploration teams to Peru, Bolivia, and Argentina and engaged in ventures in South Africa, Rhodesia, Canada, and Mexico. In a mind-set that would be echoed by many of Newmont's competitors during the rise of the environmental movement in the late 1980s, Judge Ayer became convinced that Roosevelt's New Deal labor and economic policies were going to destroy free enterprise in America and backed Searls's overseas expansion.

World War II, however, focused attention back on the United States, where the demand for metals was growing at a frantic pace. Three Newmont executives joined the ranks of "dollar-a-year" men in Washington during the war. Henry DeWitt Smith, a Yale-educated engineer who joined Newmont in 1929 and would play an important role in the company in the postwar period, was in charge of the government's Domestic Metals Procurement Program. Schneider earned the Presidential Certificate of Merit for his work on several war mobilization and shipping boards. And, Searls had an office in the White House where he served with a group of men known as "the Jimmy Byrnes Brain Trust." James F. Byrnes headed President Roosevelt's Office of Economic Stabilization and later served as secretary of state under President Truman. Upon retirement from government service in 1947, Byrnes joined the Newmont board where he served until 1966.

Two Colorado mining ventures in which Newmont had taken an interest in 1938 and 1939 gained attention during the war. These were Resurrection at Leadville and Idarado at Ouray. Like the Empire-Star, these were historic vein deposits that had been mined since the 1870s. But unlike Grass Valley, these mines were in sad repair. Nevertheless, Searls loved them and believed there was more ore to be found. Despite the ascent of Daniel Jackling's theory of large mines and economies of scale, Searls, at this point, still had a soft spot for vein mines with their more easily defined ore bodies, higher grades, and long-established mining methods. Besides, these were strategic metals, lead and zinc, that the government was willing to subsidize during the war. Ironically, the government analyst who approved Resurrection's participation in the Premium Price Plan was Malozemoff, a Russian-born metallurgist who joined Newmont in 1945 and became the most influential chief executive in the company's history.

McQuiston shared one of Searls's other quirks—a preference for equipment discarded by other facilities—and built a 250-ton-per-day flotation plant at Resurrection cobbled together from "junk."

Leadville in 1942 resembled the mining towns of gold rush days with a large molybdenum mine on one side, an army camp on the other, and all the vices the men could afford in between. There were no rooms at the Vendome Hotel, so McQuiston paid 50 cents a night to sleep on the lobby floor. He later graduated to a chair for $1 a night before securing a room, complete with a rope fire escape, on the fourth floor. When the army sent out forty volunteers to help reopen the mine, McQuiston reported that after two weeks, "10 were in jail, 12 had gone AWOL, 10 had been fired, and the remaining eight turned out to be fairly good workers."[4]

Resurrection did little for the war effort or Newmont's bottom line, and with the drop in metal prices following the war the operation lay idle for years. In 1961 the mine was reorganized; two earlier partners were bought out and ASARCO came in as operating partner with a 50 percent interest. A new mine shaft was sunk to 1,650 feet, and a 700-ton-per-day flotation mill built. Earlier, the 19,600-foot-long Yak Tunnel had been extended to connect Resurrection's Black Cloud mine with ASARCO's Irene mine so the two could be mined jointly. But it wasn't until ten years later, after an investment of $15 million, that the mine's 2.7 million tons of ore averaging 5.13 percent lead, 9.95 percent zinc, 2.64 ounces of silver, and 0.084 ounce of gold per ton came into production. By the time the mine closed after sixteen years of operation, Newmont had recovered its capital and received $20 million in dividends.

Idarado (a contraction derived from Idaho and Colorado) owed its origin to a treaty with the Ute Indians in 1873 that opened the rugged San Juan Mountains of southwestern Colorado to white intrusion. Prospectors with pack horses entered the area and, as the spring snows melted, worked their way up the seventeen peaks that top 13,000 feet in search of gold and silver in quartz and pyrite outcroppings. Dozens of mines, many with colorful histories, were opened along the east side of Red Mountain above the town of Ouray and on the west surrounding Telluride. George Westinghouse built the first electric power plant in the country using alternating current near Telluride in 1891 to supply the Gold King mine. To persuade the company to make the $15 million investment, the mine's owner traveled to Westinghouse's headquarters in Pittsburgh and laid $100,000 in gold coins on the boardroom table. "I'm willing to gamble," he challenged. "What are you willing to do?"[5] The Tomboy mine, owned by British interests, was said to be one of the world's great gold mines in 1899 when Colorado ranked number one in gold production in the nation. That year some $8 million in gold and silver was pulled from San Juan and San Miguel counties.

Searls's interest was in the Black Bear mine, located above Ouray at 12,000 feet. Men and mules had pulled a fortune in silver from the mine between 1894 and its closure in 1934. But as the vein dipped deeper into the mountain, the silver gave way to zinc and lead, which at the time had little commercial value. With the war, Searls saw new possibilities and brought in Sunshine Mining of Idaho as a partner. But even with government help, the mine wasn't ready to reopen until 1945. In one of McQuiston's greatest achievements, he designed the first flotation plant for the simultaneous separation of zinc, lead, and copper concentrates. The metals react differently to reagent materials, such as cyanide, and some chemical reactions could consume rather than recover the high gold values in the ore on which the economics of the mine depended. His solution involved a complex chemical reaction between cyanide and zinc ions and calcium salts. Another challenge: winter brought 450 inches of snow, making the mine portal reachable only by climbing 2,000 feet on snowshoes.

Although drilling confirmed new reserves and mill capacity was expanded, mining was difficult and profits slim. Sunshine and Newmont were at odds. After obtaining an independent appraisal of the mine's worth at $1 million, Searls offered to sell Newmont's share to Sunshine or buy their share at that price. Either way, he said, he was indifferent, but he wanted an answer immediately. Sunshine took the cash; Searls got his vein. Idarado had always had independent shareholders and Newmont's interest was 80 percent. In 1953, Idarado purchased Telluride Mines, which over the years had consolidated the historic Tomboy, Argentine, Liberty Bell, Pandora, and Smuggler mines. Newspaper articles at the time said the purchase was

3.3. Idarado, a lead and zinc mine, at Telluride, Colorado, in 1945. (*Pete Loncar/Newmont*)

"the miracle Telluride prayed for,"[6] since the alternative was closure of the mines at a loss of 230 jobs, or 90 percent of the town's employment in the days before the ski resorts, music festivals, and tourists.

With Telluride, Idarado had two operations on opposite sides of the mountain. The distance from its office in Ouray to the Pandora Mill at Telluride was sixty-four miles by road, but only six miles if a tunnel could be drilled through the mountain. In the days before satellites and global positioning systems, general manager Arthur Hilander had to "shoot the star" by taking sextant readings of the North Star to align his borings, which were blasted out from both sides of the mountain. Several years later Pete Loncar, resident manager from 1972 to 1978, used the same technique to bring fresh air to miners working the Ajax drift, which was about five hundred feet below the surface. "I had a four-foot-diameter hole bored from the surface and installed a large fan, which helped considerably. To do that, I had a young engineer locate the spot on the surface where we'd drill. I told him to 'shoot the star' and then check his figures three times because I didn't want to miss the mark. We were only able to drill down four hundred feet because that was all the drill pipe we had. So I had another crew drive a raise from underground to meet this hole. New York didn't believe we could do that, but we hit it dead center."[7]

With the new tunnel, Idarado was able to close the Red Mountain Mill and move all the ore to the Pandora, at 1,000 feet lower elevation, for processing. By 1959, when the upgraded Pandora Mill was operational, Idarado had invested nearly $6 million in the project.

That year the American Mining Congress named Idarado the best underground mine in the United States. For years it ranked as Colorado's most productive mine. In 1968, it processed 425,000 tons of ore, producing 21 million pounds of lead, 33 million pounds of zinc, 5.8 million pounds of copper, 814,000 ounces of silver, and 16,000 ounces of gold. Sales peaked at $21 million in 1974, when Idarado earned a profit of $2.7 million. From 1958 until 1975, Idarado paid Newmont $18 million in dividends. However, with falling metal prices, the operation closed in 1978.

For the men who worked the underground veins or sat over drafting tables at the Red Mountain office, the pride of accomplishment ran far deeper than the parent company's profitability. Still hanging above the trestle at the entrance to the mine yard at the Red Mountain office in Ouray is a sign reading, "The metals mined by the men working here help to keep America strong." That fading sign speaks volumes to what mining has meant to America in terms of national security, the foundation of a modern society, and the industry's ability to provide high-quality jobs, pay taxes, and support schools and communities throughout the West.

Idarado's years of success resulted from the hard work of several mine managers to overcome enormous challenges, not the least of which was keeping the 450-man operation staffed with qualified underground miners. Loncar recalls some of the issues. The mine was a rabbit warren of tunnels and old workings with steeply dipping veins that averaged only seven feet in width. Mining was done on five levels, from the 300-foot level at Black Bear to the 2,900-foot level at the Argentine. Although all the ore was hauled to Telluride, there were separate work crews and separate foremen on each side of the mountain. Communication was difficult and productivity low. It took up to an hour and a half for men to get from the portal to the mine face to begin work. Supervisors traveled the underground workings on bicycles modified to run on the rails used by the ore cars.

Men were paid by the amount of rock moved or feet advanced. To improve productivity, Loncar brought in larger diameter air hoses to increase pressure and speed on the air drills, which long ago had replaced cumbersome steam drills. Some, like Lloyd Neilson, who earned a reputation over the course of twenty-five years as one of the mine's best workers, were thankful for the faster equipment because it increased their pay. Others complained that the new hoses were heavier to carry. Hippies were migrating to Telluride in the 1970s and while many applied, their work habits, attitude, and use of marijuana on the job infuriated Loncar. "My policy was simple: put out or get out," he says. The only women working the mines were hoist operators, called "nippers," who were razzed constantly. Everyone had a nickname—Cowboy, Tadpole, Billy Bob. Neilson was "Swede," which made his youngest daughter, Jane, "Swede Pea."

In 1977, Newmont management prepared to close the mine. Loncar had borrowed $1 million from the company to keep it going in the hope that metal prices would recover. Then he struck a break, discovering a high-grade replacement stope where the ore was flat and wide enough to be mined with a mechanized loader and removed with a small diesel truck. In January 1978, he went to New York to lay his case for more time before the Newmont board. Chairman Malozemoff ran the calculations on his slide rule. "You mean to tell me that you are going to produce ten tons per man shift? Johnny Wise, who was the best manager Idarado ever had, could only produce eight. Impossible!" He threw his pencil on the board table. Loncar returned to Idarado and told his men, "We're going to do it if each of us has to go into that mine with a shovel and wheelbarrow." He actually beat his tonnage forecast, repaid the loan, and produced a profit of $411,000 in the mine's closing year but never heard again from the chairman.

Today Resurrection and Idarado are undergoing major reclamation. Idarado has become a model for reclaiming wastes and restoring land once used by legacy mines. For years, both mines were managed jointly from Newmont's office in Ouray, which was the center of the company's operations, other than copper, in the western United States. Until his death in 1971, general manager Hilander had responsibility not only for the two Colorado operations but also for Dawn Mining, a uranium mine in Washington State, and for the new Carlin Gold operation in Nevada. It took years before Carlin was considered important enough to justify its own, on-site executive.

4

AFRICA

All that glisters in South Africa is not gold. Diamonds came first with the discovery in 1866, by children playing with a 21-carat stone, of the tremendously rich diamond pipes at Kimberley. Within five years, 50,000 men were living in squalor and digging like prairie dogs to extract the precious stones from the rocky soil. Those squeezed out by chaos and competition packed their gear and headed northeast to Transvaal, where gold had been discovered at Witwatersrand in what would become the greatest goldfield on earth, stretching 170 by 100 miles around today's Johannesburg.

The gold and diamond camps were initially run by "diggers' democracies" in which private claims and individual initiative prevailed. But as shallow mining along visible outcrops gave way to deeper underground mining requiring shafts and heavy equipment, these were soon replaced by partnerships, organized mining groups, and companies that could marshal the necessary resources and technology. The reefs, or veins, at Witwatersrand are among the deepest in the world and could only be mined on the largest possible scale. Enormous amounts of capital were required, but if successful, enormous profits could be reaped.

As mining became a corporate enterprise earlier than in North America, it took on a distinctly South African look. Veins could thin out, prices could fall, and without the benefit of today's exploratory drilling, sampling, and analysis, costly shafts could be put in the wrong place. Mining was too risky to put all one's eggs in one basket. So instead of individual companies owning individual mines, a system of cross-investment was developed where enterprises owned shares in several mines as well as non-mining ventures. It was like insurance companies spreading the risk, or for that matter like Newmont itself, except that companies that might be considered competitors also ended up as major shareholders in each other's ventures.

The two men most responsible for the growth of these mining groups and two of the most powerful figures in South African history were Cecil Rhodes and Ernest Oppenheimer. Rhodes, the son of a British vicar, was sent to South Africa in 1870, at age seventeen, for health reasons and soon joined the pursuit of both gold and diamonds. Always the scholar, it was said that when he first went prospecting, he carried with him "a pick, two spades, six volumes of the classics and a Greek lexicon."[1] In less than twenty years he had rationalized Kimberley, consolidating 3,600 mining claims into about 100; created the giant De Beers Consolidated Mines, which established a worldwide diamond syndicate controlling both the production and marketing of the precious stones; and, after buying up a number of Boer farms on the Rand, established Gold Fields of South Africa in 1887, as the country's first major gold-mining house.

Oppenheimer, a generation younger, was German born but British educated and had become a British citizen by the time he went to South Africa as a representative of a London diamond house in 1902. His arrival coincided with the end of the Boer War, which raised the Union Jack over all of South Africa, and the death of Rhodes in March of that year. Outdoing Rhodes, it took Oppenheimer only fifteen years to wrest control of several gold- and diamond-mining enterprises. In 1917 he launched Anglo American Corporation, which would become the largest gold producer in the world with a hand in most South African mining and metals pies, including holdings in both De Beers and Gold Fields. It was a subsidiary company, AngloGold, that Newmont bested in 2002 to become the world leader in gold.

It was also Newmont that put the "American" in Anglo American. The London *Times* of September 28, 1917, reported that by taking a 25 percent founding interest in Oppenheimer's venture, initially capitalized at one million pounds sterling, Newmont and its associates had provided "the first occasion on which a definite arrangement has been made for the employment of American capital on the Rand."[2]

From the outset, the Kimberley and Rand mines were built on British capital. Many mining houses, including Gold Fields, were incorporated in London. But with the onset of World War I in August 1914, the London markets ran dry, at least in their willingness to finance overseas mining ventures. New deposits were being found on the Far East Rand, but with the reefs extending four thousand feet deep, five to six years were needed to develop a new mine. Desperate for capital, Oppenheimer approached Herbert Hoover in London in the spring of 1917. Hoover turned to his New York bankers, J. P. Morgan & Company, who engaged William Boyce Thompson to organize the syndicate to find American investors. Thompson had formed Newmont Company as his private investment vehicle a year earlier and Anglo became one of its first core holdings.

By the time Newmont sold its Anglo shares in 1935, it had become involved in a number of other Oppenheimer and Anglo-related ventures. These were spurred both by Fred Searls's growing interest in the region's copper potential and Oppenheimer's social contacts with Thompson's daughter, Margaret, Mrs. Anthony J. Drexel Biddle Jr., Newmont's largest shareholder, who was living in Paris (see chapter 2, note 17). Mrs. Biddle, who wrote for such publications as *Collier's* and the *Woman's Home Companion*, was at the center of Europe's literary, political, and intellectual life and entertained brilliantly. When Massachusetts senator Henry Cabot Lodge sought in 1951 to persuade Dwight Eisenhower, then the Supreme Allied Commander of NATO, to accept the Republican nomination for president of the United States, the meeting took place at Mrs. Biddle's Left Bank home.

Newmont's most important early South African venture, one that overshadowed the company's original Anglo investment, was a 25 percent interest in Rhodesian Anglo American, formed to develop Anglo American's various copper properties in Northern Rhodesia (now Zambia). Newmont held an interest in Rho Anglo, as it was known, until 1951.

Thompson was a founding member of Anglo American's board and Searls, Newmont's vice president of exploration until becoming president in 1947, was a director of Rho Anglo. In addition, in an exercise that would set a Newmont pattern for later investments, the company lent two of its higher-ranking executives, Harold Munroe, a mining engineer, and A. J. McNab, a metallurgist and vice president of Magma, to Rho Anglo to help develop its properties and design new smelters.

While Newmont put its footprint on the continent in its infancy, the company's most important presence came in the decades after World War II when it was the managing partner of two of the most important base metal mines of the period—O'okiep (pronounced O-keep) in South Africa and

Tsumeb (Su-meb) in South West Africa (now Namibia). These mines significantly changed Newmont's scope and character and vaulted it into the ranks of the world's major mining houses. Later participation in a third mine, Palabora in South Africa's Transvaal region, became Newmont's most lucrative African investment, while a 14 percent interest in Highveld Steel and Vanadium Corporation, an Oppenheimer affiliate and the world's largest producer of this steel-hardening element, added handsomely to Newmont's earnings.

It is hard to overstate the importance of these operations. They underpinned Newmont's balance sheet for decades, provided confidence in its ability to manage overseas operations, and financed its growth into a host of important mining ventures around the globe, including Carlin. In the 1950s and 1960s when Newmont's income came primarily from dividends, O'okiep and Tsumeb poured $220 million into the company's coffers, representing 54 percent of earnings in the 1950s and 45 percent in the 1960s. In total, the four operations paid Newmont dividends of $450 million between 1946 and 1987, when they were sold for $126 million as part of a corporate restructuring. They made Newmont one of the largest U.S. investors in southern Africa and, indirectly, one of the region's largest employers. They also made Newmont the focal point of attack by anti-apartheid groups in the 1970s and 1980s.

Additionally, these mines provided the training ground for a number of men who later became senior executives of the company, most notably Gordon Parker, chief executive from 1984 to 1993, and T. Peter Philip, president from 1991 to 1994. These men guided the company through a period of extreme turmoil and refocused its efforts on gold. It was also in Africa that Newmont established a pattern of management that rigorously separated local operating decisions from corporate issues of finance, taxation, strategy, and governance. While this decentralized style served the company well for much of its history, especially when it was more of an investor than an operator of mines, it has been less easy to sustain in recent years as U.S. Securities and Exchange reporting rules such as Sarbanes-Oxley and mining critics armed with global Internet connections require the exertion of more authority from headquarters.

Newmont first became involved in O'okiep, the smallest of the African operations but the one in which the company's ownership was the highest,

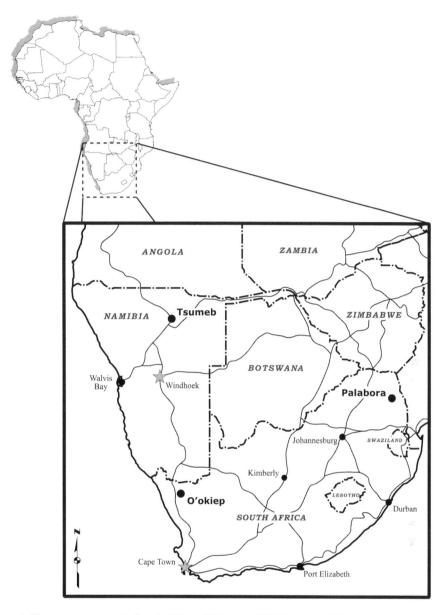

4.1. Two copper mines in South Africa, O'okiep and Palabora, and Tsumeb, a lead, zinc, and copper mine in southwest Africa (now Namibia), were financial powerhouses for Newmont in the 1950s, 1960s, and 1970s. (*Newmont Archives*)

during a visit by Searls in 1927. The Dutch discovered copper outcroppings in the Namaqualand desert, inland from South Africa's Atlantic coast, in 1685, and sporadic mining by Welsh and British groups occurred in the area from the 1850s until the end of World War I. By the time Searls visited the area, at the invitation of American Metal Company, the forerunner of Amax, the workings had been abandoned and the claims were available for $750,000. However, an exploration program undertaken by the legendary mining engineer Henry Krumb had to be shelved with the collapse of metal prices in 1932.

Newmont returned to Namaqualand in 1936 armed, according to *Fortune* magazine, with "U.S. geotechnical imagination, financial daring and managerial skill."[3] With a 67 percent interest, Newmont was joined by American Metal and briefly by Rho Anglo in investing $2.7 million in the newly incorporated O'okiep Copper Company, named for a nearby town. The financial daring had to do with taking on such a large project in a remote area when the copper price was barely 13 cents a pound. The new operation hoped to deliver 26 million pounds of refined copper a year to European ports at a cash cost of six and a half cents a pound. It came close to its production goal during its first five years and beat its cost projection by nearly a penny a pound, but did not report these numbers until 1945. With start-up occurring at the outset of World War II and all of its output sold to the British government to meet its war needs, O'okiep kept such statistics a secret. "Under present conditions, it is not considered advisable to publish the General Manager's Report covering specific details of operation," was a repeated line in O'okiep's early annual reports. What was published was that with the war driving up metal prices, the mine earned a healthy 25 percent after-tax profit on sales throughout the 1940s.

Managerial skill came from such veterans of Newmont's California gold mines as George Kervin, who became O'okiep's first general manager, and Wesley Goss, a mining engineer who had worked at a Newmont copper mine in Arizona as the first mine superintendent. Henry DeWitt Smith, a rising star at Newmont's New York headquarters, was named managing director, or president. To win acceptance by the area's Dutch-blooded Afrikaners, Smith took to calling himself "Duhvitt Smit."

Searls also set a precedent that has been observed by Newmont ever since. When entering a foreign country, the company has always engaged local talent at the highest levels possible. Newmont's choice in South Africa was Albert Livingstone, a Johannesburg attorney who was invaluable in helping establish each of Newmont's enterprises on the continent and who served on the boards of both O'okiep and Tsumeb until his death in 1970.

By the early 1940s, O'okiep was operating three mines with a combined annual output of 800,000 tons of ore at a grade of 2.5 percent copper. This was considered low-grade at the time but is vastly higher than most large copper mines today. Ore was mined at a depth of 700 feet by the open stoping method in which ore was blasted loose and allowed to fall into troughs for underground crushing before removal to the surface. On the surface, a 1,500-ton-per-day flotation mill and concentrator separated the ore from crushed tailings, which were returned to the mine to fill the empty stopes. The concentrate was heated to 2,400 degrees Fahrenheit in a reverberatory furnace before a converter turned the molten metal into the end product, blister, or 99.2 percent pure copper. Some 60,000 tons of blister copper, in the form of two-by-three-foot slabs weighing 380 pounds each, were produced for Allied weapons during World War II.

Marcus Banghart, who also began his career in Newmont's Grass Valley gold mines, replaced Kervin as general manager in 1941 and engineered a steady progression of added reserves, improved mining and processing techniques, and reduced costs. Within five years of his arrival, profits had increased 76 percent to $1.36 per ton, enabling the company to pay its first dividend. For years, O'okiep was recognized as one of the most cost-efficient copper operations in the world. In recognition of his achievements, Banghart was presented with the American Institute of Mining Engineers' Gold Medal Award in 1961.

In its early years, O'okiep also won favorable recognition in the U.S. press for its employee practices and treatment of native workers. Needless to say, this approbation must be looked at through the lens of a different time and a different culture. In 1946, the operation employed 1,575 men, 275 "Europeans" who held all the skilled and trades positions and were paid an average of $5.41 per day, and 1,300 "natives," mostly Bantus but some mixed-blood "Cape coloreds," whose average pay was $1.03 per day plus food, lodging, and health care. This was 30 percent higher than the gold mines on the Rand paid their native employees.

There were no native workers in the largely uninhabited Namaqualand, so those employed lived in compounds, as was the practice on the Rand, returning home to their families only infrequently. Newmont would have preferred to have the families live on-site, but that was prohibited by law. O'okiep also sought to train blacks in basic job skills, but, again, South African law barred them from skilled trades. However, "coloreds," those of mixed blood, were permitted to hold semi-skilled jobs.

With profits approaching $1 million a year in 1946, Newmont offered its shareholders the right to participate directly in O'okiep's success by purchasing one "American" share of the company, listed on the Curb Exchange, for each ten Newmont shares held. This raised $500,000 and reduced the company's holdings in O'okiep to 57.5 percent.

That year, American Metal brought Newmont another prospect, an abandoned lead, zinc, and copper mine 490 miles north of O'okiep in South West Africa called Tsumeb, or "green slopes" in the tribal Ovambo tongue. South West Africa had been a German colony, and from 1908 until 1939 the mine was operated on a marginal basis by a German company. Although after World War I the League of Nations awarded the country to Great Britain, to be administered by the Union of South Africa, the German company retained its mine. That ended with the outbreak of World War II when South Africa's Custodian of Enemy Property seized the mine, and after an unsuccessful effort to operate it, shut it down in 1941.

After the war, American Metal approached Newmont's men at O'okiep with a proposal to jointly dewater the flooded shafts and do some exploratory drilling in preparation for an auction the government agency was planning for 1947. But the Custodian insisted on bids being made on an "as is" basis. Deprived of the opportunity to obtain direct knowledge of the deposit, Smith and Banghart sent samples from the old German ore piles to the United States for testing. The results showed surprisingly high metal grades. Anticipating that other bidders would offer one million pounds sterling, or $4 million, Banghart upped his offer by ten thousand pounds and got the property for what turned out to be a bargain basement price of $4,040,000.

Tsumeb was incorporated with Newmont being the operator but owning only 28.5 percent. O'okiep held 9.5 percent, with the balance split between American Metal and Britain's Selection Trust. Because of their overlapping ownership, O'okiep and Tsumeb had nearly identical boards of directors for years. Tsumeb was incredibly rich, with 60 percent recoverable metal. The initial ore body averaged 14 percent lead, 6 percent zinc, and 5 percent copper, with sizable amounts of cadmium, silver, and germanium. A $5 million loan to dewater the mine and install new equipment was paid off within two years.

Tsumeb consisted of a pipe 250 feet wide and 600 feet long that pinched and swelled in irregular fashion from the surface to a depth of 4,550 feet. Geologists believe the pipe was created by fracturing and brecciation, the melding of older, angular rocks, and the intrusion of pseudoaplite or pseudoquartzite. Above the 1,200-foot level, the ore was heavily oxidized by ground water, while below 2,600 feet the deposit's plumbing produced an unusual second oxidized zone. The oxidized material contained a complex of carbonates, sulfates, arsenates, and oxides of copper, lead, and zinc, while the intermittent sulfides were equally complex.

Geologists identified 179 mineral species that have been recovered at Tsumeb, some of great beauty and many unique to the location. Among the most important were azurite, chalcocite, bornite, tennantite, malachite, cuprite, galena, cerussite, and sphalerite. Not only is this number unusually large, but a great many rank as "best of species" in the world, "not just a little better than specimens from other localities, but rather incredibly better," reported the *Mineralogical Record*.[4] "It was a metallurgist's dream, but a geologist's nightmare," says Richard Ellett, Newmont's vice president of exploration in the 1970s.[5]

In 1970 B. H. Grier, a mineralogist at Tsumeb, carefully looked under his microscope at an arsenate containing lead, iron, and zinc, and realized that it was an entirely new mineral. Noting that the International Committee on Nomenclature had already designated a mineral "geyerite," a name entirely too close to his own, and that there was also a "redledgeite," which ruled out naming it for the mine's general manager, J. P. Ratledge, Grier wrote to Plato Malozemoff, suggesting that the mineral be named "malozemoffite" in his honor. Newmont's CEO quickly demurred and the discovery was named "tsumcorite."

As with O'okiep, the company's timing was uncanny. Within three years of Tsumeb's start-up, zinc was selling for 13.6 cents a pound, up 64 percent from the mine's inception; copper was up 87 percent to 22 cents a pound; and lead had risen 178 percent to 18 cents a pound. Tsumeb soon became the second largest employer and taxpayer in South West Africa.

By the early 1960s the heart of the operation was a 2,000-ton-per-day mill that was among the most complex in the world. In addition to recovering lead, zinc, and copper, Tsumeb was also able to produce germanium, which was in increasing demand for transistors, thanks to an innovative combination flotation and magnetic separation plant designed by Frank McQuiston. Tsumeb became the second largest germanium producer in the world. Concentrates were shipped 380 miles by narrow-gauge rail, often a bottleneck, to Walvis Bay on the Atlantic Ocean, where they were shipped to smelters in the United States and Europe. But because the mix of metals could not be separated completely, the concentrate was discounted by the smelters, who had to refine out the impurities. To improve its economics, separate copper and lead smelters were added to the Tsumeb complex in the early 1960s.

In an even more remote desert location than O'okiep, Tsumeb invested more than $13 million, nearly 20 percent of its entire capital, to build a town for employees and, for whites, their families. Homes, schools, a hospital, and recreational facilities were built and a sense of community established. As early as 1950, Tsumeb was the third largest town in South West Africa with 1,800 Europeans and 4,000 natives. A company-run farm employed 240 natives, raising almost enough corn, vegetables, cattle, and dairy products to keep the town self-sufficient. Blacks from the Ovambo tribe, less skilled and lower paid than at O'okiep, sought employment as manual laborers as an improvement from the poverty of their homelands. Robert Ramsey, whose *Men and Mines of Newmont* chronicles the company's first fifty years, reported that the daily 4,500-calorie diet prepared by the mine's kitchens resulted in "an average weight gain of 20 to 30 pounds during a man's first year on the job."[6]

Over the years, both O'okiep and Tsumeb expanded from mines to mining districts. By the early 1970s, O'okiep had six mines, three mills, a smelter and a workforce of 5,000. Tsumeb opened the Kombat mine and mill 65 miles distant and later developed the Matchless mine, 225 miles to the south, near the capital city of Windhoek.

In thirty-seven years of operation by Newmont, Tsumeb yielded more

4.2. Miners at Tsumeb in South West Africa (now Namibia) report for work in 1964. (*Peter Wrinch-Schulz*)

than two million tons of lead and a million tons of copper, while O'okiep sold 1.2 million tons of copper from its start-up in 1940 to its sale in 1987. By the early 1970s, Tsumeb was averaging $75 million in annual sales (it surpassed $100 million in 1974) and generated nearly $20 million a year in profits. O'okiep, with a lower grade and a single metal, reported sales of about $50 million a year with net income averaging $12 million. Although results for both companies were volatile, each averaged a return of 23 percent on sales over several decades. What is truly remarkable is that these returns were generated from an asset base that never exceeded $70 million at Tsumeb or $50 million at O'okiep. Over a twenty-five-year period, from 1950 through 1974, O'okiep earned an average 38 percent return on assets, while Tsumeb averaged 23 percent. For base metal mines, that is phenomenal, far surpassing returns at the best mines of today.

Newmont's third African mine, Palabora, began as a 50/50 effort by O'okiep and Tsumeb, called Safari Exploration, to evaluate a large, low-grade copper outcropping near the Kruger National Park in the mid-1950s. Safari's application for an exploration license, however, collided with another filed almost simultaneously by Rio Tinto of London, which soon merged with an Australian company to become Rio Tinto Zinc, or RTZ (pronounced R T Zed in British and Australian parlance). Two other companies, one government owned, were already mining the property for vermiculite and phosphate, but had little appreciation for the deposit's copper potential. As an added complication, South Africa's Atomic Energy Commission detected high Geiger counter readings in some rocks at the Transvaal Museum in Pretoria that came from the area and began prospecting for uranium.

Given its keen interest in the final ownership and development of the property, the government forced a joint venture in which RTZ became the operator and majority owner and Newmont held a 29 percent interest. Other shareholders in Tsumeb and O'okiep also participated. However, Malozemoff, who negotiated the final agreement along with general counsel Roy Bonebrake, insisted that major decisions be approved by a 75 percent shareholder vote, giving Newmont far more control than its direct ownership indicated. For example, at Malozemoff's urging, Ed Hunt, assistant manager at O'okiep, became Palabora's first chief executive.

According to *Engineering and Mining Journal*, Palabora was "one of the remarkable mining consortiums of [the] day—pooling the technical, financial and marketing facilities of participating companies and individuals" to create "South Africa's first fully integrated open-pit copper project."[7] With an initial investment of $112 million, it was also the largest investment in a single mining operation in the country. Although the World Bank, faced with growing U.S. government opposition to bank-sponsored projects in the Republic of South Africa, turned down financing, Kreditanstalt für Wiederaufbau, or KFW, the West German bank for reconstruction, was willing to lend $27 million. A German smelter also agreed to take 36,000 tons of blister copper for the first five years of production. Of the $41 million in equity capital, Newmont's share was $12 million.

Extensive drilling over several years proved up a deposit of 315 million tons of ore grading 0.69 percent copper in a carbonatite structure of dolomitic calcite and magnetite that lay in an elliptical pipe-like body 200 feet high and half a mile in width by one mile in length. Although low-grade, a favorable strip ratio of 0.9 to 1 meant that mining costs were low as less than a ton of waste rock had to be removed for each ton of ore.

Facilities designed to mine and process 33,000 tons of ore a day and produce 80,000 tons of copper a year were put in place largely with the technical support of Newmont and Magma personnel. Production began in 1966. Two years later, a 45,000-ton-per-year electrolytic copper refinery was added along with a continuous rod caster for the production of wire bars. In addition to copper, phosphate, and vermiculite (of which it accounted for one-third of the Western world's output), the operation produced sulfuric acid and magnetite, an iron ore. In 1971, a heavy metals recovery plant began extracting uranium oxide from mill tailings, but government restrictions prevented detailed public disclosure of that side of the business.

Palabora employed 3,000 workers—800 Europeans and 2,200 Bantus. Whites lived in the bustling company town of Phalaborwa; Africans lived in two separate villages, one for married families and one for single men. The African villages were built and maintained by the South African government but received medical, educational, and recreational support from the company. According to *Engineering and Mining Journal,* "These living areas are planned and operated to conform to the special and traditional habits and preference of the Xhosa, Zulu, Shangaan and Pedi ethnic groups which comprise the population."[8]

As the only refined copper producer in South Africa and with much of its output going to growing local markets, Palabora had a distinct advantage over Tsumeb and O'okiep when world metal prices plunged in 1974 from an average of $1.15 a pound for copper in the first half of the year to 70 cents in the second half. That September, the company launched a $100 million expansion program to increase milling capacity to 82,000 tons per day and nearly double refinery output to 156,000 tons per year. To feed this expansion, lower-grade ores were tapped and mining doubled between 1972 and 1980 to more than 100 million tons, requiring an increase in the haulage fleet from thirty 65-ton trucks to seventy-five 150-ton behemoths.

During its first decade, Palabora followed O'okiep as one of the lowest-cost copper companies in the world, producing refined metal for less than 25 cents a pound. In 1974, the operation earned $66 million on sales of $135 million, giving it an after-tax return of 49 percent on sales and 35 percent on assets. But, with lower grades and higher capital employed, returns declined to under 15 percent of sales and assets in the 1980s. Furthermore, while repeated devaluations of the South African rand against the U.S. dollar and British pound kept sales and profits high in local terms, when converted to U.S. dollars, they reduced the value of dividends Newmont received. Yet over the years the mine was an unqualified success. During Newmont's twenty-two-year involvement, it produced 2.3 million tons of copper and paid Newmont $163 million in dividends.

Just as surely as dividends moved from South Africa to New York, so too did successful managers. Smith, Banghart, and David O. Pearce, who began his career with Anglo American at Witwatersrand, were successive general managers at Tsumeb and O'okiep and each ended his career in New York as vice president, or senior vice president, of operations for all of Newmont's mines. All three also became members of the board of directors. Goss, O'okiep's first mine superintendent, was named president of Magma Copper in 1953, and Brian Woolfe, who succeeded Ratledge as general manager at Tsumeb, later headed both Newmont Australia and Magma. Eric Hamer, a metallurgist who began his career as mill superintendent at O'okiep in 1974, became vice president of North American operations in 1995, while Aubrey Paverd, who joined Tsumeb in 1973, rose to vice president of exploration.

In another important step in the development of Newmont personnel, Malozemoff and Banghart initiated a scholarship program for talented South Africans to study in the United States provided that upon graduation they agreed to work for three years at either O'okiep or Tsumeb. Those interested in mining engineering went to Montana Tech in Butte, where Malozemoff and Banghart had both graduated, while those seeking a career in mineral dressing, as metallurgy was called, went to the University of Arizona in Tucson. Eighteen men participated in the program in the 1950s and 1960s, including Parker, who received both a bachelor's and a master's degree from Montana Tech, and Philip, a fourteenth-generation South African, who graduated magna cum laude from Arizona. Both men spent years advancing through the African operations and gained experiences that profoundly shaped Newmont's culture and success in later years.

Parker recalls his first assignment as a supervisor at Tsumeb in the early 1960s as being "a very different world from what I anticipated. As a recently graduated engineer, you put away all your learned knowledge and devoted all your energies to persuading others to do things. To be a mine supervisor, you probably should major in psychology rather than engineering." Workers taunted the new college graduate and language was a real barrier. "Half the craftsmen at Tsumeb spoke German and 90 percent of the rest spoke Afrikaans. Very few knew any English. Laborers spoke Ovambo, a tribal language not spoken elsewhere in Africa. Some mine workers understood 'Funaglo' a type of sign language that was the lingua franca of the South African gold mines. I only knew English. I came from the Cape, where wine is grown, not where gold is mined."[9]

He chafed at South Africa's "oppressive labor laws that limited what blacks could aspire to do. We had lots of low-paid people, but productivity was abysmally low. It didn't take a lot to figure out that if one had better-trained workers, better things would happen for both the employer and employee. If I made any impact or articulated any views back in those days it would be about the need to teach and train. 'Teach, teach, train, train,' became my theme song for most of my life. It started right there with the utter frustration of trying to get things done with an untrained workforce. It made you want to hurl your hat in the air."

As he moved into management at both Tsumeb and O'okiep, opportunities for improvement were everywhere. "My predecessors were largely autocrats," Parker recalls. "They were all competent, strong-willed with powerful intellects. But they weren't collaborators. Everyone on-site knew who the boss was." Planning was minimal and budgeting almost nonexistent. The mines generated a lot of numbers, but most were tonnage and process related, of little help in planning production, controlling costs, or improving profits. "Trying to get people to think was difficult. No one had accountability except at the very top. But many people were ready for a change. So when someone like me came along with such ideas—and the power to make it happen—it did. Of course, by then, computers were making things a lot easier."

In 1975 Parker, who had married Pearce's daughter Pamela, succeeded Pearce as managing director of both operations. Instead of being based in New York as had his predecessors, he set up office in Cape Town. But by then Newmont's great economic engine in southern Africa was running out of steam. A world copper glut was putting pressure on prices at a time when inflation was being driven by soaring energy costs. Additionally, the U.S. Internal Revenue Service forced an end to a three-decade-long arrangement under which Newmont managed O'okiep and Tsumeb, but Amax handled all metal sales. By carefully allocating costs, the arrangement had allowed Newmont to avoid paying U.S. income taxes on the profits of the two African entities. The IRS sought $44 million in back taxes; Newmont reluctantly settled for $2.7 million. Malozemoff later said he chose not to fight because "a court case would become public knowledge" that could have affected the stock price of both O'okiep and Newmont.[10] In 1978, O'okiep and Tsumeb set up a joint sales office in London and for the first time began marketing their output.

As profits turned to losses, major projects that had been years in planning were canceled. These included a large electrolytic copper refinery at Cape Town to serve both O'okiep and Tsumeb and a joint effort by O'okiep, Newmont, and later Anglo American to develop a huge zinc deposit at Gamsberg, eighty miles west of O'okiep. Thanks to a $37 million loan from the South African government, O'okiep finally was able to open the 4,200-foot Carolusberg Deep copper mine in 1983. But as losses mounted, O'okiep was forced to turn to the equity markets for financing. With heavy losses in its U.S. copper operations, Newmont chose not to fully participate and saw its ownership in O'okiep drop to 40 percent. In 1984, it turned management of the operation over to Gold Fields of South Africa, which had acquired a controlling interest in both O'okiep and Tsumeb.

In addition, a great social awakening was occurring both within South Africa and around the world regarding that country's system of apartheid. O'okiep and Tsumeb had been at the forefront of providing better social and economic conditions for their native employees. O'okiep began offering pensions and life insurance to blacks in 1972 and shortly after, Tsumeb provided the first secondary schooling for black children in the region. Native wages rose substantially. Housing and job equality, however, were more difficult. Tsumeb won official approval to build houses for black families in 1974, only to face opposition from the Ovambo tribe, which refused to let its people relocate outside their homeland. By the early 1980s, however, nearly 500 colored families were living in company housing at O'okiep as were 185 black families at Tsumeb. The greatest achievement came in the late 1970s, when the two companies became the first mines in southern Africa to eliminate a dual wage scale for black and white workers.

Philip, who succeeded Parker as general manager at O'okiep, looked at the issue from an economic as well as social perspective. With mounting losses, the workforce had been cut in half, austerity programs had been introduced, and it was imperative that the company get the most from its employees. To Philip, that meant equal pay for equal work. The government by then agreed, but the Mine Workers Union, which represented the skilled white trades, refused and staged a ten-day strike in 1979 not only against the copper mines but against the much larger gold industry as well. O'okiep prevailed, and soon "we had blacks doing work that they had never done before in the entire South African industry," Philip recalls.[11] J. A. Livingston, a Pulitzer Prize–winning international reporter with the *Philadelphia Inquirer,* called Newmont's action "a milestone in industrial relations in South Africa."[12] By 1981, Tsumeb, which had adopted its own unified pay scale, had eighty blacks employed in jobs formerly reserved for whites.

None of that, however, seemed to matter to America's opinion leaders, who were in a moral outrage over apartheid and South Africa's mistreatment of its black majority. Although Newmont had adopted one of industry's first fair employment and non-discrimination policies in 1974 and publicly stated its commitment to follow that policy, to the extent it was legally permitted to do so, in all of its global operations, church groups drew up their own codes of social responsibility, which they insisted the company adopt. Proxy proposals and protesters at annual meetings demanded acceptance of operating "conditions" drafted by Bishop Desmond Tutu, recipient of the 1984 Nobel Peace Prize. Harvard and other universities and a num-

4.3. CEO Plato Malozemoff presents a gold watch to a Tsumeb employee in 1971 in recognition of his twenty-five years of service. (*Newmont Archives*)

ber of public employee pension plans sold their Newmont stock. Church groups, columnists, and others demanded that the company withdraw from South Africa in order to exert economic pressure on the country.

In an unsigned letter to shareholders in 1974, the company stated, "We certainly take no exception to these principles as an aspiration for the world over, but their adoption as a by-law is opposed since such a by-law would also require management to seek new laws as needed for implementation of these principles, . . . would be read as a private declaration by the Corporation of an intent to interfere with policies and legislation of the government, . . . [and] might be construed as a declaration of hostility rather than a statement of high principle." In subsequent responses, the company noted that it was the direct employer of only a handful of people in South Africa and that it held only minority investments in independent South African companies. Ironically, by taking that position, it had to forgo the more compelling argument that by its presence it was doing more good for native Africans than its withdrawal would ever accomplish.

In September 1985, Parker was elected Newmont's fifth chief executive officer and four months later assumed the office of chairman. Presiding at his first board meeting on January 29, 1986, he led the board in accepting the Sullivan Principles, drafted by Leon Sullivan, a black Baptist minister from Philadelphia, as a supplement to the company's longstanding policy of equal employment opportunity. By then, however, the decision was almost moot. At the same board meeting, the company wrote down its investment in O'okiep to $8 million and within two years pulled up stakes in Africa and put its chips once again on gold, this time on the Carlin Trend in Nevada.

Minerals

Visitors to the vast mineral and gem hall of the American Museum of Natural History in New York City can be awestruck by the dazzling display of geologic beauty. What they may overlook, however, is Newmont's connection with this mineral wealth.

The most valuable stone in the museum, having been appraised several years ago at $5 million, is the Newmont Azurite. Measuring a foot high and a foot wide and containing clusters of prismatic blue-black crystals up to eight inches in length, it is said to be the finest mineral specimen in existence. Azurite is a carbonate of copper formed over millions of years by the interaction of groundwater on primary copper ores. The Newmont Azurite was unearthed at the Tsumeb copper mine in what is now Namibia in 1952.

A second specimen in the entry showcase is a seven-by-five-inch mass of beautifully crystallized leaf gold extracted in 1951 from the Empire-Star mine in Grass Valley, California. Also considered very rare, it contains 21.2 ounces of gold.

Both minerals were donated to the museum in 1979 by Plato Malozemoff, Newmont's chief executive who at the time was a trustee of the museum. Previously, they had been on display in the company's headquarters at 300 Park Avenue in New York.

But the Newmont connection runs much deeper. In fact, the core of the museum's extraordinary collection is a gift of 1,536 mineral specimens donated in 1927 by Newmont's founder, William Boyce Thompson. An avid mineral collector from his youth, Thompson had amassed one of the finest collections of the period, which filled several rooms at his estate along the Hudson. In addition to stones from mines he owned or had visited, he sought out and purchased stones of unparalleled

4.4. The Newmont Azurite, on display at the American Museum of Natural History in New York City, is said to be the most valuable mineral in the world. (*American Museum of Natural History*)

beauty, including all of the minerals from the Panama Pacific International Exhibition in San Francisco in 1915. He also gathered an exquisite collection of rare jade carvings that were donated to the museum on the death of his wife, Gertrude, in 1950. These donations were supplemented by a $70,000 endowment on Thompson's death in 1930, which continues to fund much of the museum's mineral purchases.

The Smithsonian Institution in Washington is another recipient of Newmont gold and minerals. In 1999, the institution was given a rare orpiment that was discovered in the pit wall of the company's Twin Creeks gold mine near Golconda, Nevada. Orpiment is a yellowish-orange mineral composed of arsenic and sulfur and is principally found in Peru, China, and Nevada. True to tradition, the specimen donated to the Smithsonian was labeled one of the finest of its type in the world.

Digging a Pit

Like removing a stump, digging ore from an open pit requires a larger hole at the top than at the bottom. The deeper the ore body, the more surface area must be excavated. A pit is dug in concentric circles with benches tiering down like an inverted wedding cake. Numerous computer calculations must be made to optimize the pit in order to extract the ore in the safest and most economical fashion. With a final pit size of a mile long, two-thirds of a mile wide, and a third of a mile deep, here are some of the issues at Palabora.

- **Mill size:** With a 33,000-ton-per-day operation, seven days a week, Palabora required that the pit deliver 38,500 tons of ore per day on a six-day mining schedule.

- **Ore grade:** To keep a consistent ore grade of 0.69 percent copper feeding into the mill, when grades, or concentrations of copper, varied throughout the deposit, it was necessary to mine at three different locations and blend the ore. To meet the tonnage requirements, this implied the use of thirty 65-ton trucks loaded by six cubic-yard shovels. The reach of the shovels, in turn, limited the bench height to a maximum of 40 feet.

- **Cut-off grade:** The original pit design anticipated mining 215 million tons of ore using 0.3 percent copper as the lowest grade that could be economically processed. Later, with an expansion of the mill and further understanding of the ore body, the minimum grade was reduced to 0.2 percent copper. This increased reserves to 526 million tons, but as a trade-off lowered the average head-grade to 0.5 percent copper, reducing milling efficiency. It also meant deepening the pit to 1,790 feet from 1,200 feet, necessitating larger trucks and shovels.

- **Haulage grade:** To exit the pit, a fully loaded truck could climb an 8 percent grade. Later, with larger trucks and heavier loads, a trolley-assist system was installed in which the trucks hooked onto electric power lines for added power on their ascent. This increased truck speeds and lowered costs compared with diesel fuel.

- **Waste-to-ore ratio:** Because of the configuration of the ore body and the competence of the surrounding rock, Palabora initially had a favorable waste-to-ore ratio of 0.86-to-1, meaning that less than a ton of waste had to be removed for each ton of ore mined. Later, with an expanded pit, the ratio changed to a much less favorable 2.5-to-1, or five truckloads of waste for each two of ore.

- **Pit slope:** Safety is the major consideration in the shape of a pit. If the pit walls are too steep, the slope can fail, sending an avalanche of rock onto work areas below. With competent rock, Palabora could sustain a 45-degree angle on most pit walls. With each foot down requiring only a one-foot setback, only 272 million tons of waste needed to be removed from the original pit. Had the rock been less stable, a lower 38-degree angle would have required the removal of 100 million additional tons of rock over the life of the mine at a substantial increase in cost for the same amount of ore. In the end, the ore body, and thus the pit, turned out to be much larger than originally estimated and 1.5 billion tons of rock, both ore and waste, were extracted over a twenty-two-year period.

5

PLATO

Asked to name the most influential chief executive at the end of the twentieth century, one might give top honors to Jack Welch, the successful and self-promoting CEO of General Electric from 1981 to 2001. But if asked to turn back the pages of history by a few years, Plato Malozemoff would surely be among the top contenders. And if the selection were limited to mining company executives, he would have few peers.

Malozemoff guided Newmont—some would say he *was* Newmont—for thirty-two years, from 1954 through 1985. When he stepped down, at age seventy-six, he had been at the helm for more than half of Newmont's sixty years as a publicly traded company and longer than almost any CEO in the annals of American business. More important, by intellect and personal persuasion, he "almost single-handedly . . . fashioned a small mining investment house into a major diversified international mining concern."[1]

Yet that was hardly the measure of the man. In addition to developing and operating a number of first-class mines, Newmont was a partner in many other mining and energy ventures where it had board representation and provided technical support. It was one of the world's largest copper producers, but it also controlled Peabody Coal, America's largest coal company, and was one of the largest shareholders of DuPont, St. Joseph Lead, and Phelps Dodge. Mobil Oil sought its participation in offshore exploration.

Because, as Malozemoff told the *New York Times,* he preferred "to have part of a good thing rather than all of a mediocre thing,"[2] Newmont's influence far exceeded its market capitalization in the 1980s of $1.5 billion. Additionally, Malozemoff served on the boards of numerous business, financial, and charitable organizations, putting him in touch with the important industry leaders of the day. He knew and was respected by everyone who mattered in mining. His reputation for astute project analysis and financial judgment, backed by a first-rate technical staff, meant that for more than

5.1. Plato Malozemoff, a Russian emigrant, ran Newmont for thirty-two years and greatly expanded the company's mines and global reach. (*Guy Gillette*)

a generation virtually every deal in the mining industry crossed his desk at Newmont.

He was called "brilliant," "gifted," "dynamic," and "a formidable competitor," but also a "thorough gentleman" with "great character and integrity" whose dealings were "honorable and fair." Robert Macdonald, who for many years ran Newmont's research laboratory at Danbury, Connecticut, says he was "the smartest man in the room and it didn't matter how many people were in the room."[3] *Forbes* called him a "renaissance miner."[4]

Even those who crossed swords with him in epic battles held him in high esteem. "I thought he was a great man," says Rudolph Agnew, the former chairman of Consolidated Gold Fields of London and the Newmont director credited with finally dislodging him from his perch. "You have to remember the place that Plato occupied in the mining industry and the place he occupied in his own mind."[5]

His hubris was both inherited and firmly grounded. He graduated, after three years, at the top of his high school class in Oakland, California, spent a year studying music in Europe, and then entered the University of California at Berkeley, where he graduated magna cum laude in metallurgical engineering in 1931. A year later he received his master's degree from the Montana School of Mines, again graduating magna cum laude. In accepting his first job with the Montana Bureau of Mines at $50 a month, he turned down an offer of $250 to be first violinist with the Seattle Symphony Orchestra. He spoke French and Russian fluently and learned Spanish early in his career. A master chess player, which he said helped him think strategically, he was also a fierce competitor at tennis and golf.

Like two of his predecessors, William Boyce Thompson and Fred Searls Jr., Malozemoff spent his early years in a gold-mining camp—but in Siberia, not the American West. Shortly after his birth in August 1909 in St. Petersburg, Russia (his given name was Platon Alexandrovich), his father, Alexander, was exiled to Siberia for his political opposition to the czar. A well-educated engineer with a command of Latin, Greek, German, French, and philosophy,[6] he was able to find a job and raise his family managing a gold mine on the Lena River a couple hundred miles north of Lake Baikal. With the overthrow of the czar in 1917, Alexander won his release from exile and was immediately named managing director of Lena Goldfields, a British enterprise 25 percent owned by Consolidated Gold Fields.

That year, while Thompson was heading the American Red Cross relief effort in Russia, Malozemoff was a precocious eight-year-old taking violin and math lessons while his father held one of the most prestigious mining positions in Russia, commanding a workforce of 8,000 and earning a salary that would make a bourgeois blush: 60,000 golden rubles a year.

The Bolshevik revolution arrived later in Siberia than in the cities of St. Petersburg and Moscow but brought with it the same antipathy toward capital. In 1920, while on a trip to the United States to acquire new equipment for an expansion of the mine, Alexander learned that the Communists were in control and that he would likely be jailed or worse if he returned to Siberia. He sent money to his wife, Elizabeth, and urged her to emigrate to the United States with their two sons, Plato, then eleven, and his brother, Andrew.

In separate interviews with the Bancroft Library at the University of California, Berkeley, Malozemoff and his mother told hair-raising stories of their flight across nearly two thousand miles of Siberia, Mongolia, and China to meet up with Alexander in Peking. They traveled by riverboat, barge, and horse-drawn wagon, on foot by night, across the Gobi Desert by car, and at one point stood in a filthy third-class railcar when the main line of the Trans Siberian Railway was occupied by soldiers. There were midnight searches of their hotel rooms, a house arrest, delays in obtaining transit papers, sealed borders, and ruses to get through checkpoints.

His mother was both brave and resourceful. They weren't being pursued by the Bolsheviks, but in a revolution of the have-nots, a well-dressed woman with disposable funds was moving against the current of the times. To make matters more difficult, Elizabeth insisted on bringing all her possessions—clothing, furniture, and mementos—which filled four horse-drawn wagons. At Irkutsk, they took on more luggage—presents that had been sent out by Alexander. Plato received a small Kodak camera, which he used to document the remainder of their trip, including a picture of the Great Wall of China. Once united in Peking, the family traveled to Japan, where they obtained visas for America. On December 30, 1920, some six months after leaving Siberia, the Malozemoffs steamed into San Francisco Bay to begin their new life in the Russian community in Oakland.

Two footnotes on this remarkable family. Alexander returned to Siberia in 1924 under Lenin's New Economic Policy, which allowed him to manage the mine, export gold, and pay dividends to shareholders in London. That ended in 1929 when Stalin again nationalized the mine and Alexander returned to the United States. While the teenage Malozemoff attended Oakland public schools, his mother enrolled at the University of California, earning a master's degree in French philosophy, writing her thesis in French, and later a doctorate in Russian literature, written in English. She taught Russian language and culture at Berkeley from 1936 until 1950.

For all his academic achievements, Malozemoff had a slow start to his career during the Great Depression. A job as a consultant and equipment salesman for an engineering company took him to a gold mine in Alaska and a copper mine in Arizona, but failed to impress his father. "All you are doing is peddling machines. You should get into production,"[7] Malozemoff recalled being told by his father. In 1938, he joined his father in trying to develop gold mines in Argentina and Costa Rica. Both ventures failed as did his health and he returned to the States both ill and broke in 1943.

Following an operation to remove a tumor on his leg, he found a job in Washington with the Office of Price Administration reviewing potential mining projects for government support during the World War II. Among the many mines he analyzed were Newmont's lead and zinc mines in Colorado and the Magma Copper mine in Arizona. It was during an on-site inspection of the stopes at Resurrection in Leadville that he encountered Philip Kraft. An intellectual and musician as well as a Columbia-educated geologist, Kraft took an instant liking to Malozemoff and at the war's end persuaded Searls to offer him a job at Newmont.

Not convinced that the company needed another employee in New York, Searls extended only a stingy welcome. "What are you earning in Washington?" he asked. When told it was $4,800 a year, he responded, "Then I'll offer you $4,200."[8] Malozemoff, who viewed Newmont as "adventurous and efficient," accepted and reported to work at 14 Wall Street in October 1945. As the company's only staff engineer, he found himself a lone Indian in an office of chiefs. There were ten offices, each occupied by a member of the board of directors. These included Charles Ayer, president; vice president Searls, chief geologist, and his brother Carroll Searls, assistant secretary and later general counsel; Kraft, who oversaw U.S. and Canadian mines; H. DeWitt Smith, who had developed the company's South African properties; A. J. McNab, also vice president of Magma; and Franz

Schneider, who had handled financial matters since the Depression. In addition, legendary mining engineer and longtime director Henry Krumb had an office at Newmont. With a few secretaries and accountants, that was the entire headquarters staff.

In the years immediately following World War II, Newmont was flooded with proposals for new ventures. Banks considered mining too risky to finance, so prospectors with new ideas turned to companies like Newmont that provided the venture capital of the day. As the company's staff engineer, Malozemoff reviewed as many as twelve proposals a month—rejecting 310 in the six years between August 1947 and December 1953.

His first assignment of note came in 1949 when he wrote the technical portion of a prospectus for a $3.4 million stock offering by Magma to help finance development of its second mine, San Manuel, near Oracle, Arizona. With an estimated 463 million tons, the property was thought to contain the second largest copper deposit in the United States. But at a grade of only 0.78 percent copper and lying 1,500 feet below the surface, the mine would not be hugely profitable and therefore difficult to finance. A deep split within Newmont didn't make that task any easier. McNab, who that year had become president of Magma, believed that only a large-scale operation producing 30,000 tons a day and costing $100 million would be economically viable. Searls, Newmont's president since 1947, was bitterly opposed and pressed for a much smaller operation. McNab eventually won, but the rift caused the two companies, for a period, to separate their overlapping officers and boards of directors, although they still maintained offices together on Wall Street.

The stock offering itself was a failure, with barely half the shares placed. Newmont, which had jointly underwritten the issue with Lazard Fréres & Co., ended up taking 38 percent of the entire issue, increasing its holding in Magma to 22.9 percent from 14.9 percent. In 1952, with the Korean War under way, Malozemoff helped obtain a $94 million government loan from the Reconstruction Finance Corporation, the agency's largest such financing to that date, to finally get San Manuel started.

A more rewarding experience, and one Malozemoff called "my own first success at Newmont,"[9] was the development in the early 1950s of a low-grade nickel project in northern Manitoba with Sherritt Gordon

Mines. The project's remote location meant that transportation costs for conventionally smelted concentrates would be prohibitively expensive. Sherritt, instead, sought to employ a new and less costly process that used ammonia leaching under pressure in an autoclave to produce a pure nickel powder and a salable by-product, ammonium sulfate fertilizer. When others turned down financing, Sherritt approached Newmont. Malozemoff was "intrigued" by the process and devoted several years to making it a success.

To raise $47 million in financing, he had to prove that a technically challenging process would work flawlessly while placating Eldon Brown, Sherritt's determined president.[10] (Brown's brother-in-law was John Drybrough, Newmont Canada's president.) In what would prove to be a typical Malozemoff move, he "allowed Sherritt Gordon to do the actual work, but I arranged to have the over-all assessment of process and equipment supervised by men in whose competence I had the utmost confidence—Oscar Tangel, chief metallurgist of Battelle Institute (whom I knew in 1933 at Montana School of Mines), and Eugene H. Tucker, chief engineer of Newmont."[11] Together they ran numerous pilot tests before approving final construction. For financing, Schneider introduced Malozemoff to J. P. Morgan & Company, which in turn brought in Metropolitan Life Insurance Company and the Mutual Life Insurance Company of New York. Malozemoff gave credit to Stuart Silloway, then president of Mutual Life, for stepping in to save the project when financing seemed to stall. Newmont itself invested $13 million in Sherritt Gordon and eventually acquired a 39 percent interest in the company.

In the end, Malozemoff deemed the project only mildly successful, earning enough to repay its investment and returning dividends of $41 million over twenty-five years. But the impact on Newmont was more substantial. Until 1951, the company had never invested more than a few million dollars in any one project, relying instead on its ability to arrange outside financing. "After Sherritt Gordon, Newmont began to think in larger terms. The company's executives and its board . . . became able to consider propositions calling for raising sums they once would have been unwilling to even mention," writes Robert Ramsey in *Men and Mines of Newmont*.[12] In 1959, Malozemoff asked Silloway to join the board, where he offered sage financial advice until retiring in 1984. Tangel also joined the company as vice president of research and development, adding immensely to its technical capabilities.

Newmont followed the start-up of Sherritt Gordon with a burst of activity. It put $12 million into the Palabora copper mine in South Africa, $13 million into Southern Peru Copper, $67.5 million into the Granduc copper project in northern British Columbia, and $33 million in Atlantic Cement. The Dawn uranium mine opened in Washington State, and there were investments in an asbestos company in Canada, a copper venture in the Philippines, and nickel projects in Canada and Mexico. Newmont Overseas Petroleum Company was organized to participate in an oil field in the Algerian Sahara, while Newmont Oil pursued oil and gas leases in the Gulf of Mexico and offshore California. Malozemoff was the driving force in each of these ventures and quickly rose in the estimation of Newmont's aging management, being named a vice president in 1952 and a member of the board of directors a year later.

Still, when Searls decided to step down as CEO at age sixty-six, Malozemoff was not the first pick for the top job. From Paris, Thompson's daughter, Margaret Biddle, pressed for Evan Just, who had played a role in the company's short-lived lead and zinc ventures in North Africa in the 1940s. A Washington bureaucrat, he later became editor of *Engineering and Mining Journal*. In his memoirs, Malozemoff dismisses her interest in Just as being "impressed by . . . his deliberate manner of making pontifical pronouncements."[13] Searls had his eye on two eminent geologists, Frank Cameron, then a vice president of St. Joseph Lead Company, in which Newmont was the largest shareholder, and John Gustafson, who had the discovery of numerous ore bodies to his credit, including Magma's San Manuel deposit. Henry DeWitt Smith favored Marcus Banghart, the general manager of O'okiep in South Africa. Yet, in the end, Malozemoff prevailed.

Assuming the presidency on January 1, 1954, at the age of forty-four (and at a salary of $50,000 a year set to match Banghart's in Africa), Malozemoff presented a daylight and dark contrast with Searls, who had been known as "Mr. Newmont" for far longer than his seven-year tenure as CEO. Malozemoff was urbane, small boned, soft-spoken, buttoned down, and aloof. Searls was well liked but rough-hewn, gruff, and even on

Wall Street wore the flannel shirt, blue cap, red bow tie, and yellow-topped work boots of a western miner. Malozemoff was an accomplished musician on piano as well as violin. Searls was an amateur boxer and it was said that anyone coming in on a Monday morning after having been in a barroom brawl over the weekend would rise in his esteem, especially if they had had the best of it. Searls was a world-class geologist, but thought small. Malozemoff was world-class at everything and couldn't be contained. "I would fly to the ends of the earth for a good new venture," he told *Fortune* magazine.[14]

To Searls, Malozemoff's first moves as CEO seemed brash and unnecessary. He initiated a professional compensation study, including stock options, to attract and retain the talent he felt the company needed for expansion, and he moved the corporate headquarters from Wall Street to 300 Park Avenue, across from the Waldorf Astoria Hotel. At first Searls, who remained chairman until 1966, wouldn't move. But after a while isolation took its toll and, with Colonel Thompson's old furniture, he moved uptown. The new CEO sought to be deferential, giving Searls a hand in exploration and consulting with him on major issues. Later, when Searls's memory began to fade, Malozemoff assigned men to accompany him on walks to business meetings or for lunch at the New York Mining Club to ensure his safe return.[15]

In 1955, the U.S. Securities and Exchange Commission granted the company an exemption from the Investment Company Act of 1940. The act, which had treated Newmont as a closed-end mutual fund, entailed cumbersome reporting requirements and no longer fit its self-image as a mine operator. The change significantly strengthened Malozemoff's hand as he set out to make Newmont the most diversified company in the mining industry.

He brought Banghart to New York as head of operations and named attorney Roy Bonebrake, whom he called "a pillar of strength," a vice president. The two became his closest advisors. Kraft was named chairman of Newmont Oil. While competent men kept the books and bank accounts in order, Malozemoff turned for financial advice to his board members—Silloway; William Moses, chairman of Massachusetts Financial Services, who maintained a vast library on the mining industry; and most especially

André Meyer, the savvy senior partner of Lazard Fréres, the most prestigious investment banking house of the era, who was called "Zeus" by his peers.

In his memoirs, Malozemoff cites two experiences, somewhat contradictory in their lessons, which shaped his thinking and management style throughout his career. First was his work under Antoine Marc Gaudin, a brilliant professor of metallurgy at the Montana School of Mines who had done some of the early work on the separation of metals by flotation. "Gaudin would not tolerate sloppy thinking, writing or research, and his exacting demands made me realize how important it is to be strictly logical and clear-minded and to follow faithfully the scientific method of analysis so as not to be led astray in one's conclusions. These were principles that guided my professional life and saved me from gross errors in judgment,"[16] he told the Bancroft Library's Eleanor Swent.

The second was his early observation at Newmont of how the officers, all knowledgeable and experienced, but also strong-willed and independent, could move the company forward when "they seldom agreed among themselves" on anything. The answer seemed to lie in the "grudging respect" they held for each other and the fact that they had worked together almost all of their careers: "In this diverse environment I found it possible to hone my own judgments to sharper focus. I could observe how complex was the multiplicity of variables and considerations past, present and future, and marveled how these men reached the right conclusions without painstaking analysis, mostly on hunches based on their experience . . . I adopted this method of arriving at decisions as my responsibilities grew."[17]

Throughout his long tenure as chief executive he employed some of the brightest men in their fields, men who were meticulous in their research such as Tangel and Robert Macdonald, fellow students of Gaudin's at Montana; Arthur Brant and Maurice Davidson in geophysics; Frank McQuiston, David Christie, and later Leonard Harris in metallurgy; Robert Fulton and Richard Ellett in exploration; Banghart and William Humphrey in mining; Tucker and Pete Crescenzo in engineering. Every new project had to run the gauntlet of these specialists, who individually examined things in minute detail and were encouraged to challenge conventional thinking to find solutions.

"No one has a monopoly on brains," was a favorite Malozemoff expression, according to Harris.[18] Another: "You may be right, but show me the evidence." Scrupulous in his attention to detail, Malozemoff was famous for checking calculations on his slide rule and often spent Monday mornings comparing results with his project development people after a weekend of crunching numbers. Those with the credentials and nerve could challenge the CEO—but they had better be right. He could be abrupt and abrasive. "Many people were afraid of Plato, but he respected knowledge and liked to have people around who could think and argue with him,"[19] says Jack Thompson, president from 1974 to 1984.

"With Plato, you had to be right," adds Crescenzo, "but with Plato you wanted to be right. He inspired people, and he was kind. I think he felt a deep sense of responsibility for the people who worked for him. He felt they were part of his family."[20]

Harris remembers Malozemoff's response when asked by a reporter if mining was a risky business. "No, it's not," he recalls the CEO replying, "provided that you look at every single item of a project. You start with exploration and you have to really know the geology and the mineralogy and the metallurgy and how you're going to mine it and how you are going to treat the ore. Then how are you going to get the financing and market the product and staff the project? Every one of these items is very important. If you miss one and don't really study it carefully, then mining can be very risky."

In making economic decisions, he considered financial tools such as discounted cash flow, or DCF, "inappropriate" for mining because of their emphasis on short-term results and inability to cover unpredictable financial, political, or catastrophic risks inherent in the business. "Ever since my father explained it to me in the 1920s, I have always preferred the test of cost ranking,"[21] he said. Mines that were among the lowest-cost producers in their industry could withstand down cycles in the price and therefore would be more viable over the long term than other operations. He also resisted the use of mathematical models that "partially replace personal judgment and experience."

Consequently, the thumbs up or thumbs down on a project often depended on Malozemoff's gut feel. "I speak the language of the metallurgists," he told the *New York Times*. "There is an element of my personal judgment in every decision we make."[22] He had great self-confidence and did not seek consensus. His door was open to all and he routinely consulted individually with his staff, but group meetings were rare. "He didn't bring us together to discuss big strategic issues," says his successor, Gordon Parker. "He was more of an individualist than a team leader."[23] Richard Leather, who succeeded Bonebrake as general counsel and was a close advisor to both Malozemoff and Parker, says "Plato never appeared or wished to appear uncertain. He was relatively unprejudiced and could keep an open mind, but he rarely expressed uncertainty as to how to proceed."[24]

Exploration and technology have always been the heart and soul of Newmont. Thus it is no surprise that Malozemoff took great pride in the purchase of a thirty-acre site near Danbury, Connecticut, on which the company built one of the finest research facilities in the industry. Opened in 1957 and employing sixty people, Danbury combined the geophysical center managed by Brant at Jerome, Arizona, and the metallurgical laboratory started by McQuiston at Grass Valley, California. The site was chosen because it was close to New York City, but far enough removed to avoid electrical interference with the lab's sensitive instruments. Malozemoff saw technology as differentiating Newmont in the race to acquire and develop new properties and as a means to add value to its mines and investments. Danbury also became a holding tank for people between assignments, and almost everyone with technical skills was posted to Danbury at some point in their careers.

While the metallurgists studied ore samples from the company's far-flung mines and developed processing technologies, many of them patented, to best extract the metal, the geophysicists applied science to the art of prospecting. With the odds of a discovery equating to finding a needle in a haystack, geologists needed better tools. A major scientific advance was an electronic detection device called Induced Polarization (IP), which was the first geophysical technique capable of detecting scattered or disseminated sulfide mineralization below the surface. It was first used to help define Magma's San Manuel deposit in Arizona in the 1950s.

In the field, the early geophysical equipment was bulky and awkward. Large trucks "had big insulator horns coming out of them that made it look like they came from Mars," recalls retired exploration vice president Ellett. "Every now and then they would kill some poor farmer's cow. If a cow stepped on their survey line—Pow!"[25]

Southern Peru Copper illustrated how Malozemoff leveraged his connections and Newmont's technology to obtain an interest in one of the
world's largest open-pit copper mines. Cerro de Pasco, the Peruvian subsidiary of New York–based Cerro Corporation, had begun exploring a
large copper deposit in the early 1950s but lacked the funds to fully drill
out the property. Cerro chairman Robert Koenig, a longtime associate of
Malozemoff's, sought the use of Newmont's IP technology. Malozemoff
agreed and put up additional money for exploration. The new technology
proved successful and delineated a huge deposit that was later confirmed
by drilling. In 1954, a submission was made with the U.S. Export-Import
Bank for a $100 million development loan. Almost simultaneously, how-
ever, a similar application was filed by ASARCO and Phelps Dodge, who
had joined to develop two neighboring copper deposits. The bank forced a
combination, and in 1955 Southern Peru Copper Company was organized
with ASARCO owning 58 percent, Cerro and Phelps Dodge 16 percent
each, and Newmont 10 percent. The three deposits jointly contained one
billion tons of ore at 1 percent copper.

After an investment of $237 million, production of blister copper be-
gan in 1960. An additional $726 million was invested to open a fourth de-
posit in the 1970s. An international consortium of fifty-four banks provided
$404 million; the remainder came largely from internally generated funds.
Newmont put up only another $6 million in preferred stock. At its peak
in 1979, Southern Peru produced 330,000 tons of copper, reported sales
of $550 million, and earned $254 million before tax, for a pre-tax profit of
nearly 40 cents per pound. Translated back to Newmont's books, however,
the numbers didn't look so rosy. A military coup in 1968 put a leftist junta
in charge of the government of Peru, which increased taxes on mining to
68.5 percent in 1980, imposed restrictions on currency exchanges needed
to pay dividends, and nationalized copper refining and marketing. Over a
forty-year period, Newmont received only $38 million in dividends, going
many years with no returns, before selling its interest in 1995 to ASARCO
for $116 million, representing an after-tax gain of $72 million.

Simultaneous with the start-up of Southern Peru, development began
on the Granduc copper project in British Columbia. Malozemoff was fas-
cinated by the project's complexity, but later acknowledged that it was "the
biggest failure of my chief executive responsibility at Newmont."[26] The

property was located high in the Coastal Range forty miles from the small town of Stewart and near the southern Alaska border at the head of what today is Misty Fjords National Monument. Discovered by a Scandinavian prospector on snowshoes, Einar Kvale, in 1948, the deposit was otherwise inaccessible except by helicopter. In fact, a Canadian outfit known as Helicopter Exploration Company was the first to acquire prospecting rights in the area. In 1953 Larry Postle, who had managed a Newmont nickel mine in Canada, acquired the rights and brought the prospect to the attention of Drybrough.

Searls opposed Newmont's involvement, but as Malozemoff recalled, "I did not have much opposition from the board and the board finally supported me."[27] In fact, Malozemoff rarely had opposition from his board. "I have observed that a strong CEO can sometimes achieve a degree of confidence in his judgment on the part of the board so that they will follow his recommendations even in the absence of or with inadequate DCF evaluations," he later commented.[28]

Geologist Hal Norman, who had worked for the Canadian Geological Survey, drilled out a deposit of 32.5 million tons of ore grading 1.9 percent copper, and John Wise, the chief engineer at Idarado, was brought in to select a mill site and develop a mining plan. The project cost was estimated at $55 million. Hecla Mining and ASARCO joined the venture with investments of $10 million each and Bankers Trust was tapped for $30 million. But the area's isolation and severe weather posed a daunting challenge. First, twenty-eight miles of road had to be built from the port at Stewart to Tide Lake, where a 7,500-ton-per-day concentrator would be built. Then a ten-mile tunnel had to be dug under a glacier to reach the mine site. In the end, the project cost $88 million, with ASARCO and Newmont splitting the overrun. But because development costs could be deducted from profits on other ventures before paying taxes, Malozemoff justified the expense. "We were using 50-cent dollars for development of the property," he averred.[29]

Underscoring the long lead time necessary to drill out and develop a large mine in such a remote location, construction didn't begin until the fall of 1964. Tragedy struck almost immediately. More than ninety feet of snow fell on the work camp that winter and in February 1965 an avalanche roared down on the camp killing twenty-six workers and injuring nineteen others. It was the worst mining disaster in the company's history. In his annual letter to shareholders, a shocked Malozemoff reported his "extreme sorrow" at the loss. A government inquiry cleared Newmont of any negligence or safety violations, and ten years later Granduc was designated the safest mine in Canada.

Taking its name from the nearby Leduc Glacier, Granduc finally began production in 1970 only to encounter other problems. Anticipating difficulty in mining the deposit's wide veins, Malozemoff sought expert advice from Swedish engineers who had developed a new mining method called sub-level caving. The method had been used successfully at Mt. Isa in Australia, and Newmont engineers made numerous visits to both continents. But, instead of cleanly mining out the ore veins, as the experts had predicted, the caving method took out large swaths of waste rock as well, diluting the ore in the concentrator by 35 percent.[30] Higher oil prices and a prolonged strike pushed costs far beyond the $4 a barrel and $9 an hour rate on which the mine's economics had been based. And although 212 homes were built at Stewart for married workers, turnover of skilled miners ran 30 percent a month.

Granduc was shut down in 1978, having encountered losses for most of its eight years of operation. It paid Newmont a dividend in only one year, $4.5 million in 1973. The mine was sold to Imperial Oil, the Canadian subsidiary of Exxon, in 1979 for $8 million. Imperial spent $120 million to refurbish the mine and then pumped in more to keep it going, but was never able to turn a profit. Malozemoff calculated that in total Newmont lost $20 million after tax on the project, while Imperial had to write off nearly $250 million.[31]

Far more successful was the Dawn uranium project on the Spokane Indian Reservation in Washington State. Two brothers, Jim and John LeBrett, discovered uranium on tribal lands in the early 1950s. With the help of an engineer with the U.S. Bureau of Mines, they organized a company, Midnight Mines, and contracted to sell five hundred tons of uranium to the U.S. Atomic Energy Commission in Salt Lake City. After mining the first two or three carloads, however, they ran out of ore. Through a banker in Portland who had worked with Searls in developing Idarado, the LeBretts turned to Newmont. Searls went out to investigate and assigned geologist Norman to begin an exploration program. Pete Loncar, who would later be instrumental in the start-up of the Carlin gold mine, drilled out the ore body and determined that adjacent land owned by individual Indians, not by the tribe, would also be needed for mining. Newmont acquired the land, besting an offer from Phelps Dodge, and in 1956 organized a new company, Dawn Mining, in which it owned 51 percent and Midnight Mines 49 percent.

The project was strongly supported by Senator Henry M. Jackson of Washington, a member of the Joint Atomic Committee of Congress, Washington governor Dixy Lee Ray, and the Atomic Energy Commission, which considered the Midnight mine, with an estimated 100,000 tons of uranium ore, to be one of the largest such deposits in the United States.

At a cost of less than $5 million, two-thirds in bank loans and one-third invested by Newmont, Dawn built a 500-ton-per-day mill, designed at Danbury, and began production in August 1957. It was the company's last wooden mill. In its first four months, Dawn earned a profit of $360,000. It was able to repay its entire investment within two years. Operations were suspended for three years in the late 1960s on completion of its Atomic Energy contract but resumed in 1971 after new long-term contracts were negotiated with several utilities. That year, a second Newmont mine opened in Alaska, with the ore sent to Dawn's mill near Spokane for processing. Dawn's best year was 1980, with 450,000 pounds of U308 sold for nearly $15 million and an after-tax profit of more than $4 million. Two years later, however, the uranium market collapsed. Long-term contracts expired and the spot price for uranium fell below Dawn's mining and processing costs. Operations ceased as the U.S. Department of Interior sought to impose costly, and in Newmont's mind unrealistic, mill closure and mine reclamation procedures, some of which are still in litigation.

Despite the closure issues, Marcel DeGuire, who managed the operation for several years, believes that Dawn was the most profitable operation in Newmont's history. Although tiny in comparison with copper mines of the day or current gold operations, "that company paid out $40 million in dividends [$24 million to Newmont] and $10 million in royalties [to the Spokane tribe]" over a twenty-five-year period, DeGuire says. "That's not bad for a 500-ton-a-day operation in the 1960s and 1970s. By any measure—tons of ore per day or capital cost or the number of employees [with contract mining, there were only 40 to 50]—it was amazing."[32]

Newmont needed more Dawns and a stronger domestic earnings base. The headlong pursuit of mining ventures around the world was adding value to the company's portfolio, but with income dependent on dividends, nearly 60 percent of its cash flow in the late 1950s came from southern Africa. Cerro Corporation again provided an opportunity and led Newmont into one of its largest investments to that point. In a sharp departure for a company whose entire history was based on precious or base metals and oil, Malozemoff decided to enter the cement business. Furthermore, he sought to do so using the largest equipment and building the largest cement plant in the United States. This was totally uncharacteristic of Newmont and its CEO; no one at the company had the slightest idea how to make or market cement.

The idea was the brainchild of Bernard Ulrich, a Swiss engineer, who noted that because of high transportation costs, the American cement industry relied on relatively small plants serving a 200- to 250-mile radius. If economies of scale could be applied and a big plant built with access to inexpensive barge transportation, then it could serve a much wider area. He had located a large limestone deposit at Ravena, New York, on the Hudson River south of Albany, which he thought could support such a facility. He approached Cerro's CEO Koenig who, in turn, sold the idea to Malozemoff. In 1960, the Atlantic Cement Company was formed with Newmont and Cerro each owning 45 percent, and Ulrich and his associates 10 percent. Newmont would take the lead in operations.

Assigned to get the project off the ground was Jack Thompson, who had recently joined the company as staff engineer, the same position once held by Malozemoff. Thompson, who was not related to Newmont's founder, studied at the Colorado School of Mines and had been working in Cuba for Dayton Hedges, a prominent Cuban American, since 1945. When Fidel Castro seized power, Thompson was asked to join the revolutionary government as head of Cuba's mining operations. He vividly recalls a visit to his office by Che Guevara "with his entourage of about fifty men with beards, uniforms, and guns, of which probably only two or three had actually fought [in the revolution] and the other forty-eight of them were hangers-on." At the time, Guevara was in charge of everything in the country except politics and the army. Thompson declined the offer and decided it was time to leave. Through a friend, he contacted Malozemoff who offered a job "if I could get out of the country."[33] Remarkably, when his family's belongings were held up at the port, Thompson called on Guevara at his quarters where the revolutionary leader scribbled a note providing for their safe passage.

Thompson hired marketing consultants who projected a rosy outlook for cement prices and met with shipping executives to understand the basics of barge transportation. Once again Searls was opposed, but the board approved. Silloway says he "bled" over the decision to enter the cement business, "but Plato was insistent. Sometimes he relied too heavily on his own intuition and could be gullible about things he wanted."[34] Three ocean-going barges that could carry up to 17,000 tons each were ordered with the thought of carrying cement as far as Florida, and in 1961 construction began on the largest cement kilns ever built—580 feet long and 20 feet in diameter. Production was slated at 10 million barrels of cement a year.

It soon became apparent that the projected $64 million price tag ($50 million coming as loans from banks and insurance companies) was too low. To shave costs, Ulrich, unbeknownst to Newmont, eliminated one of four planned ball mills. But without the grinding capacity, the plant could not meet its planned production. Heads on the mills cracked repeatedly and, because of their extreme length, the kilns sagged in the middle, causing the brick lining to crack. Rebricking was time-consuming and expensive. The studies forecasting a 10-million-barrel-a-year market had failed to take into account that construction is seasonal. To meet peak demand periods, storage facilities had to be built and costly inventory maintained. Others also were entering the cement business, adding to capacity and driving down prices. Tugboat operators in New York harbor were prone to strike. To make matters worse, the company found itself in the uncomfortable position of dealing with the New York/New Jersey construction trade, where bribery of politicians and Mafia ties were commonplace.

Not only did Atlantic post losses throughout the 1960s, but Newmont and Cerro were called upon for annual cash advances to keep the operation solvent. Profitability was finally achieved in 1970 and Atlantic paid its first dividend the following year. In 1973, with Atlantic reporting record earnings of $7 million on $47 million in sales, Newmont acquired Cerro's interest for $38 million. Ulrich had been forced out some years earlier. Although sales doubled over the next ten years, profits never again reached their 1973 peak and losses were again being recorded in the early 1980s. During the 1970s, however, Newmont received $28 million in dividends.

Another venture in which Thompson played a key role was Foote Mineral. Founded in 1876 by Dr. A. E. Foote of Philadelphia, the company had a long history of acquiring and selling mineral specimens to universities, museums, and collectors. Foote was also a pioneer in developing uses for such elements as titanium, zirconium, chromium, vanadium, manganese, and lithium, many of which are used in the steel and aluminum industries. With steel and aluminum underpinning a worldwide economic boom in the 1960s, Malozemoff began buying Foote stock on the open market. In 1965 Gordon Chambers, Foote's retired CEO, was invited to join the Newmont board. The next year, Thompson and Robert J. Searls, Fred Searls's son, made a trip to the company's lithium operation at Kings Mountain, North Carolina, to assess its prospects. Liking what they saw, Newmont invested $5 million in newly issued shares to acquire 19 percent of the company.

A more direct investment in steel came in 1967, when the company purchased a 14.5 percent interest in the Oppenheimer-controlled Highveld Steel and Vanadium Corporation of South Africa. At the same time, Foote, which purchased raw materials from Highveld, came under attack by another specialty metals producer, Vanadium Corporation of America (VCA), and turned to Newmont as a white knight. Malozemoff brokered a merger between the two companies and invested another $10 million to bring Newmont's holdings in Foote to 33 percent. The VCA properties, which included a number of electric furnaces making manganese, titanium, and other non-ferrous metals, never lived up to expectations and were a drag on Foote's profitable lithium business.

Malozemoff wanted Foote to sell off the unprofitable ferroalloy operations, but his demands fell on deaf ears with a succession of Foote CEOs. Frustrated, he accepted without enthusiasm Thompson's proposal in 1974 that Newmont buy the rest of the company and take control of management. Through a public tender offer, and at a cost of $29 million, Newmont increased its ownership to 92 percent. Thompson had just been named president of Newmont and "I thought it would be demoralizing to Jack to oppose his first proposal," Malozemoff later said. Besides, he added, if it turned out to be a mistake, "I guess people learn from errors."[35] That put-down, coming after both men had retired, reveals another side of Malozemoff's personality—an increasing tendency as he aged of treating loyal associates as subservient. Silloway says he "despaired of the relationship between Jack and Plato, but didn't know how to deal with it."

Performance at Foote improved in the late 1970s, and the operation, which had record sales of $185 million in 1981, paid Newmont $18 million in dividends before slumping again in the metals recession of the mid-1980s.

While both Foote and Atlantic Cement were acquired as part of Malozemoff's quest for diversity, each needed a lightning bolt of good fortune to become meaningful contributors to the company's earnings. In both cases, technology provided the potential for such a breakthrough, but in both cases it came too late.

Crescenzo, who sat on the Atlantic Cement board, promoted an innovative solution to Atlantic's economic problem. Bethlehem Steel operated one of the world's largest blast furnaces at Sparrow's Point, Maryland, on the Chesapeake Bay. The furnace produced 800,000 tons of slag a year that was considered waste by the steelmaker. But finely crushed, slag had the physical properties of cement made from limestone and shale with the added advantage of greater strength and durability. And since slag did not need to be fired in a kiln, slag cement used only one-fifth the energy of Portland cement and could be produced for $18 a ton, about half the cost at Ravena.

Yet, Crescenzo recalls, "I had to convince Plato that it was a worthwhile thing." In 1980, Atlantic invested $92 million, including a $14 million industrial revenue bond from Baltimore County, to build a plant and port and launch a new 19,000-ton barge. Production began two years later.

Foote's breakthrough came with the development of a process for producing lithium by evaporation from salt brines rather than mining. A plant at Silver Peak, Nevada, proved to be quite cost-effective. In 1975, Foote began negotiations with the government of Chile for a joint venture in the Atacama Desert, where a brine deposit five times richer than Silver Peak's had been discovered. In 1984, a $50 million facility to produce 14 million pounds of lithium carbonate annually was inaugurated by President Augusto Pinochet. The facility, in which Foote held a 55 percent interest, was the first foreign investment in Chile since the ouster of leftist Salvador Allende, who had nationalized the country's mining industry in the 1970s.

But before either slag cement or the Atacama project could become fully established, they were abandoned. In 1985, as Malozemoff was transferring power to Parker, Atlantic Cement was sold to a British company, Blue Circle, for $171 million, resulting in an after-tax gain of just $7 million. A year later, with Thompson retiring after twenty-five years of service, the company announced it was seeking a buyer for Foote. Cyprus Mines purchased the company in early 1988 for $74 million, a gain of $24 million. Thompson opposed both sales and was particularly bitter about Foote. "It should not have been sold—period. It was the largest producer of lithium outside of China, and there are more uses for lithium today than there were then." Furthermore, Atacama remains the only world-class deposit of the strategic metal.

The sales, however, had less to do with the merits or outlook of the two companies than they did with other pressures facing Newmont. The company's large copper operations were reporting mounting losses in an industry-wide recession, and by the mid-1980s Newmont had a new major shareholder, Consolidated Gold Fields, which was far more interested in gold than in a diversified portfolio.

Yet, before that occurred, Malozemoff would lead Newmont into other, even larger ventures in his quest for growth and diversification. In the end, his stubborn adherence to those two strategies overshadowed much of his earlier brilliance and left the company vulnerable to attack as Wall Street sentiment toward mining stocks and entrenched management underwent a profound change.

Doc Brant

Among the many brilliant scientists who have been associated with Newmont over the years, none was more colorful or inspirational than Dr. Arthur Brant. Of Scotch-Irish and native American (Mohawk) descent, Brant earned top honors in math and physics at the University of Toronto in the late 1920s, won a scholarship to Princeton when it was home to such intellectual luminaries as Albert Einstein, and coached the German hockey team in the 1936 Olympics while completing his Ph.D. in physics at the University of Berlin.

He started consulting with Newmont in 1946 when, as an associate professor of physics at the University of Toronto, he was working on the early application of electronics to geophysics. Newmont CEO Fred Searls Jr., a member of President Roosevelt's War Production Board during World War II, had learned of new electronic techniques, such as sonar, that could spot submarines and reasoned that similar tools might be used to detect underground ore deposits. Brant at the time was applying techniques first developed by the Radio Frequency Laboratory in New Jersey in which metal, and later sulfide ore, submerged in water were found to give off electrical discharges of considerable magnitude and duration when subjected to a pulse of direct electrical current. This developed into an exploration tool known as Induced Polarization (IP).

Brant joined Newmont in 1949 and assembled a crackerjack team of scientists and mathematicians, many of them his students from Canada. His laboratory at Jerome, Arizona, surrounded by copper mines, was described by the Society of Exploration Geophysicists as "the first significant research group in the history of mining geophysics in America."[36]

Over the years, his team obtained twenty-five patents in geophysical techniques, many derived from converting wartime electronics to applications in mineral exploration. The group did pioneering work in electromagnetics, including the first use of helicopter-borne electromagnetic mapping in 1955 and the first borehole device to test electrical resistivity of ores. Not long afterward, Newmont installed one of the first in-house computers in the mining industry, an IBM 1130 that took up an entire room. During the 1980s the company developed its own computerized imaging system for mapping and was one of the first to use Global Positioning System satellites for aerial surveys.

A bear of a man, with fingers too large to dial a telephone, Brant shot in the low 80s in golf and would play contract bridge for twenty hours at a stretch. But he also had a volatile temper. "He would come into work agitated about something at home and fire the first person he would see," only to hire them back the next day, says John Parry, who joined Newmont as a geophysicist in 1969. "Some of the people who worked for him said they had been fired four or five times."[37]

Yet in twenty-five years with Newmont, "Doc" Brant earned a reputation as "a superb leader. He saw the big picture and carefully selected some very capable people to work with him to solve the problems that he and others were defining. He set priorities and established a work environment that led to teamwork and team solutions," Parry adds.

Among his recruits were Jim Wait, who did much of the work on the IP technology; Maurice Davidson, who succeeded Brant and took his theoretical studies to a more practical level; George McLaughlin, an eccentric with a remarkable ability to build electronic equipment that worked; Misac Nabighian, from Romania, who did the theoretical calculations; and Colin Barnett, from the Colorado School of Mines, who became Newmont's third director of geophysics in 1989. More recently, Bruno Nilsson, brilliant in electronics, and Eric Lauritsen, a mechanical wizard, were largely responsible for the development of the company's airborne navigation equipment.

In 1986 the University of Nevada, Reno, established the Arthur Brant Chair in Exploration Geophysics as part of the Mackay School of Mines. The chair resulted from the collaboration of John Livermore, the geologist responsible for Carlin gold discovery, and Dr. James Taranik, then dean of the Mackay School and a director of Newmont Gold Company. Livermore had been hired at Newmont by Brant and Taranik, who was the chief scientist at NASA for the first space shuttle experiments and had worked with Brant after his retirement from Newmont. Brant at the time was chairman of the Geosat Committee formed by industry scientists to monitor the geological exploration tools aboard the nation's satellites.

5.2. President Jack Thompson listens at a management presentation in the early 1970s while geophysicist Arthur "Doc" Brant reviews notes for his talk. (*Chester Higgins Jr.*)

Livermore, who had prospered from years of prospecting, offered $500,000 in Newmont stock to fund the chair. With additional contributions from his friends and Brant's, the endowment rose to $1.8 million, the largest at the university. Taranik, currently director of the Mackay School of Earth Sciences and Engineering, has held the Arthur Brant Chair since its inception.

6

MAGMA

Newmont Mining celebrated its fifti-
eth anniversary in 1971. That was the year that astronauts rode a rover on the
moon and the microprocessor was invented. It was also the year that gold
was set free from government price controls. In August, President Richard
Nixon, faced with a rising trade deficit and declining dollar, "closed the gold
window" by repudiating the country's international obligation to exchange
dollars for gold. Subject to free market forces, the price of gold jumped in
three years from $35 an ounce to $195. It was a defining moment for gold
producers, but there was no mention of it in Newmont's annual report that
year.

The reason was quite simple; Newmont considered gold as part of its
past, not its future. In a thumbnail sketch of its history, Newmont's annual report for 1971 cited an "initial phase (under founder William Boyce
Thompson) ending in about 1933; the gold mining phase, ending about
1939; the African phase following World War II, which merged gradually
into the recent growth phase that began in the early 1950s." But growth in
what? Presumably, any mining venture the company might choose. What
the company did say was that its past strategy, however changing, had been
rewarding. The purchase of 100 shares for $4,000 in Newmont's initial
public offering in 1925 would by February 1972 have been worth $140,000
and yield $4,500 a year in dividends.

Five years later, in the annual report for 1976, shareholders were given
a first, although incomplete, breakdown of the company's earnings. With
net income of nearly $50 million, 38 percent came from copper, 16 percent
from gold (including by-product gold from its base metal mines), 8 percent
from ferroalloys and lithium, 7 percent from oil and gas, and 2 percent from
uranium. No accounting was made for the remaining 29 percent, although
the cement business was profitable that year and the company recorded a
$13 million profit on security sales. Full disclosure was not yet in vogue.

That year, to further CEO Plato Malozemoff's quest for diversification, the company put together a consortium to acquire Peabody Coal, the largest coal miner in the United States. As a result, by 1980, Newmont was describing itself in its annual report as "a diversified natural resource company" with subsidiaries and affiliates producing "28 products from mines, wells, plants and refineries in the United States, Canada and elsewhere around the world." It attributed its "strength" to investments in "mineral properties having long life, low operating costs and ready markets."

However, Joseph Flannery, chief executive of Uniroyal Holding, who joined the board in 1982 and served for twenty-one years, found all the talk of a diversified portfolio so much window dressing. Throughout that period, he says, "The company considered itself a copper company and all the rest was a sideshow."[1] Carlin got very little mention in the board meetings. The emphasis was on Magma, which was going through a horrid time.

Indeed, no company has been more closely associated with Newmont over the years than Magma Copper. Although Newmont did not add Magma shares to its portfolio until 1928, the two companies had been joined at the hip since their founding by Colonel Thompson. Except for a brief spat in 1950, they had shared overlapping officers and directors and continued to share offices in New York even after Newmont moved to the Pan Am (now Met Life) Building at 200 Park Avenue in 1983. In the early 1960s, when Newmont held a 21 percent interest in Magma but did not manage its operations, three of Magma's seven directors were Newmonters. Roy Bonebrake, Newmont's general counsel, was Magma's chairman; Malozemoff was a Magma director and vice president; and Walter Schmid, Newmont's controller, was Magma's treasurer and a director. In 1964 Magma's president, Wesley P. Goss, joined the Newmont board.

A 1922 engineering graduate from the University of California, Berkeley, Goss had a sixty-year association with Newmont, starting at Grass Valley, California. In 1953, he succeeded A. J. McNab as president of Magma, where he shouldered responsibility for the company's growth for the next eighteen years and then served as chairman from 1972 until 1984. His son, John W. Goss, described as a humble man who had to work twice as hard as others to advance under his father's tutelage, became general manager at San Manuel in 1976 and later a Magma vice president, while his daughter, Patricia, married a future Magma president, David Ridinger.

For sixty-eight years, from 1914 until 1982, Magma pulled high-grade copper ore from veins occurring in deep fault fissures in mostly quartz and limestone formations at Superior, Arizona, fifty miles east of Phoenix. By the time the mine closed, a hundred miles of drifts and tunnels had been mined out at multiple levels to tap a number of separate ore bodies. The mine had yielded 1.25 million tons of copper, 45 million ounces of silver, and nearly 750,000 ounces of gold. San Manuel, a second, much larger underground mine forty-five miles northeast of Tucson and sixty miles south of Superior, opened in 1956 and remained in operation until 1999.

The Superior mine was known as a "warm mine"; the temperature at the 2,000-foot level was 109 degrees and it reached 160 degrees at the 3,900-foot level. In 1937, Magma installed the first underground air conditioning system in North America, a unit designed by Willis Carrier of the Carrier Corporation. For that feat, the American Society of Mechanical Engineers in conjunction with the Smithsonian Institution in Washington designated the Superior mine a National Historic Mechanical Engineering Landmark.

It had other distinctions. The men and women at Magma won the U.S. Army-Navy Production Award in October 1942 for their high production of metals needed during World War II. Magma was the only western copper mine that never had a separate wage scale for whites and Hispanics, a system that prevailed until the 1940s. However, the largely Hispanic workforce of 1,200 had a hard time seeing the distinction. "There was a lot of discrimination, just as there was at Kennecott, ASARCO, and the other companies," says Frank Florez, who joined Magma in 1954 with an engineering degree from the University of Arizona earned with the help of the G.I. Bill. The lead man on most crews was a gringo and favoritism, not skill, determined who got the major share of production bonuses, he says. "It's my belief that discriminatory practices in the workforce brought the union in," Florez says of the contract won by the Union of Mine, Mill and Smelter Workers in 1957.[2]

The first copper pour at San Manuel was celebrated on January 8, 1956. Although claims surrounding the ore body were first staked in 1906, it wasn't until 1943, when the War Production Board authorized evaluation of the property by the U.S. Geological Survey, that any drilling was done. It took the Korean War, a decade later, and a loan from the government's Re-

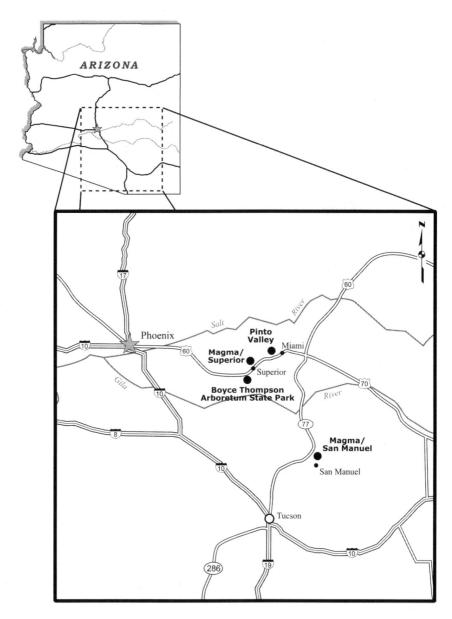

6.1. William Boyce Thompson began investing in western copper mines before Arizona became a state. The Silver Queen mine at Superior, renamed Magma Copper, produced its first ore in 1914. In 1956, Magma opened the much larger San Manuel mine and in 1982 acquired Pinto Valley to become the nation's second largest copper producer. (*Newmont Archives*)

construction Finance Corporation to finally spur the low-grade deposit into production. The $100 million project involved a deep mine, a 30,000-ton-per-day concentrator and smelter, and a thirty-mile railroad to connect with the Southern Pacific at Hayden, Arizona. Utah Construction and Stearns-Roger designed and built all the facilities, while Del E. Webb, which four years later opened Sun City, Arizona, as a haven for retirees, built a new town with 1,000 homes, four schools, a thirty-bed hospital, and a thirty-two-acre shopping center. The town was financed under a separate $12 million government loan. As operations increased, an additional 276 homes were added in 1971.

"San Manuel was by far the largest underground mine in the state. We had people pouring in from other mines across the country. It was an exploding community with good jobs," says Ridinger, who began his career as a mining engineer as San Manuel opened and became Magma's president in 1985. "I don't think miners had ever lived in a town like that before. They had an Elks Club, an American Legion and seven churches."[3] David Baker, who started as a geologist at San Manuel in 1980 and is currently Newmont's vice president of environmental affairs, remembers cinder-block homes without insulation that rented for only $60 a month, and "every once in a while you'd have to take a wet towel and put it under the door to keep the tailings from blowing in when the wind was blowing the wrong way."[4]

San Manuel was a mass of mineralized rock, chiefly granite, containing copper sulfides. The deposit covered an area one mile long by half a mile wide, but extended about 2,600 feet below the surface. To reach the mine face, workers descended in huge elevator cages carrying 110 men and equipped with redundant safety features to prevent a cage from dropping down the shaft. Ore was mined by block caving, in which a horizontal slice of ore was removed so that the ore above would fall, or cave, into the undercut. The traditional way to support the openings under each caving block was to use heavy timbers or steel sets. Extreme pressure, however, proved this method inadequate and San Manuel became one of the first mines to use concrete for structural support. Once mined, the ore was loaded on underground electric trains of fifteen cars each carrying a total of 185 tons to one of four shafts. There, 15-foot diameter drums called skips were loaded and hoisted to the surface at a rate of 3,000 feet per minute. Once in the early 1970s, 916 skips were loaded and a one-day world record of 72,000

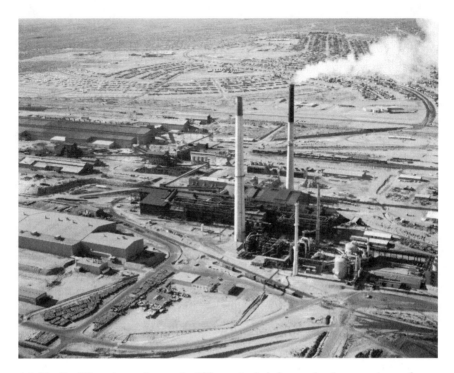

6.2. The San Manuel complex north of Tucson included not only a large smelter, refinery, and rod mill but a town (background) with all the amenities for 1,276 homes. Sulfur dioxide fumes, originally emitted from the tall stack in the center, were later processed in the acid plant at the lower right. (*Ray Manley*)

tons of ore was hoisted to the surface. Top side, a forty-car diesel train, making ten round-trips a day, hauled the ore to the mill and smelter, seven miles to the east.

In the office, engineers, geologists, accountants, labor relations personnel, and managers relied on a typing pool of five people, mostly men, who turned handwritten letters and reports into finished products, often with multiple carbon copies for filing.

In 1955, Magma's aging operation at Superior produced 24,000 tons of copper at a cost of 25 cents per pound, which it sold for 39 cents, earning record net income of $6 million on $19 million in sales. Initial production at San Manuel of 60,000 tons of copper a year was two and a half times the amount produced at Superior. But because of a much lower grade—0.7 percent versus 5 to 6 percent at Superior—the new mine had to move a lot

6.3. Headframes, hoists, primary crushers, and ore bins served the four hoisting shafts at Magma's San Manuel mine, the largest underground copper mine in the country. The service shaft at the right was used to hoist men and materials. In forty-three years of operation, the mine produced a world record 703 million tons of ore. (*Ray Manley*)

more rock. By the end of its first year of operation, the mine was extracting 580,000 tons of ore a month, an achievement never before equaled in the history of underground mining. That was 100,000 more tons than Superior mined in an entire year.

However, the new production met a world already awash in the metal, and prices fell below 25 cents a pound. Magma reported its first loss since the Depression in 1957. Two years later it suffered another loss as an industry-wide strike shut down operations for four months.

By 1961, with annual metal production at the two sites exceeding 100,000 tons and the copper price back to 30 cents a pound, Newmont decided to increase its ownership in Magma. The idea was proposed by investment banker André Meyer, a Newmont director, whom Malozemoff found to have an "uncanny" sense of timing when it came to acquisitions. Not wishing to antagonize Thompson's heirs, who did not wish to sell, Newmont made a tender offer for only enough stock to lift its holdings above 80 percent, which it purchased for $58 million in convertible preferred stock. As Malozemoff explained to Swent, "80 percent [was] the magic number because below 80 percent dividends are taxed at the full rate [then 52 percent], but above 80 percent the tax is reduced to only about seven percent."[5] The remaining shares were acquired in 1969 and Magma became a 100 percent–owned subsidiary of Newmont.

Tax planning has always been an important part of Newmont's strategy. During Malozemoff's tenure, individual companies, even when majority-owned and consolidated for financial reporting purposes, filed their own tax returns. Parent company income was primarily dividends, interest, some management fees, and gains on security sales. "Our tax policy was quite straightforward. We tried to maximize tax benefits of expenditures and minimize the tax cost of income. We did this by doing all exploration worldwide through domestic entities, thus obtaining tax deductions, while incorporating producing properties in foreign entities if possible so that only the dividends paid to the parent would be taxable in the United States," says Robert Boyce, vice president of taxes from 1966 to 1992. "As a general rule, Newmont only took the cash it needed in dividends and felt it best to leave any surplus with the subsidiary."[6]

This strategy, however, required that Newmont have enough domestic income to utilize its foreign tax credits and other benefits. The company's most important tax deduction has been the depletion allowance, which enables the company to write off a portion of its ore reserves each year as they are mined, just as it writes off depreciation on its plants and equipment. The depletion allowance has been a fundamental part of the tax code since 1929 as a means of allowing natural resource companies to recover their investments and generate the capital to reinvest in new projects.

In the early 1960s, with its African mines contributing most of its earnings and Magma restricted in paying dividends under the terms of its RFC loan, Newmont was falling short of domestic income. Therefore, one of its first moves after acquiring control of Magma was to refinance the government loan with a new one from Prudential Insurance. In 1963, Magma resumed the payment of dividends, boosting Newmont's earnings for the year by nearly $3 million. Within a few years, Magma was paying Newmont $12 million a year.

On the negative side, the acquisition triggered an antitrust suit by the federal government, which after several years of litigation forced the company to sell its 3 percent interest in Phelps Dodge (PD), the nation's second largest copper producer. Newmont had had two representatives on the PD board for many years.

As it assumed a more direct role in operations, Newmont looked at ways to increase production, particularly at Superior where old veins were being depleted. Keith Staley was named mine superintendent at Superior and began assigning more responsibility to men with technical degrees. Florez was moved into supervision and then management, becoming Superior's general manager in 1981. He believes he was the first Hispanic in Arizona to achieve such a level. In addition to Staley, he credits his advancement to Malozemoff, who took a personal interest in his career and was "farsighted on many things."

In another first, in 1978, Superior became the first mine in Arizona to employ women underground, although that came only after prodding by federal equal employment opportunity regulators. The move was met with skepticism, says Charles Freeman, the general manager at the time, not only because of the longstanding superstition among miners that women underground brought bad luck, but because of the heavy physical labor involved. Crews at the face had to place twelve-by-twelve-inch support timbers and with crews competing against each other for production bonuses, one who could not carry her weight would detract from the entire team. Yet, says Freeman, the women who accepted this challenge "worked well and willingly, for among other reasons they had something to prove."[7]

For years, Magma was pestered by a woman in Tucson who had inherited land adjacent to San Manuel and wanted Magma to buy her out. Goss saw little prospect in the land but asked her price. She said half a million; he said no. Eventually a firm backed by Houston oil interests bought the property for $1.5 million and put down several holes, locating a deposit almost as large as San Manuel's, but at considerably greater depth. Realizing that development costs would be very high, they offered to sell for $50 million. Goss was only willing to pay $10 million. At that point Malozemoff took over the negotiations and, in 1968, paid $27 million for the Kalamazoo ore body with an estimated 565 million tons of ore.

Kalamazoo, coupled with continued exploration success at the original ore body, increased San Manuel's reserves to more than one billion tons of ore, while geologists at Superior discovered a new high-grade ore reserve of 10 million tons, extending the life of that mine. That ore, at the 3,400-foot level, was in five veins separated by thin layers of limestone and only 50 feet from previous mining. A $200 million expansion program was completed in the early 1970s that increased mining at both locations and lifted milling capacity at San Manuel. The Superior smelter was closed, with concentrates shipped to San Manuel for more efficient processing.

In an important change in emphasis, rather than selling raw copper, the company invested in an electrolytic refinery to produce 200,000 tons of pure copper a year, half sold as cathodes and the balance further processed in a continuous caster to produce copper rod. The six-inch diameter rods were sold in 5,000- to 8,000-pound rolls to manufacturers such as Ford and General Motors to be made into wiring for autos.

Having never before marketed directly to end users, the company needed to attract attention. Jack Thompson, then executive vice president of Newmont, seized a way to build sales while enjoying his passion for golf. Howard Twitty Jr., who was making a name for himself on the PGA tour, was the son of Magma's Arizona legal counsel. Knowing that he would be in Tucson for a tournament in February, Thompson invited him to bring along a few other players for a pro-am event with some copper buyers. "It was a great hit," recalls Thompson, who repeated the match annually. "The first year, I think, we invited six buyers. We had twelve the second year and before long we were having a tournament with twenty-four buyers and six to eight pros."[8]

With Sherritt Gordon operating in Alberta and Manitoba and Granduc trying to get its footing on a British Columbia glacier, Newmont entered two other Canadian copper ventures in the early 1970s. The most interesting was Similkameen near Princeton in southern British Columbia, which was joined with Granduc to form Newmont Mines Ltd. A worker building the Transcontinental Highway, which ran past the property, took a piece of copper ore to a Newmont geologist in Vancouver for evaluation. John Livermore drilled out two ore bodies on either side of the Similkameen

River. Following construction of a concentrator and a bridge to link the two deposits, open-pit mining began in 1972. The project carried a start-up cost of $73 million; Newmont put up $27 million and Canadian banks and the U.S. Export-Import Bank funded the rest.

Designed as a "green" mine, special precautions were taken to protect the environment and preserve the topsoil for later reclamation. Production averaged 25,000 tons of copper concentrate a year, which was shipped to smelters in Japan. With a low grade, high labor costs, and high provincial taxes, however, the mine lost money in nine of its sixteen years of operation and only paid a dividend in three years. Its best year, 1980, coincided with a spike in the gold price, which lifted the value of its by-product gold production of 37,500 ounces to 44 percent of the mine's revenue. Newmont took a $58 million write-off in 1986 and sold the mine two years later.

The second venture, with somewhat better results, was Bethlehem Copper, also of British Columbia, where Newmont purchased a 23 percent interest from Japan's Sumitomo Metal Mining Company in 1972 for $25 million. After nine profitable years, in which it received $1 million a year in dividends, the company's interest was sold to Cominco, which had acquired a majority interest in the mine, for $53 million.

These, however, were sideshow productions to Magma's big tent operations. In its best year, 1979, Magma produced 160,000 tons of copper, racked up sales of $382 million, and earned $67 million, of which it sent $35 million to Newmont in dividends. But there were problems. In 1967, the United Steelworkers took over the Mine Workers union and shut down the entire copper industry in an eight-month strike. Industry-wide strikes lasted twenty-five days in 1971, five weeks in 1974, and four months in 1980. By then the industry was in recession. The copper price dropped by nearly a third in two years to 70 cents a pound. Once again, profits turned to losses.

In 1982, Magma laid off 2,400 of its 6,100 employees and shuttered its high-cost operations at Superior. A year later, Newmont paid $75 million to purchase a Miami, Arizona, open-pit copper mine owned by Cities Service, a Tulsa-based petroleum company. Renamed Pinto Valley Copper Corporation, the property was capable of producing 70,000 tons of copper a year at lower costs than San Manuel. Further savings came from sending the ore to San Manuel for processing.

Development of the Kalamazoo deposit was deferred. Instead, $70 million was invested in an open-pit mine to access 56 million tons of oxide ore that lay on top of the San Manuel mine—an engineering challenge—and to install a new low-cost heap leaching recovery process known as solvent-extraction-electrowinning, or SXEW. Magma was not the first to use this process, but it was the first in the western copper industry to use lined leach pads. The liner was installed to prevent acid-consuming rocks from neutralizing the leaching solution and precipitating out the copper. "We did it to increase our revenues, but it still protected the environment," says Baker.

Magma at the time was run by "some very rough, tough old boys" who had been there since San Manuel opened, Baker recalls. "It was management by intimidation." The mine manager "was one of those gruff guys who walked around with his hands in his pockets and a stern look on his face." Tough, yes, agrees Ridinger, but "we tried to be a fair company."

Labor negotiations reopened in 1986. By then Newmont's Arizona copper mines had been hemorrhaging cash for five years and losses were approaching $200 million. With labor accounting for half of its total costs, a much higher percentage than at competing open-pit mines, the company announced that it would seek substantial concessions from its employees. In 1983, Phelps Dodge fired 2,400 striking miners at its large open-pit copper mine at Morenci and replaced them with non-union workers. The move caused riots, divided the town, and required a call-up of the Arizona National Guard to keep the peace. Seeking to avoid such an outcome, Magma and its unions invited Governor Bruce Babbitt to negotiate a settlement. "Whatever he did when he was with them in the other room, I don't know, but we finally got an agreement. We took back nearly $4 an hour [a 20 percent cut in wages and benefits]," says Ridinger, who by then was president of Magma. "I always thought the union was very, very responsible to do that. But we had convinced them, 'you do that or nobody's got a job.'"

Magma had invited rank-and-file union members into its planning sessions to better understand its problems and met with families in community meetings. Bob Skiba, Magma's human resources director, hired an Atlanta group to make a video that was sent to all homes explaining the company's situation. Producers went to bars frequented by miners and then composed a song, based on the music they had heard, which addressed the need for change and what happened to dinosaurs that could not adapt. Anticipating better times, the new labor agreement included a "gain-sharing" provision that provided meaningful bonuses to the workers when conditions improved, as they did in 1988.

Hanging over all this was the heavy hand of the government, which threatened to shut down the entire U.S. copper industry unless it could come up with a way to reduce air pollution, principally the emission of sulfur dioxide gas from smelters. In 1970, Magma began studies to construct a plant to convert SO2 to sulfuric acid at San Manuel, but cost estimates and escalating demands quickly got out of hand. Newmont committed to "eliminate undesirable emissions in the smelter smoke . . . to whatever degree is necessary to protect the health and welfare of the people of the State."[9] However, the state demanded that 90 percent of the SO2 be removed, while the federal EPA had set a 60 percent level. Litigation to determine jurisdiction took two years and when the dust settled, the EPA had won, but the smelters had lost. The EPA increased its standard to 96.4 percent, a level no known technology could meet except at prohibitive cost.

Ridinger explains the problem:

> The typical smelting process in those days was the reverberatory furnace where you separate copper and slag. About 30 percent of the SO2 is released there. Then you have the converting process where another 50 percent is released. The last part is fugitives which exit through the converter roof. You have to have a gas rich in SO2 for an acid plant, so you could put an acid plant on the converter. But the reverb furnace has a weak SO2 stream and you would have to do something to concentrate that. Then you have the 20 percent that are fugitives, which are going out the roof, and you fight that until the day you die.

Involved were several huge buildings, stretching over a quarter mile.

Wayne Burt, who joined Newmont from Kennecott in 1969, and was named president of Magma in 1971 and chairman in 1985, visited a state-of-the-art facility in Finland and negotiated a licensing agreement to use its process at San Manuel. "But we never had any immediate plans to install the equipment. The cost was somewhere in the area of $200 million and we just weren't going to do it." Malozemoff's strategy, says Burt, was "delay, delay, delay,"[10] and in that he was in step with everyone else in the industry.

In 1976, the industry won an amendment to the Clean Air Act granting a five-year operating extension, with the option for a second five-year extension, to meet the regulations. That put the deadline for compliance at 1987.

As an interim solution, $41 million was invested in an oxygen flash furnace, exhaust stack scrubbers, and a sulfuric acid plant that captured much, but not all, of the SO2 and produced 300,000 tons of sulfuric acid a year. Fugitive emissions remained a problem. Monitoring stations detected when the plant was out of compliance, usually at times of adverse weather conditions, and facilities would be shut down. Cooling and reheating the furnaces was costly and in some years operations were shut down for 12 percent of the time. In addition to increasing capital cost, Magma estimated that environmental compliance was adding 15 cents a pound to its production cost for copper.

It was during Magma's struggle with emissions that Newmont established its first environmental department under Ridinger. The company soon realized, however, that compliance was only half the environmental battle. The other half was political, and in 1981 Ridinger moved to Washington as Newmont's first representative on Capitol Hill. With the EPA on a learning curve about mine pollution and with only a handful of western senators and congressmen coming from mining regions, Ridinger and his successors spent much of their time educating rule makers and legislators. At one point, an EPA representative wanted Magma to dig up a tailings pond containing mostly benign crushed rock and water and move it a hundred miles to a hazardous waste site near Phoenix. "We'd been operating for fifteen to twenty years, putting out 50,000 tons of rock a day, most of it waste, into a tailings pond that was three miles this way and four miles that way. How could we move that?" Ridinger asks. Yet that was the mentality of those enforcing the rules.

In 1983, Newmont sought a comprehensive look at all of Magma's problems in the hope of finding a permanent solution. Assigned to the task was John Parry, who had just returned from a three-month graduate program at MIT. "This was so typical of Newmont," says Parry, to take a geophysicist with a Ph.D., some exploration management experience, and just back from MIT and assign him to a totally unrelated task. Over the next three years, during which time he became vice president of corporate planning, he and Robert Zerga, a Magma engineer, ran every computer simulation they could dream up. They looked at different prices, operating rates, and cut-off ore grades. "I would wake up every Monday morning and say, 'Magma lost another million dollars last week. What have you done about it?'" Parry recalls.[11]

They found that everything was interconnected. "The cheapest source of copper was SXEW, but if we developed that we needed low-cost sulfuric acid and to do that we had to have the smelter. If we were going to have the smelter, then we had to retrofit it to meet the new EPA standards. And, if we were going to produce concentrate through the smelter, we had to be mining. We couldn't eliminate any one item. We had to do everything or nothing. And to do the whole thing required a $200 million plus investment when we had [ore reserves for] only a twelve-year mine plan," Parry says. Kalamazoo was not considered economic.

In 1984, Texaco acquired Getty Oil and decided to sell Getty's minerals operation, including a half interest in the Escondida copper mine in Chile. Parry went to Los Angeles to review the data and reported back to Malozemoff: "This is the greatest copper mine in the world." But instead of arousing the usual interest from the CEO, the report was rejected. "How can we buy Escondida when we are losing a million a week at Magma?" Malozemoff asked.

Not only had Magma become a millstone around Newmont's economic neck, but it was clouding its business judgment as well. The matter would not be resolved until after Malozemoff retired.

A Mine Fire

Frank Florez, the last general manager of Magma's Superior operations, remembers December 2, 1961, as the worst day of his thirty-eight-year mining career. He was leading a crew of five who were installing support timbers in a mined-out area on the 2,550-foot level when an electrical storm knocked out the underground fans that provided air and cooling for the workers. With temperatures soaring well above 100 degrees, spontaneous combustion of the sulfide ore ignited some old timbers.

Mine fires are always life threatening and this one quickly filled the normal escape routes with smoke and deadly carbon monoxide gas. Florez led his crew to a ventilation shaft, where they mounted a small platform not designed to carry crewmen and clung to the center support cable as the platform was pulled half a mile to the surface. Two hundred feet from the top, the platform struck a wall brace and came to an abrupt stop, throwing the men to the platform floor. Three were able to climb the rest of the way to safety, but it took several hours for workers to rescue Florez and an injured companion.

Now instead of heat, they faced a blast of cold air. "The shaft was taking in 100,000 cubic feet of air a minute that was 32 degrees," Florez recalls. He suffered a fractured pelvis, internal injuries, and hypothermia, requiring a ninety-day hospital stay to recover. The fire closed the mine for two months.

Magma had an active safety program and Florez believes a good record. But the work was still hazardous. A search of past records during his time as general manager showed that the Superior operation, with a workforce of 1,200 to 1,400 in the mine and mill, had averaged one fatality a year.

Copper

Copper, used since the dawn of civilization, is the third most widely used metal in the world after steel and aluminum. Essential to the generation and transmission of electricity, it is also used in electronics, pipes, tubes, and pots and pans. Newmont has held investments in copper companies since its formation and today, while primarily a gold producer, operates the large Batu Hijau copper and gold mine in Indonesia.

The company's best year for copper was 1979, with prices averaging 90 cents a pound. It held an interest in eight mines that produced 741,500 tons of the reddish-orange metal, equal to 9 percent of world production. The company's equity interest in that output was 300,400 tons, making it the fourth largest producer in the United States and the seventh largest in the world. A breakout of that production in short tons is shown in table 1.

Table 1
Newmont's Copper Production in 1979

Mine	Total Production	Equity Interest (%)	Equity in Production
United States			
Magma	156,700	100	156,700
Canada			
Similkameen	29,200	100	29,200
Sherritt Gordon	37,100	39.9	14,800
Bethlehem	23,500	22.8	5,400
Peru			
Southern Peru	313,200	10.7	33,500
Africa			
Palabora	124,100	28.6	35,500
O'okiep	22,500	57.5	12,900
Tsumeb	35,200	35.3	12,400
Total	741,500		300,400

These mines, which also produced other metals, paid Newmont $67 million in dividends in 1979, accounting for two-thirds of its cash income for the year. By contrast, in 2004, Batu Hijau's best year for copper output, Newmont's operations produced 358,000 tons of copper, with the company's equity share being 199,000 tons. Copper, however, accounted for 18 percent of total sales and a smaller percent of pre-tax income.

7

DESERT GOLD

The first anyone back east heard of the caper that became known as the "Great Carlin Gold Robbery" was when Robert Macdonald received a phone call in February 1974 from Jay McBeth, the resident manager of Newmont's fledging Nevada gold mine. "Bob, I want you to send me two fire assayers," McBeth pleaded. When the manager of the Danbury lab asked why, McBeth replied, "My whole assay office is in jail and I can't run this place without fire assayers."[1] In fact, federal agents had arrested the mine's chief assayer, three of his assistants, the head of the gold room where gold was poured into doré bars, and a licensed gold dealer from Sacramento, California.

Secret Service agents with the U.S. Treasury Department had noticed unusual gold buying by the Sacramento dealer. An investigation identified repeated sales by two men who happened to be employees of a gold mine. Surely this was no coincidence, even though the Carlin mine had reported no losses. A sting operation was set up and in due course the two ringleaders handed the agents three plastic-lined cardboard boxes containing 50 pounds of precipitate, a fine-grained, dark gray dirt that is an intermediate product in the refining process. The precipitate, 30 percent gold, contained 370 ounces of the precious metal worth $55,000 at the time.

Macdonald determined that the men had used an elaborate scheme that began with underreporting the head grade of ore going into the Carlin mill by 10 percent. By the time the precipitate reached the gold room for final refining in an electric furnace, there was more gold in the system than on the company's books. This the thieves removed by carrying home precipitate in their lunchboxes. When enough of the gold-laden dirt was accumulated, it was taken to a Chinese refiner in San Francisco who turned it into gold bars that were then sold in Sacramento. After a stop in Reno for a night of gambling and carousing, the men returned to their assay jobs and started the process all over again. In the four years the Secret Service believed the caper had gone on, it was estimated that the men had stolen $700,000 in gold.

That is when Bernard Sadowski, dean of Northern Nevada Community College, learned that he had been duped. A chance encounter with a mine employee he casually knew had led to a prolonged discussion over coffee. As the miner explained, Newmont encouraged its employees to seek additional education and would give pay raises to those who completed college courses. Would Dr. Sadowski be interested in teaching a two-month course in chemistry for the man and a few of his associates? The course began in November 1973 and quickly evolved into discussions of the behavior of the gold atom in chemical reactions and into various gold recovery techniques. "The men were increasingly pressing me . . . about advanced chemistry not in freshman-level courses,"[2] he later said. When the *Elko Free Press* broke the story of the robbery, Dr. Sadowski discovered the culprits were his students.

The Carlin mine in the early 1970s was turning out 150,000 to 200,000 ounces of gold a year, or 3,500 ounces a week. And each week the assayers had made off with 100 ounces. It was a huge breach of security. But then, security had never been an issue. Frank McQuiston, who supervised construction of the mill with an eye toward saving money, had not installed any security at the refinery and McBeth was known to carry gold bars to the airport for shipment in the back of his pickup truck, occasionally stopping at a bar for a drink along the way. The two benefited from one of Plato Malozemoff's quirks. Despite his reputation for toughness, the Newmont CEO had a soft spot when it came to people and personnel issues. It was said he hated to fire anyone, giving Newmont the reputation of being a hard company to get hired at but impossible to get fired from.

In truth, New York didn't concern itself with such trifling matters as security. Malozemoff, like his predecessor, Fred Searls, believed in a small corporate staff. Few people at headquarters meant fewer people to meddle in the affairs of the operating companies and that, in turn, necessitated a decentralized management style that became a Newmont hallmark. Malozemoff earned a reputation for hiring superior operating people who were given virtual autonomy over how they ran their business, but whose bud-

7.1. The Carlin gold mine in the early 1970s. (*Newmont Archives*)

gets were kept under a watchful eye by a Newmont-controlled board of directors.

From an operator's perspective, the situation was ideal, says Gordon Parker, who succeeded Malozemoff as CEO in 1985. "One of Newmont's greatest virtues was that it let its affiliates run themselves. Newmont got a huge commitment at the site because New York did not dabble in local issues." Recalling his experience in southern Africa, he says, "Tsumeb and O'okiep would each get a visit from the managing director a couple times per year and in between the companies would receive technical consultants to help out on specific issues. But the general manager ran the operations. There were not overly frequent changes at the top. General managers held positions long enough to make a difference or to be found out. Everyone knew where capital came from and where dividends were sent. We knew who set policy. But local issues were kept local."[3]

Furthermore, Carlin was considered a small, dirty, out-of-the-way operation and was rarely visited by the New York brass. "We were the bastard stepchildren compared with the rest of the company," recalls Tom Enos, who started work in Nevada as a rod man on a survey team in 1971. Yet the company "always kept me challenged and doing something different," he says.[4]

Indeed, he was made chief assayer shortly after the gold robbery, learning the trade by studying on weekends with Harry Treweek, who had analyzed the mine's original drill samples. When Carlin built its first heap leach operation, Enos was its manager. When a second mill was added, he became a superintendent. He implemented the first computerized information system linking accounting, maintenance, inventory, and ore control, and became general manager of Carlin in 1996 when production reached a record 1.7 million ounces. Two years later he was tapped to start up the huge Batu Hijau copper/gold mine in Indonesia. When he retired in 2007, Enos was executive vice president for all operations. In a company where advanced degrees are commonplace, Enos's success proves that even without such credentials, Newmont could reward bootstrap determination and a crackerjack mind. Corporate political savvy didn't hurt either.

A funny thing happened at Carlin during its first twenty years that runs counter to the way one might think a gold mine would operate. As the gold price increased, production declined. Some 337,000 ounces were produced in 1967 when the government-set price was still $35 an ounce, but when gold reached the highest price in history (prior to 2008), averaging $613 an ounce in 1980, Carlin had its lowest production ever, barely topping 100,000 ounces. Part of the reason, to be sure, was that ore grades had dropped by half, from 0.33 to 0.167 ounce per ton, as the original pit deepened and higher prices made lower grades economic. But equally important was the fact that the company was not motivated to do better. If, as the price increased, the mine could turn a profit of $10 million to $15 million a year by doing less, what was the concern? Besides, New York's attention was on copper and its rainbow of other mines, not on the pot of gold in distant Nevada.

Still, necessity spurred innovation. Faced with a lot of carbonaceous ore that could not be treated by a conventional cyanidation process (the carbon in the ore would absorb the cyanide and not free up the gold), Macdonald's group at Danbury developed and patented the first refractory ore-processing plant using elemental chlorine as the oxidant. The facility was small, using three twenty-by-twenty-foot tanks to pre-treat the ore before further processing in the mill, but it enabled the company to extract thousands of ounces of gold from material that otherwise would have been waste.

Mining began in 1974 at two small satellite mines, Bootstrap and Blue Star. Maggie Creek, twelve miles to the south, became the fourth mine when it opened in 1980. Most of the ore was hauled to the Carlin mill for treatment, but for nearly 3.5 million tons of low-grade ore, this was not an economic option.

In 1979, the company began placing ore that graded as low as 0.02 ounce per ton on heap leach sites adjacent to the mines. Leaching had been used in the copper industry, but this was the first large-scale use at a gold mine. The ore was dumped by truck on clay-lined pads; environmentally safer asphalt pads came into use in 1981, and today thick plastic liners are used. Once on the pad, the ore was sprinkled with water containing low concentrations of cyanide. As the solution percolated through the pile, the gold was leached from the ore and the pregnant solution was collected in ponds for separation and refining. To improve gold recovery, Newmont began an agglomeration technique developed by the U.S. Bureau of Mines. To keep the fine clay particles found in much of the Carlin ores from building in layers on a leach pad and blocking the solution flow, the ores were mixed with cement that bound the particles into larger pieces that would not clog the flow.

By opening new mines, finding more ore at the edges and deeper in the original pit, and adding new processing technology that allowed gold recovery from lower-grade ore, Carlin was able to prolong its life. But it was still depleting more ore than it was replacing. At the end of 1980, after having produced three million ounces of gold over fifteen years, the company reported reserves of only 1.3 million ounces of gold, two million less than when mining began in 1965.

Carlin's problem was that it had done little exploration since John Livermore and Alan Coope paced off the area in the early 1960s. The low gold price in the early years was a major factor, but so, too, was the decentralized way Newmont was structured and operated.

Essentially, a circle was drawn around each operation where the local manager had discretion in doing on-site exploration, and he could not move outside the circle. A corporate exploration team, Newmont Exploration

Limited (NEL), on the other hand, was to explore for new prospects, but only outside existing operations.

For years, exploration had been headed by Robert Fulton, a hard-driving, lone-wolf geologist who often kept his activities a secret and, it was said, never submitted a budget. When Magma Copper became a wholly owned subsidiary of Newmont in 1969, Magma's exploration geologists joined Newmont, doubling his staff. Uncomfortable with expanded administrative duties and denied his wish to manage Carlin, Fulton resigned and was replaced by Richard Ellett, who brought in a new level of professionalism.

Ellett began his career and lost much of his hearing in the tin mines of Bolivia in 1948. A communist revolution, headed by the tin miners' union, sought to overthrow the government and seized the mine. Ellett and several other professionals were herded into the union hall, where one of the revolutionaries set off some stolen dynamite. Two in his group were killed, three others were badly wounded, and he suffered ruptures in both eardrums. Before joining Newmont in 1971, he discovered several of the largest coal mines in Queensland, Australia. In 1972, he established Newmont's second technical center in Tucson, Arizona. As headquarters for NEL and later joined by the geophysical department, the Tucson office housed 110 people by the mid-1980s.

While greenfield discoveries can be rewarding, they are also rare, and Ellett believed NEL had a better chance for success by working closer to existing mines since "you know more about the geology where you're already operating."[5] Geologists call this prospecting with one boot in the pit. However, he found little cooperation at Carlin. McBeth, with the support of New York, only wanted to find near-surface, short-term deposits that would keep the mill operating; further exploration would just pull down profits.

In the wake of the Carlin discovery in the early 1960s, NEL had opened a small office in Elko, drilled several prospects, and staked some claims. One of them was Gold Quarry, which at the time was well south of land owned by Carlin Gold. Mineral rights to 522 acres of Section 35 in Township 34 North were leased from Gold Quarry Mines, one of many small groups that had sprung up in response to the Carlin discovery. Geologist Perry West put down sixteen shallow drill holes that found silicified zones of refractory ore that assayed 0.03 to 0.05 ounce per ton of gold. With gold at $35 an ounce, this was a yawner. Turning its attention elsewhere, NEL handed the property over to Carlin Gold, where McBeth and his boss in New York, William Humphrey, Newmont's vice president of operations and later the president of Homestake Mining, allowed the lease to expire in October 1971.

The original Carlin discovery was on federal land, but the surrounding checkerboard sections were private land owned by the T/Lazy S Ranch. And the ranch was not an accommodating neighbor. Containing 223,500 acres, or 349 square miles, the ranch can be traced back to 1870 when William Dunphy began running cattle along Boulder Creek. The land was not contiguous and contained old railroad property that was interspersed with another 73,400 acres leased from the government's Bureau of Land Management. After changing hands several times, the ranch was purchased for $1.25 million in 1961 by Charles "Tex" Thornton and Roy Ash, the founders of Litton Industries of Los Angeles, a conglomerate considered the Microsoft or Intel of its day. With 6,000 head of cattle and a few cowboys, the ranch was a place to escape the city, ride horses, and count one's tax deductions. Gentlemen ranchers from Bing Crosby to Ted Turner have been doing that for decades.

Wherever Newmont turned, it encountered ranch land and its prickly owners. The Bootstrap mine was on ranch property, and waste dumps and access roads encroached on ranch lands. Over the years, a series of leases were negotiated with Thornton and Ash for access and mining. The two developed an annoying pattern of short-term leases with royalty rates, based on a percentage of the sale price of any gold mined, escalating with each renewal. "If you don't really know what you're doing, do it short term," was Ash's philosophy.[6] Equally annoying was their habit of protesting anytime someone from the mine crossed onto ranch property without permission. They once sent out armed cowboys to block access to a disputed road. In a 1980 letter, McBeth had to seek their written permission "to dig a trench about a foot wide and 30 inches deep at Maggie Creek to bury a phone cable."[7]

As a result, the geologists for both the mine and NEL trod warily when chasing prospects that might extend onto ranch property. Perhaps the constant pressure also prompted McBeth to curry favor with Thornton at one of their negotiating sessions. In any event, according to Donald Hammer, NEL's manager of western U.S. exploration at the time, "Jay told him that Carlin Gold Mining Company had dropped its lease on Section 35 and that it was available for him to acquire it if he wanted."[8] Thornton and Ash picked up the property for $8,000 and unbeknownst to Newmont, certainly to anyone in New York, held it separate from their ownership of the vast T/S Ranch. Newmont would pay dearly to regain those rights later on.

With mining under way at Carlin, an entirely separate exploration group, Newmont Proprietary Limited, set up shop in Melbourne in 1965 to begin a search for gold in the Kalgoorlie district in Western Australia and for base metals throughout the Pacific Rim. This group was headed by Robert Searls, the son of Newmont's former chairman. In 1972, Newmont joined U.S. Steel and Sherritt Gordon by taking a 15 percent interest in PT Pacific Nikkel, which was evaluating a huge lateritic nickel/cobalt mine on Gag Island, Indonesia. But when development costs escalated to $1 billion as nickel prices were declining, the company withdrew its interest in 1977.

Gold had a brighter future. During a reconnaissance flight in a small plane over the Great Sandy Desert in May 1972, exploration manager David Tyrwhitt spotted "a sharp ridge of white quartz and associated iron-stained gossan with layered sediment above it. It definitely seemed to be a stratabound deposit, a distinct rock layer parallel to the bedding in the sedimentary rocks, much like a coal seam."[9] A quick landing, a grab of rock samples, and later assays in Perth gave good indications of gold, with a couple samples testing up to three ounces per ton. He quickly returned and staked a claim. It was later determined that this was the only spot in the area where high-grade mineralized reefs outcropped at the surface. The area had been looked at a year earlier by a small Australian company that had lost interest and sold its reports to Newmont for $15,000.

"Discovery is a complex phenomena," Searls later wrote. "Much of it is accidental or fortuitous and more often than not it results from a fresh look at an old, worked-over idea or piece of ground . . . but always the excitement, that first flash of realization, gives way to hard and patient work."[10] This was certainly true in the Great Sandy Desert, one of the most remote places on earth, covering 150,000 square miles of broken rock and complex geology. From the site, it took twelve to eighteen hours in a four-wheel-drive vehicle to cross the 110 miles to the nearest water hole at Woodie Woodie. The nearest town and port for material and supplies was twice that far.

Initial drilling could only be done by a small rig fitted on the back of a stretched Land Rover. But by late 1973, a base camp was established with fifty people on-site, including ten geologists and a geophysicist. A million-ounce ore body was defined, and by Christmas 1974 a feasibility study for an open-pit mine, mill, road, landing strip, and town site was completed and sent to New York for approval. A month later, Searls got the bad news. Malozemoff had turned thumbs down. With a projected capital cost of $35 million and gold selling for barely $100 an ounce, the mine would generate only a 12 percent return, which was not enough. Finally, after scaling back the project with the help of Pete Crescenzo, Newmont's vice president of engineering, to $27 million and bringing in Broken Hill Proprietary, Australia's largest corporation, as a 30 percent partner, Searls and Tyrwhitt got the go ahead in May 1975.

Searls, described by associates as a principled man, gave up his U.S. citizenship to become an Australian and over the years developed close ties with government officials in his adopted country. Australian law prohibited foreign investors from owning more than 49 percent of a mining project but allowed provincial governments to grant exceptions. Searls was able to convince Charles Cort, premier of Western Australia, that because of the grassroots nature of its discovery, Newmont merited a higher percentage. It was considered quite a coup.

Named Telfer for the provincial mining engineer who helped Searls obtain government approval, the new mine poured its first gold in April 1977. Within a year it was producing more gold than Carlin. A small leach operation was initiated in 1984 and a year later, after the discovery of additional reserves, a $26 million expansion lifted annual capacity at the mill from 525,000 tons of ore to two million. Tyrwhitt spent a brief period as exploration manager for the eastern United States and then returned to Australia where he succeeded Searls as chief executive of Newmont Proprietary in 1984. Telfer poured its three millionth ounce of gold in May 1992, just in time for the twentieth anniversary of Tyrwhitt's discovery. A second Australian gold mine, New Celebration, with an initial production rate of 40,000 ounces of gold a year, opened near Kalgoorlie in late 1986.

"The Telfer discovery captured the imagination of the exploration fraternity in Australia," says John Dow, a New Zealander who joined Newmont Proprietary as exploration manager in 1978 when Tyrwhitt moved to the United States. "It was pretty amazing because of its location and the uniqueness of its geological setting." Also striking was the fact that the discovery had been made by Newmont, a company with only a tiny presence on the continent and whose exploration budget had totaled only $11 million over nearly ten years. Furthermore, "people had been exploring the area for years looking for copper and they never looked very hard at the gold potential."[11]

One of those who had scouted the area for copper, but not gold, was Jean Paul Turcaud, who in 1970 spent several months driving a Land Rover through the desert living on wheat gruel from a 200-pound sack and water from a 44-gallon drum. He took his findings to thirteen different companies, including Newmont, without eliciting much interest. With the announcement of the Telfer discovery, he was convinced Newmont had acted on his report and demanded payment. When Newmont offered only a $10,000 reimbursement of his expenses, he became incensed and prepared a ninety-three-page document, which he sent not only to Australian government officials but to the French prime minister, Queen Elizabeth II, President Nixon, and the pope. Even in the late 1990s, Newmont offices in Denver would receive an occasional letter from this French prospector complaining of what he called the Great Australian Gold Robbery.

The Lay of the Land

Two years before George Washington became president, the Continental Congress passed the Northwest Ordinance of 1787 to dispose of lands in the western territory to help defray the cost of the Revolutionary War. This required a survey of the wilderness west of the Appalachians following a method proposed earlier by Thomas Jefferson. Lines were drawn north, south, east, and west six miles apart, creating a grid of squares known as townships, which could be further divided into sections, half-sections, and quarter sections, which contained forty acres. By the end of the nineteenth century, surveyors using a compass, a transit, and a length of chain precisely sixty-six feet long had squared off most of the country. Each parcel of land was identified on a surveyor's map and registered with a federal land office.

With the Louisiana Purchase of 1803 and the later westward migration, the survey "guaranteed the pioneers in their covered wagons legal possession of their land; it substantiated the claims of gold miners; it settled the feuds of cowboys and farmers; it financed the construction of the railroads," writes Andro Linklater, who has extensively researched the survey.[12]

Two of the most important pieces of western legislation were signed by President Abraham Lincoln during the Civil War. The Homestead Act of 1862 gave a section of land—one square mile or 640 acres—to anyone who built a cabin and farmed the land for five years. This turned over 270 million acres of public domain to private citizens. But much of the arid West was unsuitable for homesteading and remained in the hands of the federal government. Nevada has the highest percentage of federal land in the country, accounting for 87.6 percent of the state's nearly 110,000 square miles. At the opposite end of the scale, only four-tenths of 1 percent of New York State is federally owned.

Lincoln's second land act was the Pacific Railroad Act of 1864, which facilitated building the transcontinental railroad. To help obtain financing, the Central Pacific, whose tracks paralleled the Humboldt River through the heart of Nevada's gold country, and the Union Pacific were granted twenty miles of alternating sections on either side of their tracks. It was like giving them the black squares on a checkerboard, while the federal government retained the red squares. Railroads have since sold some lands and leased others to ranchers, while government lands, managed by the Bureau of Land Management (BLM), have also been leased. The railroad land grants conveyed mineral as well as surface rights, but it took a third congressional act to secure the ability to mine on public lands.

The General Mining Law of 1872, signed by President Ulysses S. Grant, gives miners the right to stake claims and to later patent, or acquire, federal lands for a nominal fee once a minable deposit has been found. The law codified mining customs and regulations that had been followed by every gold district since the California gold rush. Reviewing the history of the right of access to public lands in an 1878 case before the U.S. Supreme Court, Justice Stephen Field wrote that all states had "recognized discovery followed by appropriation as the foundation of the possessor's title, and development by working as the condition of its retention, and they were so framed as to secure to all comers . . . absolute equality of right and privilege in working the mines."[13]

In recent years, the mining law has become a lightning rod for anti-mining environmentalists who view it as archaic. Certainly fees should be increased, but access to public lands and the right to a secure title once a discovery is made need to be preserved. These are the bedrock of western mining—and for decades of the western economy. Otherwise, long-term capital commitments would be impossible. Often in entering less developed countries without such a statute, miners spend as much time at government capitals to secure land rights and titles as they do on exploration in the field.

8

BLACK GOLD

Seeing value and doggedly pursuing a controlling interest in Peabody Coal was considered by many to be Plato Malozemoff's finest achievement. It was also his most audacious. Peabody, the nation's largest coal company, had sales in the mid-1970s of $800 million a year, compared with $550 million for Newmont. It was nearly three times larger than Magma Copper and thirty-three times the size of the Carlin Gold Mining Company. Furthermore, the asking price for the company was $1.2 billion, or twice the market capitalization of Newmont. When the transaction was completed in 1977, it represented the largest corporate buyout in American history.

Besides, at the time Newmont had other major projects on its plate. Magma Copper was wrestling with the cost of retrofitting its smelter to meet antipollution requirements, the Telfer gold mine in Australia was under construction, Foote Mineral was negotiating with the Chilean government for the rights to build a large lithium facility in the Atacama Desert, and the huge Gamsberg zinc project in South Africa and the Pacific Nikkel project in Indonesia were still under consideration. Yet, Peabody was a prize Malozemoff could not resist.

Peabody owed its start to Francis Stuyvesant Peabody who, at age twenty-four, began a retail coal business from a horse-drawn wagon in Chicago in 1883. Within a few years, he was the coal dealer for the Cook County Democratic Party at a time when ward politics included many social welfare activities. He opened his first coal mine in southern Illinois in 1895 and soon thereafter signed one of the industry's first long-term supply contracts with Chicago Edison, the forerunner of Commonwealth Edison. By the time Newmont became interested in the company, it operated 47 mines (31 surface and 16 underground) in ten states. Annual production of 65 million tons of steam coal was backed by 10 billion tons of coal reserves.

But the company was unprofitable. Many of its utility contracts lacked adequate escalation clauses for the high inflation at the time and those that covered inflation had not been enforced. Frequent strikes by the United Mine Workers Union penalized productivity as did compliance with the 1969 federal Coal Mine Safety and Health Act. Yet, Malozemoff saw enormous potential with new management, and with rising oil prices, coal's future looked bright.

"Plato was a tremendous opportunist. He had a wonderful quality of believing right down to his gut that regardless of what the asset was, he could make it better,"[1] says Richard Leather, Newmont's general counsel at the time.

Peabody had approached Newmont about a merger in the late 1960s, but Malozemoff did not feel the time was right. Shortly thereafter, in 1968, Peabody was purchased by Kennecott Copper Corporation. The acquisition was immediately attacked by the Federal Trade Commission on antitrust grounds since Kennecott held undeveloped coal properties in the West. After a protracted legal battle that lasted six years, the U.S. Supreme Court ruled against Kennecott, and Peabody was put up for auction. By then, Newmont had grown to the point that Malozemoff was keenly interested. He followed the legal proceedings closely and within a day of the Court's decision called Frank Milliken, Kennecott's chairman, to say he was in the hunt, only to be rebuffed. "Plato, go away. Jump in a lake. You'll never make it; it's beyond your means," Malozemoff recalled being told by Milliken.[2]

From the beginning, Malozemoff knew that partners would be needed and that owning 100 percent was both impractical and unnecessary. "Maybe we can get a consortium together where we would have a minority interest, but still have a substantial enough interest to be viable for us,"[3] he told his staff. This was characteristic of Newmont's CEO, whose approach to acquisitions and the management of assets was to have only a minority interest but to dominate the board.

Texas Gulf Sulphur, a company Newmont had helped organize nearly fifty years earlier and whose chairman, Charles Fogarty, was a close associate of Malozemoff, was the first to sign on. But on the eve of consummating a deal, a hostile faction on its board pulled the plug. The Williams Company, a Tulsa-based pipeline company, joined at the suggestion of André

Meyer, a Newmont director and the company's investment banker. Two iron ore miners, Cleveland-Cliffs and M. A. Hanna, were approached, but they declined.

Don McCall, Newmont's assistant treasurer at the time, explains how the process worked. "Phil Walsh, a Newmont vice president, and I put together some rough numbers on the back of an envelope. It wasn't even typed, but was just in pencil. Plato lined us up to go talk to a bunch of people like the Williams Company and Cleveland-Cliffs where we would show them these numbers. Some like Cleveland weren't interested in participating, but Plato was bound and determined that he was going to get enough companies into the coalition to fund the thing."[4] Bechtel Corporation, which had built the Carlin mill and the copper refinery at Palabora in South Africa, was recruited and they, in turn, brought in the Boeing Company. Fluor Corporation, an engineering company in which Newmont later became a major shareholder, also signed on.

A new company, Peabody Holding Company, was organized to acquire the coal company. Ownership was divided 27.5 percent each for Newmont and Williams, 15 percent for Bechtel and Boeing, 10 percent for Fluor, and 5 percent for Equitable Life Assurance, which provided $500 million in financing. The partners agreed to put up $200 million in equity (Newmont's share being $55 million), and Broken Hill Proprietary stepped in to buy Peabody's Australian assets for $100 million. But that still left the consortium $400 million short of Kennecott's asking price. Although nearly everyone felt that price was too high—and in the final stages of negotiations Kennecott acknowledged that Peabody would not be able to meet its latest forecasts—its board was unwilling to accept less. With others, including the government-owned Tennessee Valley Authority, preparing competing bids and the deadline for a decision fast approaching, it was time to pull a rabbit from the hat.

John Williams of the Williams Company is credited by Malozemoff with coming up with the solution. "Why don't we give them a 30-year note bearing only five percent interest [half the going rate at the time]," he told the partners. "We wouldn't start paying it off for ten years, so really the impact of the repayment would be deferred until we can turn Peabody around to be profitable."[5] It was a gutsy move, which in the end was accepted because the other bidders were unable to arrange even that much in financing.

The move allowed Kennecott to say it had obtained its asking price while the consortium actually paid with paper worth far less than face value.

Both the process and the result demonstrated Malozemoff's legendary tenacity. "He considered himself a bulldog," says Leather. "He liked to grab hold of something and shake it and shake it and not let it go. That was his style."

However, Peabody, like Atlantic Cement, did not fit the Newmont mold. To be sure, it used huge equipment to move vast tons of earth (one twenty-story-high shovel at a Kentucky surface mine could remove 115 cubic yards of overburden in a single bucket and was said to be one of the largest self-propelled machines in the world), but mining methods were different from hard rock mining. Furthermore, exploration and technology, the lifeblood of Newmont for decades, were not considered important by the coal company. As a result, mine planning was deficient, coal quality suffered, and utilities often received shipments that failed to meet their specifications. "Peabody was this giant mining machine [with] over a hundred years of coal reserves. Yet they did not have one geologist working for them. This was a company run by engineers,"[6] says John Parry, who later became Newmont's senior vice president of exploration.

What were important were customer relations, labor relations, and, increasingly, government relations. Coincident with the Peabody acquisition, Congress passed three major pieces of legislation affecting the coal industry: the 1977 Surface Mining Control and Reclamation Act, which put coal mining under federal instead of state regulation; the Black Lung Benefits Reform and Revenue Act; and a revised federal Mine Safety and Health Act. These signaled higher capital and operating costs for the future and increased governmental oversight to ensure compliance. At the same time, pressure was mounting for a major overhaul of the nation's Clean Air Act, which occurred in 1980, to reduce emissions from coal-fired boilers at electric utilities, a move that was expected to have a major impact on Peabody's sales of high sulfur coal.

In looking for a new chief executive, Malozemoff decided "that we had to have a man with experience in Washington who could represent not only Peabody but the whole coal industry to the government in a favorable and understandable way so that the government would be more sympathetic to the coal industry as a whole."[7] His choice, after consulting with several ac-

8.1. Peabody Coal used giant draglines, like this one that could lift 115 cubic yards of dirt in a single bucket, to strip mine coal in Kentucky. (*Newmont Archives*)

quaintances including George Schultz, the president of Bechtel and the former secretary of the treasury under President Nixon, was Roderick Hills, a lawyer who had been chairman of the Securities and Exchange Commission. It was an unfortunate choice. After demanding a corporate jet, something Newmont had never had, Hills lingered in Washington for months attending to other business while the chief executive's suite at Peabody's St. Louis headquarters remained vacant. To make matters worse, when he did become involved during contract talks with the United Mine Workers Union in 1978, Malozemoff found his negotiating tactics surprisingly naive and counterproductive.[8]

Hills was replaced by another Peabody newcomer, Robert Quenon, who had been hired as chief operating officer after previously heading Exxon's coal subsidiary. While CFO Edward Fontaine, who joined Newmont from Mobil Oil in 1972, quibbled that Quenon's "oil company mentality" led to a bloated staff and an aversion to cost cutting, Malozemoff found him "an excellent manager [who] fulfilled our best hopes for a knowledgeable, competent and dynamic leader of Peabody."[9] Quenon improved quality and customer relations, which in turn enabled him to renegotiate most of the company's utility contracts on favorable terms. He sold unprofitable mines, upgraded equipment to increase productivity, and improved labor relations. Best of all, he made money mining coal. Quenon later served as a Newmont director.

Jack Thompson, Newmont's president, recalls a week he and Quenon spent in northern Arizona analyzing why a mine there was losing $2 million a year. The mine had a largely Indian workforce and while Navajos were hard workers, the Hopis were not as diligent. "Once the workers got their checks they would disappear. We'd have four hundred people who wouldn't show up the day after payday and then they'd come dragging back a couple of weeks later to go back to work. I told the manager, 'All right, if they don't come back to work you don't hire them back later. They are out and you start with someone new.'" That was great in theory, Thompson admits, but of little value in practice. There were few other workers in the area. "Finally someone else came up with the idea of giving the paychecks to the wives . . . and the problem began to disappear almost immediately."[10]

Newmont also stepped in to upgrade Peabody's "archaic" accounting system and put the coal company on a computerized system compatible with its own. "I sort of became the acting chief financial officer of Peabody,"[11] says Harry Van Benschoten, Newmont's vice president of accounting, who spent a year commuting between St. Louis and New York.

Peabody turned profitable in 1979 and within three years was earning over $100 million a year after taxes. Newmont received its first dividend of $4 million in 1983. At the same time, the company began an aggressive expansion program, signing new utility contracts and opening new mines in Kentucky and Wyoming. It acquired fourteen mines in West Virginia from Armco for $257 million and signed a long-term agreement to supply the steelmaker with metallurgical coal. The acquisition also opened the door for export sales of metallurgical coal to steel mills in Europe and Japan.

Early in 1987, the Williams Company withdrew from the consortium and sold its interest to Newmont, giving the company a 61.5 percent interest in Peabody; Fluor had stepped aside three years earlier. With coal sales by then exceeding $1.4 billion a year, Newmont did not want a majority ownership, which would have required a consolidation of assets and made Peabody the dominant company. It quickly arranged the acquisition of Eastern Gas & Fuel Associates' coal properties in West Virginia for a 15 percent equity interest in Peabody, and reduced its stake to a more manageable 49.9 percent. During the mid- to late 1980s, when copper was losing money, Peabody was Newmont's largest source of earnings and its dividends, which reached $50 million a year and were only taxed at 15 percent, underpinned the company's cash flow.

Success at Peabody also encouraged Newmont to begin thinking of itself as an energy company and to expand its oil and gas interests. With the collapse of the copper market and with its African ventures reaching the end of their economic life, Newmont was desperately grasping for a new focus. Gold, while growing, was not yet considered large enough to carry the company. Newmont had been involved in petroleum since its founding by W. B. Thompson. Why not return to its roots with more capital and a renewed commitment?

Thompson's investment in a Texas oil field in 1925 led to Newmont's becoming the largest shareholder in Continental Oil Company, and over the years the company had held shares in several other major oil companies. During the 1930s, Philip Kraft, the geologist who brought Malozemoff into Newmont, began investing with Continental and others in exploration projects in Texas, Louisiana, and the Rocky Mountain region. Incorporated under the name Alder Oil, for Thompson's boyhood home, the company soon changed its focus to the purchase of royalties on existing production. After World War II, Alder was absorbed into a new wholly owned subsidiary, Newmont Oil, which continued to acquire royalty leases. In time, royalties were held on 120 producing properties. The company was also involved in a number of waterflood wells in Texas and New Mexico where water was injected into old wells to stimulate production. While royalties and waterfloods were far less risky than wildcat exploration and produced a steady stream of income, they also lacked the rich rewards of a new discovery.

Newmont was drawn back to exploration in 1949 when it was asked by Mobil Oil to help finance offshore development in the Gulf of Mexico. Mobil was a pioneer in offshore drilling and had obtained a number of leases from the state of Louisiana in waters up to thirty miles from shore (the federal government had not yet exerted its claim over these properties) and up to fifty feet deep. But Mobil at the time lacked the cash to proceed and offered to sell a half-interest in its leases to Newmont for $18 million. As that was more than the company was willing to risk, it brought in Continental for a 37.5 percent interest while retaining 12.5 percent. Over the next thirty-five years, the MCN venture would lead to Newmont's holding a one-eighth interest in more than fifty blocks in the Gulf of Mexico offshore Louisiana and Texas. In none of these interests was Newmont the operator, and while it offered technical advice, it drilled none of the successful holes.

Like other Newmont ventures, Newmont Oil could claim several firsts. Alice Langlois, a Columbia-educated geologist, was elevated by Kraft to vice president in 1946 and served in that capacity until the company moved its headquarters to Houston in 1954. She was the first female officer in the Newmont organization and one of, if not the, first female vice president in the American oil industry. Kraft also led the first investment of American capital into Algeria, when Newmont joined three French and two other American companies in 1957 in an exploration project in the Sahara Desert. While the consortium found a promising new oil field, the operation was nationalized by the Algerian government in 1970.[12]

As Newmont was orchestrating the Peabody acquisition, Newmont Oil was a solid and predictable source of income, earning $10 million a year on sales of $30 million. Under Robert Moehlman, who became president of Newmont Oil in 1962, the subsidiary had paid its parent $36 million in dividends over fifteen years. The source of this income was an equity interest in production of 4,000 barrels of oil and 33 million cubic feet of natural gas per day. That was frosting on the cake for a company focused on mining, but the numbers were so tiny by oil industry standards that Newmont was irrelevant in the oil patch. It had to get bigger or get out, and it chose the former.

The man behind that decision was Ed Barton, who had headed the company's foreign exploration efforts before succeeding Moehlman[13] as president in 1976. He began a concerted effort to build scale and increase the company's presence at home and abroad. Dividends ceased as investments in exploration rose from $16 million in 1977 to $35 million in 1980 and $71 million in 1982.

In previous years, Newmont had stuck its toe, however small, into some of the biggest oil and gas plays of the era—Alaska's Prudhoe Bay, California's Santa Barbara Channel, the Williston Basin of North Dakota, Alberta, Venezuela, Australia, and Thailand. And it lost money on nearly every one of them. The California foray, in which it was a partner with Texaco, cost $27 million in 1958. At that point, it represented the largest investment Newmont had ever made in a single venture and, according to Malozemoff, was "one of my biggest mistakes."[14]

Despite this history, Barton was able to convince Malozemoff that the North Sea offered real potential and that a significant investment was worth the risk. Newmont began participating in other companies' ventures in 1975, and in 1981 spent $30 million to acquire a 10 to 20 percent interest in seven blocks in the Dutch North Sea. Four years later, in his last move as CEO, Malozemoff agreed to spend $165 million to acquire the Dutch subsidiary of Phillips Petroleum, which held up to a 15 percent interest in seven other blocks (Exxon was the operating partner). In his memoirs, Malozemoff chides his successor, Gordon Parker, and Barton for being timid and not wanting to spend that much. Malozemoff says he was persuaded to make a preemptive bid because the properties offered immediate cash flow, a thirty-year reserve life, and the potential for additional discoveries.[15]

The move increased the company's proven reserves of crude oil by 25 percent to 8.5 million barrels and its reserves of natural gas by 125 percent to 275 billion cubic feet. A discovery on one of the blocks in 1987 added another 10 billion cubic feet to its gas reserves.

Financing for that venture illustrates how both taxes and Malozemoff's control of his far-flung empire influenced his investment decisions. As he explained in his biographical interview with Eleanor Swent, CFO Fontaine came up with the idea of tapping into "money from Australia [because the Telfer] gold mine there was profitable and the cash flow was more than they could use. But to move it by way of dividends to the United States would have incurred a tax. Rather than do that, the Australian company used its cash to make an investment in an oil and gas play in the Dutch North Sea."[16] If David Tyrwhitt, CEO of Newmont Australia, had second thoughts about that investment, he was overruled.

But before either party could taste the benefits of that investment, Newmont, in a desperate search for cash in 1988, sold its oil and gas assets for

$403 million. Mobil took the company's Gulf of Mexico properties, Clyde Petroleum (Netherlands) acquired the North Sea interests, and a Dallas independent purchased the royalty and waterflood leases.

Newmont gained far more from its oil investments than that final sale would indicate. In 1981 Continental Oil, by then called Conoco, was acquired by E. I. du Pont de Nemours and Company and Newmont's 3.5 million shares were converted into nearly six million shares of the chemical giant. That gave Newmont a 2.5 percent interest in DuPont valued at $257 million. It was a good exchange. Five years later, Newmont pocketed $100 million from the sale of half a million DuPont shares and by using another 1.1 million shares to back debentures exchangeable into DuPont stock, the latter representing a financial strategy that allowed the company to defer tax on the gain until the debentures were redeemed. The remaining DuPont shares were sold in 1988 for $353 million.

At the time, Newmont was in the midst of a painful restructuring (which is the subject of chapter 10) and was refocusing its interests on gold. Reluctantly, in 1990, it was forced to sell its remaining energy asset, its interest in Peabody Coal, to Hanson PLC of Great Britain for $726 million ($600 million after tax). By then Peabody had sales of $1.8 billion and was nearly three times the size of Newmont's remaining assets.

Coal and oil had been jewels in Newmont's crown and offered even greater potential, but in the end they were sold to ensure the company's survival. It would take the newly emerging gold operations years to reach the scale and financial significance of these discarded assets.

9

THE END OF AN ERA

For decades, employees of Newmont Mining were convinced they were among the very privileged of their professions. It was a "great company, comprised of tremendous people," most of whom were specialists in their fields, says former president Jack Thompson.[1] "The company was run by strong-willed men who were technically sound and very involved in the technical and scientific side of mining—geology, metallurgy, and engineering," adds Charles Freeman, a New York bank analyst and former Newmont executive. "They were straight shooters. People who worked there were proud to be a part of the company."[2]

Mine managers had great autonomy. Technical staffs, a majority of whom had Ph.D.s, were the cream of the crop. Geologists traveled the world in search of copper, nickel, silver, gold, and even diamonds; metallurgists and engineers traveled the world to build complex plants and solve technical problems. "It was like the army: join Newmont and see the world," says Patricia Flanagan, who joined as a secretary/analyst in the treasury department in 1982 and rose to vice president and treasurer ten years later. She recalls with awe and amazement how "as a twenty-something analyst" being given responsibility for managing a $100 million portfolio, much of it invested in volatile long-term bonds.[3] Financial and tax planning were cutting-edge; legal work was precedent setting. "The issues Newmont frequently and inadvertently faced were more complex than anything encountered in law school or in most legal practices. It was fascinating,"[4] says retired attorney David Potter. CEO Plato Malozemoff, a director of Browning-Ferris Industries, pondered new frontiers and asked Robert Macdonald at Danbury to explore the possibility of extracting gold from garbage and seabeds.

According to Malozemoff, there were "just under 90 souls" at the company's Manhattan headquarters, including clerks and janitors, which led him to boast: "I don't think you can find another mining company with

9.1. Newmont's management team in 1981 (from left): Jack Thompson, president; Edward Fontaine, vice president, finance; Richard Leather (seated), executive vice president and general counsel; Wayne Burt, senior vice president, operations; Plato Malozemoff, CEO; and Harry Van Benschoten, vice president, accounting. (*Newmont Archives*)

management as lean as that."[5] In 1981, he was in his twenty-eighth year as CEO and showed no signs of retiring. Thompson, smart, well liked, and possessing a photographic memory, had been president for six years; Richard Leather, a graduate of Harvard Law School who rivaled Malozemoff in intellect, was executive vice president and general counsel; Wayne Burt was both president of Magma Copper and senior vice president of operations for all of Newmont; and Ed Fontaine was chief financial officer.

Everyone had nicknames. Malozemoff was "Oz" for his behind-the-scenes manipulation. Leather says he was "Cotton Mather because some people around me were thought to be held by a mere thread from the fires of hell."[6] Fontaine was "Mr. LIFO" (an inventory accounting term for last in, first out) for his banker's hours. Ruth Vanderpoel, Malozemoff's administrative assistant who tightly controlled expense accounts and once turned down Fontaine's attempt to be reimbursed for a raincoat after being caught in a London downpour, was "the wicked witch of the west." (He reworked his expense report and resubmitted it with the challenge: "Find the raincoat.")

There were ten other officers in technical and staff positions. The chance that all fifteen were at their desk at any one time was nil and next to none. "In the early years, 80 percent of the time was travel; in the end, somewhat less," recalls Thompson. "I was on so many boards I can't remember the number. I would fly to Toronto for Sherritt Gordon, to Vancouver for Bethlehem Copper or Cassiar Asbestos, to Houston for Newmont Oil, and Tucson for Magma." Peabody Coal held board meetings in St. Louis, Seattle, Tulsa, and San Francisco to accommodate its partners. There were copper conferences in London, financial meetings in Paris, operational reviews in Africa and Australia, and management gatherings at Palm Beach or Phoenix. When Foote Mineral dedicated its lithium facility in Chile, Thompson, who participated with his wife, said "every private plane in the country was chartered to bring people to the event. They brought up a tent from Santiago . . . the size of a circus tent and President Pinochet and everybody who was anybody after Allende left was there." The one place almost no one went, however, was Carlin, Nevada.

Malozemoff took pride in keeping corporate salaries low, but the trade-off was enormous responsibility and freedom. There were golf and tennis outings for the men, and after lobbying by the secretaries, an extra Christmas shopping day for the women. Illness and family issues were accommodated with whatever time off was needed. Interviewing for a job as a geophysicist in 1969, John Parry spent a week with his wife meeting people in Danbury and Toronto. He was offered the job at $16,000 a year, but needed a year to complete his Ph.D. When it came time to report, he found his salary had been "raised to $18,000 before I had worked a single day. That's the kind of company it was. It was very much a family company."[7]

Many like Macdonald believed that "Newmont was the only mining company left. The others had all degenerated into bean counters."[8] While management was certainly interested in profitability, the context was a longer time horizon than the next quarterly earnings report. Until the copper market collapsed in 1981, Newmont had shown impressive growth under Malozemoff's leadership. When he ascended to the presidency in 1954, the company earned less than $10 million on revenue of $13 million. It had $208 million in total assets and a market capitalization of only $109 million. It was a record year in 1980 as earnings reached $197 million on sales of $882 million. Assets had soared to $1.45 billion and market capitalization had risen to $1.2 billion.

But while Malozemoff was an empire builder, shareholders also were rewarded. Anyone buying 100 shares of Newmont on January 4, 1954, the first trading day under Malozemoff's tenure, would have paid $4,100. Had they continued to hold the stock until December 31, 1980, they would have had, after stock splits, 772 shares worth $33,575. Furthermore, over those twenty-six years, they would have received $16,500 in dividends. Malozemoff would have been well advised to retire when he was ahead.

Big numbers can dazzle, but they can also be misleading. Analysts looking at those numbers were beginning to notice other things. Newmont's assets were carried on its books at substantial discounts to their true market worth or replacement cost. Also, in 1954, investors paid eleven times earnings for a share of Newmont stock, whereas in 1980 the ratio had dropped to just over six times earnings. Had the same ratio prevailed in 1980 as a quarter century earlier, Newmont's stock would have been worth nearly twice as much. Had earlier investors paid too much, or was Newmont now undervalued?

With large oil companies bidding in early 1981 for Amax, St. Joe Minerals, and Kennecott, and speculation that Rio Tinto Zinc was being eyed by yet another oil giant, there was cause for concern. Concern turned to fear in March, when two South African companies controlled by Ernest Oppenheimer's son Harry, Anglo American Corporation and DeBeers Consolidated Mines, the world's largest gold- and diamond-mining companies, transferred $800 million to an investment company in Bermuda to finance acquisitions in North America. Market rumors listed the most likely targets as Phelps Dodge and Newmont.[9] In talking to a reporter a month later, Malozemoff said Newmont had not received any offers "friendly or unfriendly," and labeled the growing takeover interest in mining companies "wasteful, if not destructive."[10] In an address to the New York Society of Security Analysts he said too many investors were interested only in a "fast buck profit," while the nation's focus should be on the availability of scarce, strategic metals that could be jeopardized by foreign takeovers.[11]

In April, Newmont reported bad news: a 62 percent drop in first quarter earnings as copper prices fell sharply. And good news: Peabody Coal had signed a long-term supply contract with a Midwest utility valued at $1 billion, the largest in its history. But the most interesting announcement came on April 8. The company said further drilling at "its Gold Quarry property" had significantly increased the property's low-grade gold reserves to 4.1 million ounces from one million at year end 1980.

Russia's invasion of Afghanistan in 1979 and rising inflation sent the price of gold soaring above $800 an ounce in 1980. Although the peak was brief, it helped establish a new gold price range of $350 to $500 an ounce that lasted for nearly twenty years. With rising prices, Carlin drilled out the Maggie Creek deposit and found the ore body extended onto Section 35 in Township 34 North. This was the 522-acre Gold Quarry property relinquished to Thornton and Ash, the owners of the T/Lazy S Ranch, eight years earlier. A new lease for access and exploration was obtained and a drilling program initiated. Wary of Oppenheimer's war chest and seeking something to up the ante should there be a bid, in March 1981 Malozemoff asked Richard Ellett, vice president of exploration, to review the Gold Quarry drilling results and assess the prospects. Donald Hammer, Newmont's western exploration manager in Tucson, who joined Ellett in that review, vividly recalls what they found.

Jay McBeth [the Carlin mine manager] met us at the mine office on a Sunday. As there were no engineering staff members working that day, Jay rummaged in the files and produced logs of the rotary drill cuttings for the newly drilled holes. He also found a map showing the location of pertinent drill holes and the resource blocks that had been used in the tonnage estimate that was submitted to New York. These holes were drilled at wide intervals, 400 feet, as I recall. It turns out that the engineer who produced that estimate had drawn a cylinder 50 feet in diameter around each drill hole. He calculated the contained volume and tonnage in each cylinder, but not for the intervening ground. He added together the tonnages thus derived in order to obtain an estimate of total tons tested to that date.

Now you couldn't be sure what was between those holes, but you could be sure it was mineralized ground. Dick just blew his cork. He did a back-of-the-envelope calculation that showed instead of a few million tons of ore, we likely were looking at more than a hundred million tons.[12]

Informed of the change, Malozemoff rushed out the April 8 news release. A second announcement in November lifted the reserve estimate to seven million ounces, and by the time the 1981 annual report was published in the spring of 1982, after 580 holes had been drilled, the number had risen to 175 million tons of ore containing eight million ounces of gold. The high desert of Nevada had just become a lot more valuable.

If Malozemoff thought the announcement would cool the takeover fever, he was mistaken. In a filing with the SEC on Monday, April 27, London-based Consolidated Gold Fields said it had purchased 1.84 million Newmont shares on the open market at slightly less than $59 a share. For $108 million, it acquired a 7 percent interest. ConsGold, as the company was known, said it wanted to become "Newmont's largest shareholder" by purchasing up to 50 percent of the company and taking a commensurate position on the board.

Malozemoff was livid. He viewed Newmont as a "personal monument to himself"[13] and took the news as an attack on his leadership. ConsGold, through a controlling interest in Gold Fields of South Africa, was the world's second largest gold miner. Yet Malozemoff believed Oppenheimer was manipulating the strings since Anglo American and DeBeers each owned a 12.5 percent interest in ConsGold. He knew all the players and thought of Oppenheimer as a friend. In fact, not long before, Oppenheimer had told Malozemoff that he had purchased 200,000 shares of Newmont for his own account because he thought watching the company's growth would be "fun."[14] Newmont and Anglo were partners in several South African ventures and only a month earlier Newmont and ConsGold had considered a joint bid for St. Joe Minerals, which was under attack. The fact that Lazard Fréres served as investment banker for both Newmont and Anglo made it seem even more of a double-cross. Rudolph Agnew, ConsGold's CEO, puts a more benign spin on the purchase: "The decision to invest in Newmont was made by the executive committee of Consolidated Gold Fields of which Anglo American did not have a representative and was not aware of what was going on. It was . . . approved by the board and we acted the next day. Harry Oppenheimer wasn't in it at all. We've always been told he was extremely annoyed."[15]

ConsGold's dilemma, according to Agnew, was that it was locked into its investment in Gold Fields of South Africa, which was not paying dividends, severely crimping the parent company's cash flow. Agnew adopted a three-pronged strategy: to continue in the aggregate business, which was generating good cash flow; to start a new company, Gold Fields Mining Corporation, to search for gold in North America; and to invest in a major U.S. mining company, preferably a copper producer.

> You must remember Consolidated Gold Fields was a mining finance house, as Newmont had been earlier. We made money by buying and selling shares. We used our expertise to buy good mining shares and there was no firm view as to what the end play in a North American mining company would be. It could be just an investment, it could be a permanent investment, or it could, in my mind, (but this was not part of the recommendation), it could be a long-term merger.
>
> We looked at Phelps Dodge, which was a copper investment, and then began to get a feeling that Newmont was underpriced. Somebody told us about the Carlin Trend. And so in no scientific way, not the way chief executives like to tell you they were inspired, but probably pure blind luck, we switched to Newmont. We not only thought it was underpriced, we thought it had lost its way, and we thought it might have considerable gold potential. Now the point of investing in North America was eventually to disinvest in South Africa, not for political reasons (although the backlash against apartheid was running at a feverish pace at the time), but for cash flow reasons.

Malozemoff and the Newmont board could have cared less about what motivated Agnew and promptly sued in the Federal District Court of New York on anti-trust grounds. The proceedings carried on for months, requiring ConsGold at one point to deliver to the court eighty thousand pages of documents weighing half a ton. Leather raised an arcane issue from the federal Maritime Law that prohibited foreign ownership of commercial boats in American waters, noting that Peabody Coal owned Mid-Continent Barge Company and that Atlantic Cement moved much of its material in barges named for the wives of Newmont executives. Such legal maneuvers were legendary and gave rise to opponents saying they had been "Leathered."

In another move Malozemoff must have found galling, he began looking for a white knight on the theory, prevalent in business, that the devil unknown must be better than the devil known. Convinced that a large block of stock should only be sold at a premium, his goal was to find a buyer willing to pay $80 a share, or $1 billion, for a 49 percent stake in the company, which would have left the current management in control. Standard Oil of California and Union Oil took a serious look but said no, while Mobil, Gulf Oil, and Getty rejected the proposal out of hand.

In the end, a compromise was reached. Leather enlisted the help of Edwin Zimmerman at Covington & Burling in Washington and worked out a precedent-setting standstill agreement whereby Consolidated Gold Fields agreed not to exceed a 26 percent interest in Newmont through 1984. The agreement was renewed in 1983 and 1987 and, importantly, was found to bind subsequent purchasers of the stock in later years. Agnew and David Lloyd-Jacob, CEO of ConsGold's American subsidiary, went on the Newmont board and Malozemoff joined the board of ConsGold. Robin Plumbridge, CEO of Gold Fields of South Africa, soon replaced Lloyd-Jacob as a director. Additionally, Malozemoff persuaded ConsGold to purchase one million shares of Newmont stock from its treasury at $72 a share, putting cash in Newmont's coffers.

Newmont retained its independence, but at a cost to Malozemoff, who found his new directors vocal in their demands that he pick a successor and a retirement date. In his oral interview with the Bancroft Library, Malozemoff admitted to being stubborn, adding, "I hold stubbornness to be one of the primary factors of successful management."[16] Nowhere was this more evident, or more difficult, than in his reluctance to retire. Those inside the company and out watched good men like Thompson and Burt rise to a point where they were capable of assuming leadership, only to be left in limbo until they, too, reached retirement age while Malozemoff refused to budge.

Burt broached the subject on one of their semi-annual flights to Africa. Asked who he was thinking of as a replacement, Malozemoff, who at the time was seventy-two, answered, "There is no one." Burt continued, "Well, we are going to see a young fellow when we get to South Africa who is doing quite well. Have you ever considered bringing young Parker along?" At age forty-six, Gordon Parker was managing director of O'okiep and Tsumeb but was virtually unknown in Newmont's headquarters. Burt recalls the

CEO's reaction: "My God, the light went on like that in Plato's mind. I must say in retrospect the reason it did is that Plato saw in Gordon someone who would let him continue to run the place."[17]

While successful in South Africa, Parker knew little about American business or finance. Says Leather, "When Plato made the decision to make Gordon his successor, he started to phase Gordon in slowly. He'd say, 'It will take you a year to learn the oil business.' Then it was, 'It'll take you another year to learn the cement business.' That's when the board started to lose patience." Parker doesn't disagree. "His knowledge of Newmont in all its facets was way beyond mine," he says of Malozemoff. "When he handed the reins over to me, I'm sure he was thinking to himself, 'My God, this is ridiculous.'"[18]

Parker, described by Thompson as "a fine look in the eye and very pleasant," arrived in New York in September 1981 as vice president of operations, reporting to Burt. It was essentially the same position his father-in-law, David Pearce, had held two decades earlier. "From being a big fish in a small pond in Cape Town to the Big Apple! Wow! I made fewer decisions, but paid more for lunch," Parker quips. Malozemoff challenged him with difficult assignments, like trying to find a solution to Magma's multiple problems and negotiating a new agreement with Thornton and Ash in Nevada. "Do something heroic, please," is the way Parker remembers Malozemoff's instructions.

Changes were occurring at the vast T/S Ranch. In January 1973, Ash moved to Washington as director of the Office of Management and Budget for President Nixon and sold his half-interest in the ranch to Thornton. However, he retained his interest in Carlin's producing properties and in Section 35. Thornton, who received the Presidential Medal of Freedom from Ronald Reagan in 1981, died later that year and his son, Charles B. "Chuck" Thornton, became owner of the T/S Ranch. Faced with a large inheritance tax on his father's estate, Thornton informed Newmont in early 1982 that he was prepared to sell the ranch. Parker and Carmen Fimiani, a former helicopter pilot during the Vietnam War and at the time assigned to Newmont's corporate development staff in New York, flew to Los Angeles on April 30 to begin the negotiations. They were unprepared for what they encountered.

Not fully aware that Section 35 was held separately from the ranch, they felt Newmont had a secure lease on rights to the Gold Quarry assets. Meanwhile, Thornton and Ash, who had originally been told that Gold Quarry would probably be smaller than Maggie Creek, with 400,000 ounces of gold, were salivating over Newmont's news releases that now put its reserves at eight million ounces. They demanded among other things a higher royalty, dedicated facilities, and a $50 million capital commitment for development. "We listened to them rant and rave and when we left the meeting, I wisecracked to Gordon, 'These guys acted like they own it,'" Fimiani recalls. Subsequent research showed that the 1979 lease was for only five years with an option for another five-year extension, not nearly long enough to develop and exploit a mine the size of Gold Quarry. "Once I had finally figured out the whole story, I walked into his [Parker's] office and said, 'Guess what? They own it!'"[19]

Heated negotiations continued. "I found myself in a lion's den," says Parker. "I was supposed to negotiate for a piece of land on which gold had already been discovered and on which the owners held many of the cards. Ash and Thornton were formidable, well informed, and gave no quarter. They would have no part of a buyout agreement and insisted on a royalty. It became very complex. Every little detail of the potential operation had to be spelled out: where the mill would be located, what ores could run through the mill, and on and on. What should have taken fifty pages took five hundred."

At one point, after an extensive negotiating session with Ash, Parker thought he had reached a breakthrough. Pulling out the highest number his corporate development team could justify, he offered to buy Section 35 for $13 million. At $400 an ounce, that was the equivalent of offering to deliver a ton of gold to Ash's front door. "Roy said, 'Okay, that sounds fine to me. Let me go back and discuss it with Chuck.' Well, between his California ears and my South African accent, he thought I had said $30 million. So we were $17 million apart and couldn't bridge the gap."[20]

An agreement was finally reached on August 20, 1982. For $35 million, Newmont acquired the T/S Ranch as well as all of the surface rights and 10 percent of the mineral rights to Section 35. The company's press release and subsequent annual report said Carlin had also "renegotiated the existing Gold Quarry mineral lease with the owners of the remaining 90 percent of the mineral rights and secured a long-term lease with a fixed royalty percentage payment." What investors were not told was that the royalty rate was 18 percent, the highest in the gold industry and nearly three times the company's first royalty with Thornton and Ash of 7 percent in 1963.

Gold Quarry, with 250 million tons of ore, although grading only 0.04 ounce per ton of gold, represented a major turning point for Newmont and Malozemoff wanted to make sure the company got it right. Because of the complexity and wide variation in ore grades, he insisted on a methodical drilling and testing program to fully understand the metallurgy and re-covery rates before committing funds to a new mill. However, after more than a thousand holes had been drilled even he was showing impatience. Leonard Harris, vice president of research, recalls the CEO telling him, "You know, you are drilling the hell out of that project. Let's leave some ore for the mill."[21]

Board approval was obtained in January 1984 for construction of the mine, mill, and leach facilities costing $130 million, far more than Thorn-ton and Ash had demanded. Mill No. 2, utilizing fine grinding and a more efficient process to recover gold, was three times the size of Mill No. 1 and would produce 170,000 ounces of gold a year by processing 2.5 million tons of ore. Production began in the next summer. By the time heap leaching got under way six months later, Newmont's employment in Nevada had risen from 130 workers to 540.

With the increase in size and importance that Gold Quarry brought to Carlin, it was time for new management. In 1984, Parker brought in as gen-eral manager the man who had been his right hand in South Africa, T. Peter Philip, the general manager of the O'okiep Copper mine. Two years later Philip was named president of the Carlin operations. A small, wiry man of immense energy, a can-do attitude, and interests that ranged from glass blowing to master carpentry to snowboarding, Philip set out to change the culture of Carlin. The sleepy, family atmosphere that had prevailed since the beginning was replaced by one where "we were going at it hammer and tongs," he says.[22]

It was a step long overdue. By 1985, new gold mines were opening across North America and even with the start-up of Gold Quarry, Newmont had lost its position as the largest gold miner in Nevada. Production that year of 219,000 ounces of gold was surpassed by Battle Mountain's Fortitude mine at 225,000 ounces and Freeport's Jerritt Canyon mine at 275,000 ounces. The Rain deposit, twenty miles south of Gold Quarry and containing 800,000 ounces of gold, was discovered by Newmont Exploration Limited (NEL) in 1982, but development was repeatedly deferred by New York on the grounds that extra production was not needed.

Now, with reserves supporting the original Carlin mill quickly depleting, Philip put his boot to the back side of Nevada's geologic effort by, among other things, putting NEL in charge of Carlin exploration. There had been so much animosity between the two groups, he said, "that if a NEL geologist met a counterpart from the Carlin Gold Mining Company on the streets of Elko, one would cross to the other side."

Odin Christensen, a former geology professor at the University of North Dakota who later became Newmont's chief geologist, remembers his shock in taking over Carlin exploration.

> There were four mine geologists there and they had to ride the mine bus to work. So they would get there at 7 o'clock in the morning and had to be back on the bus at 4 o'clock. The exploration department didn't have a pickup truck. If they wanted to go to the field, they had to borrow one from one of the operations people. Needless to say they weren't very effective. The first week I was there, Fimiani [who had just been named Carlin's operations manager] and I went to Dewey Chevrolet and bought four used trucks. It cost us a few thousand dollars. But suddenly the geologists could come to work early or stay late and go to their drill rigs when they wanted to. It was for want of a nail the horse was lost and for want of a horse the battle was lost kind of thing. That investment probably spurred more exploration success than anything else we did that summer.[23]

Old drilling logs were pulled out of the files, new holes drilled, and, bingo, discoveries recorded. The Genesis deposit, three miles north of the Carlin mine with six million tons of relatively high-grade ore containing 620,000 ounces of gold, was announced in September 1985 after only twelve holes were drilled. But the story is more complicated. Frustrated after the first two holes ended in ore at 800 feet, Philip issued a decree. "I went out and said, 'I need ore in the short term because otherwise we are going to have to shut this thing [Mill No. 1] down.' I said I wanted holes put down fifty feet deep, that's all. We drilled out that surface anomaly and found enough ore for five years. We drilled it out in a matter of a month. That was how easy it was to find ore." By November, mining was under way and geologists complained that they could barely keep their drilling rigs ahead of the shovels.

The geologic thinking at the time was that Carlin-type ores did not exist at depth. But even if they did, Philip reasoned, mining could be deferred to another day. Later, that thinking, some bad blood, and a dose of arrogance caused Newmont to overlook one of the most lucrative prizes the Carlin Trend had to offer—Goldstrike.

That story begins at Post, another two miles north of Genesis, where Newmont geologists drilled some shallow holes in the 1960s but found nothing of interest. The adjacent Goldstrike property was owned by the federal government. The surface rights were leased to the T/S Ranch under the Taylor Grazing Act, which made Newmont Goldstrike's landlord when it purchased the ranch in 1982. The mineral rights, however, were available to anyone for exploration. A small Houston oil company had staked the property in the late 1960s and later farmed it out to PanCana Minerals of Calgary, which began small-scale, shallow mining in 1976. Two years later, Western States Mining joined PanCana as the operator of the Goldstrike property.

In 1984, Western States began drilling along the property line and encountered mineralization. The land had been surveyed in 1872, but the corner posts had been destroyed by range fires over the years and the boundary was unclear. After long negotiations failed to clarify the property line, Western States moved its drilling rigs onto property Newmont believed to be theirs over a holiday weekend in October 1984. Newmont sent a crew out at night to disable the rigs, Western States called the sheriff, and a nasty lawsuit ensued. It all involved just eleven feet of property. In the end a boundary was fixed that both sides could live with.

With its interest in Post rekindled by its neighbor's activity, Newmont started its own exploration effort and over the next two years identified nearly one million contained ounces on its side of the line. But it wasn't something the company wanted to mine immediately and furthermore, it believed, "the potential for additional ore [at Post] is not considered to be significant."[24]

Christensen explains the logic.

> We drilled out Upper Post that was pretty good oxide grade. Then we drilled into Lower Post and the ore went refractory and lower grade. So we would drill down and go into about 100 feet of low-grade refractory material and then stop. That was about 600 feet deep. If we had gone another 300 feet we would have hit Deep Post [a separate high-grade, refractory deposit containing four million ounces of gold]. It was the whole body of academics at the time. It was felt that the gold had formed at lower temperature at shallow levels and that the hydrothermal system hadn't deposited gold at depths. There was believed to be a geological reason why these deposits died out at depth. But the science was wrong.

Newmont passed up several opportunities to acquire Goldstrike. Joseph Rotman, a prominent Canadian oil man and investor who controlled PanCana, offered to sell his interest to Newmont in 1979 but was turned down flat.[25] Over the next several years Western States sought to enter into a joint venture with Newmont to have its ore processed at Mill No. 1, but metallurgical tests showed the ore to be refractory and not suitable for milling without expensive pretreatment. Refractory ore has not been weathered by oxidation and the gold molecules, encased in sulfides or carbon, respond poorly to conventional cyanide extraction.

Newmont looked down its professional nose at Western States. The company was owned by S. J. Groves, a Minneapolis construction firm, and the operation was more of an earth-moving exercise with used equipment than a serious mining effort. Heap leach pads were poorly constructed, improperly lined, and leaked cyanide into grazing lands along Rodeo Creek, a violation of the original lease terms with Thornton and Ash. "I was going to use this to run them out of business," says Fimiani. "Some of the staff in New York began calling me 'Rambo,' because I was so relentless with those people."

For the most part, however, this was well beyond the horizon for the folks in New York, who were facing increasing pressure from ConsGold. Public statements by the two companies were cordial, but underneath Newmont's largest shareholder was becoming restless with the widening losses in its copper operations. Earnings dropped by three-quarters from 1980 to 1984, averaging only $50 million a year. Dividends were cut in half and the stock price languished in the $40s, far below ConsGold's acquisition price. Meanwhile, with Gold Quarry and investments in North Sea oil ventures, capital expenditures were soaring.

The company remained financially strong with assets of $2 billion and long-term debt of only $200 million. But that was largely due to financial, not operating, success. Nearly $155 million was received on the sale of St. Joe Minerals stock in 1981, while a Eurodollar borrowing, the company's first, brought in $50 million in 1982. With a rising stock price in January 1983, Newmont sold nearly 2.7 million shares of common stock at $55.50 a share, providing $145 million after expenses. ConsGold acquired 667,000 of the shares to maintain its interest at 25 percent.

Early in 1983, ConsGold asked to renegotiate its standstill agreement. It did not want to wait until the 1984 deadline and felt the negotiations could be used as leverage to advance Malozemoff's retirement. The CEO had not yet set a date nor officially designated Parker as his successor. In his Denver home, Leather displays a silver bowl with a British shilling embedded in the bottom as a memento of those negotiations. Meeting with ConsGold's executives at the company's New York offices in the New York Central (now Helmsley) Building, Leather was told by CEO Agnew of his growing frustration with Malozemoff. "Successor after successor had been destroyed. Unless he went we wouldn't get a successor," Agnew says. Would Leather agree to step into Malozemoff's shoes?

"Rudolph, there's an old English saying that when you take the king's shilling, you do the king's bidding," Leather says he told Agnew. "I take Plato's shilling and I work for him and Newmont. End of discussion." The standstill agreement was successfully renegotiated with the deadline extended for another ten years. ConsGold was given the right to increase its ownership to 33.3 percent. Three months later, Leather attended a Copper Research Association board meeting in London. He and his wife, Penny, had dinner at Agnew's club with Rudolph and his wife, Whitney. "That's when he presented me with the bowl," Leather grins.

It wasn't until the board meeting of December 4, 1984, that Malozemoff finally made his first move toward the exit. Parker was named president, succeeding Thompson, who was elected vice chairman to cushion the impact of his own pending retirement. In the year's annual report, the company said the moves were made "in contemplation of Mr. Malozemoff's eventual retirement," as if there had not been time for contemplation in the previous decade. A year later, he relinquished his position as chairman and became chairman emeritus, a title that recognized the company's respect for his years of service but removed him from power.

In his last act as CEO, Malozemoff presided over the dedication of the Gold Quarry mine on September 20, 1985. He called Carlin "the nearest to my heart" of all of Newmont's operations, although the event marked only his third visit to the site in twenty years. What impressed the CEO was that over those two decades Carlin had paid $195 million in dividends to its parent. Not without sadness, he told the assembled dignitaries that in ten days Parker "will succeed me as chief executive officer of Newmont Mining Corporation [and will have the] responsibility to expand and extract maximum benefits out of this gold resource."

Parker and his successors have done that ever since. Gold Quarry turned out to be one of the richest gold mines in the world. To date, the mine has produced 10.5 million ounces of gold and still has another 10 million ounces in reserves, including one million added in 2005. Since 1985, the Thornton and Ash families have received more than $500 million in royalties. "We have tried on several occasions to buy out the lease, but each time we do our geologists find more ore proving their strategy of holding on to be correct," says Wayne Murdy, Newmont's CEO from 2001 to 2007.[26]

Lucky Len

Mining has always been a hazardous business. With heavy equipment, explosives, rock slides, deep pits, and dark underground shafts, the risk to life and limb is always present. Most accidents are avoidable and Newmont prides itself on its commitment to safety, on its training and procedures, and on its record, which for years has been among the best in the industry.

But there are other dangers that cannot be measured or easily avoided. Newmont geologists have been caught in terrorist attacks in South America and in riots in Indonesia, and were in Uzbekistan during the collapse of the Soviet Union. Robert Baldwin, a brilliant member of Arthur Brant's first geophysical team, died in a helicopter crash in Alaska in 1958. Galen Knutsen, who drilled out the Rain deposit at Carlin, Nevada, died in the crash of an AeroPeru jet off the coast of Peru in 1996.

Leonard Harris, retired vice president of research and metallurgy, encountered his first close call in 1953 when he boarded a ship in his native Australia, where both of his grandfathers had been miners, for passage to Canada. The ship sank before it could leave Sydney Harbor. Over a twenty-one-year career as one of Newmont's most widely traveled officers (his visits being eagerly awaited at each site as he always carried a fresh inventory of slightly off-color jokes), he saw more than his share of white-knuckle flights and almost lost his life in one crash.

Flying once in a small plane from the O'okiep Copper mine in South Africa to Gamsberg, a zinc deposit eighty miles away, bad weather forced the pilot to make an emergency landing on a road. A year or so later, the same plane, pilot, and passenger were forced down again on a flight from O'okiep to Johannesburg. "In all my career, I've only been forced down twice and you were onboard both times. I don't want to fly with you again," the pilot told Harris.

Twice on commercial flights from South Africa to Europe, Harris was on planes that made emergency landings for undisclosed reasons, and once, flying from the United States to South Africa, the captain announced six hours into the flight that the landing gear had jammed on takeoff and that they were returning to New York. "That was the scariest time," Harris recalls. Fire trucks and ambulances with lights flashing lined the foam-covered runway as the jumbo jet landed on its belly. Luckily no one was injured. Harris returned to the airport the next day and found the replacement plane only a quarter full. "A lot of people decided they didn't really need to go to South Africa," he laughs.[27]

His luck almost ran out, however, in January 1990 on a Sky West flight from Salt

9.2. Leonard Harris, who directed Newmont's worldwide research and development effort for nearly twenty years, also brought the Yanacocha mine into operation in Peru during a period of terrorist attacks. (*Newmont Archives*)

Lake City to Elko, Nevada. The pilot tried to land in a blinding snowstorm and struck the top of a mountain. The pilot and one passenger later died and Harris, who was pulled from the wreckage by other passengers, broke his back. Newmont sent out a Lear jet to bring him back to a Denver hospital. Six weeks later he was back at work and shortly thereafter, despite a body brace, was climbing a mountain at Yanacocha in Peru.

10

SHAREHOLDER VALUE

Like many great actors who remain too long on center stage, Plato Malozemoff had drawn the last applause from his company's performance. "Newmont was sort of a ragtag collection of assets at the time I appeared on the scene,"[1] says Gordon Parker, who, during his first month as chairman, wrote down the value of his inherited portfolio by $97 million. Combined with an even larger operating loss from its copper mines, Newmont reported a net loss of $35 million for 1985, Malozemoff's last year at the helm. It was the company's first red ink since the Depression.

While the copper market was depressed worldwide, Newmont's problem was centered in Arizona, where it cost Magma 80 cents to produce a pound of refined copper that could be sold for only 66 cents. A new low-cost SXEW plant to process surface-mined oxide ores began operation at San Manuel in May 1986, and significant labor concessions that year promised further cost reductions. But after having lost $300 million over the previous six years and facing another $200 million in mandated expenditures for pollution control by the end of 1987, Newmont's patience had run out. Furthermore, years of studies had produced no assured road map to profitability.

Unlike his predecessor, Parker sought consensus within Newmont's management team and was willing to think out loud as he grappled with major decisions. He also credits others for most of the ideas the company adopted. The solution to Magma's problems—or better stated, Newmont's way to extricate itself from those problems—came from an unlikely source: James Hill, the company's bright but combative vice president of corporate relations. "We were all trying to figure out what to do. Gordon called a bunch of us into the boardroom and we sat around the table giving our ideas. When it got to me, I said we should spin it off,"[2] Hill says. Reasoning that Magma could not be sold, he proposed giving it to shareholders as a dividend. Parker, executive vice president Richard Leather, and CFO Ed

Fontaine agreed; others, including Malozemoff, still a director but without power, were aghast. Embedded in the former CEO's philosophy were two maxims: never sell reserves and, in time, copper markets always recover.

"Newmont people were just in love with mining," says Hill. "They thought that having their hands in many mines was what was important. But investors couldn't understand the company; they wanted clarity." Malozemoff and others felt the company's diverse investments meant that a down cycle in one commodity would be offset by good results in another, giving the company long-term stability. Hill argued that investors wanted focus and an opportunity for personal financial gain, not corporate longevity. Shareholders, particularly institutional investors, could create their own portfolio by buying stocks in different companies; they didn't need Newmont to provide diversification. Additionally, if a stock threatened to tank, it could easily be sold from an investor's portfolio whereas a company like Newmont, holding a major piece of that same company, would find disposal much more difficult. Leather recalls Hill's comment at a board meeting that summer: "Like it or not, we are in two businesses, the business of running the company and the business of managing the stock."[3] Magma's continuing losses were making the latter task much more difficult.

In March 1987, Newmont implemented Hill's proposal. Pinto Valley Copper was merged into Magma, making it the second largest copper producer in the country. In addition, Newmont contributed $150 million in intercompany debt to the new company and converted another $200 million of debt into Magma preferred stock. It then spun off 80 percent of the recapitalized company on a share-for-share basis to shareholders while retaining a 15 percent interest in Magma. Five percent of the stock was set aside as an incentive for Magma's newly independent executives. With the debt removed from its books, Magma could invest in a new smelter necessary to meet environmental requirements and shareholders would be in a position to benefit when the copper market recovered, which it did the next year.

Coupled with the earlier sale of Atlantic Cement and the decision to dispose of Foote Mineral, the spin-off of Magma reduced Newmont's size by half in terms of sales[4] and Parker set about to rebuild the company. "We were trying to devise something that might have three legs to it—gold, coal, and aggregates looked interesting," he says. "There were champions within the company for different approaches and we looked at lots of things." Early in the year, the company increased its ownership of Peabody to 49.9 percent, but Parker says he "lay awake at night" worrying about the low margins earned on coal. Some favored buying an oil and gas exploration company to leverage Newmont's oil interests, but no one within the company had the experience to run such an organization and the company was unwilling to pay $400,000 or so a year to recruit such an individual. Yet, whatever the company's future, it was clear that to grow it needed an influx of cash and a higher stock price.

Investor sentiment toward gold stocks was changing in the mid-1980s. While most institutional money managers still considered gold a risky investment, a passionate few believed metal prices would soar because of reasons both fundamental—a growth in demand for gold jewelry—and emotional—inflation's erosion in the value of the dollar. Mutual funds dedicated to gold stocks were created and with a limited number of publicly traded gold companies, gold shares traded at a premium.

At a board meeting in July 1985, William Moses, the financially astute former chairman of Massachusetts Financial Services, noted that investors buying newly issued shares of Freeport-McMoran Copper & Gold paid a price-to-earnings ratio of 66, or five times the ratio for the 500 stocks in the Standard & Poor's Index. This was $2,000 per ounce for Freeport's annual production, which, if extrapolated to Newmont, meant that investors would value its Nevada mines at nearly $1 billion, Moses said.

With the start-up of Gold Quarry, the Carlin Gold Mining Company produced a record 474,000 ounces of gold in 1986 and forecast 577,000 ounces for 1987. Reserves of 12.3 million ounces were the highest in North America. Furthermore, the gold price increased $50 in 1986 to average $371 an ounce for the year. With cash operating costs of $170 an ounce, pre-tax profits from the Nevada operation surged to $67 million from $13 million in 1985.

To cash in on this good fortune and Wall Street's growing appetite for gold stocks, Fontaine, at the suggestion of George Ames of Lazard Fréres and Tom McCaughey of Salomon Brothers, proposed selling a small piece of the Carlin operation to the public. Such a sale, it was felt, would also demonstrate to investors the underlying value of Newmont's gold properties, lifting its stock price. Parker bought this advice "wholeheartedly. It was an excellent idea. We had borrowed a lot to develop [those assets] and it put the spotlight on asset values." Five percent of Carlin, renamed Newmont Gold Company, was sold in an initial public offering in June 1986 for $43 million. Ten months later, with the gold price well above $400 an ounce and the price of the new shares soaring, Newmont sold another 5 percent, this time for $143 million. A 25 percent interest in Newmont Proprietary, the company's Australian gold subsidiary, also was sold for $195 million.

Awakened to the company's gold holdings, Wall Street bid up the stock of Newmont Mining as well as that of Newmont Gold. Within a year, the parent company's stock price had doubled and in June 1987, 5.8 million shares of Newmont Mining common stock were sold from its treasury at $46 a share, bringing in $270 million. The four sales within a year added $651 million to the company's coffers. Newmont had never been so flush.

A new phrase—shareholder value—entered the business lexicon in the early 1980s in books published by college professors and management gurus. Parker, seeking a philosophical grounding for Newmont's business strategy, read books by Michael Porter of Harvard and Alfred Rappaport of Northwestern and says they "made a huge impression on me. Shareholder value is what it's all about. It's not just earnings or ROI [return on investment]. It's stock price and dividends over time. It's the net present value of an entity over time. It's hard to get your arms around, but somehow or another you have to find a way to measure it so you can guide the company to do things that will result in sustainable value." But it is also essential that shareholders understand a company's strategy.

There is an axiom in public relations that a company's best course of action is to "do good and talk about it." The same is true for achieving shareholder value. At this crucial point in Newmont's history, however, Parker and his team sought to accomplish the first half of that equation but were never committed to the second. Malozemoff had been a close-to-the-vest executive and, perhaps because of his South African upbringing, Parker wasn't any more forthcoming. The company's financial disclosure was minimal and frequently differed in format from year to year or subsidiary to subsidiary. Foreign company dividends and results might be stated in U.S. dollars one year and in local currencies—South African rand, or Australian or Canadian dollars—the next. While it met all accounting and regulatory requirements at the time, analysts complained that the company made its financial statements so opaque they were impossible to penetrate. Yet as Parker worked to restructure the company, disclosure documents became even shorter and less informative, much to the dismay of Wall Street. Quarterly earnings reports were only a few paragraphs and financial disclosure consisted of four lines—sales, net income, income per share, and shares outstanding. Reports filed with the SEC were not much more informative. (Today, detailed quarterly press releases can run twenty-five pages and SEC filings four or five times that.)

Peter Ingersoll, in 1986 an All Star metals analyst[5] with Salomon Brothers, one of three underwriters of Newmont Gold's initial public offering, remembers a road show tour he made with Parker and Fontaine to help promote the sale. Sitting in the back of a limousine from Boston's Logan Airport to a downtown hotel where they were to address a number of deep-pocket money managers, Ingersoll says he leaned over to Parker and asked, "So what are you going to tell the would-be buyers of your stock?" Parker's answer: "As little as possible."[6] When Nicolas Toufexis, an analyst for Prudential-Bache Securities, inquired what Newmont intended to do with all the money it had raised, Parker responded that it was none of anyone's business.[7]

Newmont's focus had always been on locating, acquiring, and developing promising properties or investments that would generate dividends for shareholders. It was a "trust us" philosophy that management felt no need to explain. "It wasn't about telling the shareholders the value of the company if you were to liquidate all assets tomorrow," says Leather. Yet investors in the mid-1980s were demanding that companies do more to generate immediate returns from long-term assets. If management could not get its stock to reflect the company's net asset value, the reasoning went, they should sell the enterprise in whole or in part to someone who could. And if that someone was not readily apparent, there was a new breed of investors, like jackals on the prowl, to draw blood from the flanks of underperforming companies and put them in play. Corporate raiders like Carl Icahn, Saul Steinberg, Ron Perelman, Irwin Jacobs, and T. Boone Pickens all wore Sunday suits and preached shareholder value.

Newmont had barely closed the books on its June stock sale when Parker sat down with George Melloan, a reporter for the *Wall Street Journal*, at a meeting arranged by Hill, to discuss the company's future. There has rarely been an interview like it. The first two paragraphs of the story, which ran on Tuesday, July 14, 1987, said it all.

> Gordon R. Parker, chairman, president and chief executive officer of Newmont Mining Corp., is convinced that his company is high on the target lists of all the world's corporate raiders. It has low debt, a lot of cash and a strong cash flow. More to the point, its Nevada mines have the largest known gold reserves in North America at a time when gold has taken on a new glitter for investors.
>
> "Our company must pop out of every computer study [of takeover targets] that is done," says Mr. Parker. "Analysts are saying Newmont, Newmont, Newmont. I can just see it because we're busy looking at other companies. We don't find any quite as good as us. It's a little disturbing."

Parker's management team was astounded. Graham "Chip" Clark, an attorney in the Tucson land office and later Newmont's general counsel, said he felt "a bull's eye had been pinned to our chest."[8] To this day, however, Parker insists he was "just being straightforward. We were undervalued." Just how undervalued was spelled out a week later when analyst Jim Chanos reported his findings in *Barron's* magazine. "Every professional investor's dream . . . is to stumble upon a no-brainer opportunity to turn a profit created by some inexplicable stock market inefficiency," he wrote. "And I'm convinced I've found just such easy pickings in a major arbitrage involving the common shares of Newmont Mining, which is trading around 57, and Newmont Gold, which is around 31."[9]

Chanos noted that Newmont Mining held 94.5 million shares of Newmont Gold valued by the market at $2.9 billion, while the market value of the parent company was only $3.7 billion, based on 65 million shares outstanding. This meant Wall Street was valuing Newmont's other holdings at only $800 million. Yet, the company had almost that much in cash in the bank, owned 4.2 million shares of DuPont stock worth $520 million, and had sizable holdings in Peabody Coal, Magma, Newmont Proprietary, Fluor Corporation, Sherritt Gordon, and other companies that could be sold. Even after taxes on any sales and paying off debt, Chanos concluded there would be a net gain of $2.25 billion, leaving "an unexplained $1.5 billion anomaly." What would close this gap? "A hostile takeover . . . to realize the liquidation value of Newmont Mining," he concluded.

Pickens, a Texas oil man with hangdog features, had been pillaging oil companies—Marathon, Conoco, Cities Service, Gulf, Unocal, Phillips, and Diamond Shamrock—since the early 1980s and in 1987 had targeted Boeing and Singer for attacks. His modus operandi was to (1) entice Wall Street analysts to write about a company's "undervaluation"; (2) blame this on poor management; (3) purchase a block of stock and launch a partial tender offer with questionable financing; (4) seek board representation; and (5) wait for the company to buy back his shares at a higher price—a tactic known as "greenmail"—or find a friendly buyer, or "white knight," to take it out of its misery. He never consummated an acquisition and by most accounts never had the funds to complete the transactions he announced. But the mere mention of his name sent panic through executive suites throughout the country.

On August 13, 1987, Ivanhoe Partners, a Pickens-led group, announced the purchase of a 9.1 percent interest in Newmont for $379 million, of which nearly half was borrowed from Drexel Burnham Lambert, a brokerage firm made infamous by junk bond king Michael Milken. Within a week, the partnership put up another $50 million to increase its stake to 9.9 percent. In filings with the SEC, the Pickens group said Newmont's stock price "didn't adequately reflect the value of the underlying businesses and assets" and that "there is potential for substantial appreciation in the market value of the shares."[10] Significantly, the partnership said it made its first purchases on June 18. Parker was correct; raiders did have the company in their sights. Had Chanos been tipped to Pickens's plans, or was his "easy pickings" just an amazing coincidence?

Parker, who rarely felt office-bound, wasn't one to panic. On the day of the announcement he was playing golf and had plans to leave for South Africa the next day. "I got home from golf and received an excited phone call from Goldman Sachs asking if I had seen the news wire. I told them no, but that I would see it in the office the next morning at 9 o'clock." Meanwhile, arriving in South Africa from London, Rudolph Agnew, the CEO of ConsGold, was handed an urgent message from a British Airways agent. His office wanted him to fly immediately to New York. He took the next plane out of Johannesburg and when he landed in London to transfer to

10.1. Texas oil man T. Boone Pickens used junk bond financing in a 1987 attempt to acquire control of Newmont. (*Bateman/Corbis*)

his New York flight, he says, "British Airways presented me with Pickens's autobiography. That's not bad PR is it?"[11]

It turned out that the man behind the Pickens raid was thirty-seven-year-old Robert Friedland, a bright, bold, silver-tongued promoter of gold stocks who earlier that year had formed a joint venture to exploit the Ivanhoe property, a piece of high desert real estate not far from Newmont's Carlin mine. Friedland's Vancouver-based company, Galactic Resources, had been involved in a small gold mine in South Carolina, and in 1984 began open-pit gold mining at Summitville in the San Juan Mountains of Colorado. Abandoned in the early 1990s, the Summitville mine leaked cyanide and heavy metals into the Alamosa River in one of the worst ecological disasters in the modern mining industry. "Toxic Bob," as he was labeled, sold his interest before the damage was known, but he and the mine became the poster children for environmentalists and anti-mining groups.

A roommate at Oregon's Reed College with Steve Jobs, the founder of Apple Computer, Friedland was called a "brie-and-chablis miner" by *Business Week*.[12] He took the Newmont idea to Milken at Drexel Burnham, who in turn introduced him to David Batchelder, Pickens's right-hand man. The story goes that Friedland was asked to make a presentation on Newmont to Pickens's investor group in Amarillo. When he finished, John Harbert, an Alabama coal baron who had been a partner of Pickens since his oil company forays, turned to Friedland and said, "You are one hellava snake oil salesman, and I mean that in the highest sense of the word."[13] For his introduction, Friedland was given a 10 percent carried interest in the Ivanhoe Partnership.

The big question on Wall Street was what would ConsGold do with its 26 percent ownership of Newmont? The standstill agreement included a termination clause should a third party make a raid on the company. Would ConsGold now join Pickens or counter the Ivanhoe group with an offer of its own? The answer came on August 19 in a press release from London. Agnew said he had turned down an invitation to meet with Pickens and had no intention of terminating the standstill agreement. "We strongly support Newmont management and believe it to be in our interest as the largest shareholder and in the interest of all Newmont shareholders, that management be allowed to continue to direct Newmont's affairs."[14]

Newmont's initial response to Pickens was one of disbelief. Hadn't it already enhanced shareholder value by spinning off Magma, increasing its ownership of Peabody, establishing a market for its gold companies, splitting its stock two-for-one, and raising the dividend by 20 percent? "These achievements have been reflected in the market price of the company's stock," Parker said in a press release. "During the sixteen-month period ended at the close of the market on Thursday, August 13, Newmont's share price increased nearly four times (on an adjusted basis) to $77 a share."[15]

Investor focus, however, was not on what the company had done, but on what it could do with a little more effort. "Newmont Mining applies the most rigorous and conservative standards of any North American gold producer in calculating its reserves, which we believe are understated by a wide margin," wrote John Tumazos, a metals analyst with Oppenheimer & Co. Not only did the company have a number of prospects that were not included in its reserves, but even at Gold Quarry, there had been no drilling below one thousand feet. "We believe the company's most effective takeover defense is immediately to publish a revision in its reserves . . . which should increase its published 12.3 million ounce Nevada reserve base by 25% to 100%." That, Tumazos added, would increase Newmont's "asset transfer value" to $159 to $197 per share from the $95 to $103 figure he had previously calculated.[16]

Inside the company, management quickly came to the same conclusion. T. Peter Philip, the president of Newmont Gold Company, recalls what happened. "We were all closeted trying to figure out what the hell to do with dozens of lawyers and advisors and other people around us. Toward the end of the session . . . I commented that in a year to eighteen months, I thought, we should be able to double our current production at Carlin and triple it in another year."[17] Jaws dropped. He was besieged with questions. Where is it coming from? What's the capital cost? The operating cost?

Two days after the Pickens news broke and a day after the Tumazos report, Philip called Robert Zerga, who had transferred from Magma to be general manager at Carlin, with a demand that he develop, as rapidly as possible, a new set of plans that would exploit known and probable ore reserves in as optimistic a method as possible. Working around the clock with geologist Odin Christensen and metallurgist Walter Lawrence, Newmont

Gold's operations manager, Zerga funneled numbers back to Philip in New York. "We took three days to draw up a complete plan—capital, operating, manning, production, strip ratios, the whole damn thing—three days," recalls Philip. "We were making rough estimates based on our experience, but without any real fundamental information beneath us. There was no alternative, so we did it. The investment bankers [Goldman Sachs and Kidder Peabody] jumped on our plan and said this was what the company was going to do."

The new plan was announced to the public on August 27. Based on 220 drill holes totaling more than 123,000 feet since the first of the year, Newmont Gold said its reserves had increased 14 percent to 14 million ounces and that production in 1988 of 850,000 ounces would be 45 percent higher than in 1987. It added that in 1989, it would "become the first company in the history of North American gold mining to produce a million ounces in a single year."[18] Not mentioned for another two weeks was the capital cost to implement the plan—an estimated $440 million.

Takeover battles take on a momentum of their own, and on August 31 the Pickens group launched a $95 a share bid for a minimum 28 million shares. With the 6.6 million shares it already owned, this would give it 51 percent of the company. In announcing the bid, Pickens noted that the price "represents a significant premium to recent market prices and more than 200 percent of the price at which Newmont sold its own shares to the public only two months ago."[19] But within a few days, Newmont's stock was trading down, not up, as investors questioned the Ivanhoe group's ability to raise $2.7 billion, even with Milken's junk bond support.

Legal action quickly followed. Newmont asked the federal court in Nevada to block the tender offer on the grounds that it was unfinanced and thus illegal. Ivanhoe countersued, arguing that ConsGold had illegally used inside information. Pickens also sought under Delaware corporate law to replace the Newmont board of directors with a slate of his own.

On September 11, just two weeks after issuing higher reserve numbers, Newmont announced a second revision to its business plan. Gold production in 1988 would be 913,000 ounces, not 850,000, it said, and would climb to a sustainable 1.6 million ounces in 1990. (The numbers were for Newmont Gold; the earlier sale of stock in the Carlin operations reduced Newmont Mining's interest to 90.1 percent of reserves and production.) The plan would require expanding the two existing mills at Carlin, building two new mills, and vastly increasing leach operations at two sites to handle 30 million tons of low-grade ore a year. Significantly, in a statement that went to the heart of Newmont's thinking at the time, the company said all of the production would come from near-surface deposits: "Resources of gold that may lay at depths below 800 feet have not been targeted in exploration because the tenfold growth in production between 1984 and 1990 has been and will be sustained from open pit ore deposits, which generally are more profitable than deposits mined by underground methods."[20]

If Newmont could play a higher card in this high-stakes poker game, so could Pickens. On September 15, the Ivanhoe group raised its offer to $105 per share. This was promptly rejected by the Newmont board as "inadequate," the same term it had used to reject the earlier bid.

Mondays are news days in takeover battles as both sides work frantically over the weekends to hone their tactics, which are then announced at the opening of the week's stock market. And so it was that on Monday, September 21, Newmont sealed its victory—and survival—with a pair of ace announcements. The board of directors declared a special cash dividend of $33 a share, or $2.2 billion, to be financed from internal funds and $1.75 billion in bank loans. Assistant treasurer Paul Maroni had worked with Manufacturer's Hanover Trust and Chemical Bank over the Labor Day weekend to secure the funds. But the announcement was deferred for nearly three weeks until a new ten-year standstill agreement could be worked out with ConsGold allowing it to increase its holdings to 49.9 percent. Unlike Pickens's offer, which would be available to only 42 percent of Newmont's shares and would involve some form of junk bond payment, the special dividend went to all shareholders in cash. Parker said the move delivered "substantial immediate value" to shareholders—essentially the current value of its noncore assets—while allowing them to continue to participate in the company's new focus as one of the world's premier gold producers.

Pickens sent his lawyers scurrying to Chancery Court in Delaware for a restraining order, but before the court could convene at 2 P.M., ConsGold, through its investment banker First Boston, had purchased almost 16 million shares in a "street sweep," giving it 49.7 percent of Newmont's stock. Arbitrageurs, who had been buying the stock in the hopes of cashing in on Pickens's action, were only too happy to sell for $98 to $99 cash in hand rather than wait for Ivanhoe's $105 bird in the bush. The $1.52 billion purchase set a record at the time for the total dollar value of a single company's shares purchased in one day.[21]

A Delaware judge initially called the Newmont/ConsGold action "draconian," but after a full hearing three weeks later he reversed himself and in a precedent-setting decision said the transaction had been proper and that the two companies acted reasonably and in good faith in defending the company against Pickens's coercive tactics. On October 1, the U.S. Court of Appeals, acting after the Federal Court in Nevada had refused to do so, issued an injunction blocking the Ivanhoe group from continuing its tender offer, which had been reduced to $72 a share after declaration of the special dividend.

Newmont's defense had been based on the belief that it could produce more gold and sell off non-core assets quickly to pay down the debt it had incurred by issuing the dividend. That assumption was shattered on "Black Monday," October 19, when after a devastating 9.5 percent drop in the Dow Jones Industrial Average the preceding week, the market dropped a record-shattering 508 points. Newmont's stock, which had briefly peaked at $102.25, plunged to $33. "Here I was saying we were going to sell these assets and then I blinked and the assets were worth half what they had been. It was a shock," says Parker.

Pickens kept up the pretext of a fight until November 17, when the Delaware Supreme Court upheld the lower court's decision allowing ConsGold to keep its Newmont stock. The fight cost Newmont $27 million in fees to its bankers and lawyers, and in early 1988 it paid the Ivanhoe group $7 million in an out-of-court settlement to drop all claims against the company.

The insurgents had paid an average of $64 for their shares, and had they sold immediately after ConsGold's street sweep, they would have made an estimated profit of $160 million. That includes the $33 dividend and a base stock value of $55 a share that analysts calculate Newmont would have been worth after Pickens's withdrawal.[22] By hanging on through the market crash, however, Pickens claimed the group had lost $200 million and that he personally had suffered a $28–30 million loss.[23] He did not disclose the basis for that calculation, but with a dividend check for $225 million, the group should have broken even from its raid.

Gold Fields received the dividend on its newly purchased shares, cutting its acquisition cost to $65.50 a share. Newmont advised shareholders that their dividend was taxable, part as ordinary income, part as a capital gain. Not all were happy. One shareholder wrote Parker: "If you ever feel the urge to pay out a large dividend again, please take a cold shower."[24]

Within the company, the dividend was controversial. No company had ever taken such costly action. The payout was suggested by Goldman Sachs as a means of cleaning cash out of the company's coffers. But it was Fontaine "who understood the financial dynamics of the situation and played it like an organ," says Leather. "He was the one who first realized that the company could borrow the funds, that the assets could be sold, and that the Street would support a move to build up Carlin and gold." Afterward, however, Fontaine felt the payout had been too high and that the same result could have been accomplished for less. Others, with the hindsight of the market crash, believed that Newmont had acted too quickly and that if they had held out longer, the crash would have sent Pickens packing without having to liquidate assets to get out of debt. Still others, including Malozemoff and two of his former top lieutenants, Jack Thompson and Wayne Burt, never believed Pickens had the wherewithal to pull off his threat and should have been ignored. Besides, in their view, the huge payout was orchestrated by ConsGold in order to gain control of the company.

Yet Parker, tall, urbane, and resolute, receives high praise from his board and management team for his leadership during the crisis. The Pickens fight was "Gordon's finest moment," says Leather, who credits the CEO with coordinating a top team of investment bankers and lawyers and in the end preserving the independence of the company. Jack McNally at White & Case was lead counsel and Bernard Naussbaum at Watchell Lipton, later counsel to President Clinton, was litigator.

"He took advice, he took his own counsel, and he took the measure of things and people," Leather says of the CEO. "It was his judgment that the dividend and its implications for reshaping the company were in the best interest of Newmont's shareholders. Events swept Newmont through the Pickens affair. You had to make a decision, a dividend decision was made, there was fallout from that decision, and then another decision needed to be made. The corporation was falling down the mountain and there were no brakes. Go left; go right; what next? Gordon was good at making those decisions."

10.2. Richard Leather (left), executive vice president and general counsel, and CEO Gordon Parker defended the company against a series of corporate raiders. (*Newmont Archives*)

Maureen Brundage, a young associate with White & Case at the time, recalls the chaos of the board meetings—there were six between September 1 and September 20—with multiple advisors seemingly trying to one-up each other and directors, most not having been through a takeover battle before, concerned about their personal liability as well as the welfare of the company. "It became something of a joke that they were all of a sudden saying, 'I need a lawyer. I need a lawyer,' 'Why do you need a lawyer?' 'I don't know. I just need a lawyer just in case.'"[25] Pickens's legal team harassed the Newmont directors with demands to take their depositions, and Robin Plumbridge, CEO of Gold Fields of South Africa, is convinced he and other directors were tailed by Pickens's agents when they left Newmont's offices in the Pan Am Building or ConsGold's offices across the street in the New York Central Building.

There were nine members on the board: three from management (Parker, Leather, and Fontaine); two from ConsGold (Agnew and Plumbridge); and four independents (Moses; William Turner, CEO of Consolidated

Bathurst, a Canadian paper company; Thomas Holmes, CEO of Ingersoll Rand, a maker of mining and other machinery; and Joseph Flannery, CEO of Uniroyal Holdings, a tire and chemical manufacturer). With the management and ConsGold directors excluded from some discussions by the lawyers because of possible conflicts of interest, key decisions were left to the independent directors. And with Moses about to retire, "The three of us— Tom Holmes, Joe Flannery, and myself—we got this thing thrust on us," says Turner.[26]

Despite Agnew's public statement of support, Newmont was never sure that he might not join Pickens. "We were paranoid about his intentions," says Flannery.[27] Both Agnew and Parker recognized that their fiduciary obligations to their own shareholders could put them at odds, especially if Pickens was able to back his offer with real cash. "So we were not only protecting the shareholders from Pickens. We were protecting the rest of the shareholders from both Pickens and Gold Fields," says Parker. "I recall a particular board meeting where I had conducted as far as was appropriate with the Gold Fields directors present before I asked Agnew and Plumbridge to excuse themselves. Rudolph said in jest, 'Here I am, the only director who fully understands what's happening on both sides, yet I'm the one who has to leave the room. There's something wrong with the American system.'"

Agnew says he always viewed ConsGold as part of the solution, not the problem. Yet he acknowledges that by then, "my eyes were beginning to be attracted to the idea of a full merger between the two companies." In fact, the Delaware Court found that "Gold Fields came quite close" to launching its own hostile bid for Newmont and had arranged the necessary financing for such a bid through First Boston.[28]

There was no doubt that ConsGold wanted to get Pickens out of the picture and thought the best way to do that was to put more stock in friendly hands by increasing its stake in Newmont. But with the run-up in the stock price, that was economically feasible only if Newmont itself provided part of the financing. At one point, Newmont considered acquiring a 33 percent interest in Gold Fields Mining Company, the firm's U.S. gold mining subsidiary, for $600 million on the condition that ConsGold, in turn, use the proceeds to buy Newmont common stock on the open market. But that would have required that Newmont's board was satisfied the Gold Fields subsidiary was worth that much, and there wasn't time to do the due diligence. The large dividend became the more attractive option.

Newmont told shareholders that "it had been a major and necessary precondition to the Board's approval of the $33 dividend that Consolidated Gold Fields reenter a meaningful new standstill, lest the dividend serve only to fund an Ivanhoe-Gold Fields tug-of-war over the rest of Newmont."[29] The amended agreement limiting ConsGold to less than 50 percent of Newmont but allowing it a third board seat was reached during a fifteen-minute break in the board meeting on Sunday, September 20. At 7:50 P.M. Parker reconvened the meeting. Agnew and Plumbridge were readmitted to the room and cast their votes for the special dividend, giving Consolidated Gold Fields $1.1 billion.[30]

Malozemoff, who earned $660,000 in his final year as CEO and retired with 52,000 shares of stock, was still having heartburn over being forced out by ConsGold and did not like the way the takeover fight seemed to be playing into the British company's hands. In the heat of the battle, he decided to visit Burt, who had retired to Tucson. The stock was trading at about $96 at the time. "I met him at the airport and he asked, 'What are you going to do with your Newmont stock?'" Burt recalls his former boss inquiring. "I said, 'I'm going to sell a bunch of it.' He said, 'I think I will, too.' We got to the house and he called his broker. Then we went for a swim."[31]

11

GOING CRAZY

The battle with Boone Pickens and subsequent market crash left Newmont Mining in a desperate financial position. At year-end 1987, the company had a negative net worth of nearly $500 million, was saddled with a record $1.9 billion in debt, and had committed $450 million (which later became $500 million) to accelerate production in Nevada. Paying down debt became an all-encompassing focus.

Within a year, $1 billion was raised from the sale of the company's oil operations, its DuPont stock, its interests in southern Africa and Canada, and its remaining stock in Foote Mineral. With rising copper prices, Magma Copper turned profitable in 1988 for the first time in seven years, and Newmont was able to sell its remaining 15 percent interest for $190 million in a leveraged buyout backed by the venture capital firm WarburgPincus. (In 1996, Australia's BHP acquired Magma for $2.4 billion, only to shutter operations three years later when copper prices again tumbled. By the time it closed in July 1999, San Manuel had mined 703 million tons of ore, a world record for an underground mine.)

In a significant move for a gold producer, Newmont in February 1988 entered into a syndicated gold loan, a type of hedge. One million ounces of gold were borrowed from financial institutions led by the Bank of Nova Scotia and sold immediately for $449 an ounce, to be repaid from production over the next four years. At the time, it was the largest gold loan ever made.

The intent was to balance the company's risk profile. "Up until then, Newmont had a very conservative balance sheet with little debt. They basically took the operating risk and eschewed the financial risk," explains Paul Maroni, then treasurer. But after borrowing heavily to defeat Pickens, "we recognized we had taken on substantially more financial risk and needed to reduce our operating risk. That's when we started selling gold forward and did the gold loan and some gold swaps."[1] Additionally, because of gold's perceived monetary value, the transaction reduced interest costs to only 2 percent versus 9 percent on the company's dollar-denominated debt.

Chief financial officer Ed Fontaine saw yet another plus to hedging. While CEO Gordon Parker was nearly always bullish on gold, Fontaine was one of the company's few bears. Gold, he felt, was too cyclical and its price movements too irrational to support a long-term corporate strategy. Thus, when the gold market was hot, he was willing to sell the metal short. As it turned out, the company's timing was deft. Gold soon entered a down cycle and Newmont closed out the loan in early 1992 with a forward purchase of the metal at $335 an ounce. In all, the transaction added $85 million to pre-tax profits while saving as much as $25 million a year in interest. Gold bugs, however, blamed Newmont's hedging for depressing the gold price.[2]

In Nevada, Peter Philip, president of Newmont Gold, unleashed a tornado of activity to develop new properties, build new mills, and accelerate production. "That's when everything went crazy," says Tom Enos, who in 1988 had spent seventeen years climbing the management ladder at Carlin. "It was, 'We've got to make how many ounces?' Nobody had ever produced that many ounces, ever. We built Mill No. 3, Mill No. 4, and Mill No. 5, just boom, boom, boom."[3]

Philip credits Bechtel with much of the company's success. "They are the people who could really act fast and get involved very quickly. We depended on them and used a lot of their experience other than just design." Bechtel built Mill No. 1 at Carlin in 1964 and had just completed Mill No. 2 at Gold Quarry. Mill No. 3 at Rain was a version of Mill No. 1, while Mill No. 4 at Genesis and Mill No. 5 at Gold Quarry were nearly carbon copies of Mill No. 2. "It was quicker to leave the drawings just as they were and say, 'Build it just like that,'" says Philip. He shrugs off hindsight that Mill No. 4 was unnecessary. "We took shortcuts, but it was important to take shortcuts. We had gone to the market and told them what we could do and now we had to make it happen. Number two, we didn't know how long this gold boom was going to last. It had already peaked and was coming down. Every day you lost you had a lower gold price. If we had gone slower, we might have done finer engineering or maybe made better estimates on the capital side, but we would have lost time and time was terribly important."[4]

Philip had vision and a reputation for empowering people to let them grow. "He knew what he was talking about and was very good at what

11.1. T. Peter Philip was brought in from South Africa to put the Carlin gold operations on a fast track. He later became Newmont's president. (*Newmont Archives*)

he did,"[5] says W. James Mullin, who moved to Carlin in 1989 following the closure of the Similkameen copper operation in Canada, where he had been general manager. But Philip was also feisty and thrived on chaos—a "bantam rooster" in Mullin's view. His team consisted of Eric Hamer, who started at O'okiep in South Africa; Walter Lawrence, who had been at Dawn, Idarado, and Magma; and Ken Brunk, who began his career at the research laboratory in Danbury. All three were metallurgists, very bright, strong-willed, and regularly engaged in heated turf battles. (Lawrence, Hamer, and Mullin later became senior vice presidents of operations.) When Robert Zerga, whom Philip had brought in as general manager from Magma, told him, "You have a bunch of cutthroat sons of bitches out there and you're fostering it. The infighting is absolutely terrible," he said Philip laughingly replied, "The strong will survive."[6]

Yet it was an exhilarating time. Between 1985 and 1989, nine new deposits were added to reserves, which rose to nearly 21 million ounces. Gold production jumped by a million ounces a year from 475,000 in 1986 to 1,468,000 in 1989, making Newmont the largest gold producer in North America. Everything was bigger. At Gold Quarry alone, 450 drill holes were blasted every day to access the ore. Giant shovels moved 1,000 tons of rock an hour, and a fleet of 38 haul trucks carrying 120 to 140 tons each operated twenty-four hours a day. The company's five mills processed 13 million tons of ore in 1989 and produced 890,000 ounces of gold. But the key to the operation's success came from squeezing another 578,000 ounces from 30 million tons of low-grade ore that was heap leached. Including 90 million tons of overburden removed to reach the ore, the operation moved more than 130 million tons of material during the year, or nearly 90 tons for each ounce of gold sold.

New technology was entering the picture. The old countercurrent decantation method of gold recovery used in the carbon-in-pulp circuit at Mill No. 1 was replaced with more efficient carbon-in-leach circuits at Mill No. 2, Mill No. 4, and Mill No. 5. Although the recovery rate for heap leaching was only 70 percent versus 85 percent for milling, the company was proving the feasibility of extracting gold from ores containing as little as 0.02 ounce per ton—and doing it on a massive scale. Computers were becoming available to handle the vast flow of information from drill data to ore control and inventory management. And environmental protection was improving with better monitoring, heavier leach pad liners, more controls, and better understanding and training to impress upon everyone their personal responsibility for compliance.

In an industry first, Brunk designed an automated, robotic assay laboratory at Carlin that was able to conduct over two million fire and chemical

11.2. After Pickens, everything became super-sized to meet promised production goals. Haul trucks quadrupled in size and could carry 140 tons of ore. Ten years later, Carlin was using 240-ton trucks like the one shown here. (*Joel Grimes*)

11.3. High explosives fragment rock for removal from the pit. The holes in a grid pattern on the right await the injection of explosives for the next blast. Samples from each drill hole are tested to separate waste from ore and to understand the metallurgy of the ore for processing. (*Jack Morris*)

assays a year with just a handful of people. Opened in 1989, the lab cut assaying costs by two-thirds to $3 a sample and gave the company better and faster information on where to mine and how to process ore across its thirty-one-mile stretch of mines. Coupled with a computerized dispatch system that kept trucks rolling to the proper site—mill, leach pad, refractory stockpile, or waste dump—while minimizing waiting time at the shovels, Newmont had one of the most automated mining operations in the world.

While the original Carlin discovery was based on fundamental geology and geochemistry, the newer deposits were located with the help of geophysics. Regional gravity studies and "the introduction of airborne mapping techniques, which were not new to the industry, but which we made affordable by putting them on lightweight helicopters . . . put the geology in perspective so that Newmont could realize the potential of the Carlin Trend,"[7] says Colin Barnett, who became Newmont's director of geophysics in 1989. Over the next five years, Barnett's group ran 62,500 miles of aerial surveys in Nevada.

The science of geostatistics, while dating from the 1940s, was also gaining new importance with Newmont as its leading advocate. Based on statistical analysis of sample data and heavily dependent on computers, geostatistics allows geologists and mining engineers to understand the characteristics of a mineral deposit from the location of mineralization to tonnage, grade, and recoverability. Based on the deceptively simple premise developed by South African mining engineer Danie Krige that gold values in a deposit are more likely to be similar if the samples are taken close to each other than if taken farther apart, geostatistics relies on equations to quantify this similarity and to create computerized block models of gold values in a deposit. Evaluating these blocks is called kriging. With large mines and complicated geology, kriging has become an essential tool for deposit modeling, mine planning, project evaluation, and operations. It is a system Newmont wished it had employed when evaluating the first drill results at Gold Quarry.

Jean-Michel Rendu, who retired in 2001 as vice president of resources and mine planning, worked with Dr. Krige and later taught geostatistics at the University of Wisconsin before joining Newmont in 1984. As part of the first public offering of Newmont Gold stock in 1986, Rendu was assigned an unusual task: convincing the SEC that the reserve numbers he had calculated for Gold Quarry were correct. It was the first time the SEC had reviewed a low-grade gold mine and the first time they had encountered reserves based on statistical analysis. Despite some skepticism, the agency not only accepted Rendu's methodology but has used it as the standard for reserve reporting for the gold industry ever since. Rendu was given the Daniel C. Jackling Award by the Society for Mining, Metallurgy and Exploration in 1994 for his work in the field.

Scott Barr, who retired in 2008 as vice president and chief technical officer, credits Rendu with establishing a discipline that allows the company to consistently "achieve ore reserve reliability of plus or minus 5 percent. That's tremendous. Most companies would be happy to come within 20 percent."[8]

The Carlin workforce, which had risen fourfold with the start-up of Gold Quarry, soared to nearly 2,500 by the time both Mill No. 4 and Mill No. 5 were operating in 1989. An additional fifty-five geologists and technical people worked for Newmont Exploration Limited, while during construction Bechtel and other contractors had as many as 800 workers on-site. The turnover rate, however, was "absolutely deplorable—27 percent a year," says Mullin. "We were losing 600 to 700 people a year," half of whom were fired. "The problem was that we needed so many bodies that if you could walk and talk we hired you."

With other mines opening and expanding, Elko became the fastest-growing city in America. Its population surged 21 percent in a single month in 1986. Mining wages averaged $44,000 a year, turning the Carlin Trend into a magnet for people looking to better their lives. "They pull in here with a car packed down with belongings, but no money. It's like the 1920s during the dust bowl," a community services director told the *Reno Gazette-Journal*.[9]

Of necessity, Newmont found itself in the housing business. To relieve a critical shortage, the company invested nearly $30 million to build 250 homes and 400 apartment units, open 110 lots for mobile homes, and provide dormitory space for 430 construction workers. The homes were later sold or rented to employees. To help relieve a tax imbalance caused by the fact that its mines were in Eureka County, while the population influx was overcrowding schools and facilities in Elko County, Newmont donated more than $7 million over a five-year period to Elko schools and institutions and spent $4 million more for job-training programs for everything from heavy machinery operators to craftsmen and laboratory technicians at Northern Nevada Community College.

As it raced to build facilities and bring on new production, the company found itself in a steeplechase both on the Carlin Trend and on Wall Street with an upstart Toronto mining company, American Barrick Resources. Created in 1983 by Toronto entrepreneur Peter Munk and backed in part by Saudi businessman Adnan Khashoggi, Barrick had acquired a couple of small gold mines in Canada and the United States. In early 1987, it purchased the Goldstrike property from Western States and PanCana Minerals. Joseph Rotman of PanCana was a Barrick director and persuaded Munk to send his operations manager, Bob Smith, a respected and well-liked mining engineer, to Carlin to take a look at Goldstrike.

Unable to make its shoestring operation profitable, Western States had thrown in the towel a year earlier. At the time it was producing 40,000 ounces of gold a year and had about 625,000 ounces in reserves. Offered a chance to bid, Newmont sent geologist Galen Knutsen to recheck drill hole data in the area "to see if there was any pickup of grade or rock alteration at depth, or anything else to justify deeper drilling."[10] Nothing was found and Newmont offered only a minimal bid based on the nuisance value of getting Western States out of the way. Besides, says Carmen Fimiani, the operations vice president at Carlin at the time, the 6,800-acre Goldstrike property was surrounded by Newmont land—the Post deposit on one side and the T/S Ranch on the other three—and the company felt it could prevent anyone else from mining the property by denying access or the right to lay back on Newmont land.[11] (To mine deep ores from an open pit on tightly confined land, the pit walls would have to extend onto Newmont property.)

Jaws dropped when Barrick paid $65 million for Goldstrike. "I remember hearing our people chuckling and saying, 'Can you believe what those crazy Canadians paid for that property?'"[12] recalls Parker. Jaws dropped again two months later, in March 1987, when Barrick announced the discovery of the Deep Post deposit. By drilling nearly 2,000 feet deep it had hit 620 feet of ore grading a third of an ounce per ton.

Advising Barrick on that hole was none other than Ralph Roberts, the retired U.S. Geological Service geologist whose theory of ore placement in Nevada had led John Livermore to the original Carlin discovery twenty-five years earlier. Brought to Goldstrike by Rotman, he looked at the same data Knutsen and others had reviewed but saw things differently, predicting that the property had the potential for a world-class deposit at depth.[13] Rotman pressed Western States to start drilling deeper, and between the time of Newmont's token bid and Barrick's riverboat gamble, it put down a 1,000-foot hole and found high-grade ore. Thus by the time he laid down his chips, Munk had already taken a peek at the winning card.

Shortly after Deep Post, Barrick discovered the Betze deposit, 3,000 feet to the west. That hole, which also went below 1,000 feet, found 200 feet of ore grading half an ounce per ton. At the time, Barrick credited the discovery to the first use of Induced Polarization (IP), technology on the Carlin Trend.[14] IP, which involves monitoring the discharge of electrical current applied to the surface of suspected ore bodies, had been developed by Newmont's Arthur Brant in the early 1950s. Industry chatter at the time chided Newmont for not having made more use of its own technology in finding deep deposits at Carlin. In a recent technical paper, however, Barrick's Keith Bettles acknowledges that their IP work had produced "chargeability anomalies unrelated to gold mineralization," and that the Betze discovery resulted from "a combination of the IP-resistivity data, geology, geochemistry and mineralization detected in prior shallow drilling."[15]

It should be remembered that Newmont's exploration focus at the time was on near-surface oxide ores, while IP works best with deeper sulfide ores. "There were anomalies everywhere and IP didn't appear to be a useful discriminating tool. So we put more energy into things like gravity and airborne magnetics, which I think helped more to unravel the picture and guide exploration on the Trend," says Barnett. "Newmont, with a large land package, was continuing to explore outward looking for these cheap oxides, while Barrick, because of their restricted land position, had fewer lateral distractions and only one direction to explore, which was down. They were the first to realize the deep potential [of the Carlin Trend], but I don't think you can credit IP for it."[16]

Another set of Toronto gunslingers also placed their bet on Goldstrike in 1986 and shared handsomely in its later success. The two were Pierre Lassonde and Seymour Schulich, partners in Beutel, Goodman, a Toronto merchant bank that invested in oil, gas, and mining companies primarily in Canada. In 1982, they formed a minerals exploration company, Franco-

Nevada, and raised $2 million through the sale of stock. Between deals, they found themselves drawn to the poker tables of Reno and ski runs at Lake Tahoe. "We once came close to buying a bordello up near Lovelock and were going to list it in Vancouver just as a gag," says Schulich. "One of our mantras was to have fun."[17]

But they were also shrewd businessmen and in 1986 began buying up royalty properties in known mineral belts. Royalties had been a common means of investing in oil and gas properties for decades. "The royalty formula is that you have land and other people spend a lot of money exploring on it and if they find anything you get a percentage of it. We were the first to go around and buy [mining] leases and buy out prospectors and start a business," says Schulich. Adds Lassonde, "The reason we wanted to be in Nevada is that Behre Dolbear [a mining consulting firm] had just done a twenty-five-year study of the exploration business and found that the cheapest place in the world to find gold was Nevada. And the Carlin Trend was the cheapest place to find gold in Nevada. So that's where we wanted to be."[18]

A consulting geologist called Franco's attention to an ad in the *Reno Gazette-Journal*. Intra American Oil and Gas Company, a small Houston exploration outfit, was selling two royalties it held on the Goldstrike property—a net smelter royalty paying 4 percent on all gold sold and a net profit interest that paid 5 percent after deducting production costs. Intra American had staked the Goldstrike property twenty years earlier and then farmed it out to PanCana Minerals. But the royalties were not earning much and the company had a $2 million bank loan that was being called.

Lassonde flew in to take a look. The operation, managed by Western States, was shabby, but what impressed Lassonde was that Newmont the previous fall had drilled the first hole below 300 feet on the Carlin Trend at Genesis, less than two miles from the Post-Goldstrike border, and found high-grade ore. Familiar with underground gold mines in Canada, Lassonde says, "I looked at the rock package and saw everything was dipping to the north and figured we would catch some of it and that the lease would be worth about five times the $2 million we were going to pay for it. So I called Seymour and said, 'I got good news and I got bad news.' He said, 'Give me the good news.' I said, 'We've just bought our first royalty and I think we are going to make five times our money.' 'Great, fabulous. Now what's the bad news?' I said, 'We've got no more money.'" Franco-Nevada had invested its entire treasury in Goldstrike.

Newmont remained skeptical as additional holes at Goldstrike confirmed Roberts's and Lassonde's predictions and Barrick's stock jumped twelvefold on the Toronto Stock Exchange. "Barrick grew up before our very eyes," says Parker. "There was nothing one day and the next day there was this little thing and then it was 10 percent bigger. It just grew and grew. Whenever my technical folks looked at it they thought Barrick was on the edge of disaster. They were running by the seat of their pants. We thought it might fail and we could pick up the pieces. But it did not happen."

For years, a popular game among gold company executives and mining analysts was to find the donkey on which to pin the tail for Newmont's failure to leverage its strength at Carlin to win the Goldstrike and Gold Quarry prizes. Today, with hindsight, some who were present at the time offer their perspective. Retired exploration vice president Richard Ellett says that for years, "The Carlin staff was preoccupied with the development of the Carlin mine and did not pay sufficient attention to the rising gold price and its effect upon lower grade prospects."[19] To explain why the company's drilling had only scratched the surface, Fimiani compares exploration with religion. "Dogma creeps in and suddenly dogma becomes the guiding principle for the exploration project. Curiosity goes out the window." Retired chief geologist Odin Christensen credits Barrick's success to the creative thinking of its geologists supported by an aggressive exploration budget in contrast to Newmont's more frugal mind-set, both onsite and in New York.[20]

Retired vice chairman Richard Leather thinks Newmont, with a long history, a full agenda outside Carlin, and thousands of shareholders to satisfy, was appropriately conservative but lost out when pitted against upstart risk takers like Munk and Lassonde. At the same time, he adds, "We did a miserable job of assessing what we had at Carlin. There was an inadequate amount of pressure on the exploration people and on the Carlin people. It took the coercive attack by Pickens to make people realize" Carlin's potential and then to develop it.[21] He and others also fault the company for not acquiring Barrick once Goldstrike proved to be a success.

No doubt Newmont's "we're the big boy on the block" attitude also was a factor. With its new focus on gold and its quick success in ramping up production after Pickens, Newmont became insular and dismissive of outside ideas, once the lifeblood of its exploration effort. While fiercely competitive, management viewed many smaller companies, especially Canadian juniors, as inebriated on their own hype. They, in turn, viewed Parker and Philip, South African to the core, as arrogant and the company as "the evil empire." Reinforcing that impression was the fact that the company's principal interface with the public, communications vice president Jim Hill, viewed most media or analyst inquiries as incoming missiles to be attacked at the source.

Once stood up by Parker and Philip after a scheduled meeting to discuss a possible joint venture, Lassonde flew back to Toronto vowing "never to bother dealing with those people again." However, by 2004, as Newmont's president, Lassonde could say, "Today, I look at the organization and I am so proud of it. It's turned 180 degrees."

Newmont did not begin deep drilling on the Carlin Trend until late 1987. Its first announcement, in January 1988, was eye-popping—a hole into the Post deposit had intersected 470 feet of ore grading 0.93 ounce per ton. Philip called it "the richest assay over such a long intersection in the history of gold exploration."[22] Drilling by Newmont and Barrick quickly proved up nine million ounces of reserves at Betze-Post, half of it on Newmont's side of the line. While Philip and Barrick's Smith sought ways to accommodate each other's operations, others at Newmont were not as neighborly. For some time, until a joint operating agreement could be reached, Newmont leveraged its land lock over the property by requiring Barrick to mine and deliver Newmont's share of the ore to Mill No. 4 for free in order to access its own reserves.

The flurry of activity in Nevada brought the new gold rush into American living rooms as newspapers, magazines, and TV shows reported amazement at the size and scope of modern mining in comparison with the shovel and pan days of the forty-niners. In a *20/20* program on ABC in 1989, Barbara Walters stated what most of her audience probably believed: "I didn't even know there was any gold left to mine" in the United States.[23] Lynn Sherr, who did the on-camera reporting bedecked in large gold earrings, necklace, and rings, expressed shock that companies would dig large pits and use cyanide to extract gold, whose primary end use is jewelry. Environmental

11.4. Drilling for deeper ore deposits near the Post mine on the Carlin Trend. (*Newmont Archives*)

activists and anti-mining critics, who had also grown as mining expanded, were given ample airtime as pictures of unrelated disasters elsewhere were commingled with shots of Newmont's activities in an effort to paint all miners with the same dirty brush.

Senator Dale Bumpers of Arkansas pressed for higher royalties for mining on federal land. Labeling the 1872 mining law a "license to steal," he claimed that profits in gold mining were going not to the American people who owned the land but to foreign companies. Sherr referred to Newmont as having "British and South African ownership." It didn't help that the three people assigned to escort her around the mine had pronounced foreign accents: Philip and two others who came to Carlin by way of South Africa; Hamer, from Wales; and Leendert Krol, a Dutch geologist.[24]

The central theme of the *20/20* program—the need for increased government regulation—was reinforced by repeated references to cyanide as poison. Sherr also suggested that the company refill the Gold Quarry pit, which was projected to reach a mile wide, a mile long, and half a mile deep. (Today, it is 1.9 by 1.4 miles and 1,500 feet deep.) "This must be the largest man-made destruction ever seen," Krol recalls her saying. "Oh, no," he replied. "That would be New York City. It is a much larger area that has been destroyed from its original beauty."[25] That conversation, unfortunately, was off camera.

12

GRIEF

Returning to their offices on the thirty-sixth floor of the Pan Am (now Met Life) Building after the 1988 Labor Day holiday, Newmont employees received shocking news—the company was moving its corporate headquarters to Denver, Colorado. New York had been Newmont's home since its founding by William Boyce Thompson nearly three-quarters of a century earlier and the company's worldview was New York centered. Many of the nation's largest mining companies were located in midtown Manhattan, executives regularly exchanged views at the city's two mining clubs, and law firms and investment bankers specializing in mining were only a short walk or taxi ride away.

Few in the company had ever been to Denver, and to some the prospect invoked images of a cow town where people ate lunch at diners instead of white tablecloth restaurants. In the end, not all made the move; CFO Ed Fontaine joined the Rockefeller Foundation. The company looked at other locations—Tucson, Salt Lake City, and Reno. It took CEO Gordon Parker only a five-minute drive past the casinos of downtown Reno, where a large sign welcomes visitors to "The Biggest Little City in the World," to beat a hasty return to the airport and the next flight out of town. Denver had deep mining roots, was home to several gold companies and consulting groups, and was next door to the Colorado School of Mines at Golden. Additionally, a new international airport announced shortly after Newmont's decision greatly facilitated its growth.

The move was billed as an opportunity to consolidate offices from Danbury to Tucson in one location closer to Carlin and as a means of reducing overhead expense (although much of that benefit evaporated when asbestos was found in the Pan Am suite, making it difficult to sublease the space). But Parker had a deeper, more compelling motive. "There was a need for a total shake-up within Newmont. Everyone needed to know that a fat, dumb, possibly arrogant Newmont had no future. We had committed our-

12.1. A strategic planning meeting in Tucson in April 1988 was led by Harvard professor Robert Reich (far left, second row), who later become secretary of labor under President Clinton. In the front row are Peter Philip, president, Carlin operations; John Parry, senior vice president, exploration; Gordon Parker, CEO; Edward Fontaine, senior vice president, finance; and Richard Leather, vice chairman and general counsel. (*Newmont Archives*)

selves to do all sorts of things . . . and I thought the only way it would happen was to turn the company upside down. We came to Denver not because of the mountains or skiing or to save a buck, but to change the culture of the company."[1]

Parker tells two stories that are revealing as to his mind-set and to his ability, at least after the fact, not to take himself too seriously. Shortly after the move was announced, he was visited by Phil Anchutz, Denver's leading billionaire with interests in oil, gas, and railroads and later the founder of Qwest Communications. Denver was in the throes of an energy slump and his downtown Arco Building was largely vacant. If Newmont was interested in leasing 70,000 square feet, he would gladly rename it the Newmont Tower. "Well that just cooks the deal," Parker says he replied. After Pickens, he had had enough notoriety. "There is no way we want our name on a building. Ever. We just want to sneak into town quietly and go about our business," he says he told a startled Anchutz.

On the home front, he had just moved into a new house in Connecticut, which his wife, Pam, was busily decorating. Rather than upset her, he waited until their children came home for Thanksgiving to break the news of the move. The moving van was only weeks away. If one must put up with grief, he told friends, it's better to do it for a few weeks than for three months.

If grief was what Parker wanted to avoid, the wake-up call came at 3 A.M. on Thursday, September 21. The man who roused him from his sleep was Hank Slack, Harry Oppenheimer's son-in-law and head of U.S. operations for a little-known holding company called Minorco. Calling from London where he and his associates had spent the night arranging financing and looking over legal papers, Slack announced that Minorco was launching a tender offer for Consolidated Gold Fields, the holder of 49.7 percent of Newmont's stock. Could he count on Newmont's support? Timing is everything and at that hour of the morning, Parker cursed and hung up.[2]

Minorco was the investment arm of the great Oppenheimer empire and its bid for ConsGold was part of a long-smoldering effort to move its asset base and earnings power out of South Africa. In 1981, the empire's two big powerhouses, Anglo American and De Beers, had staged a "dawn raid" on ConsGold, buying up 30 percent of its shares on the London Stock Exchange. It was the transfer of that stock to Minorco that first alerted Plato Malozemoff that Oppenheimer was on the prowl. ConsGold and Minorco considered merging in 1986, but that didn't work out, and now Minorco was pursuing its goal as a hostile suitor.

Like kissing cousins, the Oppenheimer corporate family was more than a little incestuous. Anglo, in 1988 the world's largest gold producer, and De Beers, the world's largest diamond mining and marketing organization, each owned more than a third of each other and together with the Oppenheimer family owned 67 percent of Minorco. While ConsGold held a 48 percent interest in Gold Fields of South Africa (GFSA), the world's second largest gold producer, Anglo had another 11 percent. Among Minorco's holdings were sizable positions in Engelhard Minerals and Johnson Matthey, two of the largest refiners of precious metals with major interests in platinum, and the company had just added $1.4 billion to its bank account

12.2. Harry Oppenheimer of South Africa, a longtime Newmont friend, became its adversary in 1988 when his investment unit, Minorco, sought a hostile takeover of Consolidated Gold Fields (ConsGold), Newmont's largest shareholder. (*William Campbell/Sygma/Corbis*)

from the sale of its interest in Salomon Brothers, the big New York investment banker. As the battle for ConsGold was taking shape, Julian Ogilvie Thompson, or JOT as he was known within the empire, was chairman of both De Beers and Minorco and deputy chairman of Anglo American.

Newmont had been a founding shareholder of both Anglo American and Minorco. The latter, originally known as Rhodesian Anglo American, was organized in Britain in 1928. Newmont remained a shareholder until 1951. As the independence movement rolled across Africa in the 1960s, Northern Rhodesia became Zambia, whose new president, Kenneth Kaunda, nationalized the country's copper mines, including those operated by RhoAnglo. In 1970, RhoAnglo moved to Bermuda and changed its name to Minerals and Resources Corporation, or Minorco. Shortly before its raid on ConsGold, Minorco moved again, this time to the tiny tax haven of Luxembourg. Anglo American was legally based in an even smaller and more secretive tax haven, Liechtenstein. But the strings for all of the operations were pulled from Anglo and Oppenheimer offices in Johannesburg.

In the Afrikaans language, apartheid means separateness or separate existence. Official apartheid, adopted by the South African government in 1948, established a rigorous system of racial separation that imposed limits on where blacks could live and travel, what they could be taught, and where they could be employed. These laws were superimposed on an already entrenched system of white supremacy and minority rule. The whole system was repugnant to most of the civilized world and by the mid-1980s pressure was mounting on South Africa by governments in Europe and North America. In 1986, the U.S. Congress imposed stiff sanctions: a ban on most imports and exports; a prohibition against financial transactions including loans or investments by U.S. companies in South African ventures; and cutting off direct air transportation between the two countries.

Caught in this vortex, Anglo American saw its foreign shareholder base evaporate while the limited investment pool in South Africa could not support its global reach. It desperately hoped that Minorco, Luxembourg, and Liechtenstein would provide sufficient cover to allow at least a partial escape through the acquisition of London-based Consolidated Gold Fields.

ConsGold and its feisty CEO, Sir Rudolph Agnew, quickly realized that the company, which had just celebrated its one hundredth anniversary, stood a better chance of defeating the Oppenheimers on a political battlefield than a purely financial one. Agnew labeled Minorco a Luxembourg shell and a front for South Africa. In one of the many pithy one-liners that characterized the ensuing battle, he told the British press, "You can deny your bastard sons; you can't deny your parents."[3]

Newmont was dead set against Minorco's move and supported its largest shareholder by joining in a lawsuit in the U.S. District Court in New York. Not only had ConsGold stood by Newmont in its fight against Pickens, but Newmont could see real peril to its own interests if control of its stock fell into South African hands. The standstill agreement it had signed with ConsGold in 1987 prevented Minorco from acquiring a majority interest, but public perception might not notice. Newmont had faced its own attacks by anti-apartheid forces for more than a decade and only six months earlier sold its South African holdings to GFSA, which took over Tsumeb and

12.3. Pictured at the Gold Quarry mine in Nevada, Rudolph Agnew (left), CEO of London-based ConsGold, Newmont's largest shareholder, joined forces with Newmont CEO Gordon Parker in 1988 to defeat an attack by Oppenheimer's Minorco. (*Ray Manley*)

O'okiep, and Anglo and De Beers, which jointly acquired Newmont's position in Palabora. The last thing Newmont wanted was to be dragged back into the contentious struggle over South African entitlements.

The company's biggest fear concerned Peabody Coal. In its effort to recast the company from a multi-metal mining conglomerate into a more focused enterprise, Newmont had finally settled on a two-pronged strategy. It was going to be a gold producer, but with a coal "kicker," Parker told investors.[4] Now Parker and Richard Leather, who became vice chairman in 1988, were paranoid that if Minorco became Newmont's largest share-holder, anti-apartheid forces would bring unrelenting pressure against the state regulatory commissions that had to approve Peabody's contracts with electric utilities.

Minorco's opening bid of £13.06 in cash and stock represented a 20 percent premium over ConsGold's stock price, which was already inflated by takeover speculation. Over the next seven months, as legal battles ensued on both sides of the Atlantic, the offer was twice increased. The final bid of £15.50 per share valued ConsGold at nearly £3.5 billion, or $6 billion, the largest takeover bid in British history. When the tender offer closed on April 26, 1989, Minorco had won control of 55 percent of ConsGold's stock, but that included the 30 percent it already held.

Enticing shareholders was one thing; fending off anti-trust charges that the merger would put 32 percent of the world's gold production in Anglo's hands was quite another. In addition to its interests in GFSA and New-mont, ConsGold had a U.S. mining division that had discovered gold at Mesquite, near El Centro in southern California, and at Chimney Creek, a hundred miles west of Carlin in Nevada. To clear the anti-trust hurdle, Minorco promised to "hold separate" ConsGold's interest in GFSA and Newmont until they could be sold. It went so far as to seek bids for New-mont from American Barrick and Placer Dome, at the time Canada's larg-est gold producer. With that and other arguments, Minorco eventually won universal regulatory approval—from the British Monopolies and Mergers Commission, the Competition Board of South Africa, the European Com-mission, the U.S. Federal Trade Commission, and the U.S. Justice Depart-ment. But the one hurdle it could not clear was the lawsuit in the U.S. Dis-trict Court in New York. Judge Michael Mukasey had issued a preliminary injunction against the merger in October, and Minorco made the lifting of that ban a condition of its offer.

The *Wall Street Journal* joined the financial press in London in attacking the U.S. court for presuming to have jurisdiction in a legal dispute between two foreign registered entities over a merger that had won regulatory ap-proval on three continents. Less than 5 percent of ConsGold's stock traded in the United States and there was virtually no trading in Minorco's. But Leather and outside counsel Richard Howell at White & Case argued that

Newmont's interests weren't to be trifled with; it couldn't just be assigned a box on someone's organizational chart and then left to suffer the consequences.

Minorco claimed it was independent and not controlled by Anglo American. ConsGold and Newmont countered that Anglo was "secretive, authoritarian and centralized."[5] In the end, the veil of secrecy was pierced by Oppenheimer's desire to be decent. During the heat of the battle, Thompson, Minorco's chairman, told Agnew that whatever the outcome, he would be "looked after." Agnew had learned that Oppenheimer's key lieutenants, including the directors of Minorco, were paid not by the company but from a separate Oppenheimer bank account in Switzerland.[6] A similar message was delivered to Newmont by George Ames, a partner in Lazard Frères, Oppenheimer's agent in New York. Known on Wall Street as "Georgie Porgie," Ames told Fontaine that Newmont's officers "don't have to worry," should Minorco prevail. How could such messages be delivered if Minorco was truly independent? "It was the petard that hoisted the whole Anglo deal," Leather avers.[7]

With the deadline on the tender offer quickly approaching, on April 17 Judge Mukasey made his temporary injunction permanent. Minorco, he ruled, could not be trusted to abide by its "hold separate" promise regarding Newmont and GFSA. The Oppenheimer web of companies was just too tangled and with South African laws encouraging companies to conceal the source of their overseas investments to avoid an anti-apartheid backlash, there were incentives to cheat. If the Newmont and GFSA shares were simply passed from Minorco to another Anglo affiliate, the anti-competitive issue would remain. "I have every reason to be concerned that the order (lifting the injunction) might be undermined by an Anglo group affiliate over which this court has no control," Mukasey wrote.[8] Pressed by Minorco for a rehearing, Mukasey declined on May 16. (In November 2007, Mukasey was named U.S. attorney general by President George W. Bush.)

Lurking behind the counsel tables in all of the U.S. court proceedings was a four-hundred-pound gorilla—the De Beers diamond cartel, which controlled 80 percent of the world's sparkling stones. Three times since 1945 the U.S. Justice Department had filed anti-trust charges against De Beers and a 1974 grand jury indictment for price-fixing had never been answered in court. Anglo and Thompson, chairman of both De Beers and Minorco, had signed the "hold separate" agreement that was at the center of Judge Mukasey's ruling. Yet neither had stepped foot in his courtroom to back that commitment, nor would they with the 1974 indictment outstanding. One could take Minorco out of South Africa but not South Africa out of Minorco.

The *Financial Times* called ConsGold's success an "inglorious victory."[9] In fact, there was little room for celebrating in any quarter as ConsGold's stock fell to £12.58. Minorco wanted out, immediately. On May 17, 1989, a day after the court's final ruling, Minorco CEO Sir Michael Edwardes, who had been brought in by the Oppenheimers specifically to run the campaign and who was detested by everyone at ConsGold and Newmont, placed a phone call that would end Agnew's career and give Parker even more grief than he had encountered in the previous two years. The call went to Lord James Hanson, who with Sir Gordon White had assembled Hanson PLC as Britain's largest conglomerate.[10]

Hanson held positions in chemicals, bricks, tobacco, and beer and in the United States owned companies that made industrial cranes, Jacuzzi whirlpools, cement, and garden tools. At the time of Edwardes's call, Hanson PLC had sales of £8 billion, profits of nearly £1 billion, and a market capitalization of £8.5 billion ($14.5 billion). It was flush with cash. Hanson, sixty-seven, and White, who had moved to the United States, were not just buyers of property but shrewd break-up artists who disassembled the companies they acquired, often selling off the pieces at fat profits. They had done so many deals that they were known in Wall Street investment circles as "the two lords a leaping," and because of their lifestyles—Hanson's pursuit of Hollywood stars including Audrey Hepburn had been widely publicized—as the "swinging lords."[11]

Minorco quickly accepted Hanson's offer of £14.30 a share for its 30 percent interest in ConsGold. Negotiations with Agnew took a little longer, but on July 4, while attending a company party at the London Zoo, Agnew accepted a sweetened Hanson offer of £15.50 for the remaining ConsGold shares. While some have said that Agnew capitulated so quickly because he was exhausted after his eight-month battle with Minorco, he denies it. First, he and Parker knew they could not press the same anti-trust charges against Hanson in the U.S. courts that they had levied against the Oppenheimers. Second, Agnew says, Hanson had 30 percent of his company's stock and another 25 percent had voted for change by accepting the previous offer at the same price. But most important, "The Hanson offer was much better. Hanson offered all cash, while Minorco offered this dubious share."[12] During the Minorco fight, Agnew had derided the value of the thinly traded Minorco shares as "gamma stock" that would evaporate once the merger took place and the new shares flooded a nonexistent market.

(In 1999, Anglo acquired Minorco, becoming Anglo American PLC. Over the next several years it reorganized operations, selling off or consolidating its web of South African mining interests and acquiring other companies to become a mining powerhouse with offices in London and principal trading on the London Stock Exchange. AngloGold became its 67 percent–owned gold-mining subsidiary.)

Parker viewed his new shareholder, Hanson, with dismay. "There are very few large shareholdings that are good for any public company. They think primarily about their own investment and not the whole company," he says. Hanson had never been involved in gold or precious metals and seemed most interested in ARC, ConsGold's profitable crushed stone operation. "Unlike Gold Fields, we knew they weren't going to be longtime shareholders. I didn't want to wait for them, so I began contemplating ways of diluting them," Parker says. "A merger seemed to be a potential answer." This time it was Newmont that called on Placer Dome and Homestake, but again nothing happened. In the meantime, White pressed for faster action in reducing debt and for a turnaround in the stock price, which had fallen by half since 1987. "Do something, do something, do something," Parker says he was told.

On June 30, before Agnew accepted the Hanson offer, Newmont filed an elaborate refinancing scheme with the SEC. It had the Rube Goldberg look of an investment banker's late-night doodling. Newmont would issue $575 million in high-yield junk bonds, which it would use to buy out the other partners in Peabody. Peabody would then pay Newmont a $425 million dividend and Newmont would resell a fraction over 50 percent of the coal company to Salomon Brothers and Shearson Lehman Hutton, who were handling the financing, for $75 million. At the end of the day, Newmont would have an influx of cash to help pay down its debt, while Peabody would be saddled with as much debt as its heavy trucks could carry. Before the trigger could be pulled, however, a nationwide coal strike undermined investor confidence and the transaction was postponed. During a second attempt a few months later, the junk bond market, which Newmont had railed against when it financed Pickens's foray, collapsed in the wake of an SEC clean-up effort. The deal was abandoned, but only after the company acquired Equitable Life's 5 percent interest in Peabody for $57.5 million.

Still, Peabody represented about the only option Newmont had left to satisfy the Hanson demands, and in October, Newmont began negotiating the sale of Peabody to Hanson itself. In February 1990, Hanson announced that it was buying the 45 percent of Peabody held by Boeing, Bechtel, and Eastern Enterprises for $504 million and offered $715 million for Newmont's 55 percent. Convinced that the asset was worth more, Newmont solicited a competing bid from Amax, which Hanson then topped, buying the Peabody stake for $726 million on July 2.

After thirteen years, there was no longer a coal "kicker" to Newmont's strategy. But the sale also opened the door for Hanson to exit. "I think it was a Hanson condition for getting out of Newmont," says William Turner, who joined the Newmont board in 1988. "It wasn't expressed that way in a board meeting, but it was understood they would go quietly if they got Peabody."[13]

13

JIMMY

Driven by necessity, but aided by providence, Newmont Mining entered the 1990s as an entirely new company, one focused for the first time on a single commodity—gold—that was riding the crest of consumer demand and investor sentiment.

In his annual report for 1990, CEO Gordon Parker reported that "the world jewelry market has increased its gold usage by an estimated 65 percent since 1987 and in 1990 that market alone . . . consumed nearly 10 percent more gold than was produced by all the mines in the Western World." Propelling that growth were such factors as rising discretionary income in North America and Europe and good harvests and auspicious marriage seasons in India, the world's largest consumer of gold. In India, as in much of the less developed world, gold jewelry is considered a form of savings and even today the health of the gold market hangs heavily on the necks and arms of Indian brides who traditionally receive high-karat gold necklaces, rings, and bracelets as dowries.

Total world gold consumption in 1990 was 2,615 tonnes.[1] Jewelry accounted for 75 percent of that, with the balance fairly evenly split between other fabrication (electronics, dentistry, architecture, commemorative coins, and medallions) and investment (official gold coins and bar hoarding by wealthy individuals and institutions).

While old gold scrap and sales of gold bullion by central banks are important sources of supply, most of the metal each year comes from mine production. Western world gold production (the closed economies of the communist countries did not report such numbers) rose rapidly during the second half of the 1980s, reaching 1,734 tonnes in 1990, up 25 percent in just three years. That growth was driven by the opening of new mines in the United States, where production of 295 tonnes had increased 90 percent since 1987. Leading that growth was Newmont Gold Company, by then the largest gold miner in the country, whose production jumped 185 percent between 1987 and 1990 to 52 tonnes, or 1,676,000 ounces.

The gold price fluctuated wildly during this period, trading between $490 and $360 an ounce. It rallied 12 percent to $415 in the last half of 1990 in response to Iraq's invasion of Kuwait and the subsequent Gulf War against Saddam Hussein. World chaos usually sends gold bugs scurrying to buy up more of the yellow metal.

Newmont celebrated its twenty-fifth year on the Carlin Trend in 1990 and could look at a plethora of numbers with satisfaction. Not only were production and prices up, but the cash cost of production was declining. At $218 an ounce, its cash cost ranked in the lowest third of the world's gold mines; the average world cost that year was $265. Net income of $343 million, or $5.06 per share, was the highest in a decade. Furthermore, the staggering debt taken on to defeat Boone Pickens had been cut to a manageable $300 million.

But while Newmont was investing in Carlin, it was selling its Australian gold assets. Newmont Australia, the new name for Newmont Proprietary, had found the Telfer and New Celebration mines on its own without help from New York and was fiercely independent. Furthermore, Australia had a reputation as a country that U.S. companies put money into, but one from which it was hard to bring money home. Now, with rising interest in gold stocks by Australian investors, Newmont had the opportunity to sell and repatriate the money to help pay down its debt. In 1989 and 1990, it sold 46 percent of Newmont Australia for $237 million, reducing its holdings to 24.5 percent. One 20 percent block was bought by an Australian wheeler-dealer, Robert Champion de Crespigny. It would not be his last dealings with Newmont.

In August 1990, less than two months after selling its interest in Peabody Coal to Hanson PLC, Newmont took steps to reduce Hanson's grip on the company. It planned to sell 12 million shares of stock, 3.6 million from its treasury and 8.4 million in a secondary offering by Hanson. Newmont would use the proceeds to help purchase an additional 6 million shares from Hanson. The intent was to reduce Hanson's interest from 49.1 percent to 26 percent. Wall Street, however, was not prepared for that much dilution and within a few weeks Newmont's stock price dropped 15 percent from the mid-$40s to the high $30s. The issue was scrapped in mid-October.

Simultaneous with that decision, Hanson announced that it had found an alternative solution. In what became known as the gold-for-trees swap, Hanson exchanged its entire interest in Newmont for 1.7 million acres of timberland in the U.S. West and South. The forests had belonged to Crown Zellerbach, which in 1985 had fallen victim to another of the world's great takeover artists, Sir James Goldsmith, who acquired the company and sold its paper mills but kept the trees. Goldsmith and a distant cousin, British merchant banker Jacob Rothschild, managed their investments through companies registered in the Cayman Islands, the Netherlands Antilles, and Barbados.

On October 16, Hanson's U.S. partner, Sir Gordon White, broke the news to Parker, who within minutes received a call from Paris. "I'm Jimmy Goldsmith and you may have heard of me," the caller announced, "but I'm not as bad as people make me out to be." Parker says, "I was just as charming and said, 'Welcome, and I do hope you will join our board.'" Outside Parker's office Peter Philip, who had just been named Newmont's president, and vice chairman Richard Leather listened on a speaker phone and became visibly sick. Leather, putting on the face of a dying man, ran his finger across his throat and announced, "That's the end of Newmont." Parker, more philosophical, says, "It was a bit of a shock, but you can't choose your shareholders any more than you can your relatives."[2]

Sir James, fifty-seven at the time, was a bigger-than-life British French industrial tycoon. One of the world's wealthiest men, he stood six foot four with thinning silver hair, piercing blue eyes, and a commanding presence. With only a high school education and a taste for high-stakes poker, he had shaken the U.K. and U.S. business scene since the 1970s with raids on the Grand Union supermarket chain, Goodyear Tire & Rubber, BAT Industries, and timber and paper companies St. Regis, Diamond International, and Crown Zellerbach. Goldsmith said his aim was "to remake bloated corporations by selling unproductive assets and sharpening the core businesses."[3] Targets called him a greenmailer and asset stripper. But he was also a gold bug and saw in Newmont a means of protecting his wealth in the event of world monetary collapse.

13.1. Sir James Goldsmith, a bigger-than-life tycoon, acquired a controlling interest in Newmont in 1990. (*Newmont Archives*)

Goldsmith's life was one of contradiction and controversy. His father was German Jewish but lived a bourgeois life in England; his mother was a French Catholic peasant. He shared lavish homes in London, Paris, Burgundy, Spain, and Mexico with his wife (who had been his mistress), an ex-wife, and his current mistress. Once asked what happens when a man marries his mistress, he replied, "It creates a new job opening." Involved in conservative politics in both England and France and a vehement opponent of European integration and monetary union, he later helped form the Referendum Party in Britain to advance his views. Prime Minister Margaret Thatcher called him "one of the most powerful and dynamic personalities that this generation has seen."[4] Yet, at the urging of his brother, a founder of Greenpeace, he contributed substantial sums to environmental causes, and worked with Ralph Nader in opposing the international trade agreement GATT.[5]

At Newmont, Goldsmith evoked mixed reactions. Some, like Philip, became enthralled with his enthusiasm and boundless energy. "Newmont needed Jimmy. He provided the spark and the drive that we lacked at that level,"[6] he says. But Parker found him a royal irritant in the derriere. "Jimmy was consummately bright; his mind was quick as a whip," says Parker. "The trouble with Jimmy was that he was fickle and capricious. He was obsessed with things of the moment. He could turn on a dime. He was quick to judgment and had strange ideas about management. He couldn't stand the boilerplate of business. All he wanted was deals and action." He had no office and carried no briefcase, managing his affairs from a manila folder that contained his papers of the day.

The problem for Parker, who held an imperial view of his responsibility as a CEO, was that Goldsmith was not content to deal with the company at the board level. He involved himself with day-to-day decisions, meddled in personnel matters, and circumvented Parker's authority. In what became known as "Jimmygrams," he would fax Parker letters through his secretary in New York. Always gracious and usually very short, the letters would begin "My Dear Gordon" and close "Yours affectionately, Jimmy,"[7] but in between he would sandwich his latest complaint or demand. If a Jimmygram arrived on a Friday afternoon, Parker would lock it in his desk drawer and not look at it until Monday so it wouldn't spoil his weekend.

Goldsmith intimidated the board, where he was always sure of himself and often disruptive—standing up, making speeches, issuing demands, and waving his arms. "He would walk around the room saying, 'There are six reasons why' something should or shouldn't be done. He always had six reasons," recalls Philip. He insisted that the boardroom temperature be precisely seventy-two degrees. At White & Case in New York, which hosted many board meetings, Maureen Brundage recalls sending a technician with a thermometer to check out a room before a meeting. Someone asked if he was checking the room for bugs. "That will always be my memory of Goldsmith—checking the room for bugs," she says.[8]

He could be charming, but he also could be petty and mean-spirited. Paul Maroni, who became chief financial officer in 1990, was one of the few within the company not in awe of its largest shareholder. At one board meeting in 1992, Goldsmith upbraided Maroni because he preferred to work with the commercial bankers who had supported the company through the Pickens crisis and in its first gold loan rather than Goldsmith's investment banker, Lazard Frères. When Parker backed his CFO, Goldsmith protested, "You're telling me that after I have invested $2 billion in this company, you're going to take that middle-level manager's opinion over my bankers?"[9] Maroni, who had not been happy in Denver anyway, left the company shortly thereafter to become chief financial officer of Connecticut College.

Goldsmith was bound by the same standstill agreement that Consolidated Gold Fields had signed in 1987. While that gave Newmont some degree of protection, it also meant that Goldsmith's investment in the company was not as liquid as he would like, and Parker realized that this would likely make his new shareholder more meddlesome. Parker felt Goldsmith had taken his position in Newmont with unrealistic expectations. "His view was to strip it, squeeze people, slash costs, siphon cash, and sell it. Jimmy was accustomed to buying fat cat companies with a lot of inefficiency where you could do that sort of thing. But with Newmont after Pickens, we were tight as a drum, staffs were stretched, and there was little fluff."

As he had with Hanson, Parker began to search for ways to dilute Goldsmith's position. The logical choice was a merger with American Barrick, whose Goldstrike property on the Carlin Trend was adjacent to Newmont's Post mine. Newmont had 19 million ounces of gold reserves in Nevada; Barrick had 18 million. A merger would result in significant cost savings and create a company with production of two million ounces of gold a year. With Goldsmith's support, Parker called on Barrick's chairman, Peter Munk, in Toronto and on May 18, 1991, the two companies announced that they had entered into merger discussions. An expected exchange ratio of 1.8 shares of Barrick, trading at $20 a share, for each share of Newmont Mining, trading at $36, would give the new company a market capitalization of $5 billion.

After two months, during which Goldsmith often dealt directly with Munk, talks were terminated. "Jimmy initially thought I had scuttled the merger to protect management and employees—a preposterous thought," says Parker, adding that he had agreed to step down as CEO if that would facilitate the deal. Rather, he says, the breaking points were corporate governance and control. "We had agreements and court decrees resulting from the Gold Fields and Pickens era designed to protect the minority shareholders. These were relevant and had to be honored in any new agreement." Munk, on the other hand, found these and other rules that govern American corporate boards too confining. "In the last conversation I had with him, Munk said, 'You can get on and run your company with your dammed committees, but I'm going to run my company myself,'" Parker says. Furthermore, Goldsmith would have remained the largest shareholder in the new company, and playing second fiddle wasn't something the independent minded Munk found appealing.

In early 1992, Newmont and Barrick signed a joint operating agreement for the Betze-Post Pit, allowing for unified development of the deposit that straddled their property lines. If the two companies could not combine their high-rise corporate suites, at least they could save money by working together in the pit.

Parker described what happened next. "After the aborted attempt to merge with Barrick, we had run out the course of finding a merger partner. We now needed to sit down and craft a strategy to grow the company to allow Jimmy to exit. That, of course, would benefit all shareholders. We had bankers working on this and were hoping for substantial organic growth from our exploration efforts. Once Jimmy got over his rage about Barrick, he suggested that we form a committee of the board to look at corporate strategy. I said, 'Sure, let's all sit around and talk strategy because I'm running out of ideas.'"

Goldsmith chaired the committee, and that, says Parker, "was the beginning of the end of our relationship." The audit and management consulting firm of Coopers & Lybrand was brought in by Goldsmith to study the company. "But rather than develop a strategy, it quickly became an exercise to see how they could cut overhead by 20 percent. We had reduced ourselves to the bare bones and now here comes Jimmy, this very bright guy whose mind is flying in one hundred directions and who I thought could be of great help, but who in the end only wanted to cut costs." To make matters worse, the man chosen to head the effort was Al Dunlap, whose work for Goldsmith in cutting up Crown Zellerbach had earned him the nickname "Chainsaw Al." Goldsmith wanted to put Chainsaw on the board. Parker seethed.

Director William Turner, who had worked most of his life in family-controlled companies, urged Parker to "just relax and let the consultants look over the place. They're going to find it's a pretty well-run company."[10] Besides, he cautioned, "You know, Jimmy's put a lot of money in this thing and he wants to assure himself that the company is run reasonably well. That's a perfectly legitimate thing for a new major shareholder to do."

But Parker viewed Coopers's presence as more than an attack on his prerogatives. It was demoralizing his management team. "Throughout the assignment, Coopers rode roughshod over our people under the protection of Jimmy," he says. "It was a very trying time." Timothy Schmitt, vice president, controller, and corporate secretary, explains what was going on: "Coopers insisted on looking at the company as it existed that day, which meant a one-operation company centered on Carlin. I argued day and night on behalf of the accounting department and thank goodness there were no cuts. Otherwise, we would have lost all our good players and when we started up in Peru and Uzbekistan would have had to go out and hire new people."[11]

While corporate costs were squeezed, as were operating costs at the mine site, Goldsmith supported an increase in the company's exploration budget. In that regard, director Joseph Flannery found Goldsmith to be "a forceful voice for change. He was a builder and always supported the company's strategy of exploration and growth."[12] He recalls a board meeting at which John Parry, then senior vice president of exploration, was describing the Yanacocha discovery in northern Peru. It was very early in the evaluation process, but already it looked very promising. Flannery remembers Goldsmith pointing to a map of Peru and saying, "If it's that good, tomorrow go out and lease all this land," as he ran his finger from the discovery spot near

Cajamarca all the way to the Ecuador border. "Everyone else was thinking of the land around the site necessary to open a mine and Jimmy was thinking expansively of what else might be out there."

Newmont had increased its exploration budget annually and its commitment for 1993 of $68 million was double what it spent just a few years before. By contrast, the gold industry's expenditures for exploration during the early 1990s declined sharply in the face of an uncertain gold price and increased hostility toward mining by the Clinton administration. In its annual report for 1992, Newmont said it was positioned to benefit from a dual development—"a decline in competition for even the most attractive exploration opportunities at the same time as foreign countries formerly closed to us are adopting positive programs to attract international investors to their mining industries. Because Newmont Mining enjoys a widespread reputation as a technological leader in all facets of exploration, mining, and metallurgy, we have already been invited to participate in promising ventures in some of these emerging economies."

Exploration and mine development, however, have a long time horizon, and patience was not a Goldsmith virtue. Instead of rising as he had anticipated, the price of gold had languished. Commentators said the yellow metal was in an "investment wilderness." In 1992, the Dutch and Belgian central banks sold 602 tonnes of gold, further depressing the price. With lower-priced metal, Newmont's earnings declined. In November, with gold trading at $340 an ounce and Newmont's stock price at $46, Goldsmith quietly sold 1.8 million of his 33.2 million shares in a private placement. In April 1993, in a move that improved the market and his own fortunes, Goldsmith sold 6.8 million shares, or 10 percent of Newmont, to investor George Soros for $39.50 a share, the same imputed price he had paid in his trees-for-gold swap three years earlier. The two men barely knew each other, but Soros had been following the gold market closely for some time and exchanging views with Barrick's chairman Munk, a fellow emigrant from Hungary. Soros approached Goldsmith with the offer to buy at a $2.50 discount to Newmont's market price and Goldsmith accepted within twenty-four hours.

Reporting on the transaction, the *Wall Street Journal* said "Sir James declined to comment on market speculation that he has been disappointed with Newmont's management."[13] Goldsmith promptly sent a letter of de-

nial to the editor. "I am always happy to comment on Newmont's management, which I consider to be very good. [In sending the same letter to Parker
he used the word "excellent."] We have worked together in great harmony
and I intend to maintain a significant long-term investment in Newmont
Mining."[14] News of the trade, surprisingly, triggered a rally in both gold and
Newmont shares.

When does the sale of stock at a discount justify a bull run? When two
of the world's most savvy investors say it does. Calling himself "an enormous bull" on gold, Goldsmith said he would invest the proceeds of the
sale in the metal itself by buying gold options. Soros, known for his insight
into international currency markets, had just made a billion dollars by bet-
ting against sterling. "The George Soros people are very astute," Newmont
spokesman Jim Hill told Reuters. "It's not only bullish for Newmont, it's
bullish for gold."[15]

Gold got a boost the day before the transaction when Helmut Schle-
singer, president of the German Bundesbank, held a press conference in
which he called "the gold standard . . . the fundamental currency reserve."[16]
Immediately after Soros's purchase, Lord Rees-Mogg, a longtime gold bug
and columnist for the London *Times,* wrote, "Any study of the history of
the gold standard leaves one with an awed respect for the significance of
the metal as a measure of reality."[17] Another reality: since June 1990 Rees-
Mogg had served as the non-executive director of St. James's Place Capital,
the investment arm of Goldsmith's partner Rothschild. Soon reports were
circulating that Russia, a sometime exporter of the metal, had exhausted its
stockpile, while China had become a big-time buyer. As rumors flew, investors gorged on gold options.

"No market in the world has more fanatical followers than gold, and
the news that Soros was interested brought many buyers out of the wood-
work,"[18] the London *Sunday Times* reported. Julian Baring, a respected gold
analyst with Mercury Asset Management in London, added, "I am beginning to hear the thundering hooves of investors who have not been near the
market for years."[19]

Despite his statement of long-term intentions, Goldsmith acted swiftly.
On May 10, he sold 6.5 million Newmont shares to investors in Europe and
Asia at $45.50 a share through Morgan Stanley. On July 7 another block
of 9.7 million shares was placed through Salomon Brothers at $54.75. Both

sales were made under Rule 144a of the SEC that allows the sales of large blocks without filing registration papers as long as the sales take place overseas and the shares are not resold to Americans for forty days.

In all, it was estimated that the Goldsmith-Rothschild team made more than $164 million from their Newmont investment and still held 6.5 percent of the company. Turner praises Goldsmith's exit strategy: "He managed to get out quite brilliantly and didn't depress the stock price, which I think was quite amazing." Soros, who increased his holdings to 10.2 million shares, or 12 percent of the company, did not fare so well. Possessed with a trader's mentality, he viewed the company only as a speculative investment, not a long-term creator of wealth. To many, he was a negative influence whose contacts with management were seen as self-serving. He began selling in 1997 as the gold price declined and liquidated his position in early 1998 at about $32 a share, suffering a sizable loss.

With Goldsmith gone, Parker decided that he, too, would step aside. Although only fifty-eight, he was having health problems and had endured more than his share of corporate grief. Ken Gooding of the *Financial Times* wrote that Parker "must be the only businessman who has faced up to the attentions of three of the world's most aggressive corporate raiders—Boone Pickens, Lord Hanson, and Sir James Goldsmith—and still be in his job."[20] And Gooding didn't mention Harry Oppenheimer and his Minorco maneuver.

Looking back on his eighteen years as a director, Sir Rudolph Agnew, the chairman of Consolidated Gold Fields, says, "My thinking runs like this: Gordon Parker's handling of the exit from copper, the raid by Pickens, the defense of my company, and the investments in gold were superb. Today, Newmont has emerged out of all this as a totally changed company. And the basis for all that, in my view, is Gordon Parker. He saved the company."[21]

He also made money for Newmont's shareholders. An investment of $1,000 in Newmont stock on October 1, 1985, Parker's first day as CEO, would have been worth just under $2,500 when he stepped down on October 29, 1993. Additionally, shareholders who held on during that tumultuous period would have pocketed $2,260 in dividends, most of it from the big payout to defeat Pickens. And had they held their Magma shares until the company was acquired two and a half years later by BHP, they would have received another $840.

The one thing he had not done, however, was prepare a successor. Philip had already conveyed his intention to retire, and a search was under way for a chief operating officer who might later advance to CEO. Parker says it soon became apparent that the company "could attract significantly better candidates if we let it be known that we were looking for someone to fill a CEO slot. So I recommended this approach to the board and told them I would happily step aside if it worked out that way."

The man who won the nod was a surprise to tradition-bound Newmont—no one had heard of Ronald C. Cambre. A chemical engineer from Louisiana, he was the first in his family to move outside New Orleans since an ancestor, a French soldier, settled there in the early 1700s. He had spent thirty years in management at Freeport Minerals, which like Newmont had offices in the Pan Am Building. Most recently he had been chief executive of Freeport-McMoran Resource Partners, the nation's largest fertilizer operation, but had started looking for greener pastures after tiring of Texas geologist James "Jim Bob" Moffett, who had taken control of the old-line company and merged it into his McMoran oil and gas company. Moffett loved the razzle-dazzle of exploration, and the company's Grasberg copper/gold mine in Indonesia is one of the industry's true prizes, but he seemed bored with developing and operating properties, which was Cambre's strength. (Four other senior Freeport Minerals executives left about the same time to become the CEO of other mining and petroleum companies.) Before coming to Newmont, Cambre was offered the CEO spot at Placer Dome. But there was a split on the Placer board that resulted in frequent turnover at the top. "I figured it wasn't the time in my career to be the fourth CEO to be fired in six years," he says.[22]

Cambre's career had only brushed the fringes of mining, but he had strong international experience, having worked in Spain, Australia, and Indonesia, a country where Newmont saw huge potential. Two Newmont executives also were in contention. Wayne Murdy was brought in as chief financial officer from Apache Oil in 1992 and had been told by Parker that he was a potential successor. But when Parker decided to retire early, the board chose to look for more experience. Graham Clark, who had succeeded Leather as senior vice president and general counsel, likewise felt he had been promised a shot at the top. While Murdy worked closely with Cambre over the next seven years and succeeded him as CEO in 2001, Clark never adjusted to the fact that he had been passed over and left the company within two years of Cambre's arrival.

During the interview process, while on a trip to Europe with Freeport, Cambre took time to meet with Goldsmith. Goldsmith sent his private plane, a Grumman IV with the tail letters beginning AU for gold, to meet him in Brussels. "I flew to some place in Burgundy and caught a helicopter to his magnificent chateau. There was a fountain shooting water a hundred feet in the air. It was quite intimidating, but a nice introduction to this guy who was bigger than life." The two spent the day together walking about the grounds as Goldsmith talked of his mother who was from a village just down the road. "He was just so kind and gracious, but you could tell he was a distracted person." He was ill with cancer and deeply involved in European politics.

"His interest had waned on Newmont and he had turned succession over to the board," Cambre says. "He was also a lonely person. He was all alone in that huge chateau other than the help. I walked away thinking that this was the loneliest billionaire I had ever met in my life. I felt sorry for him." Within two months of Cambre's coming to Newmont in November 1993, Goldsmith resigned from the board to co-lead a national slate in France for the European parliament.

In its annual report published in March 1994, the company praised Goldsmith's "unique contributions to Newmont," primarily his "stress on the strategic imperative for long-term investment in exploration activities." It added, "The Newmont Board of Directors and management have appreciated Sir James' insightful guidance. His successful international business experience, and his firmly- articulated convictions based on this experience, have been equaled by his boundless energy; and all have been delivered in full measure in behalf of Newmont and its public shareholders." The report represented the views of many within the company other than Parker, and was signed by Cambre and Philip.[23]

Cambre and Murdy saw Goldsmith on several occasions after he resigned and always found him supportive. "He . . . never interfered in the operation at any time, unlike his very heavy involvement with Gordon," Cambre says. Yet, he could be vocal on issues that touched his heart. On an investor relations tour in the spring of 1997, Murdy met Goldsmith at his Paris home, where he relaxed on an overstuffed sofa as the two discussed company strategy. In closing, Murdy suggested that with a declining gold price the company might consider hedging some of its production, a move that would boost short-term cash flow but would be interpreted bearishly by gold bugs. Goldsmith bolted upright with the admonition that he should banish any such thought. That evening in his hotel, Murdy received faxes from both Goldsmith and Soros, with copies to Cambre, urging Newmont to remain unhedged.[24]

It was his last communiqué with the company. A few months later, in August, Goldsmith died at age sixty-four. He still held five million shares of Newmont stock, which were sold in the high $20s by his estate in late 1999.

Marketing Gold

As if Gordon Parker didn't have enough on his plate in 1987, he was chosen that year as the first chairman of the World Gold Council, an organization formed by gold producers to provide a global advertising and promotional force for the consumption of gold.

Unlike breakfast cereal, designer jeans, and other consumer items, gold is not sold directly to retailers or wholesalers and producers do not compete on price, quality, or packaging. Rather, mines ship doré bars to refiners who turn it into pure gold that is then sold to a handful of bullion banks at the London fixed spot price of the day. Gold fabricators and mints buy from these banks. Thus producers work together to promote gold's various uses.

While jewelry has been the council's principal focus, ownership of gold coins and bullion and industrial uses of the yellow metal are also promoted. Over the years, the council has worked to lower regulatory barriers to gold imports in countries like India and China, and has been an advocate of official sector holdings—the purchase and retention of gold by central banks as a reserve currency. Recently, the council has supported new gold investment products, such as streetTracks Gold Shares on the New York Stock Exchange, that allow investors to buy a "share" of gold at the spot price.

The council is a successor to the International Gold Corporation (InterGold), which was set up by the South African Chamber of Mines in Johannesburg at a time when South Africa accounted for two-thirds of the gold produced in the noncommunist world. In 1973, InterGold began marketing the popular Krugerrand, a one-ounce, 22-karat gold coin introduced by the Chamber in 1967. Over the next twenty years, the Krugerrand absorbed 43 million ounces, or 1,338 tonnes, of South African gold[25] and became the principal way individuals could own gold.

When gold prices soared in 1980, a new gold rush began. It took time to discover and develop new deposits, but by 1986, with mines opening in North America and Australia, South Africa's share of the world gold market had fallen to 50 percent. By then, Canada had introduced the Maple Leaf and the U.S. Mint had coined the American Eagle as competing gold coins.

Equally important, in 1986 the U.S. Congress, in an effort to pressure the South African government to end apartheid, banned most imports from that country, including Krugerrands. During the first five years of the decade, America was importing $450 million to $500 million in Krugerrands a year. Anti-apartheid sentiment in Europe also caused a collapse of the market for Krugerrands on the Continent.

Faced with the loss of their most important outlet at a time when new production was pouring into the market, South African miners scrambled to find a way to uncouple gold from its long association with their country. Tom Main of the South African Chamber and Harry Conger, CEO of Homestake Mining, conceived the idea of the World Gold Council. Initially funded 50 percent by South African mines, the organization sought to encompass producers from around the globe and focused on the promotion of universal gold products, such as jewelry, instead of coinage identified with a single country.

Parker, who was born and spent much of his working life in South Africa, became the South Africans' man of choice to head the new organization and bring other North American producers into the fold. Harry Van Benschoten, Newmont's vice president of accounting, who set up the new organization's headquarters in Geneva and brought Price Waterhouse onboard as its auditors, credits Parker's involvement for both revitalizing gold marketing and giving Newmont confidence in a gold strategy. "Gordon had tremendous responsibility and accomplishment in changing the whole structure" of gold promotion, he says. "And, I think that positioned Newmont to springboard more into the gold business."[26]

Newmont president Pierre Lassonde was named chairman of the World Gold Council in 2005.

14

NEW HORIZONS

With the rapid acceleration in gold mining in the 1980s and early 1990s, anti-mining activists found plenty to rail against. In Colorado's San Juan Mountains, the Summitville mine leaked cyanide, acid, and heavy metals into the Alamosa River, while in Montana a Canadian company sought to mine on private property just outside Yellowstone National Park, the holy grail for environmental preservationists, and another company proposed mining along the Blackfoot River made famous by Norman Maclean's fly fishing classic *A River Runs Through It*. Environmentalists were not above deception, showing pictures of a pristine Yellowstone they said would be devastated by a mine leak, when in fact the Clarks Fork River near the property flows away from the park, not into it. Some companies, on the other hand, seemed tone-deaf to public opinion that not all sites are appropriate for mining, even with the state-of-the-art facilities they promised.

Yet, with attempts to block every new mine regardless of location, mining executives began to suspect that the Clinton administration was tilting the playing field in favor of their adversaries. Overly restrictive land use rules were imposed; environmental permitting bogged down in endless hearings; the 1872 mining law giving access to federal lands came under severe attack; and a moratorium was placed on issuing patents, that is, transferring federal land to miners, including for applications that already had been approved. Forced by lawsuits to grant these patents, Secretary of the Interior Bruce Babbitt stood before TV cameras to condemn it as "the greatest gold heist since Butch Cassidy," or to charge that foreign companies, of which he falsely included Newmont, "got the gold, but the public got the shaft." Miners were livid.

Feeling unwelcome in the United States, U.S. and Canadian gold companies turned their attention abroad, especially to undeveloped countries that were opening to foreign capital. What they discovered was no surprise.

Just as it had done in Nevada thirty years earlier, Newmont had gotten there first—and not by months or years but in some cases by a decade or more. Between August 1993 and March 1996, while many companies were just beginning to establish foreign beachheads, Newmont opened precedent-setting operations in Peru, Uzbekistan, and Indonesia. Furthermore, these came not to escape environmental regulation but to embrace new opportunities under the banner of U.S. environmental laws.

Newmont first became interested in Peru in 1921 with a visit by its founder, William Boyce Thompson. Its geologists had poked around the country in the 1920s and 1930s, and the company partnered with Cerro de Pasco in developing Southern Peru Copper in the 1950s. Alberto Benavides, chairman of Cerro de Pasco in the 1960s, often met Newmont's chairman, Plato Malozemoff, during board meetings of the parent Cerro Corporation in New York. Newmont's vice president of research Leonard Harris spent sixteen years with Cerro in Peru and Anthony Bowerman, an English geologist, spent nine. Both married Peruvian women and developed insights into the country's cultural, political, and geological landscape. After a leftist military junta seized power and nationalized Cerro de Pasco's operations, both joined Newmont—Harris in 1974; Bowerman a few years later. Along with Aubrey Paverd, a South African geologist with a Ph.D., they set Newmont's course for fabulous success in Peru.

That began in 1981, when exploration vice president Richard Ellett, who had spent time in the Andes, decided Newmont needed a renewed presence in South America. He assigned the task to Paverd, whom he had hired earlier at the Tsumeb copper mine in South West Africa. Paverd recalls asking Ellett where he should begin his search. "Don't ask me," the senior geologist replied. "You're the manager of foreign exploration. Go look."[1] Given such freedom, Paverd headed for Peru, which had high potential and less competition than he would face in Chile. Peru was the one country, however, that Malozemoff had banned because of political turmoil and rising terrorism.

On his initial visit to Lima that August, Paverd and geophysicist Misac Nabighian met with a law firm recommended for its English-speaking partners with knowledge of Peruvian mining, commercial, and tax law. One of the lawyers, Jose Miguel Morales, asked if they would like to meet his father-in-law, who was in the mining business. Paverd agreed and the next day found himself lunching in San Isidro over a pisco sour with Benavides,

14.1. Expanding the company's horizons were (top to bottom): Joe Kowalik, who used a vodka toast to initiate a joint venture in Uzbekistan (stockpile in background); Aubrey Paverd, a South African geologist, who led the discovery of Yanacocha, the largest gold mine in South America (view of mine from top of the Andes); and John Dow, who spent years in Indonesia before finding gold at Minahasa and Batu Hijau (mill site pictured). (*Newmont Archives; John Dow's photo from Larry Laszlo*)

who had founded Cia de Minas Buenaventura, the largest privately owned mining group in Peru. Surprised, Benavides asked, "I thought Plato said Peru was off limits." Replied Paverd: "He doesn't know I'm here."

Over the next eighteen months Paverd investigated several silver prospects in which Buenaventura had an interest. Then, in January 1983, Jacques Claveau, a French Canadian who had just retired as Newmont's senior foreign geologist, arranged for Paverd to meet in Orléans, France, with the Bureau de Recherches Géologiques et Minières (BRGM), the geological and mining bureau of the French government. Claveau had joined Newmont immediately after World War II and earned a reputation as the company's most widely traveled and erudite geologist. His global contact base was legendary.

BRGM was seeking partners for exploration projects around the world, including a base metals prospect in northern Peru. When Newmont decided not to pursue that venture, the French proffered two more prospects, one of which was a bulk, low-grade epithermal silver target called Yanacocha, or black lake, near the city of Cajamarca. BRGM's Peruvian subsidiary, CEDIMIN, in which Buenaventura held a 35 percent interest, had just taken claim to the property after it was relinquished by Kennecott.

In March, Paverd sent Bowerman to Lima to establish Newmont's first office in the country and he, in turn, hired Miguel Cardozo, a Peruvian geologist with a Ph.D. from Germany, who would add immensely to the company's exploration effort over the years. The Peruvian economy at the time was in shambles and the government of Alan Garcia had shut down foreign exchange and stopped most imports. Bowerman found the last available vehicle in Lima, a Toyota Land Cruiser, which Benavides purchased since Newmont was unable to send funds into the country. At the end of September, he decided to inspect the property.[2]

Yanacocha sits among snow-capped peaks 14,000 feet in the Andes 375 miles north of Lima. Climbing out of the old provincial city of Cajamarca, it took Bowerman several hours in the four-wheel-drive Toyota to traverse the muddy switchback trails dodging colorfully dressed campesinos and burdened donkeys to cover the thirty miles to the target site. But he liked what he saw. There is evidence that cinnabar, a mercury compound, was mined in the area as early as 300 A.D., and in the 1400s and 1500s the area was the center of Inca gold. The latter gave rise to one of the most inglorious chapters in gold's history.

In November 1592, a band of 62 Spanish horsemen and 106 foot soldiers under the command of Francisco Pizarro marched into Cajamarca from Peru's barren western coast. With the aid of small cannons, suits of armor, and horses, none of which the local Indians had ever seen, the conquistadors captured the Inca chief Atahualpa and slaughtered 7,000 of his followers. A line was drawn on the wall near the ceiling of a room in Cajamarca to the height of Atahualpa's reach. Pizarro demanded that the room be filled to that level once with gold and twice with silver to gain the chief's release. Although the ransom was paid, Atahualpa was garroted in the town square. Historical records show that with additional looting at the Inca's southern capital of Cuzco, the Spaniards melted down and shipped out 280,000 ounces of Peruvian gold and over two million ounces of silver.[3]

The history of mining is replete with examples of discoveries made in the shadow of historic mining or where previous searches for other metals failed to detect the prize. Yanacocha reflects both phenomena. Japanese geologists drilled eleven holes in the area between 1968 and 1970 looking for porphyry copper. During the same period, a British technical aid mission surveyed the area and found anomalous silver values in the stream sediments. Their effort increased the knowledge of Peru's mineral resource base, but not for any immediate economic purpose. Following up on the British results, CEDIMIN had initiated a comprehensive exploration program in 1980 that over the next three years included mapping, Induced Polarization and resistivity studies, geochemistry, and trenching to expose the bedrock. Interspersed with the government studies were commercial probes by St. Joe Minerals, Cerro de Pasco, and finally Kennecott in search of copper, lead, zinc, and silver.

A letter of intent for a joint venture owned 40 percent each by Newmont and CEDIMIN and 20 percent by Buenaventura was signed in May 1984. A definitive agreement followed in September 1985. Originally, the French wanted a 50/50 venture with Newmont, but Bowerman, finding the French "insufferable," declined. Besides, both parties agreed that political expediency demanded inclusion of a strong local partner, and Buenaventura, which already had a joint venture with BRGM, was the logical choice. Newmont was the operator and agreed to contribute $2.2 million over four years; Buenaventura would fund another $1.1 million.

Rock chip sampling and limited drilling began in 1984 and produced mixed results but tilted the focus toward gold. Moving forward, however, took tons of faith. The economy under Garcia had collapsed with hyper-inflation, food shortages, and threats to nationalize the oil and banking industries. The Maoist group Sendero Luminoso, or Shining Path, increased its campaign of terror, bombing power stations, kidnaping businessmen, and killing peasants in the mountains. Bowerman's wife and children would hit the floor of their home in Lima as terrorists fired bullets in the streets. Newmont was the only foreign company still exploring in Peru and in late 1986 CEO Gordon Parker ordered a halt to the project. It took heavy lobbying by Paverd and a renegotiation of the agreement with CEDIMIN to stretch out funding over several more years before Parker relented. Still, the company only released enough money to drill a couple holes a year and keep its toehold on the Yanacocha claim.

Newmont's board sought the advice of outside experts in Latin American politics, but they were useless, says Peter Philip, by then Newmont's president. "They were always 'On the one hand this and on the other hand that.'"[4] Positive recommendations from Harris and Bowerman, both of whose wives are named Rosa, were discounted because the New York office felt they were looking at Peru "through Rosa-colored glasses." But Philip was a decision maker and "once he became involved he put the fire under our feet," Paverd remembers.

Persistence paid off and by 1988, after drilling several locations where Yanacocha would later establish mines—Carachugo, San Jose, and Maqui Maqui—two million ounces of gold resources had been pinpointed in highly friable, granular silica rock. "We have a tiger by the tail," Paverd told Bowerman.[5] Benavides, whose high-grade vein mines tapped gold from ore containing an ounce per ton, was skeptical that anyone could extract value from Yanacocha's 0.02 to 0.04 ounce per ton material. But after Harris, who had extensively studied the metallurgy of the deposit, and Bowerman explained Newmont's heap leaching experience at Carlin, Buenaventura's chairman acquiesced. "I don't know about this sort of thing," he replied, "but if Newmont says so I'll go along."

The tide began to turn with the 1990 presidential election of Alberto Fujimori, who pledged to restore Peru's economy and stamp out terrorism. "That gave us enough safety in our investment to say we should go ahead and do it," says Philip. Still, when Newmont's president traveled to Peru he would fly to Quito, Ecuador, where Fujimori would have a military plane waiting to secretly whisk him into Lima. "I was on the hit list of the Sendero Luminoso," he says. "They figured if they could knock me off the project would die." Ecuador was Peru's archenemy, but Fujimori involved it in the ruse because "he desperately wanted the project" and correctly believed that "other multinational companies would invest in Peru if we did so successfully," Philip says.

"What tipped the scales," Philip adds, "is that the first bit of ore I saw from Yanacocha convinced me that we could put in the cheapest plant in the world and recover the gold. The ore was so freely leachable that you could take it straight from the mine to the leach pad and get out a significant amount of the gold and make money without having to do extensive crushing or building a mill. We also managed to borrow money from the International Finance Corporation [IFC; part of the World Bank] cheaply. The amount of cash that Newmont actually laid out was negligible." For its role, the IFC earned a 5 percent interest in Yanacocha, and after a reshuffling of interests Newmont held 38 percent, Buenaventura 32.3 percent, and BRGM 24.7 percent.

It's easy to overlook the role that reputation plays in starting a new venture. But without Newmont's solid credentials it is doubtful it could have obtained financing in such a high-risk environment. CFO Paul Maroni was "welcomed with open arms" by the IFC "because I represented Newmont. The mining guys there respected the people at Newmont—Parker, Philip, Jack Parry [who succeeded Ellett as senior vice president of exploration], and the exploration staff—because of . . . the environmentally conscious approach they had taken to mining." Furthermore, they knew they could bank on the company's reserve and cost estimates. "Our guys were regarded among the All Stars in the industry."[6]

On July 23, 1992, board approval was given to develop an open-pit mine, leach pad, and Merrill Crowe recovery plant. The total cost of the project, including past exploration, was $37 million, of which Newmont put up $15 million. It represented the first foreign investment in the Peruvian mining industry in twenty years. The same day, Harris recalls, nine terrorist incidents were recorded in Peru resulting in three deaths.

After a recommendation from Benavides, Harris volunteered to manage the project and bring it into production. Because of his past experience in the country, he was able to assemble an all-Peruvian workforce, which was good since no one from the States wanted to go. Yanacocha's first operations manager was Carlos Santa Cruz, who was working for Buenaventura and holds a Ph.D. in mining engineering from Pennsylvania State University. He was named general manager of Minera Yanacocha in 1997, becoming the first national employee appointed by Newmont to head one of its overseas operations. Named a vice president in 2001 and senior vice president in 2008, Santa Cruz is now in charge of all of Newmont's South American operations.

Before returning to Peru, Harris engaged the Ackerman Group in Miami, a security firm headed by ex-CIA men, and Forza, a Lima security group, to meet Philip's requirement that personnel and property be protected. The combination of gold, explosives, and high-profile American visitors at a remote mountaintop made the project vulnerable to attack. "If we can't solve this problem, we're not going to Peru," Philip told Harris.

Harris's wife, a nurse and former police chief in La Oroya, Peru, personally interviewed each of his bodyguards before they were hired. Safe houses were set up in Lima and Cajamarca, Harris traveled in armored cars that never followed the same route, and armed command posts surrounded the mine site. Forza troops in Darth Vader helmets patrolled the perimeter on all-terrain vehicles. "The Forza group was very well trained," Harris says. "On the other hand I carried my own weapon. I told them, 'You are to protect me against the Sendero Luminoso. This is to protect me from you guys.'"[7]

The first gold pour occurred in August 1993—twelve years after Paverd's first meeting with Benavides and ten years after Bowerman's first site visit. Some 81,500 ounces were produced that year at a cost of under $100 an ounce. The mountains turned out to be covered with shallow, low-grade disseminated gold deposits and as new mines and facilities came into production, Yanacocha quickly became the largest heap leach operation in the world and the crown jewel in Newmont's portfolio. Despite an elevation that taxes breathing and throttles the efficiency of internal combustion engines, Yanacocha has always benefited from high productivity. Production surpassed Newmont's Nevada operations in 2003 and topped three million ounces in both 2004 and 2005. Cash production costs have consistently been half of those in Nevada, and since 1996 when Newmont increased its interest to 51.35 percent after a protracted legal battle with BRGM (see

14.2. To protect its workers and facilities at Yanacocha from the Sendero Luminoso guerrillas, Newmont employed a private security force, called Forza, which patrolled on all-terrain vehicles. (*Jack Morris*)

chapter 17), Yanacocha has been Newmont's most profitable operation. With 9,000 employees, Yanacocha also is one of Peru's largest employers and taxpayers ($284 million paid in 2006).

Through 2008, Yanacocha had sold nearly 27 million ounces of gold, while reserves of 25 million ounces remain to be mined. From its humble beginning, the operation now involves an investment exceeding $2.5 billion.

Those numbers far exceed anything the early participants could have imagined. But Harris deserves credit for more than just getting the operation started on a firm foundation. He and his wife helped shape Newmont's commitment to community service. For years, Cajamarca had been a center for radical protests centered on the local university and the Catholic Church, which at the time had a number of foreign priests practicing what became known as liberation theology, a form of socialism. Early demonstrations against the mine spurred on by the mayor convinced Harris that the project had to be more than just a fair employer. At the same time, Rosa, listening to the concerns of other wives, was convinced that Forza could not protect the workers unless Yanacocha won the hearts and minds of the people. "We wanted to weave a security blanket around our husbands and friends working in the mine,"[8] she says. Her answer: Adaminya, an organization of wives and women employees to help the campesinos and subsistence farmers near the mine site.

Harris threw the company's support behind health and education, but was soon told by his wife that his approach would not work. "I asked why, and she said, 'These kids are starving.' I said, 'What are we supposed to do?' and she said, 'Feed them.' I said, 'But if we get into that how will we ever get out of it?'" Sociologists were consulted and the relief agency CARE was brought into the equation. Under the Harrises, Newmont worked out a philosophy of "giving a hand up, not a handout." CARE provided the food, the company supplied materials for stoves and construction, and men in the community were engaged in building schoolrooms and mothers in cooking meals.

The number of children attending local schools was 200 in 1993. Five years later it was 3,500, with girls attending in significant numbers for the first time. Malnutrition, which afflicted more than half the children in 1995, was sharply reduced with more than 2,000 students receiving daily meals. Newmont's commitment to the communities in which it mines has

14.3. Len and Rosa Harris began Newmont's community relations program in Peru. (*Len Harris files*)

expanded immensely since 1993, as have public expectations (see chapter 19). But much of its approach began in the mountains of Peru and was born of a necessity seen by Len and Rosa Harris.

Newmont also found success, although on a smaller scale, in Mexico, where a joint venture with Peñoles, Mexico's largest silver miner, began in 1987. After searching several years for gold in the mountains of southern California, geologist James Mayor followed a geologic fault line southeast into Mexico, which allowed foreign companies to engage in mining ventures only as minority partners. Coincidently, Peñoles, which operated underground mines, was looking for a means of entering the rising gold market and was seeking a partner with open-pit experience. Newmont became a 44 percent partner; Peñoles was the operating partner. A 1.7-million-ounce oxide deposit called La Herradura (horseshoe in Spanish) was discovered in northern Sonora Province in 1991. Geologist Allen Cockle, as project manager, brought the mine, heap leach plant, and Merrill Crowe recovery plant into production in 1998 at a capital cost of $74 million. By

2000, with the addition of a crushing plant for harder ores, the facility was producing 115,000 ounces of gold per year at a cost of $131 an ounce. It continues as one of the company's smallest mines, but with potential for major expansion.

The company's Indonesian experience has a time line nearly as long as its history in Peru. John A. S. Dow, a New Zealand geologist who joined Newmont Proprietary in Perth, Australia, in 1978, moved to Jakarta in 1983 to undertake a three-year greenfield exploration program. He ended up staying thirteen years and overseeing two major discoveries—Minahasa and Batu Hijau. To support his effort, Dow and his wife, Linda, took language classes in Bahasa Indonesian, becoming among the many at Newmont who are multilingual.

Companies have limited exploration dollars, and though Ellett during Carlin's infancy thought they were best spent looking close to existing mines, his successor, Parry, Newmont's exploration chief from 1987 to 1992, argued that only greenfield exploration could find company-making deposits. He cites the work of two mineral economists at Queens University in Canada, Brian Mackenzie and Michael Doggett, who looked at every base metal discovery in Canada and Australia over a hundred-year period through 1988. By developing a mine plan for each economic deposit based on then-current prices, they created a cumulative profit curve showing which mines were most profitable. Of 129 mines in the study, 12, or 9 percent, produced 68 percent of the profits and 25 mines, or 20 percent, generated 80 percent of the profits.[9] The Pareto Principle is alive and well in mining. Furthermore, in a proven district like Carlin, Parry believes, only one or two mines—usually discovered early in the process—will contain 80 percent of the reserves. Gold Quarry with 30 million ounces of gold (not all classified as reserves) and Betze-Post with 50 million ounces are the giants of the Carlin Trend; the rest, he says, are pygmies by comparison.

Therefore, Parry says, even when money was lean in the days after Boone Pickens and when so much effort was being spent building up Carlin, "My focus [as head of global exploration] was always on new districts and going into new areas to make sure we found the big ones first."[10]

By the early 1980s, the geological community was beginning to take notice of gold deposits around the Pacific Rim, and while some high-grade epithermal deposits were well-known, most of the region had not been explored. When Newmont decided to take a look, Dow, who had spent three years in Indonesia with Kennecott, was given the assignment.

There are more than thirteen thousand islands in Indonesia, many volcanic and nearly all jungle covered. Where was one to look? Not surprisingly, Dow chose a path that others had already trod. "The first year I was in Indonesia I visited every known gold occurrence except one. I went first to North Sulawesi because that's where I'd worked with Kennecott in the 1970s."[11]

The Dutch mined high-grade gold veins in the Ratatotok area around 1900. Dow went underground and took samples from the walls and pillars of these old workings and found "amazing results" that justified further exploration. Ratatotok is one of several small subsistence farming and fishing villages located near the equator sixty-five miles southwest of Manado, the provincial capital of North Sulawesi. Scattered clove, vanilla, and coconut groves covered the area. It was nearly inaccessible by road.

In August 1984, Dow applied to the Indonesian Mines Department for a Contract of Work (COW) covering two thousand square miles of ground around Ratatotok and other areas of similar geology elsewhere on the island. Indonesian law required applications by foreign companies to include a local partner, and if a company did not have one, the Mines Department would suggest someone. The man Dow was told he should see was Jusuf Merukh.

Unlike Benavides, a man of substance and impeccable credentials whose family has been close friends of Newmont's senior management for years, Merukh was an enigma. Born on the small eastern island of Roti near Timor, he was trained as an agricultural scientist, served as a government bureaucrat, was elected to the lower house of Parliament as a member of the Christian party, from which he later had a falling out, and operated in the shadowy world of Jakarta businessmen. He was a partner in unspecified joint ventures, engaged in the import and export trade, and hauled gravel by barge to construction sites in Singapore. He became interested in minerals long before anyone else in Indonesia and applied for mining claims (or KPs as they were called) in many areas of the old Dutch mines. At one point he held twenty-seven KPs across the country. Then in the 1980s, when foreign companies like Newmont came to Indonesia and located areas they wanted to explore, they found that Merukh already had an application on file for the ground.

Merukh became a 20 percent carried partner in a new company, PT Newmont Minahasa Raya, in which Newmont owned 80 percent but put up all the money for exploration and later development. A year later, Merukh repaid the favor by offering to partner with Newmont on a COW in the province of Nusa Tenggara, which included the island of Sumbawa and a portion of Lombok. He had originally filed an application for the entire province with CSR, an Australian mining company that had begun life as Colonial Sugar Refineries, but the provincial governor did not want so much land in a single concession and ordered Merukh to cut his holdings in half and find another partner. Dow had already targeted western Sumbawa as an area of geological interest and was delighted when CSR chose the eastern half of the province and allowed Newmont, with Merukh as a 20 percent carried partner, to take the west.

The Mines Department was facing an avalanche of mining applications, and to sort it all out it declared a moratorium on new permits from mid-1985 through most of 1986. No one was sure they would get their applications and without published maps it was impossible to tell what land was covered by preexisting applications. "You couldn't tell if there were any shenanigans going on in the Mines Department, which was an absolute hotbed of re-drafting," Dow says. When Newmont finally got its permits in December 1986, it received only a small portion of its original application at Minahasa, the bulk of the area being awarded to Aneka Tambang, the Indonesian state mining company. However, its COW did include the ground it had sought around Ratatotok. In Nusa Tenggara the entire application was approved except for a 25,000-hectare (98-square-mile) block on Sumbawa, which was subject to prior application.

The gap between government permission to explore and actually finding a minable deposit is measured in years of hard work. Dow assembled a multinational team of geologists to do the ground work and evaluate the results. It took more than a year to do the first-pass fieldwork at the two sites and a third location that had been staked on the west coast of Sumatra.

Each concession was divided into catchment areas of one to two square miles. The field geologists then walked up every stream or ravine in each catchment to collect representative soil and rock samples. Four tests were performed. A silt sample was taken with minus eighty mesh screens in a geochemical technique developed in the Philippines by Alan Coope, one of the discoverers of the Carlin deposit, for his doctoral thesis in the 1960s. Second was a new BLEG (bulk leach extractable gold) test in which bucket-size samples of bulk material from streambeds were collected for a laboratory cyanide test to detect microscopic particles of gold. The third test was to collect samples of rocks and boulders washed down from further upstream to assist with subsequent interpretation of the geochemical analysis. Fourth was conventional panning to collect samples of heavy minerals. Several hours of work were required at each sample site and then the samples, with the aid of local laborers, had to be hauled back to camp.

"My instructions to the troops was this," says Dow. "The big expense is getting you guys into the field. Assays cost peanuts by comparison. I don't want to have to go back to any site because you screwed up the sampling. I only want to go back because you found something."

The field testing was designed to detect anomalies of gold and possibly base metals like copper and nickel. Dozens of potential targets were identified in the Minahasa concession, but while the rock samples had tested as much as an ounce of gold per ton, twenty diamond drill holes ended in barren rock. A local farmer presented the team with a gold nugget he had found while plowing his field, setting off another search, this time with a bulldozer to dig a trench across the farmer's field. Again good gold values were found in the surface soils and in the trench, but when diamond drilling went deeper there was only barren limestone—"tombstone stuff," according to Dow. "It got to the point you'd scratch your head and say, 'This is ridiculous—there's gold everywhere, but no obvious source.'"

Steve Turner, the team's chief geologist, then tried something different. He gathered dozens of specimens of gold-bearing rocks that had been collected in the area and laid them out on a table. The local field hands, drivers, and helpers who had been hired from the local villages were asked to take a look to see if they could recognize any of the rocks. One man with a Dutch name, Hein Piet Emor, instantly recognized a cream-colored limestone rock as coming from an area a day's drive away and the next day led a geologist to the spot. It turns out he had driven a logging truck over the area several years before and the truck kept bottoming out on a large outcropping in the road. Emor took a sledgehammer and broke off the top of the rock so he wouldn't bang his truck. That piece was identical to the rock on Turner's table. Newmont called it "Hein's find."

The August 1988 find wasn't quite a discovery, but it was sufficient to cause the team to relocate its camp and redirect its effort. Subsequent drilling in 1989 located Mesel, the largest of three ore bodies at Minahasa, in hilly terrain just a few hundred yards from Hein's find in rocks that had not been exposed enough to be detected by the initial drainage geochemical surveys. The anomalies the team had spent a year and a half drilling were lateral extensions of the Mesel deposit that had eroded away. Hole 27, with an impressive mineralized intercept of 350 feet beginning just below the surface and testing more than a third of an ounce of gold per ton, convinced Dow that his team had made a significant discovery. In all, some 2.1 million ounces of high-grade (0.204 once per ton) refractory ore were found in the three deposits.

However, with Carlin requiring all of the company's available capital, Newmont was in no hurry to develop a small mine in such a remote location. Site preparation at Minahasa did not begin until November 1994, and with a grinding mill, small roaster, gold recovery plant, and port as requirements, $130 million was invested before the first ounce of gold was produced. That came in March 1996, twelve years after Dow first chipped samples from the old Dutch workings in the area.

A similar exploration regimen was followed for the Nusa Tenggara concession. Forty anomalous sample sites were located and ranked according to their gold values, with a couple of copper anomalies thrown in for later evaluation. After more than two years following the most promising gold prospects without significant results, attention shifted to copper. The best samples came from a stream draining off a high hill that was in the center of the ground that had been excluded from the original COW. "My instruction to our exploration guys was, 'If you want to get fired, just step over that boundary,'" Dow says. "No one wants to find a discovery on somebody else's ground. At that point we could not find out who held the ground and I didn't want to go directly to the Mines Department in Jakarta without that knowledge for fear that it might arouse someone else's interest." During a subsequent meeting with the regional chief of mines in Lombok the subject was casually broached and to Dow's surprise he was told that the original applicant had never paid the security deposit and that the land was available. He quickly applied to amend the COW to include the vacant ground and, once the legal amendments had been signed by the government, sent a team to the site to begin follow-up exploration.

In May 1990, geologist Bob Burke was the first to walk up the 1,750-foot hill while checking stream sediment anomalies and panning for gold in the streambed. When he neared the top, he found that supergene-enriched porphyry copper mineralization cropped out into the stream with a spectacular display where leaching groundwater had left a green copper precipitate on logs, branches, leaves, and rocks. "Across this brightly colored outcrop ran a very well-worn footpath. Local hunters had obviously been there before but didn't know that this was anything other than the way rocks there had always been," Dow marvels. It didn't take long for this new discovery to be named Batu Hijau (green rock in Indonesian). Although its location on the southwest corner of Sumbawa was uninhabited, it is not that remote. The Gunung Agung volcano on Bali is visible from the top of the hill.

All of Newmont's work in Indonesia had been done under the auspices of Newmont Proprietary, based in Australia. When it floated a 25 percent interest in its Australian assets to create Newmont Australia Limited in April 1987, the firm's exploration activities in Indonesia and Papua New Guinea were excluded. The Macquarie Bank, which handled the IPO, reasoned that investors would not pay much for these early stage projects. Newmont Australia continued to second its staff and manage the Indonesian exploration on behalf of the parent company even as Newmont moved to further reduce its Australian holdings. With exploration taking an increasing share of the Australian company's human resources, John Quinn, chief executive of Newmont Australia, issued Parker an ultimatum: either share the fruits of the discoveries with his company or find someone else to manage the Indonesian projects. Parker chose the latter and in 1990 Dow and his entire team moved to Newmont Mining's Denver payroll.

It proved to be a hugely beneficial move for Newmont as years of drilling identified nearly 15 million ounces of gold and 11 billion pounds of copper at Batu Hijau. By the time production began in December 1999, $2 billion had been invested in the mine, mill, concentrator, port, power plant, and accommodation village. And while the company was looking for gold, the new mine put Newmont back in the copper business for the first time in twelve years. Today, Batu Hijau is a world-class operation and along with

Carlin and Yanacocha a symbol of Newmont's success in grassroots exploration, project development, and mine management.

The company's venture into Uzbekistan, a Central Asian country along the fabled Silk Road, was of an entirely different order, grounded in diplomacy as well as technology. It all began in late 1990 with a visit by Newmont senior geologist Joseph Kowalik to Muruntau, the largest open-pit gold mine in the world. Opened in 1972 and responsible for nearly one-third of the gold production in the former Soviet Union, Muruntau had been off limits to Western visitors. It wasn't gold that caused such secrecy but the nearby uranium mines operated by the Navoi Mining and Metallurgical Combine, Uzbekistan's state-owned mining entity. Kowalik learned of a first-ever tour while attending a mining conference in Moscow in 1990 and pressed two other geologists into joining him on the trip.

After flying to Tashkent, the Uzbek capital, the three made their way to the mine, 250 miles to the west and in the middle of the Kyzylkum Desert, in a 1948 Soviet biplane that was forced to land in a field along the way because of a heavy storm. The pit was impressive, but what really caught Kowalik's eye was the largest stockpile he had ever seen—some 240 million tons of low-grade ore standing over a hundred feet high and stretching for several miles. His hosts had carefully segregated the ore by grade, from 0.035 to 0.05 ounce per ton, but did not have the technology to process it.

Uzbek dinners are noted for their many vodka toasts and that evening with Tulkun Shayakubov, the chairman of the State Committee for Geology and Mineral Resources, in attendance, Kowalik raised his glass to Soviet-American cooperation. "One of my more lengthy toasts was that Newmont had 25 years of experience in heap leaching, that we in fact helped develop the technology to heap leach low grade ores and that if they were interested they should contact us,"[12] he said later. He left his business card. To his great surprise, in April 1991 he received a letter taking him up on his offer.

Shayakubov wanted to send four or five of his people to Nevada but could only afford to get them to New York. Was Newmont willing to pay their expenses in the States? Don McCall, one of three vice presidents of project development at the time, took it up with Parker, who under pressure from Jimmy Goldsmith to cut costs, suggested that only one make the trip. "Gordon, they don't come in ones. They only come in fours and fives,"[13]

McCall replied. Their visit to Nevada in May, the first time any of them had been outside the Soviet Union, was a huge success as they saw not only their first heap leach operation, but their first supermarket and first K-mart.

That August a Newmont technical delegation traveled to Muruntau to analyze the metallurgy of the ore they hoped to process. The team was headed by Parry and included McCall, Kowalik, Harris, and another vice president of project development, Marcel DeGuire, who would manage the project and bring it into production. After a stop in Moscow, the group took a 1 A.M. flight to Tashkent and while in the air, at 6 A.M. on August 19, hard-line Communists overthrew President Mikhail Gorbachev in a short-lived coup that triggered the breakup of the Soviet Union. Because of a news blackout, the Newmont team did not learn what had happened for a day or two. McCall remembers being "in the Kyzylkum Desert eating lunch when all of a sudden CNN came on the TV—the first time CNN had ever been broadcast there. We saw Yeltsin standing on a tank and they were saying Moscow was in flames. There were people in the room from Moscow and they were concerned."

With all flights grounded and no outside communication, the delegation went about its task. "The Uzbeks gave us first-class treatment. They gave us an expensive yurt to stay in and served us a different kind of pilaf every night," says McCall. They later learned that Rosa Harris and the other wives had been frantically calling Parker demanding that he get their husbands out. "We knew our wives were going crazy, but we were drunk as skunks, living high off the hog and couldn't go anywhere,"[14] DeGuire chuckles.

It was quickly determined that with extensive crushing, gold could be economically extracted from the stockpiled ore. The challenge was to sign an agreement that would allow Newmont to export the gold and sell it on the world market, something that had never been allowed in the Soviet Union. Vice chairman Richard Leather realized that the company had a narrow window of opportunity. Uzbekistan, which on August 31, 1991, became the first state to break away from the Soviet Union, "had not been spoiled as yet by advisor-type intervention from the U.N. or Europeans. As far as we could tell they had not yet received bad advice and their minds were open."[15]

Leather launched a diplomatic and educational mission of unprece-dented proportions. On a visit to New York in November, he arranged for

Shayakubov to meet with Thomas Pickering, the U.S. ambassador to the United Nations (whom Leather had met the year before on a rafting trip on the Salmon River in Idaho), and to stand on the podium of the General Assembly. Uzbekistan did not yet have a flag, but Newmont obtained a copy of its intended design and made up lapel pins with its green, white, and blue banner and the American Stars and Stripes. Leather remembers Pickering gesturing toward the row of flags in front of the U.N. Building, and saying, "One day, before long, we hope to see the flag of Uzbekistan flying among those of the member nations." On another visit, a Washington dinner was arranged for Shayakubov with James Woolsey, the former head of the CIA, who had joined the law firm of Shea & Gardner, Newmont's Washington counsel. These were incredible experiences for a former Soviet bureaucrat.

If that wasn't enough, Leather resorted to poetry. He found a poem by Alisher Navoi, Uzbekistan's greatest poet, about a peasant and a prince who journey across the mountains. They become totally dependent on one another and reach their goal only through such traits as friendship, confidence, understanding, loyalty, and faithfulness. Leather, who knew some Russian from his younger days as an international chess player, had the poem translated into Russian and was coached on how to read it. He then recited it at a dinner in New York.

"I said I would read it because the lessons taught by the poet illustrated Newmont's sense of what we were doing," he recalls. "I said I was sorry I couldn't read it in Uzbek and would probably mangle it in Russian. So I read it, it was maybe twenty lines, and when I finished I gave it to Shayakubov and said, 'Now Mr. Minister, will you read it back to us properly, the way the poet Navoi intended it to be heard?' He was familiar with the poem and declaimed with all the rolling alliteration that is in the language and finished by clapping the book closed in a dramatic fashion. It was a small thing, but it built confidence on a real basis. I put in the effort and wasn't overly embarrassed by butchering the language, but I wanted to convince them that we were making a moral commitment based on trust."

Parker and Leather, who met with President Islam Karimov in Tashkent in January 1992, were determined that the transaction be above scrutiny. "I told Shayakubov, 'Mr. Minister, you can take this agreement to any objective critic and you will not find one valid contention that you have been taken advantage of,'" Leather recalls saying. "'This is a normal joint venture with proper rewards for capital and proper rewards for the asset that you bring. You will be able to use this transaction as a format in any other transaction with foreign investors.'" Goldsmith, who had become a strong supporter of the project, recommended Sam Pisar, a Russian-speaking French lawyer who had handled one of his divorces, to help draft the agreement. He was joined by Alex Papachristou, a young lawyer in White & Case's Moscow office, who spoke numerous languages and was an expert on the Koran. From the Uzbek side, Sodyg Safaev, an English-speaking member of Uzbek's economics ministry who had attended MIT and later became the country's ambassador to both the United States and the United Nations, was influential in resolving differences.

Dozens of Newmont employees—technical, financial, and legal—made trips to Uzbekistan to work out the details of the agreement. All tell hairraising stories of local airplanes with metal cords protruding from bald tires, cracked windows, nonexistent seatbelts, smoking stewardesses, and drunken stowaways. Once when important papers had to be carried from Muruntau to Tashkent, a dust storm grounded the only commercial flight. There was a midnight train, but it was fully booked. One of the Uzbek negotiators had a brother who was a policeman. When the train pulled into the station, he entered the first car and removed three sleepy and vodka-sodden passengers and then ushered DeGuire and two associates aboard.

The Zarafshan-Newmont Joint Venture agreement was signed in February 1992—six months after the country's independence—with Newmont owning 50 percent and 25 percent each being held by two Uzbek state agencies, Shayakubov's State Committee for Geology and the Navoi Mining and Metallurgical Combine headed by Nickolay Kuchersky. A Ukrainian, Kuchersky was also deputy prime minister. He controlled the country's gold and uranium mines, ran the schools and hospitals in the mining districts, built the streets, collected the garbage, and had a workforce of fifty thousand. Newmont never felt it was entirely welcome on his turf.

Under the agreement, the government provided the stockpiled ore at a guaranteed grade, containing 8.7 million ounces of gold. With leach recovery rates of 50 to 65 percent, this was expected to yield 4.8 million ounces of gold over a seventeen-year period. While Newmont's gold from Nevada and Peru is refined in Switzerland, the Zarafshan gold was processed at Muruntau, which won international recognition as a certified refinery, a plus for the government, and then transported to London for sale. Newmont purchased a portion of the stockpile up front and later resold it to the joint venture to advance the Uzbek's share of the project's $250 million capital cost.

As soon as the joint venture began to take shape, Treasurer Patricia Flanagan began "dialing for dollars" and contacted the London-based European Bank for Reconstruction and Development (EBRD), which had just been established and was looking for a flagship project in which to invest. With the EBRD as the lead, she and Wayne Murdy, who joined Newmont as CFO that fall, put together a consortium of thirteen banks from around the world to provide $135 million in financing.

Selling the project was not a problem; selling the country was. W. Durand "Randy" Eppler, who worked on the transaction as a loan officer at Chemical Bank and later became vice president of corporate development for Newmont, recalls, "It was a hard deal to get done because no one in New York even wanted to spell Uzbekistan."[16] At the same time, Eppler and Chemical were working with Newmont on an innovative financing plan for a $350 million roaster at Carlin. "Wayne said if we wanted to do the roaster deal, we had to help get financing for Uzbekistan. It was all about motivation." It also helped that Newmont, in another first, obtained political risk insurance from two multinational agencies to back the loans.

From the outset, it was clear that in addition to financing, Newmont would have to provide financial education for its new partners. Ron Vance, who had handled copper sales for years and was now Newmont's third vice president of project development, introduced the Uzbeks to Barclay's Bank of London, one of the lenders, which offered help in creating an Uzbek Central Bank, and to N. M. Rothschild & Sons, where twice daily since 1919 five employees establish the benchmark London daily gold fix, or spot price, to educate them about gold pricing and marketing. At one joint venture meeting, Murdy found he had to digress from his presentation to explain compound interest.

Ground was broken in October 1993 for an operation that included a four-stage crushing circuit to reduce 42,500 tons of rock per day to fine ore, a large conveyor-stacking system, lined leach pads, and a Merrill-Crowe recovery plant. Bateman Engineering designed the facility. Logistics for the project, the largest construction job in Central Asia, was an incredible feat requiring the delivery of 45,000 tons of steel, machinery, and earth-moving equipment. Gerald Hartzel, Newmont's director of administration, arranged for material from the United States to be flown out by giant Antonov aircraft or shipped from Houston to Finland and then on to the site by the Russian rail system. To protect large pieces of equipment, the Russians made plywood templates and placed them on railcars toward the front of the train. Then if the template struck an underpass or the side of a tunnel, they would stop the train to reroute the equipment. Steel came from Korea over the Trans Siberian Railroad and pipe from South Africa was trucked across Iran. At its peak in the bitterly cold winter of 1994, 1,366 workers were employed on the project. Later, much to its chagrin, Newmont learned that many of those workers were prisoners assigned to the project by the government.

DeGuire, a burly French Canadian who says that he looks more like an Uzbek than the Uzbeks, was the only one within Newmont willing to take on the assignment as general manager and credits Hartzel for keeping him supplied with frozen steaks and canned goods when the local markets served up little that met with the American palate. "Gerry was the guy that no matter where you were in the world and you said you needed something and needed it the next day, he would get it for you. He was the glue that kept Newmont together." DeGuire established an excellent rapport with Newmont's partners and developed a genuine fondness for the Uzbek people. After leaving Newmont, he brought his wife and children to the country for vacation.

Production began slowly in 1995 after a $100 million construction cost overrun, but expectations were high. At a gala dedication celebration in Tashkent on May 25, Newmont CEO Ronald Cambre thanked the company's two Uzbek partners for their dedication in bringing the project into operation. "This is an important moment for Newmont," he said. "Not only does it mark the beginning of a new source of gold production, but I am confident it is the beginning of a long and successful period of economic cooperation between our company and the Republic of Uzbekistan that will open the door to other opportunities."[17] It was the same hope that had led Leather to recite poetry.

That, however, never happened. Several attempts to enter new ventures bogged down in seemingly endless negotiations, while the difficulty of

14.4. Dressed in traditional Uzbek robes, CEO Ronald Cambre (right) and Nickolay Kuchersky, Uzbek deputy prime minister and head of Navoi Mining and Metallurgical Combine, at the 1995 grand opening of the Zarafshan joint venture. (*Bill Lyons*)

working in the shadow of a command-and-control economy always took its toll. Zarafshan-Newmont had its best year in 2002 with production of 512,000 ounces of gold, half for Newmont's account, at a cash cost of $134 an ounce. But output declined thereafter, in part because with higher prices the government began delivering lower-grade ore.

Then, in June 2006, the government retroactively changed its tax law, which a state court immediately upheld, and assessed the joint venture $48 million in back taxes. This was a violation of Decree 151, which the government had issued as a condition of the joint venture agreement, guaranteeing that there would be no change in tax laws during the life of the project. In August, the government issued involuntary bankruptcy proceedings against the joint venture, halted gold exports and the payment of foreign debts, and seized all gold and inventory on the premises. The action amounted to an expropriation of the company's assets. The company immediately removed its last expatriate employees from the country and in September 2006 wrote off the book value of its investment, taking a pre-tax loss of $101 million.

Newmont was swept into Uzbekistan on the winds of independence when President Karimov saw closer ties with the United States and increased foreign investment as important developments for his country. But Uzbekistan has never been as independent as many had hoped. By 2006, with rising unrest within its Muslim population, with continued U.S. criticism of the country's civil rights abuses, and with Karimov's ties to Russian president Vladimir Putin strengthening, the country was less willing to share its natural resources with the West than it had been a decade earlier. And with a higher gold price, it was also willing to breach a contract with an American company.

Still, Colonel William Boyce Thompson, who earned a reputation for making money from others' scrap heaps in Arizona, would be proud of Newmont's accomplishments in the Kyzylkum Desert.

Benavides

Successful, long-lived companies often depend on lasting relationships that can withstand business cycles and changes in administration. Newmont Mining's corporate picture would not be complete without a portrait of Peru's Benavides family.

Newmont has been a partner with the Benavides, the principal owners of Compañia de Minas Buenaventura, since 1984 when the two companies joined forces to search for silver and gold in the northern Andes. That venture led to the discovery of the huge Yanacocha gold mine, one of the largest in the world. But the relationship goes back much further, to the 1960s, when company founder Alberto Benavides was also chairman of Cerro de Pasco Corporation, which was a partner with Newmont in Southern Peru Copper.

Benavides obtained a master's degree in geology from Harvard University in 1944 and founded Buenaventura in Lima nine years later. Over more than fifty years he shepherded its growth into one of the top ten miners of precious metals in the world with annual sales approaching $1 billion. Benavides is a name rich in Peruvian history; Oscar Benavides served as the country's president from 1914 to 1915 and again from 1933 to 1939. Alberto is not a direct descendent; his aunt, also a Benavides, was Oscar's wife. But in modern Peru, the Benavides who comes first to mind and tongue is Alberto, not Oscar. While he remains Buenaventura's chairman, day-to-day operations are in the hands of his two sons, Roque, president and CEO, and Raúl, vice president of corporate development, and son-in-law, Jose Miguel Morales, who is general counsel. Aubrey Paverd, the Newmont geologist who directed the exploration team at Yanacocha, is a Buenaventura director.

"When we went in, we were fortunate that we had a Peruvian national partner of excellent reputation,"[18] says former Newmont CEO Ronald Cambre. "The Benavides

14.5. Alberto Benavides (right), a friend of Newmont's since the 1960s, was a founding partner in Yanacocha. He is pictured in 1995 with Newmont CEO Ronald Cambre and Carlos Santa Cruz, who later became senior vice president of Newmont's South American operations. (*Compañia de Minas Buenaventura*)

are very, very classy people in every respect; some of the finest people I've met in my entire life." Says Roque Benavides, "Openness and transparency have been the foundation of our relationship." Speaking of Cambre's successor as CEO, Wayne Murdy, he adds, "If I call Wayne anywhere in the world, I get an immediate call back."[19]

With the success of Yanacocha, investors and analysts often ask why the two companies have not merged. The answer is mutual respect and mutual benefit from the current arrangement. When the partnership was first formed, Benavides offered to sell a quarter of Buenaventura to Newmont for $8 million. But wary of Peru's political instability at the time, then CEO Plato Malozemoff declined. Over the years, "We had discussions with Alberto and other members of the family, the next generation, to say we were a willing buyer," says Cambre. "But obviously it had to be a friendly deal." Adds Roque, "Ron and Wayne have told me and my father repeatedly that if anyone wants to make a run on us, Newmont will be there to support us. But I think that by remaining an independent company and the largest mining house in Peru, Buenaventura adds value for Newmont." Cambre agrees, adding, "I think in the end they did the wise thing. They stayed in and held on and they've reaped a whole lot of financial wealth from it."

While Newmont's 51.4 percent interest in Yanacocha helped elevate the company to world-class status, Buenaventura's 43.6 percent stake has made the Benavides very wealthy indeed. With a portfolio of several smaller mines, Buenaventura had a market capitalization in 2009 of $10 billion, of which the Benavides family held 25 percent.

15

CULTURE SHOCK

As Ronald C. Cambre took the helm as Newmont's sixth CEO on November 1, 1993, the company was on the cusp of a new era of growth. Production at Yanacocha would begin the next day. Two weeks later, ground was broken on the Zarafshan-Newmont joint venture in Uzbekistan, and a feasibility study was under way for the Minahasa mine in Indonesia. In Nevada, construction had begun six months earlier on a high-tech roaster to treat refractory ores, and for the first time exploration was looking at underground mining, where ore grades could run ten times that of surface deposits.

Immediately whisked off by Jim Hill, the company's vice president of corporate relations, to meet analysts and investors in New York, Boston, and Toronto, Cambre listened as president Peter Philip presented the company's upbeat outlook. Production was predicted to increase by one-third to two million ounces by 1997. Newmont had impressive gold reserves in North America at 25 million ounces, and, Philip noted, the industry's largest exploration budget, $65 million in 1993, with 250 geologists and other professionals searching for new prospects in North America, Mexico, Ecuador, Laos, Indonesia, and elsewhere.

Arriving in Denver for the first time a week later, the new CEO faced a more sobering reality. "If you looked at the five-year plan, we had a growth profile that we could not staff. We badly needed to recruit talent throughout the organization."[1] Senior people were retiring, while the technical lightning rods who had built Carlin over the previous six years found the transition to management difficult. Tragically, Walter Lawrence, a talented and well-liked metallurgist, died of a heart attack at age forty-eight in 1994, less than two years after moving to Denver as senior vice president of operations. He had been uncomfortable in the suit and tie world of a twenty-eighth-floor office and at board meetings in New York.

Just the opposite, Cambre would have moved the company's headquarters back to New York had Newmont been able to afford it. While Plato Malozemoff and Gordon Parker were miners who became executives, Cambre was an executive long before he put on a hard hat and boots. He thought strategically, preferred to work alone, and delegated details and mine tours to others.

He valued teamwork and a cooperative process he called "matrix management" that few could fathom. The troops wanted to know who approved their bonus checks and promotions. During his years at Freeport he rose to senior ranks, he says, without anybody having said, "'I'm your boss.' I got accustomed to not treating people like I was their boss. When I came to Newmont that wasn't understood. There were people who considered me to be an intruder. I recall people telling me that what I was proposing 'isn't the Newmont way.' You could just tell some people were thinking, 'He won't last. Then we'll get back to being who we really are.'"

Wedging between the old hands and the new CEO was one of Cambre's first new hires, Lawrence T. Kurlander, who as senior vice president of administration had few defined responsibilities but many opinions and a say on all who came, went, or advanced within the company.[2] Painfully shy, Cambre did not mingle easily with employees and welcomed Kurlander as a confidant and intermediary. Kurlander had been a prosecuting attorney in upstate New York and an appointee in Governor Mario Cuomo's cabinet, and had worked in public relations at American Express and RJR Nabisco. Quickly dubbed the "cookie monster" by people at Carlin, he knew nothing of mining, showed little respect for the company's technical heritage, and challenged conventional wisdom by, among other things, advocating fewer guns and guards at Yanacocha.

"Larry came into what was an old-line organization that was accustomed to being treated fairly gently and Larry's nature was to confront people. It didn't take long for the organization to react to him," Cambre acknowledges. Yet he helped raise the bar of professionalism in human resources, a vital but long-neglected department that had its origin in labor relations at Magma Copper. With approval from the board of directors, compensation, bonus programs, and stock options were meaningfully increased—a necessity if the company was going to attract and retain the talent Cambre felt it needed.

The company's most pressing talent shortfall was in the areas of international development and operations; with the shift to gold, there was hardly anyone left with experience in those areas. One of the first to fill that void was David Francisco, a geological engineer who had worked for both Magma at San Manuel and Granduc in Canada after graduating from the University of Arizona. He had spent the previous nine years with Freeport, the last several as general manager of its giant Grasberg copper and gold mine in Indonesia. With Newmont about to enter the country, he had ideal credentials and in 1995 was hired as vice president of international operations. He advanced to senior vice president in 1997 and to executive vice president of all operations in 2000. Cambre knew Francisco only by reputation during his years at Freeport and scrupulously avoided talking to him until he severed all links with his former employer. "Having spent thirty years with Freeport and being close to a lot of people there, I didn't want to be seen as raiding their organization," Cambre says.

Another newcomer was Robert Bush, who had spent most of his career with Morrison Knutsen, an international construction concern. Although he graduated from the University of Idaho with a degree in history, he was steeped in mining. Both his father in 1972 and his grandfather forty years earlier died in mining accidents, his father in a fire at a Sunshine Mining silver mine that killed ninety-two people. More important, he brought a background of successful project management and a passport stamped in sixty-five countries. Joining as vice president of materials management, he later headed human resources and succeeded Kurlander as senior vice president of administration before retiring in 2006.

Joining from the Jerritt Canyon mine in Nevada, formerly a Freeport operation, were Scott Barr and Richard Perry, both with master's degrees from Nevada's Mackay School of Mines. Barr, an astute metallurgical engineer with a bull-in-the-china-shop approach to situations, also had mining in his blood. His father was a miner and a great-grandfather had worked the famous Comstock Lode in Nevada. Barr was hired as vice president of mine planning, at one point headed operations in Peru, and later became vice president of technical strategy. Perry joined in a senior position in Nevada, was general manager during the start-up of the Batu Hijau mine in Indonesia, and then returned to Nevada as vice president of operations before retiring in 2005.

Cambre was appalled that nearly everyone in the company regardless of rank or background acted as independent M&A (mergers and acquisition) specialists, negotiating their own deals for drilling rights, joint ventures, or acquisitions. To elevate the M&A effort within the company, Randy Eppler was recruited as vice president of corporate development from Chemical Bank, where he had worked on Newmont financing and provided personal loans for company executives since 1980. With a master's degree in mineral economics from the Colorado School of Mines, he says Cambre told him, "You have the easiest job in the company. You don't have to explore for gold. You don't have to produce gold. You just have to grow the company."[3]

Few would question the talent of the new players or the company's need to invoke new thinking after years of fighting defensive battles. But it was a shake-up nonetheless. Some even thought of it as a Freeport takeover. "In the past, the senior people had by and large grown up within the company. You had a lot of people with fifteen, twenty, or even thirty years' tenure," observes former vice president and corporate secretary Tim Schmitt. But within a few years under Cambre, "with only a few exceptions they were all outsiders . . . so there was no unity, no history." The difference between the old Newmont and the new was also one of style and emphasis. "There is a picture in *Men and Mines*," Schmitt says of the company's fiftieth anniversary book, "in which you see all these people poring over project maps, blueprints, and designs. I never saw Ron doing that. He and Wayne [Murdy, then CFO and later CEO] would get into a room and pull out their Hewlett Packard calculators and start calculating discount rates or some such thing."[4]

Cambre's first challenge occurred in Nevada, where construction of a refractory ore treatment plant, or roaster, the largest piece of hardware in the gold industry, was behind schedule. Costs had ballooned from $197 million to $350 million. A roaster heats ore to over 1,000 degrees Fahrenheit to burn off the carbon and sulfides that encase ore that has not been oxidized by nature. Such ore cannot be processed by conventional means.

As early as 1985, Philip had begun looking at ways to treat refractory ores, which were becoming more prevalent as mining at Carlin went deeper. Barrick and others adopted autoclaves, giant steam-filled pressure cookers. This worked for sulfidic ores, but Newmont's mines also contained carbonaceous ores that did not respond well in an autoclave. Dry roasting

15.1. The refractory ore treatment plant, or roaster, at Carlin was the largest gold plant in North America when it was constructed in 1994. (*Andrew Craig*)

became the preferred option. Freeport had developed a roasting technique at Jerritt Canyon that Newmont rejected because it considered the licensing fee too high and because it believed Freeport had infringed on one of its patents years earlier.

"At the end of the day, we would have been much better off if we had swallowed our pride and done the deal,"[5] says Tom Enos, who oversaw construction and start-up of Newmont's roaster. Barr, who worked closely with the Freeport roaster, agrees, adding, "It was proven technology and probably would have saved $150 million in capital and $7 a ton on everything it processed."[6]

Original plans called for two roasters, one in the North Area near the Post deposit and the other fifteen miles to the south near Gold Quarry. But the two areas were served by different utilities, and Wells Electric supplying Gold Quarry offered lower electric rates than Sierra Pacific. As a result, the decision was made to go with one huge roaster and construct a special haul road to move ore from the north to the new facility.

The Freeport system would have treated the gas released by the roaster with lime to neutralize it. Instead, Newmont chose a design by Lurgi AG of Germany that converted the gas to sulfuric acid that could be sold to Barrick for use in its autoclaves. But it was a far more complex and costly process. In its final configuration, the refractory ore treatment plant, known as Mill No. 6, was three plants in one—a dry grinding mill, the roaster, and an acid plant—stretching 700 feet in length and reaching 100 feet in height. The grinding mill was designed by Bechtel and utilized a Krupp Polysius double rotator mill that turned the ore into talcum powder–like material. At 86 feet long and powered by a 12,500-horsepower electric motor, it is one of the largest grinding mills ever built. No one had ever tried to couple such units in a single facility. To make matters worse, Lurgi and Bechtel were often at each other's throats, while Newmont's oversight was divided between the Carlin operators and Denver engineers with Ken Brunk, the volatile vice president in the middle, threatening to fire everyone in sight.

As the facility was going through start-up in October 1994, one of two steel rings that supported the grinding mill failed under stress. A month later a fire destroyed an electrostatic precipitator used to clean gasses at the roaster. "There was black smoke coming out of a duct and we had water trucks pouring water on the thing. I was leaning on a steel girder looking at this and thinking, after all that grief, 'Why don't we just let this sucker burn down,'" says Enos. He, Brunk, and plant manager Trent Temple received the chairman's award for nursing the facility through start-up, yet it wasn't until 1997 that the roaster was able to approach its design capacity of 8,000 tons of ore per day and 750,000 ounces of gold a year.

Asked to do a postmortem on the project, Peter Crescenzo, the retired vice president of engineering, found that Newmont not only failed "to manage the various components of the project all under one head," but they also "began construction work while the flow sheet was still fluid."[7] As with his earlier projects at Carlin, Philip had followed a pedal-to-the-metal timetable knowing that with its oxide mines depleting, the company would soon have to curtail production without the roaster.

Cambre says the fiasco taught him three early lessons about the company. "First, we weren't very good at managing projects." Later delays and cost overruns in Uzbekistan added to that realization. "Number two, we didn't have the strength or depth of management we needed in Nevada. And number three, we needed to rationalize operations with Barrick to make better use of capital." While he worked throughout his tenure to build closer ties with Barrick, he addressed the first two issues with changes in personnel, among other things by putting a man with proven leadership capabilities in charge of Carlin: James Mullin, who had managed the Similkameen copper operation in Canada and had worked through the ranks in Nevada. Mullin later became senior vice president of operations, retiring in 2001.

Instead of ego and bravado, Mullin led by quiet example. "My goal was always to work longer and harder than anyone else. Getting there first and leaving last are simple things to do and everyone knows it. One of my sons asked me once why I worked longer than his friends' dads. At that point I had worked some twenty years with the company. I did a simple calculation and figured that by then I had worked an additional seven years in terms of the hours I had put in. It's a multiplier. It makes you a better person and it makes those around you better people. You can make one person work very hard with a whip, but you can make a thousand people work very hard by setting an example. Now you have a thousand minds addressing your problems with better results."[8]

To finance the roaster, the company adopted a leveraged lease plan crafted by Chemical Bank (it was Eppler's last project with the bank before joining Newmont). The roaster was sold to investors and then leased back for twenty-one years. It was a complex transaction designed to take advantage of differences in corporate tax rates. Because of percentage depletion, Newmont had a low federal tax rate and was generating tax credits it could not use, while food and tobacco companies have limited credits and therefore high tax rates. Chemical and three other investment bankers placed $265 million in debt financing and Philip Morris put up $75 million in equity capital, enabling it to utilize Newmont's unused tax credits. Newmont retains buyback options as the lease matures. A simultaneous hedge on interest rates brought the financing costs down to an attractive 6.15 percent.

Shortly thereafter, Newmont became the first company to produce gold from low-grade refractory ores using bio-oxidation. The process uses naturally occurring bacteria to oxidize the material (by eating the pyrites that encase the gold molecules), thereby freeing up the gold for cyanide recovery. James Brierley, with a Ph.D. from Montana State who retired in 2001 as chief microbiologist, holds patents on the process. He credits his success to the enthusiastic support he received from Philip, who regularly visited his lab in Salt Lake City.

Through years of experimentation, Brierley learned which organisms work best in oxidizing the ore (*Thiobacillus ferrooxidans*); how to grow them in huge quantities in large tanks; how best to inoculate the ore by spraying on the bacteria as the ore is stacked on a leach pad; how to control the air and temperature on the pad so the bacteria grow and perform; and how long to keep the process going. Initially used as a first step in heap leaching, the company now uses bio-leaching as a pre-treatment before milling. The ore is treated with the bacteria on a leach pad for 150 days (nature would do the job in a few million years) and then removed and processed at Mill No. 5 where 60 percent recovery rates can be achieved. Bio-oxidation generated 66,000 ounces of gold during its first year of operation and currently adds 120,000 to 180,000 ounces a year depending on grade.

Just as large-scale heap leaching of low-grade oxide ores had given the company a competitive edge a decade and a half earlier, bio-oxidation of refractory ores offered another way to extract value from rock that until then had been considered waste. "Anyone can make money in this business with high-grade ore. It's the ability to extract value from lower-grade material that gives you a competitive advantage,"[9] Cambre said at the time. "And if you tie that in with the fact that we have a very large, worldwide exploration program, you find a tremendous synergy. If you have the technology base and the people to extract value from whatever you find, I think you are ahead of the game."

While successful abroad, Newmont's domestic gold operations had never ventured beyond the Carlin Trend. Its first serious step outside Nevada, at Grassy Mountain in eastern Oregon, was a failure. The property was acquired with much fanfare in 1992 from Atlas Corporation, which thought it had identified a million-ounce deposit. Plans for an open-pit mine were enthusiastically welcomed in the nearby towns of Vale and Ontario, where unemployment was high. Then in 1994, environmentalists from Portland placed Measure 14 on the ballot to prohibit cyanide extraction of gold from open-pit mines in the state.

Mary Beth Donnelly, Newmont's vice president of government affairs, with the help of a Washington consulting group, waged a campaign to defeat the initiative by focusing on fairness, not mining. TV ads used plaid-shirted farmers to make the argument that folks living in eastern Oregon should not be told what to do by people in Portland. Bumper stickers read, "Vote no on 14; it's bad law." Buried among twenty-four other initiatives on the same ballot, the "bad law" image stuck and the measure was defeated by a 60 percent vote. Cambre called Donnelly to congratulate her. "Now what did this cost?" he asked. Told $3.5 million, he quipped, "Couldn't you have won by 51 percent and spent only $2 million?"[10] It was vintage Cambre.

With victory in hand, Newmont undertook its own drilling and found there was not enough ore to justify a mine. A $34 million pre-tax write-off was booked in 1995. Looking back, former CEO Gordon Parker blames "huge pressure" from Sir James Goldsmith "to do things, to expand,"[11] and for not doing proper due diligence prior to the acquisition. It was a mistake the company's founder, mindful of his father's early failure, would not have made.

Nevertheless, with the roaster advancing along its learning curve, bio-leaching moving from the lab to production and four underground mines in operation (all declines from existing pits), there was much to celebrate that July as four hundred company, state, and local leaders gathered at Carlin for the operation's thirtieth anniversary. By then, Newmont's Carlin mines had produced 16 million ounces of gold and employed 2,300 people. Among those attending were John Livermore and J. Alan Coope, the two geologists most responsible for the Carlin discovery in 1963.

On the dais with Cambre and Parker was Governor Bob Miller, who praised the company's environmental record and pledged his continued support for mining in Nevada. After leaving office three years later, he joined the Newmont board of directors. But that sunny summer day he was still a politician and, during a break in the ceremonies, leaned over to Cambre and requested a $25,000 contribution for a dinner he was hosting for President Clinton's reelection. The CEO agreed only to be told later by company lawyers that the use of corporate funds was illegal and that limits on individual contributions prevented him from writing a personal check.

Back in Denver, he called a meeting of officers and apologetically asked for their help. As Cambre explained, Miller and Nevada U.S. senator Harry Reid, who received contributions from the company's Political Action Committee, were two of the only pro-mining voices in an increasingly anti-mining Democratic Party and thus deserved Newmont's support. Would each officer consider writing a check for $2,000? Most did, but a few balked, which for a time caused some strained relations. The next day I arrived at the office with my arm in a sling. "My gosh, what happened?" Cambre asked. "I sprained my arm writing a check to Bill Clinton," I replied. And that is why for the next four years most Newmont officers received Christmas cards from the White House signed by Bill and Hillary Clinton.

A dark cloud, which turned out to have a silver lining, developed over the Carlin operations in August 1995 when Barrick flooded part of the T/S

Ranch. A flight over the normally arid land revealed what looked like miles of rice paddies in Indonesia. With Newmont's permission Barrick had built a large reservoir and other disposal systems on ranch land to handle water it was pumping from the Betze-Post pit. All deep mines on the Carlin Trend cut through underground aquifers and must be dewatered in order to be mined. But as its Meikle underground mine began operation, dewatering rose to an unmanageable 69,000 gallons per minute.

A fissure developed in the bottom of the reservoir and sucked the water underground, where it became contaminated, only to resurface in springs six miles away. Had the water flowed a short distance further into Boulder Creek, it would have been a violation of both federal and state laws and Newmont, as owner of the ranch, could have been culpable. When the company sought to plug the fissure, Barrick ringed the reservoir with haul trucks to prevent the action. Newmont brought suit in Reno, and after a seven-week hearing the judge ruled in Newmont's favor. Barrick settled by making a cash payment and surrendering certain gold reserves that were more economical for Newmont to mine. It also spent another $50 million to improve its water management.

Cambre and Murdy were determined not to let the situation sour relations with their neighbor. Convinced that the problem lay not with Barrick's Toronto executives but with the local mine manager, a French Canadian whom everyone found disagreeable, Cambre urged all employees to show good will toward Barrick as they worked to resolve the issue. In 1999, using the dewatering dispute as a point of departure, Murdy negotiated a land swap agreement with Barrick under which the two companies exchanged surface rights and two million ounces of reserves in order to optimize operations and minimize potential future conflicts. Under the agreement, Newmont was given the right to access its high-grade Deep Post underground deposit from a decline at the bottom of Barrick's Betze-Post pit rather than having to dig a shaft. It was cooperation at its best.

The land swap also gave Newmont 100 percent ownership of the 4,000-acre High Desert property between Betze-Post and the original Carlin mine where 2.6 million ounces of reserves have since been found at a depth of 1,400 to 2,100 feet. Years earlier, a small Canadian concern, Polar Resources, had done a little surface mining on the property. But when the ore ran out and it wished to sell, Newmont, which at the time was only looking for shallow oxide deposits, was not interested. The property was acquired by a couple of savvy speculators, Sean and Lee Halavais, two of the most colorful characters to ever walk the Carlin Trend.

The Halavais, from La Jolla, California, appeared in Carlin in the late 1980s with a briefcase full of gold nuggets and a pocketful of cash. To accommodate their high-stakes gambling, the Red Lion Casino in Elko would block off entire rows of slot machines for their exclusive use and provide complimentary meals, including fillets to go—"with no grill marks"— for their ever-present Chihuahuas, Fifi and Pee Wee.[12]

Newmont agreed to explore the property and earned a 60 percent interest by doing $18 million in work. Then in late 1995, with the land showing promise, Barrick paid the Halavais $120 million in stock to acquire the remaining 40 percent. Four years later, that interest was transferred to Newmont in the land swap. Since 2002, the company has invested $220 million to develop the Leeville mine on the property, its first mine at Carlin to be accessed by a shaft. Production began in early 2006 and is expected to average 450,000 to 500,000 ounces of gold a year over a seven-year life.

As Newmont began to make its mark on the international mining scene, the company realized that its corporate structure posed an impediment. All of its new ventures were owned by Newmont Mining Corporation, which now faced large capital costs, but all of its income came from the Nevada operations of Newmont Gold Company, which had an independent shareholder base. Lawyers cautioned of a possible conflict of interest. Since it could not afford to buy back the 10.8 percent of Newmont Gold stock in public hands, the two companies entered into an unusual transaction. In early 1994, Newmont Gold acquired all of the non-Nevada assets of Newmont Mining, while Newmont Mining declared a 1.2481-for-1 stock split in order to equalize the number of Newmont Mining shares outstanding with the 85.9 million shares it held in Newmont Gold. As a result, the company said, "shareholders of both companies have identical interests in the reserves, production and earnings of Newmont Gold's worldwide operations and management can pursue its goal of increasing shareholder value with a single focus."[13]

The transaction, called Optimize, was more complicated than it appeared. It required that the two independent directors of Newmont Gold, James Taranik, then president of the Desert Research Institute, a part of the Nevada System of Higher Education, and Robert Quenon, the former CEO of Peabody Coal, make a thorough study of all of the properties held by Newmont Mining. They engaged Dillon Reed as their investment banker and employed their own lawyers. Then, on behalf of their shareholders, they had to negotiate a fair price with their associates on the Newmont Mining board.

It wasn't until the task was completed that Taranik and Quenon could join the other directors at dinner. For years, Parker had hosted a dinner for the Newmont Mining directors at the Sky Club in New York before each board meeting. But in one of life's absurdities, the two directors of Newmont Gold were excluded. With the consolidation behind them, Cambre welcomed them, as well as members of management, to board dinners where discussions ranged from business to politics to the latest NFL standings, all sprinkled with the new CEO's delightful sense of humor. In October 1998, Newmont Mining issued 10.7 million shares to acquire the minority interest in Newmont Gold—again after negotiations between the two boards—to once again become a single entity.

It had been years since Newmont had operated abroad and the company quickly discovered that there are perils as well as pearls in foreign endeavors. In November 1993 the company learned that the Bureau de Recherches Géologiques et Minières (BRGM), one of its partners in Peru, planned a public auction of its assets. While the outlook at Yanacocha was promising, the mine had just begun operation. Production that year was 81,500 ounces of gold, which was backed by 3.5 million ounces of reserves. In addition to its 24.7 percent interest in the mine, BRGM was selling several exploration projects in Africa and elsewhere. To test the waters, Newmont lobbed an $80 million offer, which was haughtily dismissed. After further due diligence, the offer was more than doubled to $180 million, which was also rejected. In September 1994, BRGM announced that it was selling to Normandy Poseidon, an Australian company headed by Robert Champion de Crespigny. As with other de Crespigny transactions, his offer included little cash and an exchange of assets in various entities that made it difficult to decipher and almost impossible to value.

At the same time Newmont and Buenaventura notified BRGM that any attempt to sell or transfer the assets would trigger a preemptive rights clause in Yanacocha's bylaws that gave each shareholder the right of first refusal on the disposal of any other shareholder's interest. When BRGM ignored the claim, the two sued in Peruvian court, where they won after a trial in September 1996.

At that point Newmont and Buenaventura exercised their rights, increasing their ownership to 51.4 percent and 43.6 percent, respectively (the IFC continued to hold 5 percent), and Newmont began reporting Yanacocha's results on a consolidated basis. An independent appraisal of the property by Barings Bank, which the court accepted, set the purchase price at $109 million, which the two partners deposited in a bank designated by the court. The French appealed to the Superior Court of Lima, which ruled against them in February 1997. Newmont's Peruvian counsel advised that under the country's newly adopted rules of civil procedure, commercial cases like this could not be heard by the Supreme Court. The matter appeared to be closed.

Instead, that's when things got ugly. Over the next several years, Newmont learned two painful lessons: that the tenacity and duplicity of the French in legal matters can try men's souls, and that the rule of law in many parts of the world, even at the end of the twentieth century, could not be taken for granted. "I didn't understand the culture. I didn't understand the system," Cambre admits. "You relate to everything in your own mind-set and say, if this were in the judicial system in the United States, it would be fair. You wouldn't have to worry about people being bribed or judges giving you a biased ruling. It's hard for foreigners to put themselves in that situation." Yet that was the situation and the two officers Cambre assigned to worry about it were Joy Hansen, who had just been named vice president and general counsel, and the senior vice president of administration, Kurlander, who looked for a political solution in nearly every crisis.

Keeping the Scientific Edge

In early 1997 Newmont opened a $16 million technical facility south of Denver, the first facility of its kind built in North America in twenty-five years. With the death of longtime chairman Plato Malozemoff later that year, the facility was named the Malozemoff Technical Center in recognition of his leadership in the development and implementation of exploration and extractive technologies.

The 68,000-square-foot building brought the company's geophysical, metallurgical, mineralogical, biological, and analytical departments under one roof for the first time since the Danbury lab had been the focal point of its research in the 1970s.

In recognition of the company's cutting-edge capabilities, the National Aeronautics and Space Administration that year used a pair of Newmont potassium magnetometers on a high-altitude flight to record the earth's magnetic field for the U.S. Geological Survey. The magnetometers, which had to operate at -70° Celsius, were considered the most accurate sensors available and were used by the company for exploration. Newmont was the only company using the device, which director of geophysics Bruno Nilsson and his staff had refined from an original Russian design.

Between 1997 and 2002, three Newmont scientists and a former scientist were elected to membership in the prestigious National Academy of Engineering, which, according to the peer-ranked organization, is "one of the highest professional distinctions that can be accorded an engineer."[14] The four, all with Ph.Ds, and all retired are listed below.

- Jean-Michel Rendu, vice president resources and mine planning, for "contributions to theoretical and applied geostatistics for improved ore reserve quantification and grade control"

- Rong-Yu Wan, manager of metallurgical research and known as the "soul of the Newmont research effort," holds four patents including a Newmont patent for ammonium thiosulfate processing; recognized for "accomplishments in metallurgical research and industrial practice and for teaching, supervising and inspiring students, researchers and industrial colleagues"

- James Brierley, chief microbiologist, for "recognizing the potential of high-temperature biomining and for innovative industrial biomining practices"

- Corale Brierley (James's wife), a Newmont scientist in the early 1990s, for "innovations applying biotechnology to mine production and remediation"

16

VISION

Some men are satisfied with the status quo. Others see growth as essential to life. As CEO, Ronald Cambre stood firmly in the latter camp. For him, Newmont's future lay not at Carlin, which he felt was at a plateau without an acquisition, but in the international arena. In 1996, Newmont celebrated its seventy-fifth anniversary as the fifth largest gold producer in the world. But in Cambre's view that was not a sustainable position. If the company did not grow, it would be acquired by someone with a more aggressive agenda.

Cambre's vision for Newmont lay on the jungle-covered island of Sumbawa, 950 miles east of the Indonesian capital of Jakarta. "I saw Batu Hijau as the sort of hurdle Newmont had to cross to be seen as a major player and to grow into a big company. We weren't going to get there developing Minahasas. We had to do something significant." Batu Hijau, discovered in 1990, was one of the largest undeveloped copper/gold deposits in the world, with 11.2 billion pounds of copper and 14.7 million ounces of gold. But the grades were anemic—0.012 ounce per ton for gold and 0.53 percent for copper—meaning that over twenty years three billion tons of rock would have to be mined and processed to unlock the value. "I knew it was going to be risky and was going to be tough working in Indonesia with the Suharto government . . . but you have to play the hand you're dealt."[1]

When David Francisco, senior vice president of international operations, and others questioned the project, Cambre had a ready answer. "There are levels within the company where it is appropriate to ask questions and there are levels where it is necessary to find solutions. You need to find solutions."[2] Francisco and his team did just that.

Three early challenges had to be addressed simultaneously. The first was governmental—to be assured that it could win the necessary permits and then build and operate a mine in a remote area where skilled labor was scarce. To test these conditions Newmont gave the go ahead for the small Minahasa project on the island of Sulawesi. With 1.9 million ounces of

16.1. Richard Grasso (left), head of the New York Stock Exchange, joined CEO Ronald Cambre in ringing the opening bell on July 17, 1996, in honor of Newmont's seventy-fifth anniversary. (*New York Stock Exchange*)

high-grade but refractory ore Minahasa had a projected life of less than ten years. After Newmont promised to make environmental decisions on an equal footing as in the United States, Minahasa became the first mine in Indonesia to have all its environmental permits in place before ground was broken in November 1994. It was also the first in the country to use a sub-sea tailings system to deposit the crushed rock left after gold extraction on the ocean floor rather than in an on-land impoundment that could be damaged by earthquakes or torrential rains. Australian mining engineer John Eltham assembled a workforce of 1,600 people, many from the local villages of Ratatotok and Buyat, for construction. After extensive training, including a four-month technical program for tradesmen, he brought the plant into operation in March 1996 with only 30 expatriate employees and 400 Indonesians. At its peak, it employed 700 people.

Instead of project financing similar to that employed in Peru and Uzbekistan, Newmont paid for Minahasa itself but entered into a hedging contract for 125,000 ounces of gold a year for the first five years of production. Treasurer Patricia Flanagan caught an updraft in the market and sold the gold forward at $454 an ounce. It was a fortuitous decision as the price soon declined. In addition, the company raised $250 million through the sale of 4.65 million shares of common stock in early 1996 to shore up its balance sheet.

Batu Hijau's second challenge was technical—to complete a feasibility study and then design and build the most efficient facility on time and on budget. There would be no more Carlin roasters or Zarafshan cost overruns. Fluor Daniel Engineering began work in July 1995 with turnkey responsibility, meaning it would maintain control from design through start-up nearly four and a half years later. But with construction under way in late 1997, it predicted a $250 million cost overrun that it said could not be avoided. "Well, we couldn't stand that and it turns out there was something we could do about it," says Francisco. "We changed the contract with Fluor. Scott Barr [in mine planning], Alan Fitzpatrick [who had come onboard from BHP as project manager], and Bob Bush [with contract administration and procurement] took over control of the project and drove it to an on-time, underbudget conclusion."[3] Fluor changed its contract team as well and shared in the project's successful conclusion, earning a $36 million bonus for its effort.

The third challenge was financial. At $1.9 billion, Batu Hijau was the largest project in Newmont history and was more than even a resurgent gold producer could swallow. Flanagan arranged $1 billion in project financing from the Export-Import Bank of Japan, the United States Export-Import Bank, and Kreditanstalt für Wiederaufbau (KFW), the German export credit agency that had helped finance the Palabora copper mine in South Africa years earlier. The loans became non-recourse to Newmont once the project passed its completion test. But even with that it was clear that a deep-pocket partner was needed. Its Indonesian partner, Jusuf Merukh, held a 20 percent interest, but Newmont was obliged to carry his share of the capital cost, which would be paid back from future dividends. Randy Eppler spent the better part of his first year at Newmont talking to all of the major copper producers before finding a receptive partner in Sumitomo Corporation, one of Japan's leading trading companies.

With a six-hundred-year history, Sumitomo offered tangible and intangible benefits as a partner. First of all, Sumitomo had a keen interest in marketing Batu Hijau's copper concentrate. It had been a decade since Newmont sold Magma Copper and there was no one left at the company with copper marketing experience. In addition, in recognition of Newmont's discovery and early expenses, the new partner paid $100 million for a 35 percent interest in PT Newmont Nusa Tenggara (PTNNT), the official name of the partnership, and then funded a disproportionate share of future expenses. Furthermore, with Newmont retaining a 45 percent interest, Sumitomo was willing to let the company manage the operations without micromanaging every decision, which Newmont feared other copper companies might do. Because of Merukh's carried interest, Newmont had a 56.25 percent economic interest in the project to Sumitomo's 43.75 percent.

Partnership discussions went remarkably smoothly. "We were told we would never be able to get a deal done with a Japanese company within a year, yet we negotiated the term sheet with Sumitomo in two days and signed the final joint venture papers four months later," says Eppler. "To avoid cultural pitfalls, we made a whole set of principles that would guide the deal. We said language would not be a barrier. We didn't want someone conceding something and then concluding later that they had misunderstood the issue. So we said everything in the agreement could be renegotiated until the entire document was signed. We also decided we would have ample cigarette breaks. Quite a number of the Japanese were smokers, and it provided just enough of a break that issues could be discussed in small groups with less formality. Importantly, they had chosen team members who had experience outside Japan."[4]

In the midst of negotiations, news broke that Sumitomo's head copper trader, Yasuo Hamanaka, had engaged in unauthorized trades that eventually cost the company $2.6 billion. Sumitomo called Cambre and expected a return call. Eppler says he advised the CEO that "We should stand tall with these guys. We had a lot on the table. To back out would have delayed the project by a year. I said we were going to be partners for twenty-five years and that we shouldn't let one event, which we had been told would not break them financially, alter our relationship. Ron called them back, said all the right things and reaffirmed our commitment to the partnership and we signed the agreement." An escape clause gave them the right to back out if the Indonesian government failed to grant the required permits by the end of March 1997. As that date came and went, metal prices were declining.

Yet Sumitomo never questioned its commitment to the project. Eppler says he learned later from friends at Sumitomo that "after we had stood by them, it was unthinkable that they not stand by us."

As Batu Hijau was moving forward, Cambre began pursuing an opportunity to significantly increase the company's presence in Nevada. Every industry has its trade organizations and gold in the mid-1990s had three— the World Gold Council, which promoted gold sales, the Gold Institute, which focused on mining's image with lawmakers, and the Denver Gold Group, which brought gold company executives together with financial analysts and institutional investors for annual company presentations and one-up bragging rights. Meetings of these organizations operated on two levels, the general sessions open to all attendees and private meetings arranged by executives to feel each other out about potential mergers. Because events were attended by nearly every CEO, almost all gold mergers began with a little back-room romance at one of these conferences.

And so it came to pass that at a Gold Institute meeting on April 1, 1996, Cambre approached Patrick James, chairman and chief executive of Santa Fe Pacific Gold Company, about a possible "business combination," the euphemism preferred by lawyers when initiating acquisition talks. Newmont had been eyeing Santa Fe, a second-tier producer with large Nevada landholdings, for some time. "Anyone who looked at a map of Nevada could see that these two companies would fit together," Cambre says. While James initially rebuffed the offer, a declining gold price was putting a squeeze on his high-cost operations. On September 30, while attending the Denver Gold Group's annual investment forum, he called Cambre with a request for a meeting, which took place the next day at Cambre's Cherry Creek home.

Santa Fe traced its history to the 1880 creation of the Atchison, Topeka and Santa Fe Railroad, which had been given vast tracts of land in a checkerboard pattern extending twenty to forty miles on each side of its tracks. It discovered uranium on its lands in New Mexico in the 1950s, leased land for oil exploration in the 1960s, and in the 1970s and 1980s became a sizable coal producer. In 1983, Santa Fe acquired the Southern Pacific Company, giving it several million additional acres of railroad land in Nevada and California where it began looking for silver and gold. Its first gold discovery, Rabbit Creek, came in 1986, followed two years later by

Lone Tree. Production began in 1990. Both mines are in Humboldt County west of the Carlin Trend.

A turning point occurred in 1993 when Santa Fe exchanged its coal properties with Hanson PLC of Great Britain for the U.S. gold properties Hanson picked up in its acquisition of Consolidated Gold Fields several years earlier. Hanson had acquired Peabody Coal from Newmont and other owners in 1990. The exchange gave Santa Fe the Mesquite mine in southern California, Mule Canyon near Lone Tree, and the Chimney Creek mine adjacent to and later merged with Rabbit Creek to form the Twin Creeks mine. In mid-1994 with Santa Fe's merger with the Burlington Northern Railroad, the gold operation was spun off as Santa Fe Pacific Gold, which soon thereafter raised $250 million in an initial public offering of stock on the New York Stock Exchange. Its seventy-person headquarters was in Albuquerque, New Mexico.

Santa Fe in 1996 was a little over a third the size of Newmont with production of 852,000 ounces of gold and reserves of 18 million contained ounces. In later legal documents, Newmont described Santa Fe Gold's history as a publicly traded company as "lackluster: production has declined while costs have increased, [and] there have been no major discoveries,"[5] just the opposite of its own performance. Still, Newmont saw substantial potential through the combination of operations in Nevada, the elimination of duplicate staffs, and from new discoveries on Santa Fe's vast lands.

Significantly, October 1 was the first day Santa Fe was eligible to use pooling of interests accounting in a merger, a favorable treatment that allowed the buyer to avoid amortizing the goodwill associated with a purchase. Accounting rules prohibited this method in the first two years after an IPO. With a declining gold price, pooling was the only way a large gold merger would be economic. Meeting at Cambre's house in addition to the two CEOs were Wayne Murdy, Newmont's CFO who had just been elevated to executive vice president, and David Batchelder, an outside member of the Santa Fe board and the former right-hand man of corporate raider Boone Pickens. Discussions and later due diligence continued on a friendly basis through November. Any merger would be through a tax-free exchange of shares, making the exchange ratio the key issue. James said his company was interested in talking only to Newmont; Batchelder promised not to "shop" Newmont's proposal to other suitors.

On November 21, Newmont formally offered 0.33 of a share of its common stock, trading at $50, for each of Santa Fe's shares trading at $12.25. It represented a 35 percent premium for Santa Fe's shareholders. The Santa Fe board was expected to act quickly, but two days later James informed Cambre that his board would not meet until November 26, when it would also consider a proposal from another company. Cambre and Murdy felt betrayed and that feeling only deepened as telephone calls went unanswered and the clock passed mid-afternoon the next day, as the Thanksgiving holiday approached. When the call from Albuquerque finally came, Santa Fe said it had rejected the offer. James and Batchelder were curt and offered no explanation.

Mergers involve numerous economic and business considerations and must cross a number of legal hurdles, but in the end it is strategy and tactics that win the day. Advising Newmont on Santa Fe were two of the most nimble minds on Wall Street—Steven McArthur Heller of Goldman Sachs and David Katz of the Wachtell, Lipton law firm. Newmont's management and board were ready for a fight. The rejection and betrayal "sort of got the juices going," says Cambre. "There are times a company has to demonstrate that it's not going to sit on the sidelines and be pushed around."

In a move that took the industry and Wall Street by surprise, on December 5 Newmont went hostile with a preemptive strike. It sent the Santa Fe directors what is known as a "bear hug" letter, which it then made public. The letter spelled out the Newmont offer, said the merger would create the largest gold company in North America, and pointed out that Santa Fe stockholders would benefit from both "a substantial valuation premium for their shares and a continuing equity interest in a premium gold mining concern." The directors were further told, "It is our strong preference to work with you toward a friendly transaction [but] in any event, we want you and your stockholders to know that we are fully committed to completing this transaction." Signed by Cambre, the letter was intended to put shareholder pressure on the Santa Fe board.

Four days later, as nearly everyone anticipated, Santa Fe announced it was merging with Homestake Mining through an exchange of stock valued at $2.3 billion, or $250 million more than the Newmont offer. Both boards approved the transaction, which would make James the president and chief operating officer of Homestake, a position not offered in Newmont's proposal.[6] On January 7, Newmont countered with an increased offer of 0.4 of a Newmont share for each Santa Fe share, representing a 40 percent increase over the target's December 4 stock price and a 13 percent premium to Homestake's offer. It also filed a registration statement with the SEC to begin the public solicitation process.

With competing bids, Newmont set out to prove that its offer was superior. Over the next two months, Cambre, exploration vice president Jeff Huspeni, and I traveled to fourteen cities to make group or individual presentations to Newmont and Santa Fe shareholders. The team had to convince three sets of shareholders. First were the arbitrageurs (arbs), Wall Street's bottom-feeders who make a market in stocks that are "in play" but rarely continue to hold shares after the deal is done. By late February, arbs held a quarter of Santa Fe's stock and were pressuring both sides to raise their bids. Second were the remaining Santa Fe shareholders, including many retired railroad employees, who could be persuaded to keep Newmont shares after the merger if the prospect of long-term value was compelling. And third were the Newmont shareholders, who had to approve the merger and needed assurance that the company was not overpaying.

The task of maintaining the highest bid was made difficult by a declining gold price and by the nature of stock-for-stock transactions where prices fluctuate daily. In addition, arbs routinely short the stock (i.e., sell borrowed stock) of the buyer and buy the stock of the target. This can lock in large gains with little risk if the merger succeeds. When there are competing bidders, the expected winner is shorted more than its rival. That Newmont's stock price was under tremendous selling pressure during the first quarter of 1997 was a vote of confidence by Wall Street but a painful pat on the back when the company was trying to stay above Homestake's offer. On some days the two offers were only pennies apart.

The longer-term story was easier to tell but pitted Newmont against one of the nicest gentlemen in the gold patch—Jack Thompson Jr., the chairman and CEO of Homestake. The son of a longtime Newmont president, Thompson had worked at Magma and Granduc and was manager of the Dawn uranium mine from 1978 to 1981. But like Santa Fe, Homestake had been a mediocre performer, and with few operations in Nevada it had little in the way of merger synergies to offer. Victor Lazarovici, a gold analyst with Smith Barney Shearson, captured the futility of Homestake's hopes by likening it to the belief that "two ugly ducklings can become a swan."[7] Speaking later to the *New York Times* about the prolonged battle, Thompson said, "All in all, I thought it was pretty professional, but not a pleasant thing to go through."[8]

Under pressure from shareholders, James invited both suitors to make final presentations to the Santa Fe board in Albuquerque on Saturday, March 8. After a last-minute conference, Cambre and Murdy increased the Newmont offer to 0.43 of a share for each Santa Fe share, which became the winning bid. Santa Fe's board rescinded its agreement with Homestake and on Monday, amid smiles and handshakes, announced a new agreement with Newmont. The merger closed on May 7. Newmont issued 57 million shares, then trading at $39 a share, giving the transaction a value of nearly $2.25 billion. In addition, the company spent $163 million in fees and transaction costs, including $65 million paid to Homestake to terminate its merger agreement and $27 million in asset write-downs.

Santa Fe breathed new life into Newmont's Nevada operations, generating $100 million a year in operating savings. It increased the company's production in the state to 2.8 million ounces a year and its global output to 4 million ounces, making it second only to AngloGold of South Africa.

It also lifted spirits in the Denver office, where a due diligence fatigue had set in. The company had looked at acquiring Stillwater, a platinum producer, in the early 1990s and lost a bid for Lac Minerals, a Canadian gold producer, to Barrick in 1994. "We looked at a lot of things in the post-Pickens era, but nothing was ever good enough," says retired corporate secretary Tim Schmitt. "People began to say, 'How many more of these exercises are we going to go through?'" Aggressively pursuing Santa Fe "got people pumped up," Schmitt says. "Finally, we were doing something fun."[9]

As the merger was closing, the first of two huge autoclaves at Twin Creeks was being commissioned while the second was making the 370-mile journey to the mine from its construction site in Salt Lake City. Weighing 950,000 pounds each, the autoclaves were the largest loads ever trucked across the highways of Utah and Nevada. The move required special trailers that were pulled and pushed by ten heavy haul tractors. Each unit was 416 feet long, 26 feet wide, and 20 feet high and rode on 100 tires. It took a crew of sixteen nearly two weeks to make the trip.

Once in service, the giant pressurized vessels had a throughput capacity of 4,400 tons of ore per day, the largest in the industry. Coupled with the world's first inert gas flotation plant at Lone Tree, Santa Fe's operations provided new processing options for refractory ore across Nevada. Rich Perry at Carlin and Garry Simmons, Santa Fe's chief metallurgist, realized that significant savings could come from matching the company's various ore types with the processing option—autoclave, roaster, flotation, or bio-leach—that provided the highest gold recovery rate. Complicating the equation, the roaster generates heat by burning the sulfur found in many refractory ores, requiring the company to mine for fuel as well as gold. A complex computer program was developed to optimize the ore placement, and today green ore trucks move tons of material across Interstate 80 between Carlin and Golconda to help Newmont reduce costs and maximize production.

Newmont was committed to giving the Santa Fe employees a fair shake in the new organization even as total staffs were reduced. "We tried to keep the best of the best—we called them BOBs," says Jim Mullin, who with the merger became senior vice president of North American operations. Still, he says, "the best thing I did was to assign Carlin people"—Trent Temple and Ali Soltani, respectively—as mine managers at Twin Creeks and Lone Tree. "I also gave them a support person so there were two of them at each mine. By having a group of two they could control what was going on and implement Newmont standards. That's how we achieved the synergies as quickly as we did. The key was having good people on the ground."[10]

Among the many talented Santa Fe people who made a difference in later years at Newmont were Simmons, who headed the company's research laboratory outside Denver; Bruce Hansen, a mining engineering graduate from the Colorado School of Mines with an MBA in finance from the University of New Mexico who was chief financial officer from 1998 to 2005; and Linda Wheeler, who became vice president and controller.

As the battle for Santa Fe became fully engaged, a fight of a different sort developed on the opposite side of the globe over Batu Hijau. That threat came not from another gold or copper company but from the Suharto government, which in its final days had become openly greedy. Suharto had been president of Indonesia since 1968 when he replaced Sukarno, who had ruled the country since its independence at the end of World War II. While regarded almost as a king by the Indonesian people, Suharto ruled with a heavy hand, an ever-present army, and a low tolerance for dissent. Before entering the country, Cambre sought the advice of the only Muslim on New-mont's board, Moeen Qureshi, a former prime minister of Pakistan and senior officer of the World Bank.

"I recall Moeen talking about the great things that had been accom-plished during the Suharto years for Indonesia," Cambre says. "He noted how education had advanced, how income had advanced, and how living conditions had advanced. Moeen said Suharto had done a great job for In-donesia." By providing good jobs and new tax revenue, Newmont should be welcomed, he reasoned. Francisco, who had managed Freeport's huge cop-per and gold mine on Irian Jaya, also felt the country risk was manageable.

Then came Bre-X. In the declining gold market of 1996, the only "buzz" was about Bre-X Minerals, a tiny Calgary-based company that claimed to have found the gold mine of the millennium at Busang in the jungles of Borneo. As company executives and Canadian mining analysts hyped the stock, institutional investors gorged on its shares, which soared from $4 to over $200. At $4 billion, Bre-X had a market capitalization ap-proaching Newmont's. But while the company reported ever-increasing "reserves"—30 million ounces, now 40, maybe 100—it had no Contract of Work (COW), employed only a few Filipino site geologists, and had no funds for development. If North American investors were getting rich, shouldn't there be something in this for Indonesia?

That was the rationale given by the Suharto government as it sought to force Bre-X to merge with a company capable of managing a $1.5 billion project. The government's first choice was Barrick, which had no presence in the country but had engaged in high-powered political lobbying to curry favor with the Suharto regime. Former Canadian prime minister Brian Mulroney and former U.S. president George H. W. Bush were among Bar-rick's emissaries. In a meeting with mines minister Kuntoro Mangkusub-roto on November 14, 1996, it was decreed that Barrick would take 75 per-cent of Busang with Bre-X retaining 25 percent. The government was to be cut in for 10 percent. But under pressure, Bre-X had already given 10 per-cent to Sigit Harjojudanto, Suharto's oldest son, while Barrick had taken on Siti (Tutut) Hardiyanti Rukmana, the president's daughter, as a 10 percent carried partner. In January, the two Canadian companies were told that Bob Hasan, a Suharto crony who already held a 5 percent interest in Free-port's Grasberg mine, needed to be given a piece of the Busang pie as well.

While Barrick pondered how many slices there are in an Indonesian pie, two other Canadian miners, Placer Dome and Teck, sought to muscle in with bids to buy Bre-X. Finally, in January 1997, Suharto replaced Barrick with Freeport, which had agreed to give Hasan a 30 percent slice. Two months later, the pie vanished. Freeport drilled its own holes and discovered a massive fraud. The Bre-X ore samples had been salted; there was no gold.

Bre-X collapsed into bankruptcy and criminal investigations, while investors gnashed their teeth or claimed to have sold ahead of the collapse. Bre-X found a fall guy in its Filipino field geologist, Michael de Guzman, who fell or jumped from a helicopter on his way to the site. (A body was found, but never identified.) The company's two hard-drinking and increasingly evasive executives—chief geologist John Felderhof and CEO John Walsh—cashed in millions of dollars in stock options earlier and moved to the Bahamas and the Cayman Islands, which do not have extradition treaties with the United States or Canada. Walsh died of a stroke in 1998 at age fifty-two. Felderhof was eventually tried in Toronto for insider trading and was acquitted in 2007.

John Dow, Newmont's senior vice president of exploration who had spent thirteen years in Indonesia, repeatedly told Cambre that the Busang site could not possibly hold the reserves Bre-X was reporting, but says even he had begun to doubt his own logic as everyone else bought into the story. Disclosure of the fraud brought a sigh of relief.

Newmont's situation was entirely different. It was already mining successfully under government permits on the island of Sulawesi. It had a COW for Batu Hijau, where it had already invested $150 million in exploration and early development, and it had the financing in hand to complete the project, all of which came because its reserves were good as gold. Bre-X, however, had emboldened the Suharto government, which began to pressure the company for a piece of the action by holding up the necessary permits. The Newmont board had not been terribly enthusiastic about Batu Hijau, which showed only marginal returns at a gold price of $400 an ounce and a copper price of $1 a pound. Now with gold at $350 and copper slipping, Cambre was being asked if the company had missed the market. Some on the board who had lived through copper's last down cycle also questioned whether Batu would jeopardize the company's gold rating on Wall Street. "We realized that it was a bet on metal prices. But we also realized it was something that was strategic for the company," says Francisco. The company

16.2. Wayne Murdy, chief financial officer and later CEO, posed with a cutout of New-mont founder, William Boyce Thompson, at a party for analysts marking the company's seventy-fifth anniversary in 1996. (*Newmont Archives*)

could not stand further delays. But, by then, Santa Fe was also important. So, while Cambre crossed the country to sell the Nevada merger, Murdy made eight trips to Indonesia in five months to secure Batu Hijau.

"We started out thinking we could work with the government and then it became evident that there was something more sinister involved. Ultimately, they wanted another 10 percent. We knew the project couldn't stand another 10 percent; it didn't have the economic power. So we took a very hard line on it,"[11] Murdy says. Eric Hamer, who had been named president of the company's two Indonesian projects, says "the requests would come from people in the Ministry of Mines, from friends of the Suharto family, and from people at the ambassador level. It was all very subtle, never direct. But I could rely on the Foreign Corrupt Practices Act and our Code of Ethics and say we weren't permitted to give this or that. I became known as 'Mr. No.'"[12]

Cambre also made several trips to Indonesia during this period and at one point was asked to meet with a wealthy Chinese businessman who arranged many of the president's business deals. Suharto was an avid golfer and was frequently given golf clubs when he traveled. This man was the custodian of the clubs and had a hundred bags on display in his Jakarta home. Even for someone from Louisiana, Cambre says it was the only time he recalls meeting a real bag man.

It was suggested that the company's Indonesian partner, Merukh, was not appropriate and that his interest should be stripped away and given to Suharto's daughter. "We said we couldn't do that," says Cambre. "He was legally entitled to his share under our COW. We said, fine if she can buy it from Merukh and he is agreeable, but we are not going to do anything that is illegal to advance this project." Newmont had the first right of approval on any sale. On several embarrassing occasions, Merukh traveled to New York, Toronto, and Vancouver to try to sell his stake on the sly. Several groups, including Placer Dome, signed deals with him only to be told by Newmont that their contracts were illegal. When confronted, Merukh apologized, but it left the would-be buyers in an awful rage.

One evening after a long flight home from a fruitless meeting in Jakarta, Murdy received a call from someone close to the government. "He said that it had come down to a money issue and that the permit was not going to be signed unless a $20 million advisory fee was paid. I said, 'Well, that's not going to happen.'" Reminded that the company already had a sizable investment in the country, Murdy says he replied, "'If that's the way business is going to be done, I'd rather write off $150 million than invest another $2 billion.' If you ever give in to anything like that, it never stops." After hanging up, he says he told his wife he thought the company had lost the project.

Cambre recalls what happened next. "We were agonizing how to break this logjam when I suggested that we go and see Suharto. I had never met him. I said, 'Everybody keeps saying he's the ultimate decision maker, so let's go see him.'" Newmont's Indonesian advisor was aghast. "You can go in and have an audience with him and allow him to make a decision," Cambre says he was told, "but if he decides against you, you're done." The Indonesian way, he was told, was to work out a compromise acceptable to Suharto. "But it got to the point where we were so stretched that I said we had to get it over with one way or the other."

Hamer arranged to take Cambre and Murdy to the presidential palace. "At the time my company car was a Honda, but I was told I could not enter the presidential gates unless I was in a Mercedes. So I rented one. But before Ron and Wayne went to the palace they wanted to stop at the Catholic Cathedral in Jakarta. It's a big place right next to the central mosque. So here I am a Baptist taking these two Catholics to make their peace with God or pray for success in the negotiations or whatever before seeing Suharto, who was Muslim. It was weird."

The trio was cordially received. Cambre brought a commemorative ten-ounce gold coin minted from the first gold pour at Minahasa a year earlier, which he presented to Suharto. "He lectured us about our responsibility to Indonesia and our responsibility to the environment. Then he wished us well and said that we would get all the cooperation we needed from his government," Cambre says. "We had spent thirty to forty-five minutes with him. We walked out and it was like the sun came out. Everything got back to normal. We got our permits and there was no more pressure to shift equity. We had lucked out. What would have happened had we not gotten his approval? I guess we would have folded our tents and pulled out."

The permits arrived on May 7, 1997, the same day the Santa Fe merger closed. Construction began almost immediately and at the peak Fluor Daniel and other contractors had 19,000 workers on site. There were a few problems and one rock-throwing incident as some workers did not understand the differences in pay between skilled and unskilled workers or why those coming from off the island received transportation allowances while those from nearby villages did not. Early on, Fluor sought to keep the mostly Muslim workers from stopping to say midday prayers. Calming the waters and addressing the worker's concerns was Richard Ness, whose mining roots are in the iron range of Minnesota. He had spent several years with Freeport in Indonesia, married an Indonesian, and developed an excellent understanding of local customs. He became PTNNT's first general manager.

By the time permanent workers were being hired in mid-1999, Batu Hijau had become known as a honey pot for job seekers. When the first 800 jobs were posted, 90,000 applied. Knowing that the company had agreed to hire 60 percent of the workforce from the province of Nusa Tenggara, mayors in some of the closest villages—Maluk, Benete, Jereweh, and Taliwang—began selling local residency papers.

Batu Hijau was one of the largest grassroots start-up mining projects in history and occurred during a time of upheaval in Indonesia's economy. Logistics and coordinating the arrival of materials and supplies was critical with equipment coming from around the world and many large items assembled on-site. Prestripping the mine site took twenty-four months and involved removing 120 million tons of material, more than was mined at Minahasa over its entire life. A team of Australians, many with Indonesian mining experience, and headed by David Lilley from Darwin, trained the permanent workforce. Remarkably, each of the 4,200 permanent workers had at least a high school education and many are college graduates. Reading and math skills are essential in operating equipment as even Caterpillar 793 haul trucks carry onboard computers.

By 2002, eight giant electric shovels and a fleet of a 126 240-ton haul trucks were removing 250 million tons of material a year from the open pit. Two-thirds of the rock is waste and is placed on dumps that are continuously contoured and planted with local vegetation to resemble the existing terrain. The mineral-bearing ore is crushed and sent by a four-mile-long conveyor to a concentrator, where, at the rate of 150,000 tons a day, it is ground to the consistency of fine sand. Five flotation tanks use seawater—an industry first—and detergent-like chemicals to separate the copper and gold from the tailings. A ten-mile-long pipeline carries the concentrated ore to the port at Benete Bay, where it is dried and shipped to smelters around the world. Although low-grade, containing only 30 percent copper and less than half an ounce of gold per ton, the concentrate is very pure and highly desired by smelters making it easy to market. Tailings—basically sand—are pumped to a deep-sea canyon below the level of aquatic life where they pose no threat to the marine environment. Gravity works in the operation's favor as the mine is at an elevation of 1,475 feet and everything flows to the ocean. A town site provides housing for most of the employees while a 160-megawatt coal-fired power station supplies enough electricity to light up 100,000 homes.

The first shipment of concentrate was shipped to smelters in Japan in mid-December 1999. While that technical accomplishment brought applause, accountants had their fingers crossed. The copper price had been falling throughout construction and by start-up "was below 70 cents a pound and we needed 78 cents to break even," says Francisco. He gives "kudos" to

16.3. The port and power plant at Batu Hijau. (*Jack Morris*)

two seasoned Carlin hands, Tom Enos, who had pushed the roaster from problem to production and who was named president of PTNNT succeeding Hamer, and Perry, who as operations director put together "a great operating team" and got Batu Hijau off to a fast start. "We challenged them to find a way to be cash flow positive for five years. That was the goal," Francisco says. With the help of Barr, the mine plan was redrawn with the location of dumps and roads changed to reduce haulage distances. The fleet was enlarged and the mining rate increased to 600,000 tons per day from 480,000 in order to reach deeper, higher-grade ores faster. Lower-grade ore was stockpiled for future use.

Perry describes the start-up as the most exhilarating time of his life. "It was like grabbing hold of a fire hose." Key to the success, he says, was his team of thirty experienced people from Nevada. "It was sort of a Noah's Ark job—four mill foremen, four mine foremen, and one of each kind of engineer—people who knew Newmont's procedures and could work together."[13]

Yet he scoffs at those who suggest that mines should take time training managers to be team players: "You've got to be able to get things done and there's going to be friction with that." While both he and Barr came from Freeport's Jerritt Canyon mine in Nevada and respect each other's talents, they fought over such things as the location of dump sites. "Scott would fly in and march up the hill and tell the mining engineers to do something different than what I had told them," Perry says. "But I got him one time. The safety group had speed guns and anyone caught speeding on a mine road lost their license. Well, they got Scotty coming up the hill too fast and he lost his license. So at least for that visit I could control where he went."

In its first full year of operation, Batu Hijau produced 521 million pounds of copper at a cash cost of 57 cents a pound, after giving credit for selling 320,000 ounces of gold, and generated positive income for Newmont in the second half of the year. Throughout the ordeal, Cambre kept his confidence that Batu Hijau would be a world-class mine. "Some day," he would tell anyone who raised the subject, "a future CEO will look back and thank us for doing this."[14] It almost became a mantra.

Today Batu Hijau is one of the company's most profitable assets. The mine's best year thus far was 2004, with production of 717 million pounds of copper and 719,000 ounces of gold. Cash production costs of $129 an ounce for gold and 60 cents a pound for copper generated a pre-tax profit of nearly $300 million after minority interest. By late that year, Batu Hijau had recovered its cumulative losses and began paying dividends, of which 6 percent went to Merukh. He received almost $1 million in cash after taxes in 2004 and $4 million in 2005, the first real money he had seen since signing his first COW with Newmont in 1986.

Although production declined by a third and costs doubled between 2004 and 2007 as the pit grew larger and deeper, requiring the removal of more waste rock and longer hauls, the copper price that had been so troubling during the early years rose significantly. Copper reached $1 a pound in late 2003 and kept on climbing, averaging above $3 a pound in both 2006 and 2007. Surprising shareholders, however, Newmont let much of that gravy flow off the table through a hedging strategy that, while prudent at the time, quickly went sour (see chapter 20). Consequently, Batu Hijau received only $1.99 a pound for its copper sales in 2006. Fortunately, the hedge was short term and expired in early 2007, allowing realizations to jump to the market price.

With cash finally flowing in his direction, Merukh, in mid-2007, was able to obtain financing through BNP Paribas, a French bank, to repay his partners for his carried interest in the project (Newmont received $161 million) and he now shares a full 20 percent of the mine's profit. The move reduced Newmont's interest to 45 percent from 56.25 percent when the project began. Sumitomo's interest declined to 35 percent.

Under their COW, Newmont and Sumitomo have been required since 2006 to offer to sell down portions of their interests each year to other Indonesian entities at a fair market price. That requirement ends in 2010 when their joint interest could be reduced to 49 percent. But as it moved to implement this requirement, the government began what director James Taranik calls "a kabuki dance"[15] to pressure the transfer of shares to a government entity without cost and cancel the mine's COW. Newmont took the matter to arbitration, where it finally was resolved in mid-2009 with the government placing a $3.5 billion to $4 billion value on the operation.

In addition to price, there was the question of who would buy. The government maintained that it had the right to designate the buyer and in late 2009 chose PT Bumi Resources, which under Ari Hudaya, a well-connected Jakarta businessman, has become a fast-growing natural resource company and Indonesia's largest coal producer. Heading a consortium that also includes minority participation by several local government entities, the Bumi group paid $391 million ($220 million being Newmont's share) for 10 percent of Batu Hijau and committed to pay $494 million for an additional 14 percent. If it subsequently purchases the shares required to be offered in 2010, the Bumi group would have a larger ownership than either Newmont or Sumitomo individually, although Newmont expects that PT Newmont Nusa Tenggara will continue as the operator of the mine. That, however, may depend on how the unpredictable Merukh sees the future.

Over the years, Newmont has proven its ability to extract value from a low-grade deposit on a jungle island and has set standards of excellence in environmental protection and social responsibility (see chapter 19). But maintaining its ownership rights in an emerging economy with an increasingly nationalistic view toward the ownership of natural resources will be an ongoing challenge. Nevertheless, with higher metal prices than anyone could have imagined in the mid-1990s, Cambre's vision has become a reality.

17

FAITH, HOPE, AND HEDGING

In 1997 CEO Ron Cambre started whistling past the graveyard. "It is the nature of those of us in this business to remain bullish on the gold price,"[1] he told shareholders in his annual report letter published that March. His assertion followed a drop in the gold price to $350 from $415 an ounce during the previous twelve months and a drop in the company's stock to $43 from $55 a share. Yet, the company had invested $1 billion over the prior three years in mine development, was pursuing permits for the $2 billion Batu Hijau project in Indonesia, and only days earlier had committed almost $2.5 billion to acquire Santa Fe Pacific Gold. If it didn't have faith, what was there?

A year later, with gold at $300 and the stock trading at $27, he told shareholders, "There are sound reasons to believe that such fears [a further decline in the gold price] are overblown." Earnings in 1997 of $68 million, while down 30 percent from the prior year, were still better than most in an industry that suffered losses in the declining gold market. Newmont coped by significantly reducing expenditures and cutting the quarterly dividend to three cents a share from twelve cents—the first reduction in fifteen years.

By March 1999, gold had dropped to $280 an ounce and the stock price was down to $17.50. Cambre's letter to shareholders stated: "While our faith in a market upturn is soundly grounded, it also necessitates a disciplined and creative approach to managing our cash flow until the price cycle turns." During 1998, the company wrote off $425 million in assets impaired by the gold price, primarily in Nevada, and reported a loss of $393 million, its first loss since 1985. Yet, it retained an investment grade credit rating.

The bright spot in the company's portfolio was Minera Yanacocha in Peru, in which Newmont held a 51.4 percent interest. By 1998, with annual production of 1.35 million ounces of gold, the company's share—690,000 ounces—amounted to 17 percent of its total output, but a much higher percent of earnings. Blessed with a low strip ratio, high recovery rate, and minimal processing, cash production costs of $95 an ounce were less than half the $200 average for the rest of Newmont's mines. In just five years, Yanacocha had become the largest gold operation in South America with four mines, three leach pads, and two gold recovery plants. Reserves, which had increased every year despite higher production rates, stood at 21 million ounces. Seven million ounces were added to reserves with the discovery of the La Quinua deposit, a huge valley filled with 275 million tons of low-grade glacial till that centuries earlier had been pushed off nearby mountains. By just scooping it up and placing it on a leach pad, the gravel-like material flowed gold. "If the price goes any lower, we're all moving to Peru since it will be the only place left that's profitable,"[2] Cambre told employees only half in jest.

Then, from that bed of roses came the smell of manure. In September 1997 the Peruvian Supreme Court voted, against all expectations, to hear an appeal by the Bureau de Recherches Géologiques et Minières (BRGM) and its ally Normandy Mining of a Superior Court ruling that granted Newmont and its Peruvian partner Buenaventura the right to acquire the French agency's 24.7 percent interest in the mine. At the same time, the company began hearing rumblings that the French were trying to pressure the court, or as Larry Kurlander, Newmont's senior vice president of administration, told the *New York Times*, "that the French were behaving inappropriately in the litigation," which was "unseemly at best and corrupt at worst."[3]

Since joining Newmont in 1994, Kurlander had been making the rounds of the state and commerce departments and various embassies in Washington to advance Newmont's overseas interests. He now began contacting people in government and diplomatic circles in Lima who might have their ear to the ground. In early January 1998 the Supreme Court, which is divided into panels, ruled 3–2 against Newmont. But the court required a two-vote majority for a verdict, so a sixth judge was appointed to the panel. Kurlander and Newmont general counsel Joy Hansen set up temporary quarters in Lima in the hope of getting control of the matter.

Kurlander had taken over global security and hired former CIA, FBI, and army intelligence officers as well as the former sheriff of Elko County, Nevada. Some now joined him in Peru, where he also enlisted the help of local intelligence and security experts for surveillance. While Hansen and Yanacocha's lawyers delved into legal strategy, Kurlander was immersed in

17.1. At the top of the Andes, the Yanacocha mine in Peru is the largest gold mine in South America. (*Andrew Craig*)

the shadowy world of intrigue and innuendo where rumors circulated of conspiracies, clandestine meetings, and evildoers in high places.

"I have with my own eyes seen a letter from Jacques Chirac [the president of France] to President Fujimori asking for his intervention in the case,"[4] Kurlander later told Lowell Bergman in a PBS *Frontline* interview. Peruvian sources picked up rumors of a French plot to bribe the Supreme Court judges.[5] Fearing his phone was tapped and his room bugged, Kurlander installed encrypted telephones, spoke in hushed tones, and in calls to Denver recited what sounded like the middle chapters of a suspense thriller with alternate pages ripped out. His intelligence staff began speaking in codes.

Secrecy was not new to Newmont. In the 1920s and 1930s the company's head of exploration and future CEO, Fred Searls Jr., created a series of code books to enable geologists and engineers to communicate their findings and intuitions to headquarters without detection. The company's Empire-Star gold mine in California was referred to as "YFFSH," Bank of America was "YFEKV," and Searls himself was "YFKWO." The leather-bound books still reside in the corporate secretary's office, but no one knows how to use them.

Cambre, who received daily reports from Peru, says his two officers reacted very differently. "Sending Larry down there was like sending a kid into a candy store. I mean, Larry excelled at that. He enjoyed it, thrived on it, and, in his mind, it became the most important thing in the history of Newmont. That's great! You want the soldiers who fight the fight to feel like this. Joy, on the other hand, was down there not enjoying it, trying to get the problem solved, wanting to get on with life. When I talked to them, I had to mentally interpret where they were coming from. Larry was telling me this would put the Battle of the Bulge down into an appendix of the battles of the world." With other items on his agenda, the CEO limited his conversations. "There was nothing I could do from Denver. I would listen and give some advice and then put the problem aside. I knew Larry was working on it twenty-four hours a day, giving it his all, enjoying the hell out of it, and wanted to talk about it nonstop."[6]

As the clouds of suspicion grew more ominous, Kurlander says, "I went to my government and asked them for their help, wrote a letter to the president of Peru asking for his help. I went all the way up to the undersecretary of state of the United States. I went to the embassies, we went to the FBI, we went to anybody who would listen to us." His goal, he and Newmont insist, was not to tip the scales of justice in Newmont's favor but to "level the playing field, that's all."[7] The State Department followed up with a warning to Peru's prime minister that "A politically tainted decision would adversely affect U.S. investment in Peru."[8] But, as Kurlander told Bergman, eventually both governments told him "the only one who can stop this is Montesinos."[9]

And so it was that on February 28, 1998, the former prosecutor sat down and pledged to be "a friend for life"[10] with one of the most notorious men in Peruvian history. Vladimiro Montesinos was President Alberto Fujimori's unofficial intelligence chief and the go-to man for political decisions. He had been on the payroll of the CIA for helping the United States in its fight against drugs. But he was also corrupt and, as later investigations showed, regularly engaged in extortion, bribery, political payoffs, and drug trafficking of his own. As Montesinos's former mistress translated, Kurlander spoke of his own ties to the intelligence world and offered to lobby his fellow Jews in the United States to back off from pressure they were bringing against the Peruvian government for shutting down an anti-government television station owned by a Jewish businessman. In return, Montesinos pledged to help with the court "voting," although the nature of that help was never specified.

Nine weeks later, on May 8, the sixth judge ruled in favor of Newmont and Buenaventura, creating a 3–3 tie on the court. Jamie Beltrán Quiroga was named as the seventh and deciding member of the panel, and the next day was summoned to Montesinos's office. Montesinos reminded him that the case was a matter of "national interest" since the U.S. government was involved in settling a border dispute between Peru and Ecuador. He also suggested that a promotion for the judge might be arranged. Beltrán issued a lengthy opinion in favor of Newmont and Buenaventura two weeks later.

Details of those conversations are known because Montesinos tape-recorded meetings with everyone who came to his office, possibly for future blackmail. The tapes became public in 2000, bringing down the Fujimori government and his spy chief, who is now in jail. Kurlander, who took pride in his integrity and had not known he was being recorded, was mortified. He is adamant that "no one at Newmont . . . did anything inappropriate. I can further say that no one at Newmont knew of any inappropriate behavior by anyone connected with our side."[11] Although allegations later circulated that Buenaventura or its chairman, Alberto Benavides, paid Montesinos $4 million, the Lima bank against which the supposed checks were drawn said it was "a gross frame-up"[12] since no such bank accounts existed. Disinformation flowed freely. The U.S. Justice Department investigated the case, as did the Peruvian government; both dropped the matter without taking action.

As the drama unfolded, a mysterious actor came from the shadows and sought center stage. He was Patrick Maugein, a Frenchman with an unsavory past and close ties to President Chirac. A book published in France,[13] which he claimed Newmont inspired, implicated him in a murder plot, while it was later learned that he had been part of the U.N.-Iraq oil-for-food scandal.[14] During the wait for a court decision, he began writing Cambre with vague suggestions that he could resolve the case but without saying whom he represented. In time, his letters turned to accusations of wrongdoing on Newmont's part and demands for settlement. Later he sued Newmont in U.S. District Court in Denver for damages in excess of $25 million. After a hearing on September 11, 2003, the case was dismissed.[15]

It turns out he had been hired as a consultant by Robert de Crespigny, the chief executive of Normandy Mining, the would-be buyer of BRGM's interest in Yanacocha. An accountant, de Crespigny had founded Normandy in 1985 and named it for his Norman forebears. Although his family had lived in Australia for generations, he sought to parlay his French ancestry by moving to Paris during the BRGM discussions. Cambre, also of French heritage, never considered leaving his homes in New Orleans and Denver but traveled to Paris when discussions warranted. In an early negotiating session when there was still hope for a settlement, Cambre commented that de Crespigny had gotten in hot water with the Australian equivalent of the SEC on a previous deal. But he apparently misstated the temperature of the water and de Crespigny sued in a French court for slander. Two years later, I was in Cambre's office when attorney Hansen came in with the verdict. It was a good news, bad news report. "The court ruled against you and said you did slander Robert," she reported. "But they assessed damages of only one franc." Symbolic victories are common in cases of honor in France. "So what do I do now?" Cambre inquired. "Send him two francs and slander him again," I said.

The *New York Times*, Public Broadcasting's *Frontline*, and the *Denver Post* reported extensively on Newmont's actions in Peru after the Montesinos tapes surfaced, and the Stanford Graduate School of Business made it a case study. Legitimately, it was a major business story and raised serious questions about the company's behavior. But there was a presumption in each of the reports that Newmont had only won because *it* had corrupted the court. It appears that none of the reporters read the Minera Yanacocha bylaws or asked an attorney with competence in contract law to do so. The wording seems straightforward, and when the trial court and appellate court in Peru considered the matter, Newmont and Buenaventura won on the merits. An objective review of the matter would most likely conclude that the final Supreme Court decision was the correct one.

The news reports highlighted the fact that victory allowed Newmont and its partner to pick up a quarter of one of the most profitable gold mines in the world for only $109 million when it was worth much more. But under the corporation's bylaws, the preemptive rights were triggered when BRGM put the property up for sale, which was 1993, not at some later date of its choosing. Furthermore, that figure had been set by an independent appraisal by a respected London bank. No one noted that had BRGM won, it would have sold to Normandy at a price negotiated in 1994 that likewise would have been far below the current market value.

Finally, none of the reports mentions what else was happening in Peru that may have diverted President Fujimori's attention and led to suggestions by his government that Newmont discuss its concerns with Montesinos.

There is no denying what happened, but events do not happen in a vacuum. On December 17, 1997, shortly before the first Supreme Court ruling, fourteen Maoist revolutionaries stormed a state dinner at the Japanese embassy in Lima, taking several hundred hostages including a Supreme Court justice and ambassadors from several countries. They were held for 126 days—until April 22—when Peruvian Special Forces liberated them, killing the rebels. After the siege, a triumphant Fujimori, whose parents had emigrated from Japan, stood outside the compound to welcome the hostages' release.

Then in late January 1998, torrential rains blamed on El Niño caused the worst flooding in Peru in fifty years, leaving 70 dead and 22,000 homeless. The rains, floods, deaths, and displacements continued through the spring as President Fujimori traveled across the country to view the devastation, talk to aid workers, and offer comfort to the victims. Minera Yanacocha provided crews and material to help rebuild roads and power lines washed out by the floods and to transport supplies to stranded villages. In all the company spent $5 million for services well outside its area of operation.

But after the hostages were freed, the waters receded, and the court's ruling dutifully recorded, the case was still not over. The French would not let go. In October 1998, they filed a request for arbitration against the Republic of Peru with the International Center for Settlement of Investment Disputes in Brussels, part of the World Bank. BRGM and Normandy claimed the Supreme Court's action had wrongfully deprived them of their interest in Yanacocha, which they valued at $560 million. Newmont felt the claim was baseless but also believed that if Peru lost, Lima would look to Denver and to Buenaventura for payment and relations between Yanacocha and government regulators could sour. To analysts asking when the matter would ever end, I had a ready answer: "Whenever someone teaches the French how to say 'uncle' in Spanish." Meanwhile, Buenaventura won a unanimous arbitration ruling (including a vote by the French arbiter) against BRGM involving the same facts before the International Chamber of Commerce, but again the French pressed on.

Finally in the fall of 2000, a settlement was reached under which BRGM and Normandy dropped all claims against the two companies and Peru in return for $80 million, half paid by Buenaventura in cash and half paid by Newmont by issuing 2.6 million shares of stock selling at the time for $15.50 a share. This brought BRGM's total compensation for Yanacocha to $189 million, just $9 million more than Newmont had offered six years earlier. (If BRGM still held the stock in 2006, the shares would have been worth $150 million.)

Newmont settled with stock because it had little cash. The prolonged price slide was taking a heavy toll on the entire industry. A cartoon at the time showed two men looking at the rubble of a collapsed bank building labeled "Gold Market." The first asks, "El Niño?" to which the second replies, "El price!" Cambre's optimism was based on the fact that the industry was not replacing its reserves and was depleting its resources and that true market forces were being masked by short selling and speculation.

Commodity cycles can behave in strange ways, but the gold market in the late 1990s was bizarre. "It was the perfect storm with all the negative impacts hitting us at once—a strong U.S. dollar, strong equity market, central bank selling, producer hedging, and low inflation,"[16] recalls Newmont vice president and treasurer Thomas Mahoney. Furthermore, the price decline came against a rise in demand for the metal—up more than 20 percent between 1994 and 1999—with a much smaller increase in mine production.

Gold Field Mineral Services, a London research group that compiles annual statistics on gold market trends, reported that the 1990s were marked by a huge transfer of gold from the official sector, which had lost sight of the metal's monetary qualities, to the private sector, which was buying in record quantities, primarily for jewelry. The amount of gold moving out of government vaults during the decade was 7,200 tonnes, or 231 million ounces, with most of the outflow occurring after 1995.[17] A little over 40 percent of that represented outright sales by central banks. But well over half came from bank lending to support option trading and producer hedging.

European banks saw the road to monetary union paved with the sale of gold. To reduce their national debt in preparation for a single currency in 1999, Belgium sold more than 800 tonnes of gold, Austria sold 334 tonnes, and other countries sold lesser amounts. Canada virtually eliminated its gold reserve. Some bankers spoke of converting a non-interest-bearing metal that was collecting dust in their vaults into U.S. dollars, or later, Euros, that could earn interest. In May 1998, Switzerland announced plans to sell half of its 2,600 tonne reserve. If the gnomes were selling, was there any hope for gold? A year later the Bank of England said it would sell 415 tonnes in auctions of 25 tonnes each every second month, sending gold to a $10 loss for the day. "What the Bank of England thinks it has achieved, God knows," Kelvin Williams, executive director of AngloGold told Reuters News Service. "They have now devalued the 700 tonnes of material they have got. It strikes me as an extremely inept way of managing your assets."[18] Newmont agreed.

Then came the do-gooders. The International Monetary Fund (IMF), which was founded along with the United Nations in 1945 to promote monetary stability and economic growth, dusted off a proposal to sell part of its 3,500-tonne gold reserve to help reduce the debt of the world's seventy poorest countries. The proposal had the support of the Clinton administration and Britain's Chancellor of the Exchequer. Cambre and other gold executives were alarmed. If the IMF's vaults were breached, would Fort Knox, with 8,150 tonnes of gold representing 72 percent of the U.S.'s monetary reserves, be far behind?

The World Gold Council and a Washington lobbying effort by Newmont's vice president of government affairs, Mary Beth Donnelly, and Barrick's Michael Brown swung into action. Winning a bipartisan coalition of both houses of Congress, legislation was passed in August 1999 that requires a vote of Congress for the IMF to sell its gold. Donnelly proudly notes that both Jesse Helms, the conservative senator from North Carolina, and the chairman of the Black Congressional Caucus sent letters to the IMF on the same day opposing the sale. Helms supported gold as the cornerstone of fiscal responsibility, while the Black Caucus was moved by the fact that many of the world's poorest countries are also major gold producers. If the sale had gone through, it would have driven the price of gold even lower, thereby hurting the very countries the sale was intended to help.

Central bankers were not the only ones sending gold into a downward spiral—gold producers were doing it to themselves through hedging. Gold is a unique commodity in that it can be borrowed from bullion banks and sold immediately with a promise to repay in-kind in future years. During the late 1990s, lease rates for this borrowing were extremely low, often around 1 percent, while the proceeds could be invested in higher-yielding Treasury bills. The difference between the two interest rates, called the "contango," multiplied by the years the loan was outstanding was income for the producer. This enabled active hedgers like Barrick to report gold sales realizations, including hedging income, of $100 or more an ounce higher than the spot market. If the price declined further, the hedge looked all the better because it would be repaid with cheaper metal. But if the market rose, hedging gains could turn to losses and investors would lose the benefit of rising prices. To facilitate hedging, 718 tonnes of gold were borrowed from central banks and sold in 1999 alone, depressing an already declining market. Newmont promoted itself as one of the industry's few non-hedgers (the Minahasa hedge being an aberration) and blamed the hedgers, especially Barrick, for contributing to the metal's decline.

Additionally, speculators were selling gold short to jump on the bull market for equities as both the Dow Jones Industrial Average and NASDAQ were reaching new highs. Bullion bankers concocted increasingly complex derivative instruments that only a computer could decipher and with opaque risks almost no one knew how to measure or fairly report in corporate financial statements.

With maximum exposure to a rise in the metal price, investors in Newmont's shares could expect to reap hefty gains when the market turned. Yet with the price spiraling downward, it was hard for management not to think about the extra cash that forward sales could bring. "If the market gets back to $350 an ounce, don't you think we will want to hedge a piece of our production?" Wayne Murdy, who was elevated to president in 1999, asked at one financial review session. "No," Cambre replied, "because if gold ever gets to $350 we'll think it's going to $400."[19] It was a rhetorical question and whimsical answer, typical of the daily banter between the two executives.

Then, in July 1999, gold dropped to $253 an ounce and the company entered into two put and call option contracts to provide a measure of price protection. To obtain a floor price of $270 an ounce for 2.85 million ounces, the company promised to deliver 2.35 million ounces of gold at prices of $350 to $385 an ounce in the distant future. If it had the cash, it could have bought the puts for a few million dollars and not burdened its future.

It turned out to be the bottom of the market. That September, fifteen European central banks with the approval of U.S. Federal Reserve chairman Alan Greenspan announced what became known as the "Washington Accord," under which they agreed to limit sales and lending to 400 tonnes per year over the next five years. The accord halted the decline but did not do much to boost the price, which traded in a narrow range of $265 to $285 an ounce through 2001. The agreement was renewed in 2004. Set at 500 tonnes a year, the new limit has been honored by the banks even as prices soared.

The forward commitment was defensive and not speculative and covered only 4 percent of the company's reserves. But gold bugs howled that Newmont had joined the enemy camp. Shareholders can sell when skies are gray and buy back in sunny weather. Newmont, with huge fixed assets, a monthly payroll of 9,500, and over $1 billion in debt, did not have that luxury. Furthermore, there was no assurance that speculative forces would not drive the price even lower.

"To give our shareholders the option value of higher prices, we have to be able to remain in business to deliver it," Bruce Hansen, who had just been named CFO, told analysts at the time. Furthermore, he added, "If the price ever gets up to the point that we have to deliver those ounces we will be making so much money we won't care."[20]

In early 2006 with the spot price approaching $700 and facing a commitment to deliver 1.85 million ounces through 2011 at $384 an ounce, Hansen admitted, "Today we care."[21]

During the long years without price relief, companies searched for ways to stretch their resources, cut costs, and increase productivity. Newmont initiated a program it called Gold Medal Performance in 1999 and later embraced General Electric's Six Sigma effort to energize its workforce and instill a best practices mentality. It brought together people from all disciplines and locations to review every aspect of the business. John Cole, a process superintendent at the Lone Tree mine in Nevada, received a patent and the chairman's award for a redesigned agitator for the autoclaves that increased oxygen consumption and gold recoveries. Cambre welcomed the breakdown in barriers between hourly and white-collar employees as each recognized that they could make a personal contribution to the company's success. But many found it a time-consuming distraction and there were times when Carlin truck drivers and executive secretaries from Denver found themselves in the same meeting wondering if there was enough common ground to keep the discussion going until lunch.

Appearances were also important. Under pressure from the top to "make the numbers," Jim Mullin squeezed every ounce from in-process inventories at Carlin in order to report the highest possible year-end production, J. M.

Rendu combed drilling records to add a few more marginal ounces to re-serves, and controller Linda Wheeler would step outside to chain smoke and steam as she sought ways to add a penny or two to per share earnings. "Every CEO has a responsibility to push the organization," explains Murdy. "Look at life-of-mine plans. Engineers tend to be conservative. That feels good until you look at an acquisition and everything becomes [more expensive] because the things you are looking at were done a little more aggressively and you were too conservative. That's an injustice to the shareholder."[22]

With excess processing capacity in Nevada, companies looked at ways to consolidate. One property that caught Newmont's eye in 1999 was Getchell, a mine it helped finance in the 1930s. Only a few miles from Twin Creeks, Getchell was developing a new, deep deposit called Turquoise Ridge that could provide feedstock to Twin Creeks' autoclaves. Getchell had been owned by a Mississippi chemical concern, which spun it off in 1996. Man-agement and much of its stock were in Canadian hands. The deeper the shaft sank into Turquoise Ridge, the higher the hype rose in Toronto.

Reserve expert Rendu says it took only two days to detect a pump and dump scheme, or as Cambre more politely puts it, "The mine had been overly promoted." Told to take a second look, Rendu spent another two weeks poring over the data only to come to the same conclusion. "I give J. M. full credit for keeping us disciplined and saying, 'It's not there, guys,'" Cambre says. Shortly thereafter Placer Dome bought Getchell for $1 billion only to write off much of that amount two years later. In 2004, Placer gave New-mont a 25 percent stake in a much diminished Getchell in return for pro-viding 2,000 tons per day of milling capacity at Twin Creeks. The arrange-ment added 58,300 ounces to Newmont's Nevada production in 2006.

In late 1999, Newmont began pursuing Battle Mountain Gold, which had annual production of 760,000 ounces of gold from four mines in Canada, Australia, and Bolivia and owned a large undeveloped gold/copper porphyry called Phoenix in Nevada. Two-thirds of the company's 9.6 mil-lion ounces of gold reserves were at Phoenix. "I was a believer in the empire in Nevada," Cambre says. "Had it been elsewhere I probably wouldn't have considered it."

Battle Mountain was created by Pennzoil, a Houston oil concern, at a time when oil companies were seeking minerals divisions. Later spun off, it merged with Hemlo Gold Mines of Canada in 1996, acquiring two underground mines in Ontario and a 28 percent shareholder, Noranda Inc. Cross-border negotiations were time-consuming and other suitors were in the wings. The deal was finally announced in June 2000 and consummated in January 2001, with Newmont issuing 24.1 million shares worth $545 million. The acquisition added some talented people, most notably Brant Hinze, who became general manager at Yanacocha and senior vice president of North American operations. But with Golden Giant and Holloway in Canada and Kori Kollo in Bolivia nearing depletion, it was an acquisition based on faith in the company's technical ability to extract value from Phoenix.

Located thirty miles from Newmont's Lone Tree mine, Phoenix covered an old district where shallow deposits had been mined out years earlier. Deeper drilling found reserves of eight million ounces of gold and nine hundred million pounds of copper. But hard ores and complex metallurgy created problems. Open-pit mining did not begin until March 2006; production followed six months later. Gold is extracted from crushed ore through flotation and a carbon-in-leach recovery process, while a copper concentrate is shipped off-site for smelting. Output and costs did not meet expectations until mid-2008.

In 2000, Cambre decided to retire at the end of the year. He had told his wife he would only stay five years but remained longer in the hope that the gold price would recover on his watch. At age sixty-two, he had done most of what he had set out to accomplish and besides, he says, "Wayne was ready. How long would he have been willing to wait?" Emulating his predecessor, Gordon Parker, Cambre worked to achieve "a seamless transition." As he and Murdy wrote in the company's annual report in February 2001, "We will continue to manage for cash flow, grow largely through exploration and maintain our leverage to the gold price. Those elements have been the foundation of our past success and will continue to guide our strategy going forward."

But Newmont's Nevada empire was still missing a large piece and the board asked Cambre to stay on as non-executive chairman for another year to pursue it. Was a merger with Barrick possible? Under pressure from Sir James Goldsmith the two companies had sought to come together in 1991 but could not. Now with gold and stock prices down, Cambre and the board were convinced Wall Street would reward a constructive combination of the two biggest players on the Carlin Trend. Cambre wrote Barrick's chairman, Peter Munk, who had stepped aside from day-to-day management and was living in Switzerland. The two arranged to meet for lunch in London.

Munk was charming as usual, but Cambre says he found the meeting "sort of bizarre because the usual talk of 'I'd like to explore this if you'd like to explore it' drew a blank stare. He acted like he had no idea why I had made this trip." However, as the lunch wound down, Munk began talking about an exchange ratio with an 18 to 20 percent premium that Barrick might offer for Newmont's stock. Cambre felt such a discussion was premature.

Returning home, he sent Munk a clarifying note. "If you are really interested there are just five basic decisions that need to be made. You and I have to make those." The five were: the name of the company, where it would be located, who would be CEO, the composition of the board, and whether or not to hedge. "I put in a paragraph saying there would be times when Barrick wouldn't want to be hedged and times when Newmont would and we both needed a gracious way of getting out of our positions. A merger would allow us to do that." When they next met in Munk's suite at New York's Carlisle Hotel, Munk said he was bringing his CEO, Randal Oliphant. "I said, 'Then I'm going to bring Wayne.' You could just see it crumbling away," Cambre says.

In due time, Munk replied to the five points—the Barrick, not Newmont, name would be retained; Toronto would be headquarters, not New York as Cambre proposed; and while Munk offered to make Cambre CEO for two years—a position he did not seek—he would be succeeded by Oliphant. To Cambre and the board, it was a non-starter. "If we do this, you know we will be selling out the Newmont shareholders at the bottom of the market,"[23] Murdy told Cambre. In the end, Cambre believes Barrick's heavily hedged position gave it an inflated opinion of its present value, while Newmont believed its larger landmass and resource base provided greater long-term value. The two very different perceptions of value could not be reconciled.

By the same token, Cambre's contribution to shareholder value cannot be measured with the same yardstick as that used for his predecessors. Newmont reported losses in two of his seven years at the helm as well as his last year as chairman, the stock price dropped nearly 60 percent to $17, and the dividend was cut. But he maintains with justification that he played the hand he was dealt about as well as possible. Earlier, he built Freeport-McMoRan Resource Partners into a fertilizer powerhouse during a period of declining prices. "I told my wife that I have been CEO of two Fortune 500 companies and in both situations we had the worst pricing in the history of the commodity. If the gold price had stayed at $400 the entire time, we would have made more money. But life is about facing the challenges and at the end of the day feeling like you've taken those on and done a good job. I feel good about the fact that Newmont is still here rather than being owned by Barrick."

Here are some relevant numbers: annual equity gold production from year-end 1993 to 2000 rose 200 percent from 1.7 million ounces to 5.2 million. Gold reserves rose 155 percent to more than 66 million ounces and the company added a sizable copper reserve. These speak to the company's success in building a world-class asset base. But it cost to do this, and shares more than doubled from 85.5 million to 195 million with two acquisitions and the settlement in Peru, and debt almost doubled from $543 million to $1 billion, not including Batu Hijau's $1 billion in off–balance sheet obligations. "Our greatest contribution to shareholder wealth during those seven years was the growth of reserves and production per share while reducing costs in a terrible, declining gold price environment beyond our control," Cambre says.

In Cambre's view, he also left the company largely unhedged so that later shareholders could benefit from the gold rally that he always believed was just over the hill—and beyond the graveyard. Unfortunately, when that bull market finally arrived in 2006, much of the anticipated benefit evaporated.

18

PINNACLE

Newmont shareholders began to see a little sunlight in 2001 as the company's stock price rose 12 percent against a 13 percent drop in the overall market as measured by the Standard & Poor's 500 Index. The next year was considerably better as the stock jumped 52 percent, the best showing by a large company on the New York Stock Exchange and the third-best performance by any company in the S&P 500. At $29 a share, this still left long-term shareholders underwater, but the change in outlook was a large psychological boost.

Part of that reflected an improvement in the gold price, which broke through $300 in April 2002 and climbed another $30 an ounce by year-end. Part was due to Newmont's non-hedging philosophy and its commitment to provide shareholders with the maximum leverage to an upward swing in the commodity price. And part was a positive response to the largest merger in the company's history and one of the hardest fought in the gold industry.

In simultaneous transactions in February 2002, Newmont acquired two very different companies—Franco-Nevada, a Canadian-based minerals royalty holder and one of the industry's best-performing stocks, and Normandy Mining of Australia, the leading producer on that gold-rich continent and a thorn in Newmont's side during years of litigation over Yanacocha. Franco brought an entrepreneurial spirit and a boatload of badly needed cash, while Normandy came with some good properties and even better prospects. The three-way transaction vaulted Newmont for the time into the number one position among gold producers, with production, reserves, market capitalization, and shareholder potential surpassing those of all of its rivals.

It was an improbable combination resulting from Newmont CEO Wayne Murdy and Franco executives Seymour Schulich and Pierre Lassonde finding that their paths converged after having exhausted other options for improving their stock price at the bottom of the gold cycle. At age fifty-six

Murdy had spent eight years with Newmont, six as chief financial officer and two as president, before becoming the company's seventh chief executive in January 2001. An avid surfer in his youth, he graduated from California State University at Long Beach, spent time in public accounting, and rose to executive positions with Getty Oil and Apache before joining the gold company.

While retiring CEO Ron Cambre was accustomed to viewing the world from the balcony of life, Murdy was down-to-earth, approachable, and often showed up for work in a golf shirt. "People respected him because he was genuine," says retired treasurer Patricia Flanagan, who found his "optimism very inspiring for everyone."[1]

Settling behind his desk on the twenty-eighth floor of the Wells Fargo Bank Building with a panoramic view of the snow-capped Rocky Mountains, his thoughts could easily have turned to his retreat in Vail and the ski slopes he loved. Instead, he contemplated Newmont's future and realized that the company needed a jolt to get back into the race. Cost-cutting and productivity improvements had gone about as far as they could go. Exploration and technology would continue to add value but were unlikely in the near term to move the stock price. Without a significant increase in the gold price, the company had to look elsewhere.

"I looked at the company through the eyes of Wall Street, and the investment community was not very pleased with us," he recalls. "We weren't in dire straights by any means, but we had cut the dividend, the stock price was down to the low to mid-teens, and we weren't doing much for our shareholders. Wall Street was critical of us because of our high debt and high political risk."[2] Peru still looked stable after President Alberto Fujimori left office under a cloud of scandal, but Indonesia post-Suharto was in a state of turmoil. The currency had collapsed, there were riots between Muslims and Christians, and a power struggle, called Reformasi, was under way between the provinces and the central government in Jakarta.

"I thought I could address both of Wall Street's concerns with an acquisition," says Murdy. "If we could acquire a company with some cash and low debt, it would improve the balance sheet, and if the company had most of its assets in North America or Australia it would improve our political profile."

Assigned to scout out possibilities, Randy Eppler, vice president of corporate development, told his boss, "Over the next year there are two people you've got to get to know—Jack Thompson [the CEO of Homestake] and Pierre Lassonde."[3] That May, Merrill Lynch held a metals conference for analysts in Dublin and Murdy arranged private dinners with both men.

He was immediately attracted to Homestake. While its flagship underground mine in South Dakota was winding down, it had a solid position in Australia and Canada and a property in Argentina that was sought after by Newmont's geologists. Homestake also had a large German shareholder who was rumored to be unhappy. "So they were under pressure and I thought they might be amenable to a merger," Murdy says. In fact, Thompson immediately warmed to the prospect over dinner and by dessert was asking Murdy for a price he could take back to his board. Murdy wanted due diligence to come first.

Back in Denver, he took his case to the Newmont board, which encouraged him to pursue the opportunity. Discussions between the two parties moved swiftly with Thompson professing to welcome the combination and Newmont preparing to offer a 20 percent premium to Homestake's stock price, or just under half a share of Newmont stock for each Homestake share, resulting in a purchase price of $2 billion. Then things went silent, telephone calls were not returned, and Murdy and his advisors got the feeling it was Santa Fe all over again. On Saturday, May 23, Thompson called to say they had received another bid. On Monday, without the benefit of due diligence, Barrick announced that it was acquiring Homestake for $2.2 billion in stock, a 31 percent premium. "I was just sick," Murdy says. "Here, as the new CEO, I had gotten a commitment from our board and then couldn't make it happen. But I was never tempted to up our offer. We just couldn't see higher values."

Murdy knew far less about Franco-Nevada and its co-CEOs, Lassonde, fifty-three, and Schulich, sixty-one, although Franco held a royalty on two of Newmont's Nevada mines, Deep Post and Deep Star. Dinner in Dublin had not included merger talk but rather a discussion of the gold market, which left Murdy impressed by his guest's views and knowledge. Lassonde, who authored *The Gold Book*,[4] a widely read guide on gold and investing in precious metals, is considered an authority on the subject and in 2001 was convinced the market was about to turn up. Furthermore, Franco-Nevada was even more adamantly opposed to hedging than was Newmont.

Shrewd investors, Franco had acquired, at a deep discount, a large piece of debt of Echo Bay Mines, a once prominent gold producer that had fallen on hard times. In late August, Echo Bay began preparing a new stock offering to retire the debt, making Franco its largest shareholder at 49 percent. Lassonde contacted Murdy to see if Newmont had an interest in Echo Bay's properties.

Just as Newmont's founder, William Boyce Thompson, had named his company for the link between Wall Street and his birthplace in Montana, Franco-Nevada chose the Franco portion of its name for Lassonde's French Quebec heritage and the leverage it believed that would give the new company in selling shares in Paris.[5] Over the years, Franco (which for a few years operated a sister company, Euro-Nevada) had become the largest minerals royalty company in the world with income from some of North America's best gold, platinum, and diamond mines and since 1993 a growing interest in oil and gas properties in western Canada.

From the outset, Franco had funded a small exploration effort, but without much enthusiasm. It did so solely to satisfy the SEC, which otherwise would have classified Franco as a Passive Foreign Investment Company, making it difficult for U.S. institutions to own the stock. For ten years geologist Ken Snyder spent a few dollars a year poking around the Nevada hills without success and earning the moniker "Dry Hole Snyder." In 1992, the company began acquiring property at the north end of the Carlin Trend around an old mining camp known as Midas and began a series of drill holes. "We really liked the address,"[6] says Schulich, noting that he and Lassonde were being called "the Midas Brothers" in Toronto financial circles for their royalty picks.

The sixth hole, in August 1994, struck a high-grade vein hosting about one ounce of gold per ton. "What we found was a structure about as wide as this table and 300 feet down at a dip of 78 degrees. It was like finding a needle in a haystack," Schulich recalls. Newmont and others had prospected the area years before but were looking for disseminated gold, not a narrow underground vein. After an investment of $84 million for a mine (named the Ken Snyder mine to appease the company's much-derided geologist) and mill, production began in early 1999. By 2001, Midas was producing 216,000 ounces of gold and 2 million ounces of silver a year at a gold cost of $114 an ounce. Reserves stood at 3.3 million ounces of gold.

While good, it posed a dilemma. Franco-Nevada's twenty-one employees were merchant bankers, not miners, and an effort to convert from contract to owner mining "was killing us," Schulich says. "Craig Haase [executive vice president] and Pierre were going to have nervous breakdowns." Also troubling was that "the royalty niche had played out. There were very few royalties available that could have a material impact on the company" at a low gold price.[7] The company had become a victim of its own success. Over the years it had put together one of the best growth profiles in the industry with net income of $73 million (all numbers are in U.S. dollars, although Franco reported in Canadian currency) on revenue of $183 million. It had cash and marketable securities of $700 million and no debt. Although it had a market capitalization of $2 billion, its stock price had suffered with the rest of the industry and it saw no relief.

Convinced that gold had bottomed, Schulich and Lassonde began to explore ways to leverage their capital to take advantage of rising prices. "The most undervalued stock at the time was Gold Fields of South Africa. The stock was about $3.25, giving it a net worth of about $600 million. That's nothing," says Lassonde, who was convinced Franco could quickly double or triple its investment. "It was a no-brainer."[8] Franco had a good relationship with Gold Fields' executives and soon negotiated a merger that would have created a large, well-financed gold producer. But the deal ran into opposition from the South African government, which took ten months to finally say no. "They just strung us out," Schulich laments. Flying back after making a final and fruitless pitch to government officials in late January 2001, Lassonde says, "I went home and cried for two days because we had worked so hard on this thing."

As a fallback, Franco began looking for an experienced miner to take over Midas in exchange for a piece of a larger company. Four companies were approached and Normandy, which had been seeking a way into the United States for years, "was the keenest to do a deal," says Lassonde. In exchange for Midas, Franco was given a 19.9 percent stake in the Australian company, with production of 2.3 million ounces of gold a year and reserves of 26 million ounces. Lassonde joined the Normandy board and Schulich became an advisor.

They quickly discovered that Normandy, which had been cobbled together by its CEO, Robert Champion de Crespigny, through a series of contentious acquisitions, was the proverbial can of worms. Its mines were held in complex joint ventures, some of which were publicly traded, accounting was opaque, the dividend had been reduced, and the company was losing money, having ventured into offbeat projects such as Australian Magnesium, a company seeking to utilize new technology to become the world's largest supplier of lightweight magnesium alloys for the auto industry.

"Robert was one of the brightest people we have ever seen, but the guy had worn out his welcome everywhere and there was no one to tell the emperor that he had no clothes," says Schulich. "We were trying to rationalize the company. Robert came to Toronto and over a four-hour dinner told us how the government of Australia had agreed to put $100 million in this magnesium operation. He went on and on about how great this was, patting himself on the back. Then he and Pierre fly to Australia and after twenty hours on the plane and an hour before they land, he announces that Normandy had to put up $100 million, too. We were trying to get this guy's balance sheet in shape and it was like pouring water in a leaky bucket. Every time we'd pour in a cup of water, Robert would punch another hole in the pail."

Then on September 5, South Africa's AngloGold, a subsidiary of Anglo American and for years the world's largest producer, made a $1.7 billion bid for Normandy, offering shares worth A$1.42 for Normandy stock that had been trading at A$1.10 the day before. Anglo already owned nearly 10 percent of Normandy and believed that de Crespigny, an outspoken advocate of consolidation, welcomed the offer. Schulich and Lassonde, however, felt insulted that AngloGold's chairman, Bobby Godsell, had not consulted with them as Normandy's largest shareholder. "He really thought we were in a corner and were captive," Lassonde says. After their experience with Gold Fields, Franco wanted nothing to do with South Africa and began an immediate search for alternatives. Was its Toronto neighbor Barrick interested in entering a bidding war for Normandy? Still absorbing Homestake, the answer was no. The two Franco executives then called Murdy. Would Newmont be interested in expanding talks beyond Echo Bay? This time the answer was yes, and on September 11 Murdy and Eppler planned to fly to Toronto to explore the possibilities. "I remember getting out to the airport and watching TV in the executive lounge as the planes crashed into the World Trade Towers," Murdy says. "Obviously, we didn't make the trip."

Newmont had no interest in bidding for Normandy alone—it, too, had high debt and was heavily hedged—and while Franco's strong cash position had caught Eppler's eye, it didn't make sense to pay a premium just to acquire cash. "But the more I thought about it, the better it looked to acquire both companies," Murdy says. A three-way merger would not only make Newmont the largest producer in an industry where size counts, but it would meet his objectives of improving Newmont's balance sheet and political profile while adding new world-class properties in Australia and new exploration prospects worldwide. It also would provide a steady stream of royalty income of $50 to $60 million a year (much of it coming from Barrick's Goldstrike property) as a natural hedge against another market downturn.

The Denver Gold Group was hosting its annual investment forum beginning Monday, October 1. Murdy asked Schulich to come down a day early and join him for Sunday breakfast at the Cherry Hills Country Club to discuss his thoughts. "A couple of things struck me about that breakfast," recalls Schulich. "What Wayne said at that meeting was the template for the entire deal. What he said would happen, happened."

A room was set up at the Westin Hotel, site of the Denver Gold Group's forum, where separate meetings were held with the two parties. "We'd have different people come to the room at different times and knock twice to get in," Eppler says. Neither Newmont nor Franco wished to include the temperamental de Crespigny until the ground rules had been established. Left out of an early meeting, "Robert was on the phone, jumping up and down and screaming that he wanted to attend," Schulich laughs. "Finally, I said, 'Robert, I am sure as a boy you would do this with your mother and she would give in. Well, I'm not your mother. I'm not giving in and you're not going to attend the damned meeting.'" At another meeting with de Crespigny present, Cambre, who was still chairman and had lost a slander lawsuit to the Australian during the battle for Yanacocha, walked in. "I have some things to discuss with this man," Eppler recalls him saying, "and I have a pocket full of francs."

As with most Wall Street deals, code names were assigned to the players. "We called Newmont 'Delta' for Denver, Normandy was 'Alpha' for Adelaide, its headquarters in Australia, but Franco insisted on being called 'Fox' because they thought they were so crafty," Eppler says. "Seymour and

Pierre were called 'S&P,' so we started calling Robert 'Moody.' It really fit, but he hated it, so we changed it to 'RCdC.'"

Working through the details of a merger with strong-willed executives on two continents governed by three different sets of legal requirements was a nightmare. Franco relied on its co-CEOs, senior vice president David Harquail, and Ron Binns, vice president and CFO. Two Toronto financial institutions, National Bank Financial and CIBC, were brought in as advisors. Normandy's team included de Crespigny and the two men who managed his corporate development projects, Robert Greenslade and John Richards, and Australia's Macquarie Bank. Murdy took the lead for Newmont, assisted by Eppler, senior vice president and CFO Bruce Hansen, and Britt Banks, who had just been named vice president and general counsel. JPMorgan and Goldman Sachs were the financial advisors, while David Katz of Wachtell, Lipton managed legal strategy with a brilliant mind and boundless energy. "He was enormously helpful . . . a key to the deal's success," says Eppler. Adds Murdy, "Newmont will never do another merger as long as I'm around without involving Wachtell. They were the tops." Newmont also benefited from a very supportive board of directors.

Teams of lawyers, accountants, engineers, and geologists flew from Denver to Toronto and Australia to examine Normandy's properties and Franco's royalties. Due diligence accompanied by tough negotiations over terms took six weeks. Schulich says he found "Wayne to be a super negotiator. He never got personal or emotional and never took personal umbrage at anything we did. Yet he negotiated very hard. He was very effective and didn't burn any bridges. We bonded very fast." Lassonde responds similarly. Watching Murdy in action "was amazing," he says. "He was so composed, the consummate statesman, and doesn't wilt under pressure. I'm just the opposite, more of the Latin type. I get hot under the collar."

By mid-November, Newmont and Franco had agreed on an exchange ratio of 0.8 of a Newmont share for each Franco share, valuing the Canadian company at $2.8 billion. Australian takeover law required board approval from the subject company, and de Crespigny said it would take a significant premium over Anglo's offer to win such approval. The number finally agreed upon was 0.0385 of a Newmont share plus A$0.05 for each Normandy share, with the nickel in cash being contingent on receiving 90 per-

18.1. Although Robert de Crespigny, CEO of Australia's Normandy Mining, agreed to the merger with Newmont, he proved difficult to deal with throughout the negotiations. (*Bryan Charlton/Fairfax photos*)

cent acceptance of the Normandy shares. This valued Normandy at A$1.70 a share, or $1.9 billion, an 18 percent premium to Anglo's offer. A joint press release with a dateline reading Denver, Adelaide, and Toronto was issued on November 14 before the opening bell at the New York and Toronto stock exchanges. It was 10:30 P.M. in Australia, getting the news out well ahead of trading there on the November 15.

While the Newmont offer was superior, AngloGold had a six-week head start in wooing Normandy's shareholders (it was not interested in acquiring Franco). For Newmont, it was important that everyone "was mentally in this deal. It was going to be three ways or no way," Murdy says. Key to his strategy was locking up Franco's position in Normandy so that even if the deal fell apart, Newmont would own that stock. Murdy and Franco were surprised that Anglo never sought to do that or to secure a recommendation from Normandy's board.

The next two months, which included Thanksgiving, Christmas, and New Year's, were exhausting. "We had a tough fight with Anglo," Lassonde says. "There was a sixty-day period where I had fifty-eight boarding passes for planes. I did two round-the-world trips to sell the deal to investors. It was hard, really hard." Six times AngloGold filed objections with the Australian Takeover Board and lost each one; twice it raised its offer only to be topped by a higher bid. Newmont's final offer did not change the exchange ratio but raised the cash component to A$0.50. This valued Normandy at A$2.04 a share or $2.4 billion, 12 cents a share more than the implied value of Anglo's final bid.

While the price was important, so was liquidity. "We knew we were in a good position when Normandy's stock moved from individual to institutional hands since Anglo's stock was thinly traded," says Murdy. With two-thirds of AngloGold's stock held by Anglo American, AngloGold traded only a few hundred thousand shares a day, meaning arbitrageurs would have no way to get out. By contrast, it was not uncommon for two million shares of Newmont stock to trade each day on the New York Stock Exchange. With the completion of the transactions, five-million-share trading days became the norm and Newmont listed its stock on the Toronto and Australian exchanges to provide further liquidity for its foreign shareholders.

Anglo folded in late January 2002, and with a favorable recommendation from Normandy's board Newmont quickly completed the transaction. Franco and Newmont shareholders gave their approval the next month. Three Franco directors—Schulich, Lassonde, and Haase—joined the Newmont board as did two Normandy directors—John Prescott, a retired managing director of Broken Hill Proprietary, Australia's largest company, and Michael Hamson, retired joint chairman of McIntosh Hamson Hoare Govett, a brokerage firm now called Merrill Lynch Australia. De Crespigny was offered a seat but declined.

A $19 Newmont stock price on the January record date (down from $22.50 when the offers were announced) put the purchase price for the two companies at $4.3 billion. This included 197 million Newmont shares and $552 million in cash (including $90 million in transaction costs). The transaction doubled the company's shares outstanding, effectively giving Franco and Normandy shareholders half of the expanded company. The cash payments nearly depleted Franco's treasury. Since the Santa Fe merger in 1997, the SEC had opposed pooling of interests accounting, so these mergers were accounted for as purchases. As a result, the $3 billion difference between the fair market value of assets acquired and the purchase price was treated as goodwill. Most of that related to Franco's royalty business. But those were just footnotes in the annual report; the numbers Murdy and Lassonde emphasized in the company's 2002 annual report presented the new Newmont as a far stronger company.

- Market capitalization of $11.6 billion was up more than 200 percent from $3.7 billion a year earlier.

- The ratio of net debt to total capitalization was down to 20 percent from a choking 42 percent prior to the mergers.

- Gold reserves of 87 million ounces were 45 percent higher than in 2001 and 66 percent were in countries ranked AAA for their credit standing and political stability according to Standard & Poor's.

- The company's global land package of 94,000 square miles, much of it in known gold belts, was equal in size to the United Kingdom.

Lassonde was named president and Harquail, Lassonde's right-hand man at Franco, became vice president of merchant banking, handling royalties and applying an entrepreneurial eye to the management of the company's vast assets. "The thing I liked about Franco was that they were smart people, very strategic. Pierre and Seymour made their shareholders a lot of money," says Murdy. "Pierre has a tremendous knowledge of the industry and can smell new mining districts. It was essential that they be part of the new management . . . and make it work. I didn't want this to appear as a way for the Franco people to bail out." He adds, "I sometimes joke that I'm like a coach of an NBA basketball team with these superstar talents." The analogy was apt. At their first board meeting after the merger, Murdy presided with 18,000 Newmont shares while Lassonde held 2.9 million and Schulich 8.2 million.

The long plane rides to win shareholder acceptance provided time for the two leaders to begin laying out the strategy for the new company. "Traveling around the world together, we were fully connected at the hip," says Murdy. "We had a lot of time to put numbers together, to think things through and get our thoughts aligned about the new company. The term we used was transformation rather than integration because we were going to transform the entire company. At the same time, we had Seymour, the back-room guy, faxing us messages all the time because he was thinking about it." By the end of the campaign, Lassonde says, "We had a common vision."

At the depth of the gold depression, a few months before the three-way merger was conceived, the company offered an early retirement package under which ninety-one senior people (including me and six other vice presidents) left the company. Other officers retired within the next year. It was a costly miscalculation as the company soon faced a huge expansion with a shortage of both technical and managerial talent. As part of the post-merger transformation, John Dow, who had joined Newmont in Australia twenty-four years earlier and had been executive vice president of exploration, moved back to Australia as managing director. He brought along a number of financial, legal, and planning executives to help infuse Newmont attitudes Down Under. In turn, three of Normandy's senior officers moved to new posts in Denver. Four years later, none remained.

Newmont's first task was to sort through Normandy's convoluted or-

18.2. Pierre Lassonde (left), a co-founder of Canada's Franco-Nevada, and CEO Wayne Murdy bonded quickly during merger negotiations. Lassonde became Newmont's president in 2002. (*Tejada Photography*)

ganization, which involved 236 corporate entities and a 10-million-ounce hedge book that in a rising gold market was a looming liability. (Future deliveries were capped at $319 an ounce.) The company moved quickly to reduce the hedge obligation and by year-end 2003 the position had been largely eliminated, in part by buying out most of the liabilities related to Normandy's Yandal operation for 50 cents on the dollar and removing the balance through a brief voluntary bankruptcy procedure.

Within a year, $480 million was raised from the sale of non-core assets, including Normandy's cobalt mine in Uganda and a small interest in the Lihir gold mine in Papua New Guinea that Newmont had acquired with Battle Mountain. Franco's shares in Echo Bay and Normandy's interest in a joint venture with TVX Gold in five mines in Canada, Brazil, and Chile were transferred to Kinross Gold of Canada for $180 million and a 13.8 percent stake in what became the seventh largest gold company. Over the next three years, the company received $336 million from the sale of its Kinross shares and another $147 million from the sale of a copper and zinc mine in Australia. Following Franco's philosophy of selling equity when the market was hot, Newmont raised $1 billion overnight in late 2003 by selling 24 million shares to the public at $42.40 a share to pay down high interest debt. The oversubscribed issue was managed by JPMorgan and UBS Investments. On the other side of the ledger, the company worked its way out of its Australian Magnesium position at a cost of $140 million.

In reentering Australia after an absence of more than a decade, Newmont obtained an interest in operations that produced 1.8 million equity ounces of gold—equal to two-thirds of its production in Nevada—at a cash cost in 2002 of $191 an ounce. The best-known operation, Kalgoorlie, located 325 miles east of Perth in Western Australia, was the largest gold mine in the country. Its Super Pit is mining out a halo of low-grade ore surrounding old deposits along the Golden Mile, where gold has been mined since 1893. Newmont has a 50 percent interest with Barrick, which had acquired the other half in its purchase of Homestake.

Other operations included underground and surface mines in Queensland, Western Australia, and the Northern Territory. Some are located near such colorful points on the map as Dead Bullock Soak and are so remote that crews live in camps and work on a fly-in, fly-out schedule. The high-grade Pajingo underground mine, south of the old gold mining center of Charters Towers, was discovered by Battle Mountain in 1983 and had been operated as a joint venture with Normandy since 1991. In 2002 it was the company's lowest-cost mine at $99 an ounce. The Tanami operation in the desert region of Northern Territory utilizes the largest road train in the world, a 330-foot-long string of ore trailers powered by diesel tractors, to link its spread-out mines with a carbon-in-pulp processing plant at the Granites. In 2003, Newmont began using a smaller version of the road train in Nevada to haul ore between the Deep Post mine and the roaster at Carlin. Tanami was part of a publicly traded company that was 89 percent owned by Normandy. Newmont bought out the minority shares in 2003 for $115 million.

As part of the same transaction, Newmont became the 100 percent owner of the small Martha mine in New Zealand. Located in the town of Waihi sixty-six miles southeast of Auckland, Martha is one of the oldest operating gold mines in the world, having started production in 1878.

Normandy also held an interest in several early stage projects that Newmont has since expanded and developed. The most promising is Boddington, located eighty miles south of Perth in a greenstone belt of volcanic and sedimentary rocks similar to the geology of Kalgoorlie and believed to host one of the world's largest undeveloped gold deposits. A small open pit operated on the property from 1987 until 2001. Subsequent drilling, which tripled the size from Normandy's feasibility study, identified reserves of 17 million ounces of low-grade gold (0.023 ounce per ton) and 1.5 billion pounds of copper, but only tested a portion of the geologic structure that is twenty-one miles long by three to six miles wide.

In February 2006, Newmont acquired a 22 percent interest in the deposit from Newcrest Mining for $173 million to lift its position to 66.7 percent. At the same time, the board approved $1.5 billion for a complex mill using high-pressure grinding rolls to crush the hard rock and a combination of flotation and carbon-in-leach recovery circuits to extract the metal. Cost overruns, much of it associated with the appreciation of the Australian dollar against the U.S. currency, pushed the final price to $2.9 billion before the project was completed in mid-2009. With reserves increased to 20 million ounces of gold, Newmont acquired the remaining one-third interest in the mine from AngloGold for $1 billion; $750 million paid immediately in cash, $240 million due at year-end; and up to another $100 million in royalties dependent on the mine's future profitability. Annual production of nearly one million ounces of gold and 70 million pounds of copper will make it the largest gold mine in Australia.

Boddington represents the latest example of Daniel Jackling's principle—put into action at a Utah copper mine a century ago—that even low-grade ore can be mined economically if approached on a large enough scale. Yanacocha has made a fortune processing similar grade ore by heap leaching, which involved both low operating and capital costs. Boddington, with much harder rock, will try to do so from a high-capital cost mill.

Another high-potential, but low-grade, opportunity almost got lost in the early sifting of Normandy's assets. As part of its deal with the Bureau de Recherches Géologiques et Minières (BRGM) in 1994, Normandy picked up a portfolio of early stage exploration projects in West Africa, including two in Ghana. Work had begun the year before by Gencor of South Africa. Normandy did little with the properties until it put itself up for auction in 2001, when it put 3.3 million ounces of reserves on the books at Yamfo-Sefwi, now called Ahafo. Newmont and Murdy had a strong aversion to Africa and put the properties at the top of their list to be sold. Geologist Cindy Williams was sent to Ghana in October 2002 to analyze the ground and in a matter of months turned the company's thinking 180 degrees.

Williams began by examining Normandy's past drilling results and mine models and found they "had not been done the way Newmont would do it. So I re-logged some 270,000 feet of drill results and the models changed a lot. The geometry of the high-grade ore at the bottom of the deposit was found to hold better potential than we originally thought,"[9] she says. A rising gold price allowed the new models to look at deeper pits, and by assuming owner, instead of contract, mining costs were reduced. She presented her findings to Murdy in early 2003 and began to "push hard" for money for an extensive drilling program. Her voice carried some weight. With a master's degree in geology from Colorado State University, she was the director of mine geology at Yanacocha during a five-year period when 16 million ounces of gold were added to reserves. She was primarily responsible for unraveling the complex geology of the 7-million-ounce LaQuinua deposit.

Funds in hand, Williams scouted the world for available drilling rigs and soon had seven at work at Ahafo, where 160,000 feet was drilled by year-end. "Everything we drilled exceeded our expectations. Then when the reserves began to explode, people got excited. The flywheel was spinning with good results generating more good results," she says. At the end of 2003, Newmont reported nearly 12 million ounces of gold reserves at two locations—7.6 million at Ahafo and 4.3 million at a second location, Akyem. Three years later, the number was 20.3 million ounces (60 percent at Ahafo), exceeding Newmont's interest in Yanacocha's reserves. Murdy gave Williams his chairman's award in 2004.

Ghana is home to the Ashanti people, who have mined gold for hundreds of years. As a result, Ghana's schools turn out excellent geologists and Williams credits the help of several men who had worked on-site from the beginning for her quick success. However, with no mining tradition in the immediate area—80 miles for Akyem and 180 miles for Ahafo—northwest of the coastal capital of Accra, Newmont launched extensive community relations programs to educate local people and address their concerns prior to mining. Mineral rights in the country are controlled by the government, but surface lands are occupied by tradition and administered by local chiefs. Subsistence crops for palm oil and citrus along with cocoa support the local population. There were no defined fields or owner's plots, but people could point to specific trees or bushes they had harvested in the past. It made compensation difficult. The issue of relocation was challenging as well, as the population increased in both areas as word of future jobs spread, and many in the area live nomadic lives without fixed housing.

Eppler and John Gaensbauer, a young attorney in the Denver office, made more than twenty trips each to Ghana over a two-and-a-half-year period to work with various ministries and negotiate the necessary agreements, while Paul Lahti, the former general manager at Minahasa, began on-site groundwork. "Randy and I presented Newmont to the government as a company the country would want to do business with," says Gaensbauer. In a country with little foreign investment, Newmont's proposed $1 billion investment in the two projects "created real excitement," he says. "We wanted the broadest possible community and government support and I am so proud that this was done in the most open and transparent way with the Parliament voting unanimously in 2003 for the agreement. It's the most rewarding thing I've done in my professional life."[10] Greatly helping the negotiations were Dorothy Gyamfi, a lawyer in Accra who knew the intricacies of government decision making, and the fact that English is Ghana's official language.

18.3. Geologist Cindy Williams discusses the LaQuinua deposit with analysts in Peru. She later won the chairman's award for an exploration program that proved up large reserves in Ghana. She was named a vice president in 2009. (*Jack Morris*)

Under the agreement Newmont will pay a 3 percent gross royalty and will be taxed at the country's statutory rate, currently 25 percent. The government will receive 10 percent of the net cash flow after the company has recouped its investment and has the right to acquire up to 20 percent in the projects at fair market value after fifteen years. Part of Akyem is in an area designated by the government as a forestry preserve, although the Forestry Commission found it to be "devoid of any special protected biological areas" or endangered species. One observer describes the preserve as looking "no different than any of the surrounding area. Trees are sparse and stick out of the landscape like large umbrellas, not the dense canopy associated with a forest."[11] Nevertheless, Newmont has agreed to a slightly higher royalty and to undertake extensive reforestation elsewhere in the area if granted a permit.

Minority partners at both locations were bought out and an initial $125 million loan from the International Finance Corporation put in place. Each site will contain multiple pits and a carbon-in-leach gold recovery system. Production at Ahafo, which covers 620 square miles, began in mid-2006. Output is expected to average 450,000 to 500,000 ounces of gold a year, somewhat less than originally planned due to lower grades and recoveries and difficulties with the country's chronic power shortages. In 2007, the company joined with other gold producers to build a $45 million power plant to supplement local power in the area.

In late 2006, development of Akyem was deferred as the company addressed a number of engineering issues, including power shortages in the area, and is still awaiting a final mining permit.

The company also faced escalating power costs in Nevada and in 2000 began studying the feasibility of building a power plant of its own in the Carlin area. Natural gas was the preferred fuel source, but when a pipeline from the Rockies could not be arranged, the company turned to coal. In 2005, it began construction of a 200-megawatt plant—25 percent larger than the plant at Batu Hijau. By the time it came on line in 2008, costs had escalated by more than 40 percent to $620 million. Still, it could be one of the company's highest-return investments as it is expected to save $25 an ounce, or $75 million a year, in energy costs. The facility will also supply one-third of its power to the local grid, helping meet the growing energy needs of the region. Elko mayor Michael Franzoia cites the plant as an example of the company's leadership in Nevada.

As Newmont adapted to its role as the world's gold leader, it expanded its horizons into new business ventures, as well as new locations, as it responded, in part, to the entrepreneurial input of its Franco-Nevada executives. A few are listed below.

- To hedge the cost of diesel fuel—the company's operations consume more than 175 million gallons a year—Newmont took a 6.5 percent interest in the Canadian Oil Sands Trust in 2004 for $200 million. The purchase essentially locks in an oil price of $27 a barrel for fifty years, Lassonde told *Barron's* magazine.[12] With rising oil prices, the position had quadrupled in value by mid-2006, prompting *Barron's* to call the move "positively brilliant." Two years later, as the price of oil doubled again, the investment was worth $1.3 billion and was paying Newmont $120 million a year in cash.

- Another $10 million investment in an Alberta Heavy Oil project was sold in 2006 for a whopping $280 million. The man behind both investments was Schulich, who in addition to being a Newmont director was chairman of Newmont Capital, which managed the company's portfolio of royalty holdings and alternative opportunities. "Seymour is clairvoyant when it comes to finding ways to make money,"[13] says Thomas Mahoney, Newmont treasurer.

• Large positions were taken in two overseas gold refineries that together process metal for 20 percent of the world's fabricated gold products. Being involved in downstream markets gives the company a unique eye on the gold market in Asia and India. Other investments have been made in coal, iron ore, Arctic gas, and diamonds, while equity positions were acquired in a number of junior gold exploration and production companies in the hope of piggybacking on their success.

In many ways, the company was rediscovering its past. Under William Boyce Thompson, Newmont managed a portfolio of mining and oil investments operated by others, not unlike Newmont Capital. With Batu Hijau, Phoenix, and Boddington, Newmont is once again becoming a significant copper producer.

Also for the first time in years, its name is being associated with philanthropy. Thompson and his close associate Henry Krumb gave hugely to universities and other institutions during the company's early years and Carlin discoverer John Livermore helped endow Nevada's Mackay School. But until Schulich and Lassonde, both of whom had become exceedingly wealthy, joined the company, officers did not have personal fortunes at their disposal. Schulich had given $150 million to various Canadian and U.S. universities by 2004 and says he is "on a path to give away either during my life or posthumously half my money." Lassonde helped fund the Lassonde Institute of Engineering Geoscience at the University of Toronto, where Arthur Brant began his early work in geophysics, and has pledged nearly $15 million to the University of Utah, from which he holds an MBA.

By masterminding the three-way merger and the transformation of the company, Murdy established himself as a leader, wiping out some early misgivings. "When Ron retired, Wayne was the obvious choice, although we had quite a discussion about his lack of mining experience. Now, I'm convinced the board made the right choice,"[14] said director Joseph Flannery, who became one of Murdy's most vocal supporters and a close confidant, in 2003. Dow, speaking on the eve of his retirement later that year, was even more impressed: "As number two there was little evidence of how he was going to behave when he became number one. I have to tell you that I wasn't really sure Wayne could be strong enough and independent enough to succeed Ron. Man, I couldn't have been more wrong. Wayne has become a leader of the industry, he certainly is a leader inside Newmont, and he is managing the board dynamically. The thing that has gotten the board and executive team fully behind Wayne is his ability to articulate the issues so clearly and to lay out a plan to get it done."[15]

Wall Street agreed. Longtime gold analyst Leanne Baker praised Newmont's "non-hedge stand during the bear market" under Cambre and Murdy as "a huge show of leadership. Their willingness to adopt a philosophy to support the metal showed that they understood what investors wanted in a gold company." She also applauds Lassonde and Schulich for staying with Newmont after the merger. "They put their life's savings—everything they had worked to build—on the line in the belief that there would be a bull market in gold. Investors noticed; it speaks volumes to shareholders."[16]

They and other shareholders were rewarded. In the first five years under Murdy and Lassonde Newmont added 7 million ounces of gold to its reserves, bringing the total at year-end 2006 to 94 million ounces. Gold production reached a record 8.8 million ounces in 2004, with the company's equity share at 7 million ounces. That was 40 percent higher than in 2001. With rising metal prices, revenue rose from $1.7 billion in 2001 to $5 billion in 2006, when net income reached a record $791 million, or $1.75 per share.

The company raised its dividend in 2003 and again in 2004 and 2005. The current quarterly payout of 10 cents a share is the highest in a decade. Its stock hit a high of $62 a share in early 2006. From 1998 through 2001, Newmont and Barrick traded in close parity on the New York Stock Exchange—in the high teens to low twenties. After the mergers, Newmont pulled steadily ahead so that by early 2006 NEM was selling for double the price of ABX. That's the sunshine Newmont shareholders had long awaited.

19

A GOOD NEIGHBOR

The *Wall Street Journal* recently asked: "What obligations do companies have to be socially responsible?" Chief executives, the article said, "know their primary mission is to make profits, but they also feel pressured to demonstrate that their businesses have a social conscience."[1]

Newmont Mining's philosophy was summed up a few years ago by then CEO Wayne Murdy, who said the company strives to be "a model of how an ethical company should behave,"[2] and is committed to "act with integrity, trust and respect" in all of its activities. "From the day we begin exploration, our success is tied to our ability to develop, operate and close mines in a manner that improves the lives of the people in the surrounding communities in a safe and environmentally responsible manner."[3]

Newmont has an excellent, and verifiable, safety and environmental record and invests millions of dollars each year—$45 million in 2008 alone—for schools, health care, infrastructure improvements, and other community projects. It has won numerous international awards for its efforts and in 2007 became the first mining company to earn inclusion in the Dow Jones Sustainability Index—World, which selects the best of 2,500 global companies based on their long-term economic, environmental, and social performance.

That is just the tip of the economic benefits that it brings to its mine sites around the globe. Through job creation, local purchases, taxes, and community projects, the company pumped $19 billion into local communities in 2006, 2007, and 2008—Ghana received $750 million, Indonesia nearly $2.5 billion, and Peru $4 billion.

Yet the company has faced unrelenting opposition from nongovernmental organizations (NGOs), many with an anti-development bias, that use inflamed rhetoric and unsubstantiated charges in an attempt to discredit it. Accepting such charges, which are widely circulated on Web sites, as fact, reporters have vilified the company while searching out those who feel by-passed by progress rather than those who have benefited.

"Our employees care deeply about the communities in which we operate [and] we work closely with local governments . . . to ensure that the highest environmental standards are upheld," Murdy wrote in a December 2004 letter to the editor of the *Denver Post*. The newspaper had just published a series of articles attacking the company's global environmental record in a way, Murdy said, that "portrays a company largely unrecognizable to us."[4]

Mining is open to legitimate public concern, especially in undeveloped areas. This extends beyond the immediate environmental impact of mineral extraction. Land compensation, employment, potential health impacts, eventual mine closure, and threats to the local hierarchy are also issues. Managing expectations is critical in areas where government services are few, needs are great, and the company is seen through local eyes as having immense wealth. This is all made more difficult when governments are remote or corrupt; when there is no history of legal rights, land titles, or conflict resolution; and when savvy NGOs with global Internet connections are eager to exploit any perceived misstep. Every mining and energy company has run this gauntlet, but Newmont's experience has been one of the most bruising.

The company's approach to social responsibility is based on core values developed over time. Safety has always been number one and in 2007, nearly three-quarters of a million hours, or the equivalent of fifty hours per employee, was invested in safety training. This is particularly important at new mines in underdeveloped countries where local workers often lack an appreciation for even the basic safety requirements. The company believes that all accidents are preventable and major incidents become case studies in how to improve procedures and prevent future injuries. "We value human life in all that we do at Newmont and we will not sacrifice a safe workplace for any reason," says the current CEO, Richard O'Brien.[5]

A second core value, environmental stewardship, was championed by Peter Philip. When he became president in 1991, he worked to ingrain that ethic into Newmont's mind-set by formalizing a "Mission Statement for Environmental Compliance," which said it was "the intent of Newmont to set standards of excellence with regard to environmental matters" wherever it operated. Compliance began with the commitment of senior management, and performance would be enforced through tracking, training, and audits, all of which are now integrated into its activities.

When the company moved abroad, it committed to a third core value— hiring local workers and supporting them with extensive training. In 2008, 31 percent of employees and 55 percent of contractors were drawn from local communities, while an additional 68 percent of employees and 44 percent of contractors were nationals of the country. Thus Yanacocha, with 9,000 workers, has a nearly 100 percent Peruvian workforce and Batu Hijau's workforce of 7,200 is 98 percent Indonesian. Wages as well as the number of women in professional and technical positions at all mines far exceed national norms.

The newest core value is sustainability, a concept that seeks to balance local concerns over the social and environmental consequences of mining with both the needs and expectations of future generations and the company's ability to secure land and raise capital. Sometimes called CSR (Corporate Social Responsibility), it seeks an integrated approach to corporate decision making that embraces a triple bottom line—people, planet, and profit. Transparency and open dialogue are mandatory for its success. Needless to say, it is a concept that came from schools of social science, not mining and engineering.

Today the company's efforts are closely monitored by the board of directors with assistance from panels of global leaders drawn from environmental, community relations, and human rights organizations. Using measures developed by the International Organization for Standardization (ISO), the U.N. Global Compact, and other multinational groups, the company rates and ranks progress at each site on a number of criteria and then develops programs to achieve continual improvement. Goals, programs, and results are published annually on the company's Web page. "In areas of the environment, social responsibility, and sustainability, Newmont is way out in front of all the mining companies," says James Taranik, who chairs the board's Environmental and Social Responsibility Committee.[6]

So what is the company's record?

In safety, results have been outstanding. The company-wide lost time accident frequency rate declined by two-thirds between 2002 and 2008, when it was 0.10 for every 200,000 hours worked. A total reportable accident rate of 0.74 worldwide compares with a 2006 rate of 4.4 compiled by the U.S. Department of Labor for the metals and mining industry in the United States alone. Furthermore, the company includes contractors in its reporting statistics, which not all companies do.

Nevada operations won the first award from the U.S. Department of Labor's Mine Safety and Health Administration (MSHA) for its performance in 2005. Through mid-2007, Nevada had gone six years without a fatality, although there have been three since then. Yanacocha, Batu Hijau, and Pajingo in Australia have earned their countries' top safety awards. Through 2004, Kalgoorlie, also in Australia, had gone four million hours without a lost time accident, but suffered a fatality in early 2009. Across the company, there were 15 fatalities from 2002 through 2008. Over those years, 550 million hours were worked at the company's facilities, equal to 36.6 million hours per fatality. Recent deaths resulted from an underground subsidence, truck accidents, the fall of machinery in a repair shop, and lightning striking a contractor working on a community project in Peru. Newmont has grieved each loss.

Significantly, after forty-four years of operation in Nevada and the movement of four billion of tons of earth, Newmont has never had an environmental accident of consequence. But, just as there are scrapes and bruises that require no more than a band-aid, there are minor environmental incidents—a spill of diesel fuel, a rock slide—that are reported and cleaned up quickly. The most serious was a leach pad failure in June 1997 that allowed 18,000 gallons of water with a low concentration of cyanide to reach a creek on the company's T/S Ranch. The creek is not a source of drinking water and water quality was not in danger. Newmont immediately notified the Nevada Division of Environmental Protection (NDEP), which fined it $23,500 but praised its quick response. To mitigate the release of 400,000 gallons of storm water run off at the Phoenix mine in 2006, Newmont spent $21,000 installing bat gates at historic mine workings in the area.

"Have we been perfect in all respects? Absolutely not," says John Mudge, director of environmental and social responsibility for North America. "But when we have a problem, we identify it, report it, correct it, and then change our procedures to prevent it from recurring."[7]

The company addresses its environmental challenges up front, at the permitting stage, and conducts concurrent reclamation throughout the mining process. Thousands of acres along the Carlin Trend have been returned to their native state after exploration or mining. Reclamation bonds are established for each project and a reclamation fund—currently $2 an ounce in Nevada—is set aside solely for cleanup. The amount is updated regularly to make sure sufficient funds are available. At year-end 2008, Newmont carried a reclamation reserve of $716 million for its worldwide activities.

The company has won numerous state and federal awards for its reclamation and mitigation activities, including reseeding 1,300 acres of mule deer winter range devastated by wildfires and repairing 82 miles of stream channels and 2,000 acres of riparian lands for the benefit of a variety of fish and wildlife. As general manager at Carlin in the late 1990s, Jim Mullin changed the bonus program to include environmental stewardship and community service.

Nevertheless, applications for mine permits routinely bring lawsuits from opponents of mining. Most are resolved in the company's favor, although some go all the way to the Nevada Supreme Court before that happens.

A look at a recent concern in Nevada and surrounding states regarding the release of mercury from various processing plants into the atmosphere provides a case study on environmental charges and Newmont's response. Mercury, often associated with gold ore, is a by-product of mining. Elemental mercury is not very toxic, but when evaporated and breathed or absorbed by fish that are then eaten, it can be poisonous. Since 1998, mines have been required by the EPA to report all releases of toxic material from their operations. Under the definitions, the movement of rock during mining counts as a release if it contains naturally occurring trace minerals such as arsenic, manganese, nickel, and mercury. Because mining involves huge numbers, reported releases are likewise huge.

What took everyone by surprise was that when the EPA published its first Toxic Release Inventory data in 2000, it showed that ten tons of mercury had been released into the atmosphere in Nevada in 1998. That was within the permitted levels of the U.S. Clean Air Act, but it was still a big number and the NDEP and the gold industry set out to do something about it.

A joint effort, called the Voluntary Mercury Reduction Program (VMRP), was established to monitor, test, and reduce mercury emissions in the state. In a 2006 analysis, the NDEP said the program had "resulted in significant and rapid mercury reductions . . . [that] met or exceeded its goals."[8] The four participating companies—Newmont, Barrick, Placer Dome, and Anglo-Gold—were given the EPA's Environmental Hero Award in 2003.

Newmont produced a third of Nevada's gold in 1998 but released only 10 percent of the mercury. "Our part was easy" under the voluntary program, says Mudge. "We shared our knowledge with other producers." Newmont installed mercury controls at its gold refinery in the 1980s as part of its industrial hygiene program and included a mercury scrubber on the roaster when it opened in 1994. With improved controls at the Twin Creeks autoclaves, which had just come into operation in 1998, emissions have since been reduced to about 500 pounds a year. Another six tons of mercury are recovered each year at the company's Nevada facilities, which it sells to industrial users.

In 2006, as the Nevada legislature was considering mandatory mercury controls, environmentalists in Nevada, Idaho, and Utah began an anti-mining campaign calling for further study. Newspaper articles accused the gold miners of exporting pollution across state lines as the prevailing winds blew east toward Salt Lake City and north toward Idaho's Salmon Falls Creek Reservoir, a popular tourist site, where fish were found to contain high concentrations of mercury. A spokesman for the Idaho Conservation League called it "a significant health threat" and said the Nevada mines had chronically underreported their mercury emissions.[9]

Then Glenn Miller, an environmental professor at the University of Nevada–Reno and one of the industry's more prominent critics, did his own mercury testing by sticking a measuring device out a car window near several gold mines, including Newmont's.[10] The *Las Vegas Sun* published his findings under an alarmist headline: "Nevada's Gold Diggers Mucking up the Air."[11]

The reports turned out to be grossly inaccurate. A study of sediments at the bottom of the Salmon Falls Creek Reservoir conducted by the U.S. Geological Survey (USGS) for the Idaho Department of Environmental Quality found that mercury levels in the water were "lithologic (or geologically derived versus anthropogenically derived)."[12] Specifically, it found that the highest concentrations of mercury came from periods dating back to 1912 when there had been upstream erosion of soil as a result of high precipitation. One key sample showed less mercury accumulation during the period of 1990 to 2005 than in the remainder of the core. Water samples also showed mercury concentrations "significantly below" established drinking water or aquatic standards. Overall, the USGS found that the "average concentration of total Hg [mercury] in the Reservoir is generally lower than that for the upper continental crust." In short, the lake wasn't polluted. Some three thousand water bodies in the United States contain fish with high mercury levels and most are nowhere near a gold mine.

Miller's contribution to the debate drew a swift rebuke from Leo Drozdoff, the NDEP administrator. In a public letter to the professor, Drozdoff said his "study" exhibited a "complete lack of methodology . . . no quality assurance . . . no peer review, and the inclusion of inflammatory conclusions that are not supported by the data or other peer reviewed works." He noted that "one of the most egregious and inflammatory misstatements is the claim that the numbers reported 'approach concentration where impacts to worker health and safety, particularly to women of child bearing age, should be assessed.'"[13]

Of course it was the accusations, not the scientific rebuttals, that made the headlines, and that is what the public remembers.

Even if pollution levels are low, what about land disturbance? Doesn't mining with all that earth movement and large pits represent an affront to the environment? No, as long as companies are environmentally responsible, says Helen Hankins, northern Nevada field manager for the federal Bureau of Land Management (BLM). "In this district there are 7.3 million acres managed for the public and roughly 30,000 to 35,000 are disturbed by mining. What is that, less than half of 1 percent?"[14] Furthermore, almost everything in our lives is built with metals or material mined from the earth. Fortunately, most gold mines, as in Nevada, are in remote and often desolate areas.

What is important is water. "Environmental issues in mining are all about water," says David Baker, Newmont's vice president of environmental affairs since 1991. He foresees no problem of groundwater contamination from any of the company's waste dumps or leach pads once mining ceases and the sites are reclaimed. At the Phoenix project, a multimillion-dollar perpetual trust was created to provide funds for remedial action in the unlikely event that mining ever affects the groundwater. "The biggest challenge we will have long term is managing the pit lakes," Baker says. During mining, water is constantly pumped from the pits, creating what is called a cone of depression where the water table has been lowered around each site. After closure, the water table will recover and the pit will slowly fill with water. "At Gold Quarry, we will have a pit lake that's going to be 1,800 feet deep. We'll be monitoring the water quality for the next hundred years."[15] Could recreational lakes be part of Carlin's future?

The company has worked diligently to build a reputation of trust with the agencies that regulate its activity. The NDEP regards the company as a "leader" in the environment and "responsive" to the agency's concerns, citing its role in the mercury program as an example. The BLM's Hankins finds the company "environmentally responsible and proactive." A geologist with forty years of experience, she says "Newmont ranks as high, or higher, than any company I have ever dealt with. John Mudge and [his assistant] Paul Pettit are good communicators and are concerned about doing the right thing for the environment. I appreciate their integrity."

She cites recent work on an Environmental Impact Statement for a new mine at the south end of the Carlin Trend. Near the end of the process the federal EPA wanted new tests to determine the extent of acid-draining rocks at the site. "The thing I liked is that Newmont said right up front, 'Let's do more testing.' It cost Newmont a lot of money and time." Although the tests provided no new information, Hankins says, "It was just another example of how they are proactive and want transparency in what they do."

Hankins also oversees Newmont's T/S Ranch and applauds the company for its management of that asset.[16] Nationally recognized ranch manager Dan Gralian is the president of the Nevada Cattlemen's Association.

Michael Franzoia, an Elko businessman and the city's mayor since 1995, finds Newmont to be a good neighbor. "Newmont is a real leader," he says. "They always let me know what they are doing that impacts the community."[17] He likes the diversity mining brings to Elko with well-educated people from around the world who with their families become active in churches, schools, youth organizations, and the orchestra. Lee Hoffman, head of strategic planning for Nevada operations, served on the Elko City Council for sixteen years and in 2006 Mary Korpi, the company's director of external relations and ambassador extraordinaire, became chairman of the Chamber of Commerce.

Does the mayor worry about his town when the gold is gone and the mines close? "We think about it all the time, especially when gold is below

$300 an ounce," Franzoia says. But there have been predictions ever since the 1970s that the Carlin Trend had only a ten-year life. Today with higher prices and added reserves, the outlook is much brighter. "There are no guarantees," the mayor says. "There are opportunities with mining for local businesses to make hay while the sun is shining. Put some money away. That's just good conservative business planning." He hopes that Great Basin College, which has received significant support from Newmont, can be a catalyst for new jobs once mining is over, but does not believe it is the responsibility of Newmont or any other company to provide jobs for the future. "The mines aren't governments. It's too easy to let things fail because [we think] the mines will bail us out."

The Nevada example is what Newmont envisioned for itself when it went abroad. "When Newmont went back overseas as a gold company in the early 1990s, we made a conscious decision that we had to work to the same level of environmental protection that we used in Nevada," says Baker. "Nevada had the most sophisticated mining regulations in the nation. So when we went into Peru and Indonesia, we brought those standards with us. Other mining companies at the time were saying they were leaving the United States because they couldn't do business under those regulations. It was the wrong message." Baker and others are infuriated that newspaper articles accusing the company of environmental irresponsibility invariably state, without documentation, that the company moved abroad largely to avoid environmental regulation.

The company holds up Batu Hijau, built in 1999, as world class in every respect as it met the most demanding environmental hurdles imposed by law and its bankers, including the World Bank. Batu Hijau receives more than ten feet of rainfall a year and spends nearly 10 percent of its operating budget on water management, sediment control, and water treatment. In 2005, Batu Hijau was the only mine in Indonesia to earn a green rating from the Indonesian Ministry of the Environment for a level of environmental stewardship that exceeds legal requirements. It was the mine's second such award.

Yet the company has made mistakes and has not always lived up to its own ideals. Admits Baker, "We didn't always execute as we should have." No issue has galvanized Newmont's environmental consciousness more than the mercury spill at Choropampa, fifty-three miles southwest of Yanacocha.

On June 2, 2000, a contractor's truck carrying casks of mercury from the mine to a buyer in Lima spilled 332 pounds of the liquid metal along a twenty-six-mile stretch of winding mountainous road. The mine was not notified until the next morning when townspeople found children playing with mercury in the street. The driver had not realized his load had shifted and that a spill had occurred. Yanacocha immediately sent a team to investigate and by the end of the day had crews engaged in cleanup and in warning local residents of potential harm. Employees went door to door asking villagers to return any mercury they had found, and a town ambulance equipped with a bullhorn made similar pleas. They met with little success. Mercury is used by indigenous miners to extract gold, and the fact that the company was making such an effort to get it back convinced some that it had value. Increasing the potential danger, some boiled it on kitchen stoves in the hope of finding gold, while others simply hid it in their homes where temperatures were high and there was little ventilation.

The first health problems were reported on June 9. Local doctors and health officials were quickly mobilized, a consulting physician was flown in from Lima, and fifteen world experts on mercury poisoning, treatment, and cleanup were contacted. Some people were taken to a hospital in Cajamarca and one was airlifted to Lima. Others were treated at a local clinic and medical screening was offered to all. One woman sustained permanent damage, but the rest recovered and the Peruvian Ministry of Health foresees no future issues.

Nearly 140 people combed the road for traces of mercury and located spills at sixteen locations where the road was either washed or repaved. In all, 2,814 homes were tested for mercury and 115 in three villages required remediation. In some cases that meant removing dirt floors and replacing them with concrete. A total of 312 pounds of mercury were recovered.

Minera Yanacocha made payments to more than a thousand people and built schools, sports facilities, and water systems in the three towns affected. It also paid a $500,000 fine to the Peruvian government. Expenditures related to the cleanup and compensation exceeded $20 million. Nevertheless, 1,100 Peruvians, many who had signed settlement agreements, sued Newmont in U.S. and Peruvian courts. Nine years later, all but 200 cases had been settled after the U.S. cases were submitted to binding arbitration and the Peruvian Supreme Court upheld the validity of the earlier settlements.

The World Bank's International Finance Corporation, which is a 5 percent owner of the mine, conducted a thorough investigation and issued
twenty-two detailed recommendations ranging from protocols for handling
mercury to establishment of emergency medical teams to better community involvement and communication. Minera Yanacocha has implemented
most of the recommendations. Vehicles carrying hazardous material are
now escorted along their route and must stop for inspections at safety checkpoints. Contractors and employees are trained in handling and transport-
ing such material. Furthermore, Yanacocha has made the spill a case study
in transparency, publishing an eighty-two-page booklet in 2001 that provides minute details on the accident and its response.[18]

Reflecting later on the evolution of Newmont's thinking, Murdy remarked, "In the safety and environmental arenas, what we do is scientific.
It is measurable. We can be objective. The social arena is much more difficult. At one point we said providing people with training, offering good-
paying jobs, and operating our properties in a safe, clean, and healthy manner was great. Being responsible citizens, paying taxes, and doing certain
things in the communities was great. Today we have to go way beyond what
we may think is necessary."[19]

Today CSR is a thriving industry with social planners, social anthropolo-
gists, foundation representatives, and others eager to participate in shaping
corporate policies and practices. But in its early years abroad the company
found little objective outside guidance as global NGOs that seek to participate in development issues in the third world, such as Oxfam, also fund
anti-mining protests.

As a result, such matters were largely left to the discretion of mine
managers—geologists and engineers—who made it up as they went along.
While there was corporate support for community programs at each site, it
was largely defensive in nature and limited in scope. Buenaventura, Newmont's partner in Peru, advised against moving too aggressively on social issues; the company chose to "come in under the radar" in Indonesia to avoid
the human rights and environmental problems Freeport had encountered in
Irian Jaya; Uzbekistan had a socialist government that provided cradle-to-
grave services, and a declining gold price limited available funds.[20]

Fortunately, over the years Newmont's site managers have done a remarkable job and programs have grown from the helping hand concept pio-
neered by Len and Rosa Harris at Yanacocha to major endeavors, follow-

ing consultation with local leaders, which address a wide range of needs at each location. Batu Hijau has a company-funded foundation that has won plaudits for its ability to forge alliances between the company and local communities.

Among Newmont's accomplishments, malnutrition, prenatal health issues, and measles, which were major problems around Yanacocha, have largely been eradicated. A public health program at Batu Hijau reduced the incidence of malaria in the surrounding villages from 80 percent in 1998 to less than 1 percent by 2004. In entering Ghana, an outreach program was initiated to attack HIV/AIDS. CARE, Project Hope, and Doctors Without Borders have been engaged to assist in these programs and Murdy sought help from the University of Colorado Health Science Center to do baseline health studies around the company's mines. Money is provided for schools at every Newmont site, but often local funds are not available for books and teachers. "Governments would be happy for us to do everything,"[21] says Tom Enos, who retired in 2007 as executive vice president of operations.

Yanacocha has developed extensive programs to promote economic and social development around the mine. In 2000 it established a jewelry manufacturing business in Cajamarca that trained 1,300 low-income women how to weave gold chain and make other items in their homes. Some 2,000 farmers have benefited from a cooperative program to improve dairy farming, while 1,000 more now have access to a twenty-two-mile Newmont-built road through the mountains connecting twenty farming villages with city markets. Previously markets were a day's walk over rugged footpaths that limited sales to what a donkey could carry. Since establishing a nonprofit corporation in 2003, the mine has fostered 280 small businesses and created 10,000 new jobs.[22] Assistance is provided to eighty villages.

Elsewhere the story is much the same. Inti Raymi, the 88 percent–owned Bolivian company that operated the Kori Kollo mine, won the Excellence in Social Responsibility Award from the Latin American Mining Association in 2004 and the National Chamber of Industries' Award for Sustainability in 2007. Now in closure, the operation found meaningful jobs for 80 percent of its laid-off workforce and supports a technical institute that trains others for work in construction and small businesses. Its pit lake has become a wildlife habitat and may become a tourist site. Newmont offers aboriginal scholarships and an arts program in the Northern Territory of

19.1. Students in Peru attend a school built and supported by Newmont. (*Newmont Archives*)

Australia. Batu Hijau works to protect native sea turtles, built an irrigation system for local farmers, and initiated agricultural programs called "subsistence to surplus" that doubled rice yields. There is a fish-processing facility at Minahasa and concrete reef balls are made at both Indonesian locations to help restore coral reefs.

However, no company can address every third world need or satisfy every grievance, and it is easy for NGOs and sympathetic reporters to present the trials and tribulations of daily life in impoverished areas as calamities brought on by mining. The false impression they seek to leave is that local people do not want mining. "It's not friction between the local people and the company," says Enos, who managed Batu Hijau during its start-up. "You have the NGOs and the company, and the local people are in the middle. Generally the local people want to see development and want to see that their lives are better. But when you have problems, the NGOs seek to drive a wedge between the people and us."

That is what happened when Yanacocha allowed a water issue to escalate out of control. By the time it was resolved, both Newmont and the mine had lost valuable community support and some moral high ground.

Streams near the mine were primarily used for agriculture and in wet seasons were filled with sediment. As part of an early community outreach program, Carlos Santa Cruz, later the mine manager and a Peruvian of Indian heritage, worked with several mountain communities to install filtration systems and provide potable water where none had existed before. Newmont monitored water quality surrounding the mine and says it always met U.S. drinking water standards.

However, as the mine grew and impacted more streams and more people, water quality deteriorated and did not always meet the more stringent U.S. standards for aquatic life. It gave opponents an argument that Newmont was doing things differently in Peru than in the States. A drought dried up some streams as mining advanced, convincing many that the two were related.

In September 2004, an activist priest without a parish but with a populist following led angry protests against the mine. The road from Cajamarca to the mine was closed and police were called in. The focal point was Cerro Quilish, a mountain where Yanacocha had a drilling permit. Locals believed, and Newmont disputes, that mining would have threatened the city's water supply. When an agreement was reached, the mine, in an unprecedented move, relinquished its permit and wrote off 3.9 million ounces of gold reserves (nearly 2 million of which were Newmont's). It also agreed to build five large dams and reservoirs at a cost of $27 million to control its own water and provide water to the area. The effort won an award from the Peruvian National Environmental Council in 2007.

With five open-pit mines, four leach pads, three processing plants, and a land package of 666 square miles, Yanacocha rivals the Carlin Trend in size and has brought rapid change to the area. Once narrow streets and dirt roads open only to foot traffic and donkeys are now paved and clogged with four-wheel-drive vehicles. In his 2004 community relations report, general manager Brant Hinze wrote: "We acknowledge that we have not always understood the magnitude of those changes and at times did not hear the legitimate concerns expressed by the people of Cajamarca."[23]

The priest, who was flown to Denver on several occasions by NGOs opposed to mine expansion, met with Murdy at the company's annual meetings. Yet he was also a participant when another mob stormed mine property in August 2006, this time demanding more jobs. Despite a concerted effort by mine management to keep tensions down, one protester was shot and killed by police (the company's Forza security force was not involved), and two mine employees were kidnaped and later released. NGOs also opposed the start-up of mining at Ahafo in Ghana, where in 2006 a demonstration by unskilled job seekers turned ugly and a participant was killed by police.

In Turkey, the Ovacik mine acquired with Normandy was sold at a $16 million loss in 2005 after failing to overcome local opposition to the use of cyanide. The small open pit and underground operation, which had produced 350,000 ounces of gold in four years, was the first modern gold mine in an ancient gold-mining region. Despite a clean record and an enthusiastic workforce of 450, lawsuits and endless permitting delays forced a shutdown. The leader of the opposition was described on an NGO Web site as a "peasant" who is "a strong opponent of Neo-Liberalism and the New World Order" and who "used civil disobedience particularly well."[24] In 1999, Newmont withdrew its exploration team from several highly prospective sites in the Philippines after anti-mining advocates succeeded in winning passage of a new mining law that gives blanket veto rights to any indigenous group even if a majority of the people in the area support development.

Newmont's most difficult encounter with NGOs has come in Indonesia, where both the Minahasa and Batu Hijau mines came under attack by Jatam and Walhi, two Jakarta-based anti-mining/environmental activist groups with international funding. In May 2002, the NGOs sought to capitalize on the UN World Summit on Sustainable Development by sponsoring an Indonesian People's Forum in Jakarta. Showcased was a Sumbawan woman with a litany of woes—she had been forced off her land near Batu Hijau without compensation, her family suffered as local farmland and fishing had been destroyed; impoverished families were fleeing the area. In a lengthy article the forum claimed that only thirty-two local people had been hired by Newmont, while a doctor associated with one of the NGOs said arsenic poison from the mine soon would produce "a generation of idiots."[25]

A Cornell University anthropologist researched Newmont's community interaction at Batu Hijau and found all the claims to be fabricated from whole cloth, or in the woman's case, tattered cloth since she acknowledged taking only her shabbiest clothing on the 950-mile journey to the capital. The researcher determined that the woman and her family had moved to a neighboring village in 1991, years before mine development began; her sons were among hundreds of locals employed at the mine; her husband was the village representative on the Newmont-sponsored foundation; and she had been accused by community leaders of misusing a $2,500 foundation grant to help women in the area. As a result, villagers viewed the NGOs as outside agitators. The work of the foundation and Newmont's hiring of sons and daughters of village chiefs as community relations representatives also helped its cause.

Nevertheless, in keeping with much academic thought today, the anthropologist, whose focus was on "advocacy networks supporting indigenous rights and environmental agendas against the forces of capitalism," found a way to justify the lies. In publishing her findings, she wrote, "Whatever its shortcomings, the article did deal with a set of environmental and social problems of grave concern to local residents, highlighting issues felt most acutely by villagers marginalized by geography and social position."[26]

While the NGOs received little traction on Sumbawa, they gained a much firmer foothold in North Sulawesi two years later when they began subjecting the communities around Minahasa to "unwarranted fears over health risks."[27] In contrast with Batu Hijau, Minahasa at the time was preparing for closure with the loss of several hundred jobs. The NGOs focused on the poorest of the local villages where people were marginalized not by Newmont but by their neighbors, and they targeted a specific, high-profile environmental issue—the subsea tailings disposal system that was installed after consulting with experts around the world and with the specific approval of the Indonesian government.

Rather than place the tailings in a surface impoundment, which would have filled a valley, removed a wildlife habitat, and been subject to failure under Indonesia's heavy rains and seismic activity, the tailings were piped half a mile into the bay and deposited on the sea floor 270 feet below the surface. Before disposal, the finely ground rock—it looked like sand—was treated to remove any cyanide. Batu Hijau, which does not use cyanide but has a much larger processing volume, uses a similar system and deposits its tailings in the ocean at an even greater distance and depth.

Despite numerous community meetings prior to construction to explain the system to local residents and extensive monitoring and objective studies that have since attested to its safety, critics refuse to accept that conclusion and contend it would not be allowed in North America. In fact, subsea disposal has worked well at a copper mine near Vancouver and the example most often cited for the United States is not comparable. In what is considered a landmark environmental case, a federal judge in 1976 forced Reserve Mining to stop dumping taconite tailings in Lake Superior north of Duluth. But the mine did not use a deep-water pipeline and instead dumped tailings on the surface near shore where it built up into a man-made delta.

A few residents had complained of declining fish catches and health problems from the start. As the mine began closing in 2004, the NGOs recruited a flood of complaints from a squatter's village the government did not want to legitimize. "We were walking a tightrope," says Hinze, who was general manager at Minahasa from 2001 to 2003. "The community had no water or sewage facilities and what people were doing from a hygiene perspective was quite alarming. Our desire was to go in and help them but the other villages didn't want that. We finally supplied them with a water source and an outdoor septic system."[28]

Health problems, Newmont believes, were always the result of poverty and malnutrition and from cooking indoors over open fires. International health organizations found the rashes, lumps, and dizziness of which the residents complained to be common ailments in coastal villages in Indonesia.

Likewise, fishing conditions are similar to those all along the coast where fish bombing—throwing sticks of dynamite into the water and waiting for the dead fish to surface—is common practice. To prevent damage to sensitive coral reefs, Newmont initiated police patrols to stop it at Buyat Bay. Other fishermen, collecting exotic specimens for sale to aquariums, sprinkle diluted cyanide in the water to stun the fish. It makes fishing easier but kills the coral.

The hills around Minahasa are dotted with crude tents fashioned of bamboo and blue plastic tarps under which perhaps a thousand indigenous miners dig for gold. Coconut shells are used for panning and when enough gold is accumulated, it is taken into villages where it is milled in rotating drums called trommels. Gold recovery is done with mercury amalgamation. Much of the mercury is burned off, but 25 percent is released into streams

19.2. The Minahasa mine and roaster with Buyat Bay in the background. (*Andrew Craig*)

flowing into the local bays. Paul Lahti, general manager in 1999, bought a small gravity separator and gave it to the miners so they could stop using mercury. They never used it.

In July 2004, the NGOs flew four villagers to Jakarta and helped them file police complaints against PT Newmont Minahasa Raya, the legal name of the mining operation, claiming that they were suffering from mercury poisoning. Additionally, they claimed a baby had died from Minamata disease, an accumulation of methylmercury in the bloodstream. The Indonesian ministries of mining, health, and the environment immediately investigated but found no evidence to support the claims. The baby's death was considered to have resulted from malnutrition. Nevertheless, the two NGOs filed a $543 million lawsuit against Minahasa on behalf of the villagers.

The World Health Organization, the Minamata Institute of Japan, an authority on mercury poisoning, and Australia's Commonwealth Scientific and Industrial Research Organization were asked to investigate. Hair and nail samples of the villagers, fish tissue samples, and water and sediment samples were analyzed. Again, no evidence of mercury or arsenic poisoning was found. The Ministry of the Environment brought together a team of government, university, and NGO representatives to review ten years of studies of the bay and announced that it was not polluted. But the ministry later issued a "revised" report saying the tailings had adversely affected ocean sediments. That report was not signed by all the original participants and, according to Newmont, ignored some evidence and misinterpreted much of the rest. A year later, the University of Manado brought together scientists from several Indonesian universities to take another look at the data and again found no evidence of pollution.

On June 14, 2004, *Fortune* magazine listed Newmont among "America's most admired companies," based on key attributes of reputation including social responsibility. Three months later, in an effort to tarnish that image, the *New York Times* weighed in with a front-page story about Minahasa headlined: "Spurred by Illness, Indonesians Lash Out at U.S. Mining Giant."[29] The two thousand six hundred-word article blamed the company for the baby's death, for sickness, poverty, the loss of fish, misery, and deprivation, but said nothing about the scientific studies refuting such claims that Newmont had provided it.

"It was one of my worst days as a CEO. I was absolutely shocked," says Murdy. "There is a range of criticism we will always get from the NGOs. They can push for higher standards and better practices—that's their role. But this was so mean-spirited, so unfair, and so sensational. I was just sick." Two weeks later his sickness turned to anger as five mine employees—three Indonesians, one Australian, and an American—were jailed by the national police. The police, it turns out, conducted their own tests at Buyat Bay and came up with much higher levels of mercury and arsenic than any of the scientific studies. Assisting the police in their water sampling was one of the NGO activists who had earlier sued the company.

With a $2 billion investment in Indonesia, Newmont will not discuss possible motives for the police activity. It is worth noting, however, that Transparency International consistently ranks Indonesia as one of the world's most corrupt countries, barely ahead of Haiti, Iraq, Myanmar, and Uzbekistan. It is widely known that other companies operating in the country have faced shakedowns and paid bribes to avoid problems. KKN, the Indonesian initials for corruption, collusion, and nepotism that prevailed under Suharto, did not end with his departure but morphed into what some have called the "democratization of corruption" as power and potential for graft shifted from the palace to government agencies and the provinces.

Murdy flew to Indonesia almost immediately and visited the employees in jail. Over their five-week confinement, he called once a week to check on their well-being and boost their spirits. U.S. ambassador Robert Boyce met with Indonesia's president Megawati to urge their release on the grounds that they and Newmont were fully cooperating with the investigation.

Newmont sued three NGO leaders for defamation and they quickly recanted and withdrew their lawsuit. "It's like dealing with a bully," says Murdy. "At some point you have to say, 'I've had enough.'" The Jakarta doctor most vocal in denouncing the mine later told the Indonesian police that her allegations had been "premature" and that "there was never any scientific, comprehensive, detailed and integrated proof" of the poisoning she had claimed.[30] About the same time, the Jakarta District Court found that the police investigation and detention of the employees had been illegal.

That would be a nice ending, but, unfortunately, the case continued. The Indonesian Supreme Court reversed the lower court and in July 2005, Richard Ness, president director of PT Newmont Minahasa Raya, was indicted for polluting Buyat Bay. The fifty-six-year-old, who had spent much of his life in the country, faced up to ten years in prison. The prosecutor called his first witness in October 2005 and the case dragged on for nineteen months with weekly hearings in Manado. Murdy sat in on one session in May 2006 while his wife, Diana, gave comfort to Ness's wife.

With future investments by U.S. companies at stake, a member of the U.S. embassy attended each court session. Reporting on the trial, the Associated Press, working on a presumption of guilt, wrote: "Environmental activists have long targeted Newmont in Indonesia and abroad, and they are eager to see if the government will punish a multinational mining company for the first time in recent history."[31] Newmont, on the other hand, saw a silver lining in the ordeal. "We need to go through this trial where we will be able to prove that there is no pollution and no wrongdoing," said Enos.

Finally, in April 2007, the court acquitted Ness and Newmont on all charges. Saying that the case never should have been brought to trial, Judge Ridwan Damanik told a packed courtroom, "The police evidence doesn't stand up."[32] *Forbes* magazine credited the decision to "an apparent outbreak of the rule of law" in Indonesia.[33] The *Wall Street Journal* editorialized that the "flimsy 'evidence' didn't stop NGOs (one of whom was the local affiliate of Friends of the Earth), environmentalists and the *New York Times* from whipping Newmont into a major scandal."[34]

A separate civil suit brought by the same NGOs against Newmont was later dismissed by a different judge, while a $134 million suit brought by the Indonesian Ministry of the Environment was settled in early 2006 after the mine and the government signed a "goodwill agreement." Both parties pledged to participate in yet another scientific study of the bay with the company promising to pay for any remedial measures if it is found that pollution did occur. Newmont also promised to invest up to $30 million in unspecified community programs over the next ten years. With legal fees, the Buyat Bay fiasco has already cost Newmont $110 million, far more than the Minahasa mine earned over its seven-year life.

In the midst of all this, in July 2006, the Tourism Office of South Minahasa released a 150-page guidebook to diving sites in the area with color photos of coral formations, reefs, and aquatic life. "Unfortunately, in recent years Buyat Bay has gained notoriety because of the incorrect reporting that the Bay has been degraded by PT Newmont Minahasa Raya's operations," writes the director of tourism. "Far from it, the area boasts some of the best and healthiest coral reefs in Indonesia and the world."[35] Newmont assisted in producing the book, but it carries endorsements from the governor of North Sulawesi and the bupati (or regent) of South Minahasa.

Many of the complaints against mining, the company believes, come from government matters beyond its control. For instance, the Western Shoshone, whose native homelands include acreage around Newmont mines in Nevada, say the U.S. government has not honored the 1863 Treaty of Ruby Valley, which to them was a peace treaty not a land transfer agreement. The federal government has been trying to settle the dispute since 1950 and in 2004 offered $125 million plus 25 million acres of land. The tribes, who could not agree among themselves, rejected it. Still, Shoshone representatives routinely picket Newmont's annual meetings with signs reading, "Gold, Greed and Genocide."

A major concern overseas is that taxes on mining historically have been paid to central governments and not used for local needs. At one point, a bupati in North Sulawesi tried to tax waste rock at Minahasa as road material since all the taxes on gold production went to Jakarta. Recently, Peru

19.3. Protesters organized by anti-mining NGOs picket Newmont's annual meeting in Denver in 2006. (*Jerry Cleveland/Denver Post*)

has adopted procedures to remit half of all mine taxes to local communities if they have the capability to use it. In 2006, Yanacocha agreed to pay 3.75 percent of its net income—$22 million that year—for community improvements.

In a major change, Newmont and others have agreed to "Publish What You Pay" to highlight government taxes and royalties. The numbers for 2006, 2007, and 2008 are revealing—nearly $2 billion in total government payments, or more than 40 percent of pre-tax earnings before minority interest and special charges. Both Indonesia with $705 million and Peru with $503 million received more in taxes than the United States at $486 million.

Additionally, Newmont has joined other major mining concerns in seeking to lift its commitment to social responsibility to a higher level and provide assurances to communities and governments that mining brings sustainable benefits. Former CEO Ronald Cambre helped launch the Global Mining Initiative in the late 1990s and Murdy served as 2006 chairman of an offspring effort, the International Council on Mining and Metals (ICMM), which has codified ten principles of sustainable development that member companies follow.

When Tiffany's, in a bow to green pressure, declared it would not buy gold produced with cyanide, Newmont became a founding member of the Council for Responsible Jewelry Practices to give jewelry purchasers confidence that its gold is ethically produced. The company uses 26,000 tons of cyanide a year and was one of the first to commit to the International Cyanide Management Code, developed by a U.S. environmental group. As a supplement to the Sullivan Principles, which it signed in 1986 to guarantee the right of employees to fair practices, the company has recently adopted a number of multilateral agreements on human rights, including the United

Nations Global Compact, which addresses such issues as the use of security forces and respect for indigenous people. The company is also a founding member of the World Economic Forum's Partnering Against Corruption Initiative, which commits member companies to a zero-tolerance policy on corruption and bribery.

None of these initiatives changes the company's previous commitment to best practices, ethical behavior, and upholding the law, such as the Foreign Corrupt Practices Act. With participation by the World Bank, international labor organizations, and a number of NGOs, there is a United Nations/European Union feel to the groups with secretariats, surrogate members, protocols, and plenary sessions in Rio de Janeiro.

Future observers will have to determine whether these alliances strengthen the company's credibility or curb its flexibility while submerging its own moral authority in the collective group-think of people who have no responsibility for or stake in the outcome of events. Baker, the environmental vice president, strongly believes it will be the former: "It helps shift the industry. It gives us a framework that was developed through a multi-disciplinary, multi-stakeholder, and global model of engagement that we now can embrace." A major objective is to ensure that corporate actions are transparent and achieve their promised goals.

In 2007, the company put that to the test by agreeing to a shareholder proposal at its annual meeting for an independent study of its community relations policies and practices. Involving twenty-four CSR experts from around the world reporting to a special committee of the board of directors, the study took nearly two years and examined six sites in depth. The committee's 180-page Community Relations Review with detailed recommendations is available on Newmont's Web site. Two of the board's advisors on the project came from Oxfam and Earthworks, NGOs that had run campaigns against Yanacocha in the past.

Overall, the report was quite favorable, saying "the study directors believe that Newmont's current standards and policies are quite good."[36] The authors appear almost surprised to find that in Nevada "the apparent level of trust between the company and the community is remarkable. . . . [M]any refer to the company as a 'law abiding citizen.'"[37] The misuse of security forces has the potential to poison relations between companies and communities, but the team concluded that at Batu Hijau "the security paradigm and manner by which it is implemented is one of the best currently operating in Indonesia with strong emphasis on avoiding confrontation and addressing the roots of conflict."[38] The team recognized that in Ghana, the Ahafo mine is so new that the company has been able to install the best practices from its other mines and as a result, "the mine demonstrated a strong commitment to community relations through a highly trained and effective" CSR staff that "has sought to engage with community stakeholders on the basis of core values of fairness, transparency and participation."[39]

Eight lessons, each with a number of recommendations, were laid out. Some seem obvious, such as the need for a comprehensive and integrated community relations plan at each site that assesses risk and assigns responsibilities. Others could have been written by marriage counselors a continent away—conflict is inevitable, improve communication, treat your adversaries with respect even if you don't think they deserve it. There is the politically correct admonition that each site should have a special program for women, not women employees or those with special needs, but women in the community separate and apart from community programs in general. And as with most consultants, the report said more study is needed to fully understand the issues the team had just spent two years studying.

Some criticism of past practices was on target, such as saying that management at Minahasa had relied too much on its technical truths (e.g., the subsea tailings system worked) than on addressing public perceptions. I recall a visit to the mine site before production began. From Buyat Bay one could see the big red cut in the side of the hill where stripping had begun, while a stream poured red mud into the bay. "Not our problem," the mine manager told me. "We have a retaining pond. This is coming from illegal logging operations on the other side of the mountain." My response: "It doesn't matter. Unless it is stopped, you will be blamed."

In other cases, the authors missed the mark. Citing Choropama, for instance, Yanacocha, is criticized for ignoring local communities prior to the protests and for the perception that it "has not fully taken responsibility for its 'past mistakes.'"[40] Yet, the mercury spill occurred fifty-three miles from the mine on the road less traveled—to Lima, not Cajamarca. Why should that community have been engaged prior to the spill? One would also be hard-pressed to say what more Newmont should have done after the spill

19.4. CEO Wayne Murdy meets with tribal leaders in Ghana. (*Newmont Archives*)

to address health issues or community concerns. Far more serious transport accidents occur on U.S. roads and rails without companies being obliged to adopt the surrounding community for life.

More important, because of the leftist orientation of the CSR fraternity, the report left no doubt that indigenous rights should trump corporate rights; that it is the company's responsibility to address every need, every want, and every perceived slight within miles of its mines; and that dialogue is the only option for resolving differences. There was no acknowledgment that some demands have been outrageous or that protests were staged by outside organizations. Furthermore, it offered no guidance on how the company should respond when future demands escalate beyond its willingness or ability to pay.

CEO O'Brien says Newmont knowingly accepted this bias because it was the only way to give credibility to the study. He gives Murdy, Baker, and former general counsel Britt Banks "kudos" for accepting the shareholder resolution and having the faith in the company's record to push it forward. "I truly believe that we have taken this on in a way that will see our benchmarks improve. We are reengaging with the communities, telling them what we found out, and making sure that what they told the researchers is still what they have on their mind. By taking a more proactive approach, we hope to avoid the issues like we had at Yanacocha."[41]

Given all that Newmont has done and all that it has endured to establish its leadership in social responsibility, the *Wall Street Journal*'s question at the beginning of this chapter seems naïve. No company today, especially a large company in the extractive industries operating in emerging economies, can expect to do business without a commitment to sustainability—and the CSR mind-set that comes with it. Says O'Brien, "We must embrace the tension among profitability, sustainability, and responsibility."

Leaving a Proud Legacy

Across the American West are hundreds of so-called legacy mines, the remnants of old workings that produced precious and base metals prior to World War II. Some are now historic tourist sites, while others are eyesores where piles of acid-leaching rock threaten the environment. Few companies have had more success turning the latter into the former than has Newmont at Idarado in the San Juan Mountains of western Colorado where mining was carried out from the 1870s until 1978 (see chapter 3). In 2006, the mine received the first award issued by the U.S. Department of Interior's Bureau of Land Management for its implementation of the principles of sustainable development.

Prodded by a Superfund lawsuit in 1983, Idarado's restoration owes its success not only to Newmont's ingenuity but to the levelheaded thinking of former Colorado governor Roy Romer, a pragmatic Democrat, and former state attorney general Gale Norton, who later became U.S. secretary of the interior under President George W. Bush. Together they had the political will to make a decision and see the issue through to a practical conclusion.

The heart of the problem was a 150-acre pile of old mill tailings that lay at the base of a box canyon at the east end of Telluride. At the time, Telluride was just beginning the transition from a rundown mining village into today's pricey destination resort. The city drilled two water wells near the tailings pile and picked up excess amounts of chrome 6 that had been dumped during the final days of the mill's operation. About the same time, a high school science project tested soil in the area and found the presence of lead. Newmont, still based in New York City, immediately flew out a medical team from Sloan-Kettering Hospital to do a blood-lead study and found the children to be perfectly safe. Galena, naturally occurring lead sulfide, does not dissolve into the bloodstream. But, with the issue of contamination twice raised, a lawsuit was inevitable.

The state's initial solution was to dig up the tailings, all twelve million tons of it, and haul it to a site in Utah. Environmental chief Mac DeGuire and senior vice president and general counsel Graham Clark Jr., with the help of a lobbyist from Hill & Knowlton, spent eighteen months on a campaign to educate city leaders, the state's technical team, and environmental groups and win their support. "We did the arithmetic and said, 'Hey, guys, it's a truck load of dirt every twenty minutes for twelve years through the only road in town. Do you really think this is a good idea?'"[42] says DeGuire.

Later, the state proposed digging up a large area on the other side of town and using that soil to cover the tailings pile. Governor Romer was holding town hall meetings called "Dome of the Range" across the state and found this plan the subject of discussion when he came to Telluride and Ouray. Clark recalls the governor being struck by several large aspen trees on the site of the good soil, and saying, "I come from Sterling [on the state's eastern plain] where trees are pretty rare and you want to take all these trees down to move the soil? How many think we should give Newmont's plan a chance?"[43] A show of hands was 60–40 in Newmont's favor.

Newmont's $20 million plan, called direct vegetation, began on an experimental basis and received technical support in agronomy from Dr. Edward Redente of Colorado State University. Instead of adding topsoil, Idarado created its own by tilling in large amounts of hay, fertilizer, and limestone and then seeding the area with natural grasses and wildflowers. To reduce the potential for acid drainage, water runoff was addressed at its source by building ten miles of concrete channels to divert snow melt away from the tailings. It has all worked flawlessly, even in 1995 when Telluride received a near-record 505 inches of snow, and today the area is a lush meadow, while water quality in nearby streams has improved significantly.

Additionally, Idarado has turned 5,500 acres of land on Red Mountain over to such groups as the Trust for Public Land, which transferred it back to the National Forest Service. Now hikers and other outdoor enthusiasts can enjoy the beauty of the mountains while viewing historic mining sites.

"I was always very impressed with the Idarado settlement," says San Miguel County Commissioner Art Goodtimes. "It was one of those rare win-win situations where the company reached a better and cheaper settlement, while the cleanup

19.5. Idarado's former tailings pond has been reclaimed as a lush meadow at Telluride, Colorado, in a success story for cleaning up legacy mines. (*David Baker/ Newmont*)

protected the environment, helped the community of Telluride, and met state and federal requirements."[44] David Baker, Newmont's vice president of environmental affairs, says the Idarado case shows what can happen when there is "collaboration and cooperation of the local community and government regulators." Too often, he says, innovative solutions are rejected by regulators because "they won't accept risk. So you end up in litigation and just hope to prevail in enough areas that you can get to the negotiating table in a serious way."[45]

The political will that was so important at Idarado has not been present at the 51 percent–owned Dawn uranium mine in Washington State where operations ceased in 1982 and closure is still involved in a Superfund lawsuit. Located on the Spokane Indian Reservation, the mine falls under the jurisdiction of the U.S. Department of Interior and the Bureau of Indian Affairs, with the Bureau of Land Management, the Environmental Protection Agency, the State of Washington, and the tribe all involved. The EPA has proposed digging up all remnants of mining and hauling it to a nuclear waste site used for spent fuel rods 150 miles away at a cost of $150 million. Baker calls this "nonsense."

Former CEO Ronald Cambre says he found Dawn "distressing" during his seven years at Newmont as a succession of senior managers worked full-time to resolve the issue without success. Corporations want to close such matters and move on he says, but "We're dealing with the Indian nation, the lawyers, and the government and no one wants to resolve it. It falls into the category of Mission Impossible."[46]

20

SUSTAINING SUCCESS

As the gold market gained strength, passing a ten-year high in 2003, surging above $500 an ounce in 2005 and continuing to climb, Newmont's strategy looked prescient. "We now have a new paradigm," boasted Randy Eppler, who had just retired as the company's vice president of corporate development.[1] "After 9/11 and with a weakening dollar, gold has reestablished itself as a major currency and Newmont has established itself as the industry leader." It stood tall, after the Normandy and Franco mergers, as the world's largest gold miner.

Life at the top, however, is not always easy. "One might have the perception that with gold above $600 an ounce, a person sits back, puts his feet on the desk and waits for the money to roll in," says Thomas Mahoney, vice president and treasurer since 2001. "But it isn't that way. The stress on the organization is as great, or greater, than it was when the gold price was low." When gold was rock bottom, investor expectations were low. "People would say, 'They didn't do well in this quarter, but who can do well in a $255 gold environment?' Today the market has less tolerance for any sort of performance difficulty. If you don't hit production targets, there's almost no excuse."[2]

In 2006, Newmont began missing its guidance to investors and repeatedly lowered its quarterly projections. Production from 2004 to 2007 fell 30 percent to 6.2 million ounces (with Newmont's equity share being down 25 percent to 5.3 million), while costs applicable to sales nearly doubled to $406 an ounce. Equally frustrating, for all its non-hedge rhetoric, Newmont had stealth hedges and when the long-awaited bull market in metals arrived, the company couldn't deliver the leverage it had promised. With higher prices, margins were a record $300 an ounce in 2006 and only slightly lower in 2007, but that wasn't enough to satisfy Wall Street, which expected far better. The stock price fell to $38 a share in mid-2007, and the premium over its archrival, Barrick, nearly evaporated.

Higher costs for energy, labor, tires, steel, and other inputs were impacting the entire industry. "Suddenly $400 is the new $200 when it comes to costs,"[3] lamented CEO Wayne Murdy. Also important, the company's largest operations were aging, with declining grades and increasing waste-to-ore ratios. In Nevada, the average grade dropped by a quarter between 2002 and 2007, from 0.1 ounce per ton to 0.076. In 2002, the Nevada mines blasted out and hauled away 3.8 tons of waste for every ton of ore; by 2007 it was 4.5. Combined, it meant that 92 tons of rock had to be mined for each ounce of gold produced, nearly 80 percent more than the 52 tons required five years earlier.[4] At Yanacocha, each ton of ore carried an overburden of 0.37 of a ton in 2002. Five years later, the waste-to-ore ratio was 1.13-to-1, production had dropped by half and cash production costs of $345 an ounce were up 65 percent.

"In the past if things went sour elsewhere we could pull a rabbit from the hat at Yanacocha. Well, Yanacocha is mature now and there are no more rabbits,"[5] explained William Zisch, vice president of planning, in 2007. Adds Murdy, "I will tell you with perfect hindsight that I wish we had gone slower at Yanacocha. I think we pushed that harder than we had to." The consequence: depleting reserves and huge stress on the community.

Knowing that its mines were maturing, the company had counted on new projects to refresh its production stream. Then two large projects in Nevada, Leeville, an underground mine that faced difficulty obtaining skilled workers, and Phoenix, a copper and gold deposit with complex geology, fell behind schedule as capital costs escalated.

Phoenix became an embarrassment. J. M. Rendu, the company's former reserve expert, was called back from retirement to assess the problem. He found that the company had tried to rush into production before technical issues were resolved in the hope of getting a better rate of return. Furthermore, Newmont had relied on the drilling results of the previous owner, Battle Mountain Gold, and did not do its own ore sampling until after production began and it found itself in trouble. While Wall Street expected Phoenix to be one of Nevada's lowest-cost mines, initial production came in at over $800 an ounce.

"There was an attitude at Newmont that we could do things better than anyone else. When our metallurgists looked at what the previous owners were going to do, they said we could do it cheaper and faster by bringing in an old plant from Lone Tree [a nearby mine where operations had ceased]," says Rendu. "That attitude also led to overpaying for acquisitions in the first place. We would look at the seller's model and think we could do things they couldn't so we could afford to pay more for the property. But we seemed to forget that the sellers had already inflated what they had."[6]

After drilling 230 new holes, remodeling the mine plan and adding a huge new gyratory crusher, the operation finally achieved acceptable operating performance in mid-2008—two years behind schedule and 50 percent over its capital budget of $235 million. While that brought operating costs in line with the rest of Nevada's mines, it also lowered production by 30 percent from the original plan to 200,000–250,000 ounces of gold and 20 million pounds of copper a year. With a lower grade, reserves fell by 2 million ounces.

In late 2005, Newmont had an opportunity to leap frog over its problems at Phoenix and secure its position as the world's gold leader. But it turned it down. Instead, Barrick acquired Placer Dome for $10.4 billion and vaulted into the number one spot.

"We always liked their properties in Nevada and their Australian properties looked good," Murdy says of Placer Dome. "But we didn't want to be in South Africa or Papua New Guinea and didn't see much value in their Canadian assets. Once Barrick made its bid, we were invited in to do due diligence and formed a very good relationship with the Placer people. We knew it would be difficult, but then the adrenalin of the deal would kick in and we would think we could make it work. In the end, we didn't find the value was there. We weren't going to overpay just to be number one."

As management turned its attention back to its business, things were not going well. Shortly after becoming CEO, Murdy encouraged his officers to read *Good to Great*, management guru Jim Collins's effort to identify the traits that propel companies into the top tier of success. Among his findings: great leaders had determined what they could do better than anyone else and then developed simple strategies that they "implemented with fanatical consistency."[7]

Newmont's strategy was focused "on large mining districts . . . where we can obtain the economies of scale and operating synergies to remain a low-cost leader," Murdy told shareholders in the company's 2001 annual report. World-class operating skills and a willingness to make major investments based on that talent has been a Newmont signature. But, it leaves little margin for error. "Newmont has made the decision that it wants a few large mines," says Scott Barr, the company's chief technical officer until his retirement in 2008. "Large, low-grade mines operating at high volume and requiring lots of capital put a premium on operating skills. We seem to tread along that precipice and depend on our good operating skills to keep us from tipping over."[8]

Another of Collins's observations: great companies didn't start by deciding where to drive the bus, "they first got the right people on the bus (and the wrong people off the bus) and then figured out where to drive it . . . if you begin with 'who' rather than 'what,' you can more easily adapt to a changing world." Collins adds, "Great vision without great people is irrelevant."[9]

Unfortunately, many of Newmont's top technical and operating people got off the bus with the early retirement program in 2001 and their seats were not filled. As the company grew after the three-way merger, operating complexity grew as well and the company was neither staffed nor organized to deal with it. The tug and pull that exists in every organization between corporate staffs and operators gave way to a decentralized model in which self-sustaining geographic fiefdoms were established and corporate oversight and support reduced, although pressure continued for the highest possible production. That was the model established by CEO Plato Malozemoff in the 1960s and 1970s, but then Newmont was a diversified company and seldom owned 100 percent of its mines.

David Francisco, who became executive vice president of operations in 2000, was always considered an outsider by the people in Nevada. When Tom Enos, who honed his skills and guile during the dog-eat-dog days of Carlin's early growth, moved to Denver in 2002 and became second in command of operations, he and Francisco couldn't agree. Operators received mixed signals, while top management and the board were given conflicting views of what the company could accomplish.

President Pierre Lassonde was energetic (he was turned back by illness from climbing Mount Kilimanjaro in 2002) and always optimistic about the gold price. He sought to rally the troops with "be all you can be" goals. But built on shaky assumptions, the company adopted plans "that were too optimistic and in order for them to work you had to have all the stars and planets align,"[10] says Guy Lansdown, who became senior vice president of project development in 2007. Without an operator's instincts, Murdy let his subordinates battle over who should be driving the bus and where it was headed. Frustrated and facing health problems, Francisco retired in 2005. He was succeeded by Enos, whom Murdy credits for starting to standardize procedures and bring control back to Denver.

Lead director Glen Barton, the retired CEO of Caterpillar, says of Murdy: "I've never met a kinder, better, or well-intended man than he is."[11] Others echo Rendu, who says, "Wayne was too nice of a guy when what the company needed was a tough, decisive person who would make changes and clean things up."

Management was losing credibility with Wall Street and the board and its hedge position did not help. As commodity prices rose to new heights, Lassonde, insightful on the subject and backed by international trade and monetary statistics, predicted they would go even higher. By mid-2007, he was talking about gold at $1,000 an ounce. Yet, if the company believed that, why did it hang onto its hedges? After all, it had moved quickly to eliminate the Normandy hedges once that transaction closed.

"I never thought of Newmont as a hedged company," says Murdy, who considered its position defensive, not speculative. Twice in five years, to protect its assets, it had taken hedge positions in gold and copper (see chapters 16 and 17). Then as metal prices soared, these commitments required the company to sell a significant portion of its production at below-market prices. It lost more than $250 million in revenue in 2005 and 2006 and faced future losses of another $525 million—much more if the price continued to rise. (By contrast, Barrick, which profited hugely from hedging during the 1990s, reported large losses from its hedging activities in the rising market. Even after significantly reducing its forward commitments, its hedge book at year-end 2006 was $3.2 billion underwater.)

Actual losses were mostly in copper, but the scary potential for future losses was in gold. In late 2004, the company entered into a copper collar, a form of hedge, to lock in a price between $1.10 and $1.39 a pound. At the time, Indonesia was not a friendly place to do business. Employees were jailed on trumped-up charges and government agencies appeared to be engaging in shakedown tactics. The hedge price enabled the company to recover its large investment in Batu Hijau by the end of 2006. Since mines cannot be moved, management had a powerful incentive to recover its invested capital quickly.

Furthermore, unlike the previous gold hedge that was taken at the bottom of the market, this time Newmont thought it was locking in the top price. "If you look back historically, there was never a time in the history of the metal that it would have stayed at that level for an extended period of time," says Mahoney. Yet, copper shot above $4 a pound in 2006. The price, fortunately, remained above $3 for another year after the hedge expired in early 2007.

A more creative approach to political risk was taken in Peru. To support continued expansion at Yanacocha, in 2006 the company put together a $100 million commercial bank loan in Peru followed by an over-subscribed $100 million bond issue, one of the largest industrial financings in the country. "We wanted to use the Peruvian financial markets to expand the local stakeholder base in Yanacocha," says Mahoney. Pension funds, which purchased 80 percent of the bonds, widely publicize their holdings, "so now not only do we have Buenaventura as a partner, but we have a local bank and local investors through their pension funds." With shared risks and rewards, the company hopes there will be broader support for Yanacocha.

The gold hedge was a sleeper. In 2001, when it put a floor price of $270 an ounce under 2.85 million ounces of production, the company had agreed to pay back 2.35 million ounces at an average price of $377 an ounce through 2011. The first delivery of 500,000 ounces was in 2005 at a price of $350 an ounce, or $94 an ounce below the spot market average for the year. The next delivery of one million ounces was not due until 2008.

Newmont's hedges were considered off-book and did not have to be marked-to-market at the end of accounting periods, so no liability was recorded on the balance sheet. But as the delivery date approached and the gold price moved up, investors and the board became increasingly nervous.

Newmont Capital had taken a stake in Miramar Mining, a Canadian exploration firm that was drilling the Hope Bay deposit—a huge greenstone resource of high-grade oxide ore—on the Arctic coast of Nunavut Province.[12] In April 2007 Murdy flew up to take a look and suffered a detached retina causing a loss of sight in his left eye. It was three days before he could return to Denver for surgery. Recovery required that he lay face down for ten days and then was confined for several weeks. While boring, it provided time for reflection and for discussions with his wife about his priorities.

"Newmont had had some setbacks and I saw a turnaround coming in 2008. My ego said that would be a good time to go out. But we had done a lot of work on succession planning, so Diana and I concluded that this was probably a good time to call it quits. It was time for a change." Burdened by years of NGO pressure in Indonesia and Peru, Murdy says that once he made his decision "the weight came off me like that." After a meeting with directors at Denver's Brown Palace Hotel, his retirement was announced on June 5, 2007. He was a month shy of turning sixty-three. (According to SEC filings, Murdy began selling his stock a year earlier when it reached a high of $60 and sold 165,000 shares on which he had options for a profit of $6.6 million prior to the announcement.)

One factor in his decision, Murdy says, was the incredible traveling required by the job—250,000 miles a year. In fact, his last day as CEO, June 30, was spent in Tashkent signing papers with the Uzbek government relinquishing Newmont's interests in the Zarafshan joint venture (see chapter 14). The government was bound by international treaty to present its case for expropriation of Newmont's assets to arbitration. Under the advice of Washington council, however, they decided to negotiate, and prohibited from traveling because of his eye, Murdy negotiated by phone until the agreement was reached. Newmont received $80 million, or about "30 cents on the dollar," says Murdy, but it was the best that could have been hoped for.

Lassonde had retired at the end of 2006, after five years as president, and Schulich stepped off the board in early 2007. David Harquail, who ran Newmont Capital and was an executive vice president, would have liked to succeed Murdy, but he is an investment banker not a miner, and his group had never been fully integrated into the company. Another contender, Bruce Hansen, had been eased out of the CFO position and later became CEO of General Moly, which is developing a large molybdenum deposit in Nevada. A well-liked, knowledgeable, and effective leader, he had the misfortune of initiating both the gold and copper hedges and of being the strongest early proponent of the Phoenix project.

Instead, the corner office went to Richard O'Brien as both Murdy's choice and the board's. O'Brien, who was named president only a few months earlier, joined the company as chief financial officer, replacing Hansen in late 2005. A decade younger than Murdy, O'Brien has an economics degree from the University of Chicago, a license to practice law in Oregon that he has never used, and a background in finance in the coal and electric utility

20.1. Richard O'Brien, who became CEO in mid-2007, explains his turnaround plans for the company during an interview on CNBC in early 2008. (*Omar Jabara/Newmont*)

industries. The board had grown to respect his judgment during his two years as CFO, and that, directors say, outweighed his lack of mining experience. "As we went through the process, we didn't surface anyone on the list that we were certain could do a better job or that we had more confidence in than Dick," says director Barton.

Murdy remained chairman until the end of the year, at which time the board decided to split the offices of CEO and chairman, handing the latter position to Vince Calarco, the retired chairman of Crompton Corporation, a specialty chemical producer. Calarco, a Newmont director since 2000, is the first outside chairman in the company's nearly ninety-year history. Eager to be seen at the forefront of trends in corporate governance, the company, a year earlier, embraced a shareholder resolution calling for such a move.

Looking back on the past few years, director James Taranik says, "In these jobs, timing is everything." During Murdy's last few years, he had become "withdrawn and silent. Two things really affected Wayne: one was managing the upside, which is an extremely difficult task to do well because the options are not clearly defined. He was pretty much a hands-off kind of guy and may have missed some important signals. And second, we should have taken some risk and done the Placer Dome acquisition. What deflected him from that were all the environmental problems in Indonesia and the political problems in Uzbekistan. Those problems made him risk-averse."[13] Besides, others say, Murdy was a deal maker and he badly needed an encore.

O'Brien moved swiftly. On July 5, Newmont announced that it had spent $578 million to buy back its hedge position. The company also jettisoned its merchant banking business and took a $1.7 billion write-off for good will. While keeping Newmont Capital's investments in oil sands and other mining interests, the company's royalty assets were sold in an initial public offering in Canada for $1.3 billion in December. That company, once again named Franco-Nevada, is headed by Harquail. Additionally, Newmont raised $1.15 billion in convertible senior notes, its largest financing since fending off Boone Pickens twenty years earlier, and at year-end 2007 made a successful $1.5 billion bid for control of Miramar Mining.

Owning royalties made sense in a low gold market by providing a steady stream of income, although some, like former CEO Ronald Cambre, believed Newmont had grossly overpaid for Franco-Nevada's assets. But with higher metal prices and major projects to be developed, O'Brien reasoned that shareholders would rather see the company's money invested in gold. Wall Street confirmed his instincts and as gold approached $900 an ounce in early 2008, NEM was again trading at $55 a share—restoring $7.5 billion to its market value in just six months. (By the summer of 2008 the gold price eased off its euphoric high and Newmont's stock returned to the $40 range.)

O'Brien inherited some of the industry's best assets and an enthusiastic workforce. "I wake up every morning singing the company anthem,"[14] says Brant Hinze, senior vice president of North American operations and the veteran of numerous NGO battles in Indonesia and Peru. But he also faces a plethora of problems, some common to the industry, others where he will have more direct influence.

The first challenge is reserves replacement. Reserves are the life blood of mining companies and Newmont has one of the highest reserves in the world at 85 million ounces of gold,[15] a number that will increase in 2009 with the acquisition of the minority interest in Boddington. In addition to Hope Bay, with an estimated ten million ounces of contained gold, the company also has a number of early stage projects under evaluation that could become reserves in the future. Furthermore, two large deposits already in reserves, Conga in Peru and Akyem in Ghana, could move into production in the not too distant future once final permits and economic issues (assured electrical power at Akyem, for instance) are resolved.

Stephen Enders, a Ph.D. geologist who joined Newmont from Phelps Dodge in 2003 and was soon elevated to senior vice president of exploration, notes that while the company produces about 5.5 million ounces of gold a year for its own account, it needs to find nearly twice that much to replace depletion. That's because it must also replace its partners' share of production in jointly owned mines and because metallurgical recovery rates average under 80 percent. "Only 2 percent of all the known gold deposits in the world are ten million ounces or more. So we need to find a world class deposit every year just to sustain ourselves,"[16] he says.

The company has found more gold than it produced in most years—at an amazingly low cost of between $15 and $20 an ounce over the past decade—but much of the new reserves have been incremental additions near existing mines in Nevada and Yanacocha where the future is limited. To grow, Enders says the company must discover new greenfield sites, like Hope Bay, that are more difficult to find. As a result, he says future exploration budgets will have to be significantly higher than the $177 million the company spent in 2007.

O'Brien, on the other hand, believes the company's big mine mentality is too restrictive and would like Newmont to be able to find, develop and operate smaller mines with equal efficiency. As a result, Hope Bay, which has both surface and underground potential and the likelihood of being the most costly project in the company's history, probably will be developed gradually over a number of years as was Yanacocha in the 1990s. Difficulties of working in a remote area covered by Arctic permafrost have already pushed back the date for a development decision by a year or more.

Closer to home, the company has found new pay dirt just across the Mexican border at La Herradura. Geologist Joseph Bartolino, a twenty-year Newmont veteran who had been part of the original discovery in 1991, persuaded Enders to let him reassemble the old team for a new look. Lying under the deep sands of the Sonora Desert, the discovery was made without the benefit of 3-D exposure. Returning in 2003, Bartolino was able to observe the mineralization from the pit which had been in operation since 1998. "It was apparent from the new rock exposures that gold mineralization occurred as anatomizing 'pitch-and-swell-style' quarts veining on all scales and across a broad area," Bartolino says. Satellite images showed that the structural pattern repeated itself over a 3-by-12-mile area.

"The real battle for me was to find an executive who wasn't prejudiced by the longstanding perception that La Herradura was small and since we only had a 44 percent non-operating position, why bother? Steve had the sharply-tuned sense for what I was driving at—that this thing might be BIG."[17] Extensive drilling utilizing an Australian rotary air blast technique for rapid, cost-effective penetration of the sand cover has located a resource of seven million ounces that is now undergoing reserve evaluation. The goal is to increase production from 85,000 to 500,000 ounces a year within a few years and extend the mine life for another decade.

Capital is a second major challenge as costs for both new projects and to maintain current production are rising faster than inflation. Capital spending rose from $300 million in 2002 to $1.9 billion in 2008 as the company worked to develop Boddington and Phoenix and complete the power plant in Nevada. Sustaining capital at Batu Hijau is between $100 million and $150 million a year and Yanacocha, which operated for years as a heap leach operation requiring little in capital expenditures, spent $340 million in 2007 and 2008 to build its first mill (which improves recoveries) to help arrest production declines.

Looking at Newmont's numbers since it beat back Pickens and put its attention on gold in 1987 can be discouraging. Over the twenty-one-year period through 2008, the company earned $2.4 billion after write-offs, but invested almost $12 billion in capital. Even with rising metal prices over the past five years, the company has been able to achieve a 5 percent return on assets only twice—in 2006 and 2008. The stock price over the past two decades has grown by less than one-third of the overall market as measured by the Standard & Poor's 500 although, as one would expect, it has done considerably better than the market since both the bottom of the gold cycle in 2000 and the top of the stock market in 2007.

Wall Street has complained for years that the gold industry is over capitalized and must find ways to get more value from existing assets. O'Brien is attacking the problem by initiating a rigorous "stage gate" review process for new projects that requires 30 percent of the engineering be completed before funding is approved, versus 10 percent in prior years. Joint ventures are also being considered. For instance, the hope is that Conga, which has large copper reserves, can consolidate with adjoining property owners to build one large mill, much as Southern Peru Copper did fifty years ago. More emphasis also is being placed on planning and standardizing procedures to create a "one Newmont" approach to operations. To set clear targets and then "do what we say we are going to do . . . planning and process are two things we just have to do better," he says.

But, he adds, a higher return on assets is not the total solution. "We provide something different than other companies" in an investment portfolio: "the option value of gold."[18] Thus underlying all of his efforts is the desire to add more flexibility to production schedules so that the company can benefit from changes in the gold price (the "option value") and not strain to produce every marginal ounce.

At the bottom of the gold market in 2000 and with the support of Zisch in planning, I authored a memo of frustration urging that the company reduce production rather than "sell its plums as prunes." Why not leave reserves in the ground for later when they could be sold for more? we asked. That, however, would have required layoffs and jeopardized debt repayments. It also was counter to the company's business model which placed cash flow above a return on investment and to Wall Street's favorite measurement, net asset value, which discounts future production for inflation.

"Today, Dick gets it and the reason the stock is improving is that the company is not producing ounces that aren't profitable," says Taranik. "He has applied order and structure to everything Newmont is doing and he clearly has a strategic vision."

There will always be the challenge of getting the right people on the bus. To better prepare the next generation of leaders, Murdy in 2004 initiated a Harvard Management–type program with Denver University's Daniels School of Business that over several years involved all of the company's senior officers and high-potential individuals. The program, which Murdy regards as one of his proudest legacies, was designed to broaden the perspective of men and women with technical backgrounds.

But Taranik, who heads one of the nation's top mining schools, wonders where the technical talent will come from. There are growing shortages of mineral exploration geologists, extractive metallurgists, and mining and geological engineers, he says. More than half of those employed throughout the industry will retire in the next five years while fewer and fewer students are pursuing such degrees.

"At the turn of the 20th Century, over 2,500 mining engineering students were enrolled in approximately 60 . . . (schools) in the United States . . . (which) produced approximately 500 graduates per year," Taranik writes in the prologue to *Mackay Memories, 1908–2008*.[19] Today there are only about 300 students at a hand full of schools, which graduated only 87 people in 2004. The Mackay School had 85 students in 2007, while there were 700 students in the University's biology department and classes in criminal justice were overflowing. Young people today, Taranik laments, want to save the world from global warming or do "really fun stuff" like they see on the CSI television series rather than find and develop new metal deposits.

As O'Brien became CEO, Enos retired. Although only fifty-six, he was the company's longest serving employee with thirty-six years. Britt Banks, who had worked closely with Murdy as general counsel for seven years, also took early retirement. For more than a year the company had no chief operating officer and for the first time in its history had only one member of senior management with a technical degree—senior vice president Lansdown, who holds a civil engineering degree from South Africa.

Having lost many top scientists, the Malozemoff Technical Center is engaged in less cutting-edge work. "Part of it is that we want to change the focus of our R&D and not do everything ourselves, but to be more collaborative with research institutes," says Lansdown. Instead of being the leader, "our approach is to be fast followers."

In September 2008, O'Brien announced his leadership team by elevating five men to the office of executive vice president. Two are newcomers— Brian Hill, with a degree in mining engineering from Queens College in Ontario and an MBA from the University of Western Ontario and who had joined the company nine months earlier as vice president of Asia Pacific operations, became chief operating officer, while Alan Blank, a Portland attorney who came aboard as general council in June, now heads legal and external affairs. Two are fast track achievers who began their careers in the treasury department fifteen years ago—Russell Ball, from South Africa, who is chief financial officer, and Randy Engel, who earned his MBA from the University of Denver at night while working for Newmont, heads strategic development. The final member is Lansdown, also a fifteen-year veteran, who was given responsibility for exploration, project development, and technical services. Supporting this group are four seasoned senior vice presidents—Enders in exploration and in operations, Hinze for North America, Jeff Huspeni for Africa, and Carlos Santa Cruz for South America. In 2009, Tim Netscher, a chemical engineer from South Africa who has worked in both Australia and Indonesia, was brought onboard as senior vice president of Asia Pacific operations.

Late in 2008, the company moved its headquarters from downtown Denver to new suburban quarters in Greenwood Village near the Technical Center, giving it a fresh identity and an opportunity to rebuild its strengths under new leadership.

Rekindled investor interest in gold has presented Newmont and other producers with a surprising new competitor—gold ETFs, or Exchange Traded Funds. The largest such fund, streetTracks Gold Shares, is sponsored by the World Gold Council and trades on the New York Stock Exchange under the symbol GLD. Launched in 2003, gold ETFs enable investors to purchase and trade shares of gold-backed securities at the spot price. The gold is purchased and held in trust by banks. ETFs are more practical for individuals than buying and storing bullion itself and make pure gold investments affordable to small investors. They are also less risky, but potentially less rewarding than holding shares of producing companies. The brain child of Australian investment banker Graham Tuckwell, gold ETFs are also traded on exchanges in Australia, the United Kingdom, France, Mexico and South Africa. As of June 30, 2009, these funds held 1,694 tonnes, or nearly 55 million ounces, of gold. That is equal to about 20 percent of U.S. gold reserves.

Change comes quickly and from all directions. AngloGold merged with Ashanti Goldfields of Ghana in 2004 and now vies with Newmont for the number two spot in gold production, while Goldcorp, a Vancouver-based company with a stellar growth profile, has moved into second place behind Barrick in market capitalization. Mega mergers gained much press during the commodities boom of 2007 with the proposed $142 billion acquisition of Rio Tinto by BHP Billiton, whose main assets are in iron ore, copper, and aluminum. The deal crumbled with metal prices a year later. Will Newmont be a consolidator in the years ahead or absorbed by a larger, perhaps multi-metal player? In a maturing industry with escalating costs and difficulty replacing reserves, can gold producers retain their high stock multiples? Or if multiples fall, will that ease a move toward diversification?

Newmont is a much different company than it was just a few years ago, but faces challenges unimagined by its former leaders. These challenges must be met in a very public arena, both on Wall Street and in the third world. Furthermore, the tenure of CEOs in America is shortening, leaving less time for men to make their mark before burnout sets in or a misstep sends them packing. High executive salaries and exit packages further discourage longevity at the top.

Shortly before his retirement, Murdy met with a group of the company's young executives, the up-and-comers for whom the Denver University program was designed. "I told them they were the future of the company," and would set the pace for future generations. "I said we are an old line company and that I am very proud of the company's history, but, anything less than a desire to be in business for another 80 to 100 years would be a failure."

So, too, would be anything less than being the industry leader, recognized for the talent and dedication of its people, rewarded for its success, and admired for its integrity wherever it does business. Increasing long-term shareholder value also should be a priority.

APPENDIX: OFFICERS AND DIRECTORS

Since its incorporation in 1921, Newmont Mining Corporation has had eight chief executive officers, although that term was not used by the company until 1974. Those with the final authority, their title, years at the top, and backgrounds are listed below.

William B. Thompson, chairman, 1921–30, Wall Street promoter
Charles Ayer, president, 1930–47, attorney
　(For most of his tenure, Ayer managed as part of a three-member executive committee that included Fred Searls Jr. and Franz Schneider, a mining engineer and financial reporter, who served as chairman of the committee.)
Fred Searls Jr., president, 1947–54, geologist
Plato Malozemoff, president (and later chairman and CEO), 1954–85, metallurgical engineer
Gordon R. Parker, president, chairman, and CEO, 1985–93, mining engineer
Ronald C. Cambre, president, chairman, and CEO, 1993–2000, chemical engineer
Wayne W. Murdy, president, chairman, and CEO, 2001–7, accountant
Richard T. O'Brien, president and CEO, 2007–present, finance
In addition, in 2008 Vincent Calarco, a chemical engineer, became the company's first outside chairman.

Over that period, Newmont has had 90 directors. Seven represented the Thompson family following the founder's death (see chapter 2 sidebar, *All in the Family*), 36 were senior members of management and 47 were outsiders, although that includes several from affiliated companies or suppliers, and representatives of major shareholders, for example, Consolidated Gold Fields and Sir James Goldsmith. Outsiders have constituted a majority of the board since the early 1970s, and today of 12 directors, only CEO O'Brien is a company employee. Seven directors have been women, including Thompson's widow and three descendants. Two women were elected to the board in 2005.

The company has been able to attract a number of outstanding and long-serving directors, many of whom have been CEOs of publicly traded companies. Investment bankers, heads of investment companies, and former officers of international financial organizations, such as the World Bank and the European Bank for Reconstruction and Development, are or have been Newmont directors, as have two college deans and one college president. Recently, the company has again sought out members with mining experience.

Serving the longest, with their years of service, were: Henry Krumb, 37 years (1921–58), a mining consultant; Stewart Silloway, 28 (1959–87), former CEO of Investors Diversified Services; Robin Plumbridge, 25 (1983–2007), retired CEO of Gold Fields of South Africa; William Moses, 23 (1966–89), former CEO of Massachusetts Financial Services; Joseph Flannery, 21 (1983–2004), retired CEO of Uniroyal; Thomas Holmes, 21 (1978–99), former president of Ingersoll-Rand; and Frank Coolbauch, 20 (1967–87), former CEO of Amax. One of the most influential directors, André Meyer, senior partner with investment banker Lazard Fréres served 16 years (1960–76). Of the current directors, Dr. James Taranik, director of the Mackay School of Earth Sciences and Engineering at the University of Nevada–Reno, has the longest service, 22 years, including his time on the Newmont Gold Company board.

Several directors have had gold plated public service backgrounds. James Byrnes, a director for 19 years (1947–66), had one of America's most distinguished careers. He was elected to the U.S. Senate from South Carolina, appointed an associate justice of the U.S. Supreme Court, and served President Franklin Roosevelt as director of the Office of War Mobilization during World War II, and President Harry Truman as secretary of state. He was governor of South Carolina from 1951 to 1955, during which time he continued to serve on the board of Newmont and a number of other companies.

Lucius Clay (1950–55) was one of the nation's top military officers during and after World War II and was the architect of the Berlin Airlift of 1948, which kept the city fed during a Communist blockade. Moeen Qureshi (1994–2004), a longtime senior officer of the World Bank, served briefly in

1993 as prime minister of Pakistan during which time the country returned to a democratically elected government. Bob Miller, a director since 1999, was Nevada's longest-serving governor, from 1989 to 1999.

Executive compensation has been an issue of public debate for years as chief executive pay has risen to rival that of movie stars and top athletes. For most of its history, Newmont executives received pay packages, which, while not exactly modest, generally were below corporate norms. With the company's growth in recent years, that has changed.

Malozemoff, always frugal with corporate funds, earned $453,000 in 1980 ($1.1 million in 2006 dollars). Because he was past the normal retirement age, he received no stock options. That year Newmont realized a price of $613 an ounce on its gold sales, had earnings of $197 million, or $7.64 per share, and the stock price closed the year at $46.50. Shareholders received $2.03 per share in dividends.

Twenty-six years later, there was some commonality with those numbers. The average gold price in 2006 was $638 an ounce and Newmont's stock closed at $45.15. Net income was $791 million, but with far more shares outstanding, per share earnings were only $1.76 and the dividend was 40 cents a share.

CEO Murdy received a salary and bonus of $2 million and another $1 million in stock awards, and was granted options on 90,000 shares in addition to existing options on 580,000 shares he already held. Under current disclosure rules on corporate governance, the estimated value of those options and his retirement plan brought his total implied compensation for the year to $12.6 million. With an enhanced retirement package, his implied total compensation for 2007, his last year in office, totaled $23.1 million. Such disclosure rules and calculations did not exist in Malozemoff's time and the true value of Murdy's stock options will depend on the stock's future performance.

Pay for directors has also increased substantially as responsibilities dictated by new SEC rules have made the job much more time demanding. In 1980, the company's seven outside directors received $10,000 each and were paid $500 for attending meetings. In 2007, outside directors received a base retainer of $50,000, and with additional compensation for chairing committees and attending meetings, most received much more. Lead director Glen Barton, retired CEO of Caterpillar, received $117,000. In addition, each director was given $75,000 a year in company stock, or 1,536 shares based on the stock's closing price for the year. Beginning in 2008, the annual retainer has been raised to $80,000, the stock compensation increased to $120,000, and Calarco will receive $185,000 as outside chairman.

Retired CEO Parker recalls a conversation he had with Malozemoff in the early 1980s. An issue had arisen that Parker suggested should be placed on the agenda of the next board meeting. "Oh, no," Newmont's legendary leader responded, "that's much too important an issue for the board to consider."[1] How the times have changed.

NOTES

Preface

1. In inflation-adjusted dollars, it would take a gold price of $2,120 an ounce in 2008 to equal $850 an ounce in 1980.

2. The standard measure for gold in the United States is a troy ounce. There are 14.58 troy ounces to one standard avoirdupois pound. Globally, gold is usually measured in grams and metric tons, or tonnes. At first Newmont poured 92-pound doré bars. Today it uses smaller molds and the bars weigh 72 pounds.

3. Coope, *The Carlin Trend Exploration History,* 2.

4. *The Nevada Mineral Industry, 2007,* Nevada Bureau of Mines and Geology Special Publication, 15.

5. *Reno Gazette-Journal,* April 21, 2002.

6. David Potter, interview by the author, December 2005.

Chapter 1

1. John Livermore, interview by the author, August 2004.

2. Roberts, *A Passion for Gold,* 93.

3. Greek: "I have found it." "The reputed exclamation of Archimedes when, after long study, he discovered a method of detecting the amount of alloy mixed with gold in the crown of the king of Syracuse; an exclamation of triumph at a discovery" (*Random House Dictionary of the English Language*).

4. Livermore, *Prospector, Geologist, Public Resource Advocate.*

5. Coope, *The Carlin Trend Exploration History,* 5.

6. Newmont's penchant for secrecy went way back. When Jack Thompson joined Newmont in 1960, he discovered that Fred Searls had saved every telegram that had been sent or received since the early 1930s. "If a guy in the field sent a wire saying he was leaving Minneapolis for Calgary and would be at such and such a hotel, the message was kept—in code. There were five code books in the library. Fred and the field people were very, very secretive," Thompson told the author in a September 2003 interview.

7. Vanderburg, "Placer Mining in Nevada," 178.

8. Coope, *The Carlin Trend Exploration History,* 9.

9. Pete Loncar, interview by the author, September 2003.

10. Gerald Hartzel, interview by the author, March 2004.

11. Robert Shoemaker, oral history included in McQuiston, *Frank Woods McQuiston,* 164.

12. Ramsey, *Men and Mines*, 267.

13. Crampton, *The 100 Best Small Towns in America*.

14. W. James Mullin, interview by the author, January 2006.

Chapter 2

1. *Wall Street Journal*, January 12, 1926.

2. Remarks by Executive Vice President Richard B. Leather to management meeting of Foote Mineral Company, October 22, 1984, Newmont history files.

3. Quoted in Crowell, "A Digger for Facts."

4. Hagedorn, *The Magnate*, 25.

5. Ibid., 77.

6. Ibid., 83.

7. Quoted in Lynch, *Mining in World History*, 189.

8. Hagedorn, *The Magnate*, 139, 152.

9. Letter to Shareholders in Magma Copper Company Annual Report, May 17, 1915, Newmont Archives.

10. Hagedorn, *The Magnate*, 235.

11. Ibid., 267.

12. Ibid., 238.

13. Crowell, "A Digger for Facts."

14. *Engineering and Mining Journal-Press*, July 1925.

15. Hagedorn, *The Magnate*, 169.

16. *New York Times*, June 30, 1930.

17. Margaret Biddle's death at age fifty-eight in Paris in June 1956 put the spotlight of the American and French press on her extraordinary life. Three years later, it became the stuff of tabloid journalism as a police investigation sought to untangle "L'Affaire Lacaze." Possessed with intelligence, charm, influence, and immense wealth, she had been at the center of European intellectual, diplomatic, and social life for more than a decade and had directed the American Red Cross Clubs for Women in London during World War II. She wrote for a number of American publications and maintained homes in Paris, London, Fontainebleau, the French Riviera, and New York. She collapsed in the early morning hours after returning from a gala honoring the king and queen of Greece and the day before a scheduled visit to the south of France with the duke and duchess of Windsor. The Supreme Commander of Allied Powers, Europe, three former French premiers, and several ambassadors attended her funeral.

Accompanying her to the opera that evening were Jean Lacaze, her escort since the divorce of her second husband, ambassador Anthony J. Drexel Biddle Jr. in 1945; Lacaze's sister Domineca Walter; and Mme. Walter's companion, Dr.

Maurice Lacour, a society psychiatrist. L'Affaire involved ownership of the fabulously rich Zellidja lead mine in Morocco, which was principally owned by Mme. Walter's husband, Jean, and later managed by Lacaze. Mrs. Biddle reportedly obtained a 4 percent interest in the mine in 1946 after Fred Searls Jr., Newmont's top geologist and later president, provided technical help and brought Newmont into a joint venture with Zellidja and St. Joe Minerals to further explore the area.

Mme. Walter married well. Her first husband, Paul Guillaume, an art dealer, drowned in the early 1930s under what the Hearst newspaper syndicated called "curious circumstances," leaving her with a fortune in French paintings—more than one hundred Cezannes, Picassos, Matisses, Renoirs, and others. They had no children, but she later adopted a son, Jean-Pierre Guillaume, from whom she became estranged after he turned eighteen. A year after Mrs. Biddle's death, Jean Walter, while on a drive in the country with Domineca and Dr. Lacour, stepped in front of a passing car and was killed. Mme. Walter inherited another $175 million, and under French law her adopted son would inherit it all upon her death.

Soon, on the testimony of a prostitute and other shadowy figures, police indicted Lacaze on charges of trying to frame Jean-Pierre to deprive him of his inheritance, while an ex-army officer accused Lacour of hiring him to kill the adopted heir. Both denied the charges and in turn sued Jean-Pierre and their accusers for slander.

Mrs. Biddle's death had hastily been attributed to a stroke, but no autopsy was performed and with the presence that evening of Lacaze and Dr. Lacour, questions were raised. Furthermore, there had been unconfirmed reports that her private office had been rifled at the time of her death and that she was unhappy with Zellidja's management. In March 1959 after a ten-day review, police announced they were satisfied that her death was completely natural and would not exhume the body as they returned to sorting out other aspects of L'Affaire Lacaze.

Newmont's joint venture with Zellidja, Nord Africaine du Plomb (NAP), came to little and was shut down in 1964. But because of Mrs. Biddle's involvement, "the North African operation received for years more attention and staff time than it really deserved" (Ramsey, *Men and Mines*, 120).

Chapter 3

1. Lassonde, *The Gold Book*, 25.

2. This is a reference to 1 Kings 10:11 and to the legendary location, possibly in southern Arabia or the eastern coast of Africa, of King Solomon's mines.

3. David Potter, interview by the author, December 2005.

4. McQuiston, *Frank Woods McQuiston*, 67.

5. *Daily Sentinel* (Grand Junction, CO), February 10, 1959.

6. *Denver Post,* May 12, 1953.

7. Loncar interview.

Chapter 4

1. Johnson, *Consolidated Gold Fields,* 13.

2. Gregory, *Ernest Oppenheimer and the Economic Development of Southern Africa,* 89.

3. Jorgensen, "Nababeep and East O'okiep."

4. Wilson, "Tsumeb."

5. Richard Ellett, interview by the author, September 2003.

6. Ramsey, *Men and Mines,* 143

7. *Engineering and Mining Journal,* November 1967.

8. *Engineering and Mining Journal,* May 1971.

9. Gordon Parker, interview by the author, July 2003.

10. Malozemoff, *A Life in Mining,* 291.

11. T. Peter Philip, interview by the author, January 2004.

12. Livingston, "A U.S. Company's Breakthrough against Apartheid."

Chapter 5

1. *Wall Street Journal,* September 23, 1980.

2. *New York Times,* October 23, 1981.

3. Robert Macdonald, interview by the author, August, 2003.

4. *Forbes,* August 21, 1978.

5. Rudolph Agnew, interview by the author, March 2004.

6. Like his son, Alexander Malozemoff was an accomplished violinist and studied at the St. Petersburg Conservatory under one of the greatest violin teachers of his day, Leopold Auer, who also taught, among others, Jascha Heifetz and Efrem Zimbalist.

7. Malozemoff, *A Life in Mining,* 88.

8. Ibid., 108.

9. Ibid., 120.

10. Rather than build a new mill and town at the deposit's Lynn Lake site, Brown, in an unprecedented move, packed up 208 buildings from a depleted mine, including a bank, post office, school, two churches, 150 houses, and a concentrator, and moved them 200 miles. Ramsey, *Men and Mines,* 195.

11. Malozemoff, *A Life in Mining,* 120.

12. Ramsey, *Men and Mines,* 198.

13. Malozemoff, *A Life in Mining,* 128.

14. *Fortune,* October 1965.

15. Jack Thompson, interview by the author, September 2003.

16. Malozemoff, *A Life in Mining,* 67.

17. Ibid., 117.

18. Leonard Harris, interview by the author, December 2003.

19. Jack Thompson, interview by the author, September 2003.

20. Pete Crescenzo, interview by the author, December 2003.

21. Malozemoff, *A Life in Mining,* 250.

22. *New York Times,* October 23, 1981.

23. Gordon Parker, interview by the author, July 2003.

24. Richard Leather, interview by the author, July 2003.

25. Richard Ellett, interview by the author, September 2003.

26. Malozemoff, *A Life in Mining,* 240.

27. Ibid., 242. Joining Banghart for a site visit, Malozemoff said he had the most frightening experience of his adult life. A float plane from Ketchikan dropped them at the mouth of the Unuk River where a helicopter was supposed to be waiting. But it wasn't. Instead there was only wilderness and bear tracks. With no radio contact, silence and shivers filled the two and a half hours until the chopper finally arrived.

28. Ibid., 282.

29. Ibid., 245.

30. Ibid., 248.

31. Ibid., 251.

32. Marcel DeGuire, interview by the author, October, 2004.

33. Thompson interview.

34. Stuart Silloway, interview by the author, September 2003.

35. Malozemoff, *A Life in Mining,* 220.

36. Clark, "Arthur Brant."

37. John Parry, interview by the author, March 2004.

Chapter 6

1. Joseph Flannery, interview by the author, July 2003.

2. Frank Florez, interview by the author, November 2005.

3. David Ridinger, interview by the author, September 2003.

4. David Baker, interview by the author, March 2004.

5. Malozemoff, *A Life in Mining,* 199.

6. Robert Boyce, interview by the author, August 2003.

7. Charles Freeman, interview by the author, January 2004.

8. Thompson interview.

9. Letter to Shareholders, Newmont Mining Corporation Annual Report, March 15, 1972, Newmont Archives.

10. Wayne Burt, interview by the author, September 2003.

11. Parry interview.

Chapter 7

1. Robert Macdonald, interview by the author, August 2003.

2. Memo from Sadowski, Newmont public relations files, Newmont Archives.

3. Gordon Parker, interview by the author, July 2003.

4. Tom Enos, interview by the author, September 2003.

5. Richard Ellett, interview by the author, September 2003.

6. Guzzardi, "The Huge Find in Roy Ash's Backyard."

7. McBeth to a representative of the T/S Ranch, November 5, 1980, Carlin file, Newmont Archives.

8. Donald Hammer, interview by the author, December 2003.

9. Tyrwhitt, *Desert Gold*, 15.

10. Quoted in ibid., 2.

11. John Dow, interview by the author, September 2003.

12. Linklater, "The Measurement That Built America."

13. *Jenison Ex v. Kirk,* 98 U.S. (453).

Chapter 8

1. Richard Leather, interview by the author, August 2003.

2. Malozemoff, *A Life in Mining*, 230.

3. Ibid., 228.

4. Don McCall, interview by the author, September 2003.

5. Malozemoff, *A Life in Mining*, 230.

6. John Parry, interview by the author, March 2004.

7. Malozemoff, *A Life in Mining*, 234.

8. Ibid., 236.

9. Ibid., 237.

10. Jack Thompson, interview by the author, September 2003.

11. Harry Van Benschoten, interview by the author, December 2005.

12. Ramsey, *Men and Mines*, 286–96.

13. In March 1986, at the age of seventy-five, Moehlman was shot and killed by a robber as he and his wife left a Houston restaurant.

14. Ramsey, *Men and Mines*, 292.

15. Malozemoff, *A Life in Mining*, 159–60.

16. Ibid., 162.

Chapter 9

1. Jack Thompson, interview by the author, September 2003.

2. Charles Freeman, interview by the author, January 2004.

3. Patricia Flanagan, interview by the author, December 2005.

4. David Potter, interview by the author, December 2005.

5. Plato Malozemoff, presentation to New York Society of Security Analysts, April 13, 1981.

6. Richard Leather, personal communication with the author, December 2005.

7. John Parry, interview by the author, March 2004.

8. Robert Macdonald, interview by the author, August 2003.

9. *New York Times,* April 13, 1981.

10. Dow Jones News Service, April 13, 1981.

11. Plato Malozemoff, presentation to New York Society of Security Analysts, April 13, 1981.

12. Donald Hammer, interview by the author, December 2003.

13. Wayne Burt, interview by the author, September 2003.

14. Malozemoff, *A Life in Mining,* 168.

15. Rudolph Agnew, interview by the author, March 2004.

16. Malozemoff, *A Life in Mining,* 275.

17. Wayne Burt, interview by the author, September 2003.

18. Gordon Parker, interview by the author, July 2003.

19. Carmen Fimiani, interview by the author, March 2004.

20. Parker interview; deposition of Gordon Parker on April 6, 1978, in the case of *Newmont Gold v. T Lazy S Ranch et al.,* U.S. District Court for the District of Nevada.

21. Leonard Harris, interview by the author, December 2003.

22. T. Peter Philip, interview by the author, January 2004.

23. Odin Christensen, interview by the author, June 2004.

24. Prospectus for initial public offering of Newmont Gold Company stock, June 24, 1986, Newmont Archives.

25. Rumball, *Peter Munk,* 236.

26. Wayne Murdy, interview by the author, October 2004.

27. Harris interview.

Chapter 10

1. Gordon Parker, interview by the author, July 2003. The write-downs included Magma's Superior mine, O'okiep Copper, Idarado Mining, Dawn Mining, and Foote Mineral.

2. James Hill, interview by the author, June 2003.

3. Richard Leather, interview by the author, July 2003.

4. By treating Magma and Foote as discontinued operations, sales in 1986 were $380 million versus $760 million in 1979.

5. *Institutional Investor Magazine* annually surveyed pension funds and other money managers to determine the best analysts in their fields. Analyst salaries and bonuses were based on who had made the publication's "All Star Team."

6. Peter Ingersoll, interview by author, September 2003.

7. *Wall Street Journal,* September 22, 1987.

8. *The Gold Standard,* Newmont employee newsletter, May 1996.

9. Chanos, "Thank Heavens for Inefficiency."

10. *Wall Street Journal,* August 14, 1987.

11. Rudolph Agnew, interview by the author, March 2004.

12. *Business Week,* August 31, 1987.

13. W. Durand ("Randy") Eppler, interview by the author, September 2003.

14. Consolidated Gold Fields press release, August 19, 1987, Newmont Archives.

15. Newmont Mining press release, August 14, 1987, Newmont Archives.

16. Tumazos, "Newmont Mining Progress Report."

17. T. Peter Philip, interview by the author, January 2004.

18. Newmont Mining press release, August 27, 1987, Newmont Archives.

19. Associated Press, August 31, 1987.

20. Newmont Mining press release, September 11, 1987, Newmont Archives.

21. *Wall Street Journal,* October 16, 1987.

22. *New York Times,* September 23, 1987.

23. Reuters, October 30, 1987.

24. Gordon Parker, interview by the author, July 2003.

25. Maureen Brundage, interview by the author, January 2004.

26. William Turner, interview by the author, March 2004.

27. Joseph Flannery, interview by the author, July 2003.

28. *Wall Street Journal,* October 16, 1987.

29. Chairman's letter to shareholders, Newmont Mining 1987 annual report, Newmont Archives.

30. Newmont Mining board minutes.

31. Wayne Burt, interview by the author, September 2003.

Chapter 11

1. Paul Maroni, interview by the author, February 2006.

2. *Northern Miner* (Toronto), February 8, 1988.

3. Tom Enos, interview by the author, September 2003.

4. T. Peter Philip, interview by the author, January 2004.

5. W. James Mullin, interview by the author, January 2006.

6. Robert Zerga, interview by the author, March 2004.

7. Colin Barnett, interview by the author, February 2006.

8. Scott Barr, interview by the author, November 2004.

9. *Reno Gazette-Journal,* June 25, 1989.

10. Donald Hammer, interview by the author, December 2003.

11. Carmen Fimiani, interview by the author, March 2004.

12. Gordon Parker, interview by the author, July 2003.

13. Roberts, *A Passion for Gold,* 176.

14. "Mining Edition," *Elko Free Press,* June 1988.

15. Bettles, "Exploration and Geology, 1962–2002, at the Goldstrike Property, Carlin Trend, Nevada," 275–98.

16. Colin Barnett, e-mail correspondence with the author, January 2006.

17. Seymour Schulich, interview by the author, April 2004.

18. Pierre Lassonde, interview by the author, May 2004.

19. Richard Ellett, interview by the author, September 2003.

20. Odin Christensen, interview by the author, June 2004.

21. Richard Leather, interview by the author, August 2003.

22. *Mining Journal,* January 29, 1988.

23. Walters, "Gold Mining."

24. Krol, who retired as vice president of exploration in 2001, was born in Indonesia where both his father and grandfather were mining engineers. When the Japanese invaded Indonesia in 1942, Krol's father was imprisoned, while he and his mother spent three and a half years in an internment camp.

25. Leendert Krol, interview by the author, July 2003.

Chapter 12

1. Gordon Parker, interview by the author, September 2003.

2. Jamieson, *Goldstrike!* 132.

3. Ibid., 140.

4. *Financial Times,* November 2, 1988.

5. Jamieson, *Goldstrike!* 156.

6. Ibid., 173–76.

7. Richard Leather, interview by the author, August 2003.

8. Jamieson, *Goldstrike!* 182.

9. Ibid., 209.

10. Ibid., 211.

11. W. Durand "Randy" Eppler, interview by the author, September 2003.

12. Rudolph Agnew, interview by the author, March 2004.

13. William Turner, interview by the author, March 2004.

Chapter 13

1. *Gold 1991* (London: Gold Fields Mineral Services).

2. Gordon Parker, interview by the author, July 2003.

3. Smith, "Billionaire with a Cause."

4. "Flamboyant Goldsmith Dies of Heart Attack," *BBC Politics,* 1997, http://www.bbc.co.uk/politics97/news/07/0719/goldsmith.shtml.

5. Smith, "Billionaire with a Cause."

6. T. Peter Philip, interview by the author, January 2004.

7. Parker interview.

8. Maureen Brundage, interview by the author, January 2004.

9. Paul Maroni, interview by the author, February 2006.

10. William Turner, interview by the author, March 2004.

11. Timothy Schmitt, interview by the author, August 2003.

12. Joseph Flannery, interview by the author, July 2003.

13. *Wall Street Journal,* April 26, 1993.

14. Goldsmith to the *Wall Street Journal* (European edition), April 26, 1993, Newmont Archives.

15. Reuters News Service, April 26, 1993.

16. Cook and Raw, "Kicking up Gold Dust."

17. Ibid.

18. Fallon and Bethell, "Gold Fever."

19. Ibid.

20. Gooding, "Parker Picks His Own Leaving Date."

21. Rudolph Agnew, interview by the author, March 2004.

22. Ronald Cambre, interview by the author, December 2003.

23. Philip retired in May 1994 and was named president of Bendigo Mining, a small Australian exploration company backed by Goldsmith. Today, while still working with Bendigo, he manages a game preserve in South Africa. Leather, whose legal and strategic advice shaped Newmont's success and image for twenty years, had retired two years earlier. In 1995, his fifty-one-foot yacht *Columbine* placed third, after a handicap adjustment, in the Cape Cod-to-Bermuda race. But typical of his competitive spirit, he and his eight-man crew crossed the finish line first, winning the Blue Water Trophy.

24. Personal observation by the author.

25. Lassonde, *The Gold Book,* 94.

26. Harry Van Benschoten, interview by the author, December 2005.

Chapter 14

1. Aubrey Paverd, interview by the author, September 2003.

2. Paverd, "Yanacocha Project Chronology."

3. Hemming, *The Conquest of the Incas.*

4. T. Peter Philip, interview by the author, January 2004.

5. Anthony Bowerman, interview by the author, August 2003.

6. Paul Maroni, interview by the author, February 2006.

7. Leonard Harris, interview by the author, December 2003.

8. *The Gold Standard,* March 1996.

9. Mackenzie and Doggett, "The Mineral Wealth of Nations," 351–58.

10. John Parry, interview by the author, March 2004.

11. John A. S. Dow, interview by the author, September 2003.

12. *The Gold Standard,* July 1995.

13. Don McCall, interview by the author, September 2003.

14. Marcel DeGuire, interview by the author, October 2004.

15. Richard Leather, interview by the author, August 2003.

16. W. Durand "Randy" Eppler, interview by the author, September 2003.

17. *The Gold Standard,* July 1995.

18. Ronald Cambre, interview by the author, January 2004.

19. Roque Benavides, interview by the author, September 2003.

Chapter 15

1. Ronald Cambre, interview by the author, December 2003.

2. Kurlander and I joined Newmont on the same day in March 1994 and for the first half of my time with the company, I reported to him.

3. W. Durand "Randy" Eppler, personal communication with the author, September 2006.

4. Tim Schmitt, interview by the author, August 2003.

5. Tom Enos, interview by the author, September 2003.

6. Scott Barr, interview by the author, December 2003.

7. Peter Crescenzo, interview by the author, December 2003.

8. James Mullin, interview by the author, January 2006.

9. *The Gold Standard,* January 1995.

10. Observation by the author.

11. Gordon Parker, interview by the author, July 2003.

12. Enos interview.

13. Newmont Mining annual report, 1994, Newmont Archives.

14. National Academy of Engineering, http://www.nae.edu/.

Chapter 16

1. Ronald Cambre, interview by the author, January 2004.

2. Observation by the author.

3. David Francisco, interview by the author, June 2005.

4. W. Durand "Randy" Eppler, interview by the author, September 2003.

5. Prospectus filed with the SEC for the exchange of Newmont Mining common stock for that of Santa Fe Pacific Gold, January 7, 1997.

6. Associated Press, December 9, 1996.

7. Victor Lazarovici, conference call with the author, December 9, 1996.

8. Quoted in Bagli, "The Civilized Hostile Takeover."

9. Tim Schmitt, interview by the author, August 2003.

10. Jim Mullin, interview by the author, January 2006.

11. Wayne Murdy, interview by the author, October 2004.

12. Eric Hamer, interview by the author, January 2004.

13. Rich Perry, interview by the author, July 2006.

14. Observation by the author.

15. James Taranik, interview by the author, July 2008.

Chapter 17

1. In the interest of full disclosure, this quote from the 1996 annual report as well as subsequent quotes from the 1997 and 1998 reports were written by the author.

2. Observation by the author.

3. Perlez and Bergman, "Tangled Strands."

4. Bergman, "Montesinos's Web."

5. Riley, "Shadowy Figures, Deals Marked Mine Battle."

6. Ronald Cambre, interview by the author, January 2004.

7. Bergman, "Montesinos's Web."

8. Perlez and Bergman, "Tangled Strands."

9. Bergman, "Montesinos's Web."

10. Perlez and Bergman, "Tangled Strands."

11. Bergman, "Montesinos's Web."

12. McMillan and Zoido, "Newmont in Peru."

13. Montaldo, *Main Basse sur l'Or de la France.*

14. *Wall Street Journal,* February 9, 2004.

15. *Patrick Maugein v. Newmont Mining et al.,* U.S. District Court for the District of Colorado, January 15, 2004.

16. Thomas Mahoney, interview by the author, August 2006.

17. Gold Fields Mineral Services, *Gold Survey 2000* (London, April 2000), 51.

18. Reuters, May 7, 1999.

19. Observation by the author.

20. Observation by the author.

21. Bruce Hansen, interview by the author, April 28, 2006.

22. Wayne Murdy, interview by the author, October 2004.

23. Wayne Murdy, interview by the author, June 2005.

Chapter 18

1. Patricia Flanagan, interview by the author, January 2006.

2. Wayne Murdy, interview by the author, August 2004.

3. W. Durand "Randy" Eppler, interview by the author, September 2003.

4. Lassonde, *The Gold Book.*

5. Schulich, "The Franco-Nevada Story."

6. Seymour Schulich, interview by the author, April 2004.

7. Schulich, "The Franco-Nevada Story."

8. Pierre Lassonde, interview by the author, May 2004.

9. Cindy Williams, interview by the author, June 2006.

10. John Gaensbauer, interview by the author, June 2006.

11. *The Gold Standard,* October 2003.

12. Brammer, "Golden Opportunity."

13. Thomas Mahoney, interview by the author, July 2006.

14. Joseph Flannery, interview by the author, July 2003.

15. John A. S. Dow, interview by the author, September 2003.

16. Leanne Baker, interview by the author, September, 2003.

Chapter 19

1. "Corporate Social Responsibility."

2. Letter from CEO in *Now and Beyond 2003,* Newmont Mining's corporate responsibility and sustainability report. *Now and Beyond* reports for 2003, 2004, and 2005 and *Beyond the Mine Sustainability Report* for 2006, 2007, and 2008 on the company's Web site provide most of the site-specific data in this chapter.

3. "Our Strategy," in *Now and Beyond 2004.*

4. CEO Wayne Murdy to editor of the *Denver Post,* December 13, 2004, Newmont Archives.

5. *Beyond the Mine 2008.*

6. James Taranik, interview by the author, July 2008.

7. John Mudge, interview by the author, May 2007.

8. "Nevada Mercury Air Emissions Control: Precious Metal Mining Operations."

9. "Group Says Mines Need to Clean Act on Mercury," *Salt Lake Tribune,* August 22, 2006.

10. Miller and Joyce, *Mercury Air Concentrations in Northern Nevada.*

11. "Nevada's Gold Diggers Mucking up the Air," *Las Vegas Sun,* February 14, 2007.

12. Gray, "Evaluation of Trends of Mercury Disposition in Salmon Falls Creek Reservoir, Idaho."

13. Leo Drozdoff, administrator, State of Nevada Division of Environmental Protection, to Dr. Glenn Miller, University of Nevada–Reno, March 8, 2007.

14. Helen Hankins, interview by the author, November 2005.

15. David Baker, interview by the author, April 2006.

16. In 2008, the T/S Ranch had a herd of 5,000 cows, 800 heifers, 230 bulls, 2,000 sheep, and 75 horses. In addition to being a major supplier of beef, the ranch sells hay to farmers in other states.

17. Michael Franzoia, interview by the author, December 2005.

18. Minera Yanacocha, *Mercury Spill Incident Report* (Lima, 2001).

19. Wayne Murdy, interview by the author, April 2006.

20. I participated in many early discussions as the company developed its social responsibility policies.

21. Tom Enos, interview by the author, April 2006.

22. Gare Smith and Daniel Feldman, "Newmont Mining Corporation Community Relationships Review Global Summary Report," March 2009, p. 58, http://www.newmont.com/.

23. *Now and Beyond,* Yanacocha 2004.

24. http://www.minesandcommunities.org, April 2002.

25. Marina A. Welker, "Corporate Security Begins in the Community," *Cultural Anthropology* 24, no. 1 (2009): 163.

26. Ibid., 143, 162.

27. PT Newmont Minahasa Raya, *Buyat Bay,* a response to allegations of pollution (Jakarta, December 2005); *The Gold Standard,* October 2004.

28. Brant Hinze, interview by the author, July 2006.

29. Perlez and Rusli, "Spurred by Illness, Indonesians Lash Out at U.S. Mining Giant."

30. Dow Jones Newswire, February 17, 2005.

31. Associated Press, August 25, 2006.

32. "Indonesian Court Acquits Newmont Mining," *New York Times,* April 25, 2007.

33. "Middle or Muddle?" *Forbes,* May 21, 2007.

34. "Justice in Jakarta," *Wall Street Journal,* April 25, 2007.

35. Karamoy, *An Underwater Guide to Buyat Bay and Surrounding Areas: North Sulawesi, Indonesia,* 13.

36. Smith and Feldman, "Community Relationships Review," 2.

37. Ibid., 39.

38. Ibid., 43.

39. Ibid., 57.

40. Ibid., 59.

41. Richard O'Brien, interview by the author, May 2009.

42. Marcel DeGuire, interview by the author, October 2004.

43. Graham Clark Jr., interview by the author, July 2004.

44. *The Gold Standard,* January 2006.

45. Baker interview.

46. Ronald Cambre, interview by the author, January 2004.

Chapter 20

1. Randy Eppler, personal communication with the author, August 2006.

2. Thomas Mahoney, interview by the author, August 2006.

3. Wayne Murdy, interview by the author, November 2007.

4. Not all the gold in the ore can be recovered. Recovery rates in Nevada range from 66 to 95 percent depending on the metallurgy of the ore and the processing method used. Heap leaching has lower recovery rates than milling, while ores processed by the roaster or autoclaves have the highest recoveries. The average recovery rate in 2006 was 78 percent.

5. William Zisch, interview by the author, November 2007.

6. J. M. Rendu, interview by the author, November 2007.

7. Collins, *Good to Great,* 92.

8. Scott Barr, interview by the author, November 2004.

9. Collins, *Good to Great,* 41–42.

10. Guy Lansdown, interview by the author, December 2007.

11. Glen Barton, interview by the author, December 2007.

12. The Hope Bay story began twenty years ago, in the late 1980s, when BHP became interested in the unexplored and unmapped volcanic belts of the Canadian

Arctic. After following the activity of other explorers in the region, it sent in a ten-person drill team in 1991 after others had dropped their claims. The project passed through several hands before being picked up by Miramar in 1999.

13. James Taranik, interview by the author, July 2008.

14. Brant Hinze, interview by the author, July 2006.

15. Reserves are price sensitive. The company calculated its 2008 reserves at a long-term price assumption of $725 an ounce versus $575 in 2007 and $300 a few years earlier. In its 2008 annual report, the company states that a $50 increase in the price assumption would add 3.3 million ounces, or 4 percent, to reserves, while a $50 decrease would reduce them by 8.2 million ounces, or 10 percent.

16. Stephen Enders, interview by the author, April 2006.

17. Joseph Bartolino, interview by the author, November 2007.

18. Richard O'Brien, interview by the author, November 2007.

19. Holly Walton-Buchanan with James V. Taranik, *Mackay Memories, 1908–2008* (Reno: Jack Bacon and Company, 2008), xii.

Appendix

1. Observation by the author.

BIBLIOGRAPHY

As They Saw It

This book is based on the personal observations and experiences of key Newmont officers, employees, and associates. Between 2003 and 2009, I conducted more than eighty interviews with people who were responsible for or influential in the company's decisions over the past four decades. Most interviews were in person and lasted an hour or two, a few were by phone, and some extended over several hours over the course of several days. The interviews were recorded, transcribed, edited, and then approved by the interviewee, who authorized the use of quotations in this book. A few asked that their comments be used only for background and their names are not listed below. Copies of the entire interviews with those who consented are included in a booklet, *As They Saw It*, in Newmont's Research Library at the Malozemoff Technical Center in Denver, Colorado.

The interviewees are listed below alphabetically followed by their most relevant and/or highest position with the company and their years of service.

Agnew, Sir Rudolph	director; CEO Consolidated Gold Fields	1981–97
Baker, David	vice president and chief sustainability officer	1980–
Baker, Leanne	Wall Street metals analyst	1986–
Barnett, Colin	director of geophysics	1989–2001
Barr, Scott	vice president, technical strategy	1995–2008
Bartolino, Joseph	exploration manager, Mexico	1985–
Barton, Glen	director; retired CEO of Caterpillar	2001–
Benavides, Roque	president, Compañia de Minas Buenaventura	1981–
Bowerman, Anthony	geologist; co-discoverer of Yanacocha	1983–2001
Boyce, Robert	vice president, taxes	1976–92
Brierley, James	chief microbiologist	1988–2001
Brundage, Maureen	partner, White & Case	1981–2004
Burt, Wayne	senior vice president, operations; director; chairman, Magma Copper	1972–86
Bush, Robert	senior vice president, administration	1996–2006
Cambre, Ronald C.	chairman and CEO	1993–2001
Christensen, Odin	chief geologist	1981–2002
Clark, Graham M., Jr.	senior vice president and general counsel	1983–96
Crescenzo, Peter	vice president, engineering	1971–88

DeGuire, Marcel	vice president, corporate development; general manager, Dawn Mining, and first general manager, Zarafshan-Newmont JV	1974–96
Dow, John A. S.	executive vice president, exploration; managing director, Australia	1978–2004
Ellett, Richard	vice president, exploration	1973–83
Enders, Stephen	senior vice president, exploration	2003–2009
Enos, Thomas	executive vice president, operations	1971–2007
Eppler, W. Durand	vice president, corporate development	1994–2004
Fimiani, Carmen	Carlin vice president and operations manager	1978–88
Flanagan, Patricia	vice president and treasurer	1980–2000
Flannery, Joseph	director; retired CEO, Uniroyal	1982–2003
Florez, Frank	general manager, Magma's Superior mine	1954–92
Francisco, David	executive vice president, operations	1995–2005
Franzoia, Michael	mayor, Elko, NV	1995–
Freeman, Charles	general manager, Magma's Superior mine	1972–89
Gaensbauer, John	Newmont attorney	1999–
Hamer, Eric	vice president and managing director, Indonesian operations	1974–97
Hammer, Donald	manager, western U.S. exploration	1958–88
Hankins, Helen	manager, Elko office, U.S. Department of Interior's Bureau of Land Management	1994–
Hansen, Bruce	senior vice president and chief financial officer	1997–2006
Hansen, Joy	vice president and general counsel	1992–2002
Harris, Leonard	vice president, research, development, and metallurgy; first general manager, Yanacocha	1974–95
Hartzel, Gerald	director, administrative services	1963–2001
Hill, James	vice president, corporate relations	1983–94
Hinze, Brant	senior vice president, North American operations; general manager, Yanacocha and Minahasa	2001–
Ingersoll, Peter	Wall Street mining analyst	1982–93
Krol, Leendert	vice president, exploration	1988–2001
Lansdown, Guy	executive vice president, discovery and development	1993–
Lassonde, Pierre	president and director; cofounder and co-CEO of Franco-Nevada	2002–7
Leather, Richard	vice chairman; executive vice president and general counsel; director	1970–92
Livermore, John	geologist, prospector, and discoverer of Carlin gold mine	1952–70
Loncar, Peter	mine superintendent; operations manager	1946–84
Macdonald, Robert	director, metallurgy; manager of Danbury laboratory	1966–83

Mahoney, Thomas	vice president and treasurer	1997–
Maroni, Paul	vice president, chief financial officer	1982–92
McCall, Donald	vice president, corporate development	1974–94
Mudge, John	director, environmental and social responsibility, North America	1982–
Mullin, James	senior vice president, North American operations	1968–2001
Murdy, Wayne	chairman and CEO	1992–2007
O'Brien, Richard	president and CEO	2005–
Parker, Gordon	chairman and CEO	1954–94
Parry, John	senior vice president, exploration	1969–92
Paverd, Aubrey	vice president, exploration; co-discoverer of Yanacocha	1973–94
Perry, Richard	vice president, North American operations	1994–2005
Philip, T. Peter	president and director	1958–94
Potter, David	attorney, assistant secretary	1972–89
Rendu, Jean-Michel	vice president, mine planning	1984–2001
Ridinger, David	vice president, operations; president of Magma Copper	1956–87
Schmitt, Timothy	vice president and corporate secretary	1975–2001
Schulich, Seymour	director; cofounder, and co-CEO of Franco-Nevada	2002–7
Silloway, Stuart	director; chairman, Investors Diversified Services	1959–84
Skiba, Robert	Magma Copper manager human resources	1975–87
Taranik, James	director; director, Mackay School of Earth Sciences University of Nevada, Reno	1986–
Thompson, Jack	vice chairman, president, and director	1960–86
Turner, William	director; chairman, and CEO of Consolidated Bathurst	1988–2001
Van Benschoten, Harry	vice president, accounting	1967–87
Williams, Cindy	vice president, business opportunity	1992–
Zerga, Robert	vice president, Carlin general manager	1972–89
Zisch, William	vice president, planning	1996–2009

Other Firsthand Accounts

Brant, Arthur, "Steps along the Way." Unpublished autobiography in Newmont's archives. 1985.

Kurlander, Larry. "Montesinos's Web; Interview with Larry Kurlander." Transcript of an interview by Lowell Bergman on PBS *Frontline*, http://www.pbs.org/frontlineworld/stories/peru404/pkurlander.html. October 25, 2005.

Livermore, John S. *Prospector, Geologist, Public Resource Advocate: Carlin Mine Discovery, 1961, Interview with John Sealy Livermore.* Typescript of an oral history conducted by Eleanor Swent. Berkeley: Regional Oral History Office, Bancroft Library, University of California, 2000.

Malozemoff, Plato. *Plato Malozemoff—A Life in Mining: Siberia to Chairman of Newmont Mining Corporation.* Typescript of an oral history conducted by Eleanor Swent. Berkeley: Regional Oral History Office, Bancroft Library, University of California, 1990.

McQuiston, Frank W., Jr. *Frank Woods McQuiston Jr.: Metallurgist for Newmont Mining Corporation and U.S. Atomic Energy Commission.* Typescript of an oral history conducted by Eleanor Swent. Berkeley: Regional Oral History Office, Bancroft Library, University of California, 1989.

Paverd, Aubrey. "Yanacocha Project Chronology." Unpublished report. Newmont archives. 1989.

Schulich, Seymour. "The Franco-Nevada Story." Unpublished document. Newmont archives. 2004.

Thompson, Jack E., Jr. Oral history included in *The Knoxville/McLaughlin Mine, 1978–1996, Volume VII.* Typescript of an oral history conducted by Eleanor Swent. Berkeley: Regional Oral History Office, Bancroft Library, University of California, 2000.

Newmont Archives

Newmont Mining made available a host of published and unpublished documents and granted access to files and archives. These included the following:

Annual reports

Annual reports of publicly traded subsidiaries and affiliates

Buyat Bay, prepared by PT Newmont Minahasa Raya, December 2005

Correspondence

Executive speeches

The Gold Standard, employee newsletter since 1995

The Idarado Legacy, 2005

Legal files

Mercury Spill Incident Report, prepared by Minera Yanacocha, 2001

Minutes of board meetings

News clippings and analyst research reports

Now and Beyond and *Beyond the Mine,* environmental and sustainability reports since 2003

Press releases, analyst presentations, and fact sheets

Prospectuses for the issuance of stock, debt, or acquisitions

Proxy statements for annual meetings

Reports to the Securities and Exchange Commission

Technical reports and departmental histories

30 Years of Turning Dedication into Gold, Carlin anniversary booklet, May 1995

Web site material, www.newmont.com

Books, Major Periodicals, and Professional Papers

Bagli, Charles V. "The Civilized Hostile Takeover: New Breed of Wolf at Corporate Door." *New York Times,* March 19, 1997.

Beatty, Sally. "Giving Back." *Wall Street Journal,* August 18, 2006.

Bergman, Lowell. "The Curse of Inca Gold." PBS *Frontline,* October 25, 2005.

Bettles, Keith. "Exploration and Geology, 1962–2002, at the Goldstrike Property, Carlin Trend, Nevada." In R. J. Goldfarb and R. J. Nielsen, eds., *Integrated Methods of Discovery: Global Exploration in the 21st Century.* Littleton, CO: Society of Economic Geologists, 2002.

Brammer, Rhonda. "Golden Opportunity." *Barron's,* July 3, 2006.

———. "24-Karat Play." *Barron's,* July 5, 2004.

Carter, Russell. "Newmont Automates the Assay Process." *Engineering and Mining Journal,* June 1991.

Chanos, Jim. "Thank Heavens for Inefficiency." *Barron's,* July 20, 1987.

Chappel, Gordon. *Rails to Carry Copper: The History of the Magma Arizona Railroad.* Boulder, CO: Pruett Publishing, 1973.

Clark, Robert Dean. "Arthur Brant." *Geophysics: The Leading Edge of Exploration.* Reno: Society of Exploration Geophysicists, 1984.

Collins, Jim. *Good to Great.* New York: HarperCollins, 2001.

Cook, Stephanie, and Charles Raw. "Kicking up Gold Dust." *Independent on Sunday* (London), September 19, 1993.

Coope, J. Alan. *The Carlin Trend Exploration History: Discovery of the Carlin Deposit.* Nevada Bureau of Mines and Geology Special Publication 13. Reno: University of Nevada Mackay School of Mines, 1991.

"Corporate Social Responsibility: Good Citizenship or Investor Rip-Off?" *Wall Street Journal,* January 9, 2006.

Crampton, Norman. *The 100 Best Small Towns in America.* New York: Macmillan, 1995.

Crowell, Merle. "A Digger for Facts Will Outstrip a 'Guessing Genius.'" *American Magazine* (July 1920): 41.

Danielson, Vivian, and James Whyte. "Bre-X: Gold Today, Gone Tomorrow." *The Northern Miner* (Toronto), 1997.

Fallon, Ivan, and James Bethell. "Gold Fever." *Sunday Times* (London), May 2, 1993.

Gooding, Kenneth. "Newmont's New Man Sets the Pace." *Financial Times,* July 27, 1995.

———. "Parker Picks His Own Leaving Date." *Financial Times*, August 1, 1994.

Gray, John E. "Evaluation of Trends of Mercury Deposition in Salmon Falls Creek Reservoir, Idaho, Using Reservoir Sediment Cores." *Draft of the USGS Report to the DEQ, State of Idaho.* Denver: U.S. Geological Survey, May 26, 2006.

Green, William. "Will It Recover on My Watch?" *Forbes,* December 1, 1997.

Greever, William S. *Arid Domain: The Santa Fe Railway and Its Western Land Grant.* Stanford: Stanford University Press, 1954.

Gregory, Sir Theodore. *Ernest Oppenheimer and the Economic Development of Southern Africa.* London: Oxford University Press, 1962.

Guzzardi, Walter, Jr. "The Huge Find in Roy Ash's Backyard." *Fortune,* December 27, 1982.

Hagedorn, Hermann. *The Magnate: William Boyce Thompson and His Time (1869–1930).* Superior, AZ: Boyce Thompson Southwest Arboretum, 1935.

Hemming, John. *The Conquest of the Incas.* New York: Harcourt Brace, 1970.

Jackson, Dan. "Carlin Gold." *Engineering and Mining Journal,* July 1983.

Jamieson, Bill. *Goldstrike! The Oppenheimer Empire in Crisis.* London: Hutchinson Business Books, 1990.

Johnson, Paul. *Consolidated Gold Fields: A Centenary Portrait.* London: George Weidenfeld and Nicholson, 1987.

Jorgensen, Victor. "Nababeep and East O'okiep." *Fortune,* July 1947.

———. "Tsumeb: Three-Year Wonder." *Fortune,* February 1950.

Karamoy, Drs. Rolly. *An Underwater Guide to Buyat Bay and Surrounding Areas: North Sulawesi, Indonesia.* Manado, Indonesia: South Minahasa Tourism Bureau and PT Newmont Minahasa Raya, 2006.

King, Clarence, et al. *Report of the Geological Exploration of the Fortieth Parallel.* 7 vols. Washington, DC: U.S. Geological Survey, 1870–80.

Krautkramer, Kate. "Elko, Nevada, the New Old West." *National Geographic,* October 2004.

Lassonde, Pierre. *The Gold Book.* Toronto: Penguin Press, 1994.

Lees, B. K. "Orpiment from the Twin Creeks Mine." *Mineralogical Record* 31, no. 4 (July/August 2000): 311.

Linklater, Andro. "The Measurement That Built America." *American Heritage* (November/December 2002): 42.

Livingston, J. A. "A U.S. Company's Breakthrough against Apartheid." *Philadelphia Inquirer,* April 11, 1979.

Lubin, Joann S., and Scott Thrum. "Behind Executive Pay, Decades of Failed Restraint." *Wall Street Journal,* October 12, 2006.

Lynch, Martin. *Mining in World History*. London: Reaktion Books, 2001.

Mackenzie, Brian, and Michael Doggett. "The Mineral Wealth of Nations." *Proceedings of the 1995 PACRIM Conference*. Melbourne: Australasian Institute of Mining and Metallurgy, 1995.

Matthews, Samuel. "Nevada's Mountain of Invisible Gold." *National Geographic*, May 1968.

McKay, Peter A., and Diya Gullapalli. "ETFs Stoke Investors' Gold Fever." *Wall Street Journal*, January 5, 2008.

McMillan, John, and Pablo Zoido. "Newmont in Peru." Stanford: Stanford Graduate School of Business Case Study IB-51, August 2003.

McQuiston, F. W., Jr. *Gold: The Saga of the Empire Mine 1850–1956*. Grass Valley, CA: Empire Mine Park Association, 1986.

Melloan, George. "Gold Fever Triggers Newmont's Raider Alarm." *Wall Street Journal*, July 14, 1987.

Miller, Dr. Glenn C., and Patrick Joyce. *Mercury Air Concentrations in Northern Nevada*. Reno: University of Nevada Department of Natural Resource and Environmental Science, January 2007.

Montaldo, Jean. *Main Basse sur l'Or de la France*. Paris: Albin Michel S. A. Publishing, 1998.

"Nevada Mercury Air Emissions Control: Precious Metal Mining Operations." Program Report. Carson City: Nevada Department of Environmental Protection, March 8, 2006.

"Newmont Mining's Fourth Generation of Gamblers." *Fortune*, October 1965.

Perlez, Jane. "Mining Giant Told It Put Toxic Vapors into Indonesia's Air." *New York Times*, December 22, 2004.

Perlez, Jane, and Lowell Bergman. "Tangled Strands in Fight Over Peru Gold Mine." *New York Times*, October 25, 2005.

Perlez, Jane, and Kirk Johnson. "Behind Gold's Glitter: Torn Lands and Pointed Questions." *New York Times*, October 24, 2005.

Perlez, Jane, and Evelyn Rusli. "Spurred by Illness, Indonesians Lash Out at U.S. Mining Giant." *New York Times*, September 8, 2004.

Phelps, Richard. "Newmont Mining Corp.: An Emphasis on the New." *Engineering and Mining Journal* (August 1996): 34.

———. "Newmont #1 in Au." *Engineering and Mining Journal* (March 2002): 24.

Ramirez, Anthony. "Going for the Gold." *Fortune*, November 9, 1987.

Ramsey, Robert H. *Men and Mines of Newmont: A Fifty-Year History*. New York: Octagon Books, 1973.

Riley, Michael. "Shadowy Figures, Deals Marked Mine Battle." *Denver Post*, December 13, 2004.

Riley, Michael, and Greg Griffin. "Fighting Back." *Denver Post,* December 13, 2004.

———. "The High Cost of Gold." *Denver Post,* December 12, 2004.

Roberts, Ralph J. "Alignments of Mining Districts in North-Central Nevada." U.S. Geological Survey Professional Paper 400-B. Washington, DC: U.S. Department of the Interior, 1960.

———. *Geology of the Antler Peak Quadrangle, Nevada.* U.S. Geological Survey Open File Report, 1949, with Survey Map GQ-10. Washington, DC: U.S. Department of the Interior, 1951.

———. *A Passion for Gold.* Reno: University of Nevada Press, 2002.

Rumball, Donald. *Peter Munk: The Making of a Modern Tycoon.* Toronto: Stoddart Publishing, 1997.

Smith, Sally Bedell. "Billionaire with a Cause." *Vanity Fair,* May 1997.

Snell, David. "France Again Enjoys a Notable Scandal." *Life,* March 16, 1959, p. 22.

Tumazos, John. "Newmont Mining Progress Report." Oppenheimer and Company, August 18, 1987.

Tyrwhitt, David, *Desert Gold: The Discovery and Development of Telfer.* West Perth, Australia: Louthean Publishing, 1994.

Vanderburg, W. O. "Placer Mining in Nevada." *University of Nevada Bulletin* 30, no. 4 (1936): 178.

———. "Reconnaissance of Mining Districts in Eureka County, Nevada." *U.S. Bureau of Mines Information Circular 7022,* 1938.

———. "Reconnaissance of Mining Districts in Eureka County, Nevada." *U.S. Bureau of Mines Information Circular 7043.* 1939.

Walters, Barbara. "Gold Mining." *20/20,* June 23, 1989.

Watkins, T. H. "Hard Rock Legacy." *National Geographic,* March 2000.

Wehner, Ross. "Peruvians Battle Newmont." *Denver Post,* September 14, 2004.

White, Lane. "Newmont Gold: Corporate Direction Following the Newmont-Santa Fe Merger." *Engineering and Mining Journal* (November 1997): 16.

Wilson, Wendell. "Tsumeb: The World's Greatest Mineral Locality." *Mineralogical Record,* 1977.

Other

Throughout its long history, Newmont Mining, its subsidiaries and affiliate companies, and its projects, people, and adversaries have been the subject of thousands of newspaper, magazine, and technical articles too numerous to cite. In addition to all the sources listed above, this book has used material from routine news articles appearing in publications in the United States, Canada, London, Australia, and

Indonesia. Among others, these have included the *Wall Street Journal*, the *New York Times*, Reuters, Dow Jones Newswire, Associated Press, the *Financial Times*, *Globe and Mail*, *Denver Post*, *Rocky Mountain News*, *Reno Gazette-Journal*, *Las Vegas Sun*, *Elko Free Press*, *Business Week*, *Forbes*, *Fortune*, *The Economist*, *Northern Miner*, *Mining Journal*, *New York Journal-American*, *The Times-News* (Twin Falls, ID), and *Mineweb*. In addition, all of the major brokerage firms in North America, London, and Australia have written extensive research reports on the company.

INDEX